AF321940

VESTED INTERESTS

# Vested Interests

## TRUSTEESHIP AND NATIVE DISPOSSESSION IN THE UNITED STATES

*Emilie Connolly*

PRINCETON UNIVERSITY PRESS

PRINCETON & OXFORD

Published by Princeton University Press
41 William Street, Princeton, New Jersey 08540
99 Banbury Road, Oxford OX2 6JX

press.princeton.edu

GPSR Authorized Representative: Easy Access System Europe - Mustamäe tee 50, 10621 Tallinn, Estonia, gpsr.requests@easproject.com

All Rights Reserved

ISBN 9780691240121
ISBN (e-book) 9780691240138

Library of Congress Control Number: 2025940502

British Library Cataloging-in-Publication Data is available

Editorial: Priya Nelson, Emma Wagh
Production Editorial: Elizabeth Byrd
Jacket: Heather Hansen
Production: Erin Suydam
Publicity: William Pagdatoon
Copyeditor: Brian Bendlin

Jacket Credit: Universal Images Group North America LLC / Alamy Stock Photo

Printed in the United States of America

10 9 8 7 6 5 4 3 2 1

*For AJM*

# CONTENTS

## *Illustrations*

## *Table*

## ACKNOWLEDGMENTS

MANY LIBRARIANS and archivists have saved me over the course of this project, including by delivering scans of materials when libraries were closed during the COVID-19 pandemic. I am grateful to staff at the Alabama Department of Archives and History; the American Philosophical Society; the Beinecke and Sterling Libraries at Yale University; the Chicago Historical Society; the Clements Library; the Detroit Public Library; the Filson Historical Society; the Helmerich Research Center and Gilcrease Museum; the Historical Society of Pennsylvania; the Huntington Library; the Indiana Historical Society; the Indiana State Archives; the Indiana State Library; the Library Company of Philadelphia; the Library of Congress; the National Archives and Records Administration; the New York Historical; the Newberry Library; Stadsarchief Amsterdam; the Widener Library at Harvard University; and libraries at Brandeis University, Dartmouth College, the Institute for Advanced Study, New York University, Princeton University, and the University of Pennsylvania.

This book and the dissertation it is drawn from received generous funding from the American Council of Learned Societies, the Council on Library and Information Resources and Mellon Foundation, the Institute for New Economic Thinking at Harvard University, the John E. Rovensky Fellowship in Business and Economic History, the New York University Center for the Humanities, the New York University Provost's Global Research Initiative, and the Social Science and Humanities Research Council of Canada.

I could not have written this book without the help of a number of friends and colleagues, who bear no responsibility for its errors or omissions. For insightful feedback on parts of this project, thank you to Gregory Ablavksy, Maggie Blackhawk, Kathryn Boodry, Colin Calloway, Daniel Carpenter, Ann Daly, Christine Desan, Robin Einhorn, Elizabeth Ellis, Joan Flores-Villalobos, Stefanos Geroulanos, Alexandra Harmon, Kevan Harris, Mandy Izadi, Richard R. John, Ari Kelman, Justin Leroy, Noam Maggor, Amy Offner, Jeffrey Ostler, Susie Pak, Gautham Rao, Gabe Rosenthal, Bethel Saler, Claudio Saunt, Nancy Shoemaker, Lindsay Shakenbach Regele, Rachel St. John, Tamara Plakins Thornton, Adam Tooze, and Michael Willrich. Thanks also to the American Political History Seminar at Boston University, the Early American Graduate Seminar at the

John Carter Brown Library, the History of Global Capitalism Seminar at Harvard's Weatherhead Initiative on Global History, the McNeil Center for Early American Studies Seminar, the Mellon Research Initiative in Racial Capitalism Colloquium at the University of California–Davis, the Native Cultures of the Americas Workshop at Harvard University's Mahindra Center, the United States Political Economy Lab Seminar, and the University of California–Los Angeles Seminar for Comparative Social Analysis. For sharing sources, drafts of their own, and answering questions, thank you to Daniel Carpenter, Thomas Coen, Jamie Jacobs, Robert Lee, Sharon Ann Murphy, Michael Leroy Oberg, and Christina Snyder.

Several poor souls suffered through entire drafts of the manuscript, including Colin Calloway, Paul Frymer, François Furstenberg (and his brilliant group of graduate students at Johns Hopkins University), Jane Knodell, Rachel Nolan, Sarah Quinn, Julie Reed, Christina Snyder, Michael Witgen, and—more times than I could count—A. J. Murphy. Thank you to my pandemic writing group, Elizabeth Ellis, Julia Lewandoski, and Allison Powers Useche. Emma Teitelman has read most everything I've written, sometimes more than once. Thank you to her and to Alexis Broderick for keeping me going, forty-five minutes at a time.

New York University's Department of History nurtured this project as a dissertation. Thank you to my committee, Elizabeth Ellis, Nicole Eustace, Steven Hahn, Martha Hodes, and Rachel St. John, as well as Stefanos Geroulanos, Jennifer Morgan, Andrew Needham, Guy Ortolano, and Barbara Weinstein for their support. Elizabeth Blackmar, nominally my external committee member, was so much more; thank you Betsy. I spent a delightful year at the McNeil Center for American Studies writing up the dissertation. Thank you to Kathy Brown, who served as interim director that year.

Thank you to my friends, colleagues, and mentors at the Dartmouth College Native American and Indigenous Studies Department and the Dartmouth Society of Fellows, especially Whitney Barlow Robles, Megan Black, Colin Calloway, Maurice Crandall, Mona Domosh, Bruce N. Duthu, Laurie Furch, Yui Hashimoto, Preston McBride, Jeremy Mikecz, and Donald Pease. Mona and Bruce bent rules for me when I needed rule bending badly—thank you both. For their hospitality, a special note of gratitude to the forces of nature that are Bethany Moreton and Pamela Voekel.

I am very grateful to have landed at Brandeis University. Thank you to my colleagues for their unwavering support and constructive feedback on some especially gnarly early drafts, and to Martha Cronin for saving me from many disasters. Thanks also to my work buddies, Ulka Anjaria, Brandon Callender, Greg Childs, Yuri Doolan, Brian Horton, and Howie

Tam. Three wonderful research assistants helped sort through scans for me: at Brandeis, Arthi Jacob and Natalie Westrick, and at Dartmouth, Alejandra G. Fuentes-Vasquez. Thanks also to Margarita Corral for assistance with data. Completing this book at the Institute for Advanced Study has been an almost otherworldly experience. Thanks to Suzanne Akbari, Myles Jackson, Janet Yoon, and—it must be said—the woods, for creating a perfect enclave in which to think and write. Thank you to all who have helped me with editing and production: Priya Nelson, Shane Nelson, Emma Wagh, and Audra Wolfe.

A very tender thank you to my friends who have watched me grow old with this book and stayed close: Arash Abazari, Lindsay Baukert, David Calnitsky, Jonah Campbell, Michelle Campbell, Kat Cass, Jacqui Cornetta, Laura Dean, Mitra Ebrahimi, Elizabeth Ellis, Marian Ekweogwu, Jack Fleischer, Joan Flores-Villalobos, Nader Hasan, Emily Hill, Kira Josefsson, Sam Keller, Greta LaFleur, Sarah Lemay, Marcus Lobb, Caitlin Manning, Francesca Manning, Katie Miles, Alex Moll, Caitie Moore, Alaina Morgan, Rachel Nolan, Lakeyma Pennyamon, Ted Robinson, Fischer Scherin, Eleni Schirmer, John Semley, Lauren Shelley, Ahmed Shokr, Kerry Shopiro, Oliver Silverman, Cassie Wagler, Jackie Wang, Chris Westcott, and Rocky Zanoni.

I owe it to Dr. Alexandra Golby and the nurses and staff at Brigham and Women's Hospital that I have been able to write the book I wanted to write. I am profoundly grateful to them and to my friends and family for seeing me through. To my wife, my constant collegial companion, my best friend: Amy Zanoni, no phone call is long enough to thank you in full. To Ellen and the entire Junn family, thank you for your caring encouragement and for letting me borrow the car to write at the Huntington all day. To my parents, Bob Connolly and Lucie Gregoire, and to my sister and soulmate Adele, I could not have written a word without your steadfast support and welcome distractions. Finally, to Tina, and most of all to AJ Murphy, thank you for giving me a home.

VESTED INTERESTS

Native nations discussed in this book, circa 1760. *Source:* Map created by Shane Kelley.

# Introduction

ELOUISE COBELL LEARNED the history of her Piikani Blackfoot ancestors as a child. Piikani wealth had once been measured in horses, an average of ten per family after the equine trade reached the Northern Plains around 1740. Mounted hunting transformed the Piikanis' lives, allowing them a far more efficient means of harvesting bison furs, which they supplied to British and, later, American traders. Horses made Piikani life rich but uncertain, dependent in new ways on the whims of rainfall and the health of grasslands. Starting in the mid-nineteenth century, a widening stream of settlers, livestock, and disease coursed through the Northern Plains, throwing off balance the complement between horse and bison on which Piikani prosperity had once stood firm. Then, a proliferation of factories in faraway cities drove up demand for belts made from tension-bearing bison leather until herds were nearly gone. Cobell was born in 1945, but as a child her family still spoke of the winter of 1883, when more than 550 Blackfoot perished from starvation after their Indian agent failed to distribute rations owed them by the federal government. Cobell also knew firsthand the far more recent story of her uncle's death, a death she could not help but associate with the fact that her ancestors' wealth had never really been under their own control. When her uncle fell ill one winter, his wife needed money for his medical care. She had rushed to the distant Indian agency to request funds from an account held in trust on her behalf. But once she arrived, the agent told her that the money would not be ready for two weeks. The checks came in the spring, far too late. Cobell's uncle died soon after they arrived.[1]

These stories must have echoed in Elouise's mind when, at the age of eighteen, she asked the federal Indian agent stationed on her reservation for an account of her own trust fund. The agent brushed her off, insisting that she was incapable of understanding the finances. Not one to be underestimated, Cobell set off for community college, then Montana State University, and then Seattle, where she started a career as an accountant. Eventually Elouise felt the pull of her childhood home, and in 1970 returned with her family to the northwestern Montana reservation of the Blackfeet Nation (as they were now called). Soon enough, her fellow tribal citizens encouraged her to put her training to use. Six years later, at the age of thirty, Cobell became the Blackfeet Nation's treasurer.[2]

Among Cobell's duties was to request withdrawals from the Blackfeet national fund, held in trust and managed by the Bureau of Indian Affairs, which was housed at the Department of the Interior. The Blackfeet trust had a painful history of its own, bound up with the dispossession of the nation's homelands. Lands belonging to the Kainai, Piikani, and Siksika Nations that composed the Blackfoot Confederacy had once reached from the Rocky Mountains in the West to the North Saskatchewan River in the East to the Missouri River in the South. In a series of treaties and executive orders across the second half of the nineteenth century the United States hacked away at this territory, taking tens of millions of acres and pledging annual payments and rations in exchange. A gold rush flooded Blackfoot hunting grounds and precipitated the creation of Montana Territory in 1864. Then came railroads, and more settlers. In 1871 Congress prohibited further treaties with Native peoples and through a series of statutes carved away portions of the Blackfeet Reservation, including an expanse that would eventually become Glacier National Park, where settlers could enjoy a sublime (and for the Blackfeet, sacred) landscape of lakes, rivers, and waterfalls coursing through the Rockies.[3]

The Blackfeet had been forced to sell their homelands, and no price could ever offset the loss. Yet the near-extinction of the bison that sustained the Blackfeet economy and the steady annexation of their lands by the United States entrenched poverty. Money had become essential to survival, and the Blackfeet had too little. In 1924, they sued the United States in the Court of Claims for its failure to adequately compensate the nation for lands taken almost seventy years before. As was the standard in these kinds of cases, whatever remained after court deductions, attorneys' fees, and a modest per capita distribution to members of the nation was placed in a trust fund to be controlled by the defendant—the federal government.[4]

The Blackfeet Nation trust fund, seeded by the court award, was supposed to provide much-needed revenue to the reservation. But by the time Cobell oversaw its distribution in the late 1970s, the Bureau of Indian

Affairs could barely estimate how much money it contained. Many entries were inscrutable in the trust ledgers, but Cobell noticed alarming activity, like negative interest payments and mysterious, unauthorized withdrawals. When she sought clarifications, Cobell again found her requests dismissed by the bureau.[5]

The largest insult added to these many injuries concerned the Blackfeet National Bank. After the only bank within striking distance of the reservation shuttered in 1983, Cobell decided to found the first tribally owned bank in the United States. With banking still a novelty to most Blackfeet citizens, she launched financial education programs for elementary school children, teenagers, and community college students. Gradually the bank grew, and lent out enough capital to nurture roughly two hundred Native-owned businesses. Still, the bank could only attract so many depositors from a reservation economy stunted by over a century of colonialism. Cobell thus set her sights on one potential depositor of considerable means: her own nation. The Bureau of Indian Affairs kept the Blackfeet's trust fund millions invested in a list of preferred banks, which regularly bid on Indian trust fund moneys. Cobell repeatedly bid on behalf of the Blackfeet National Bank, only to be rejected each time in favor of larger institutions whose capitalization enabled them to offer a higher interest rate. Marginal gains in interest, Cobell pointed out, hardly justified denying the Blackfeet National Bank a pool of cash that would expand its lending capacity and so deepen its impact. The money was supposed to benefit the Blackfeet, after all.[6]

In the mid-1980s, as Cobell and other tribal leaders grew more vocal in their criticisms of Indian trust fund administration, Congress held hearings to investigate the Bureau of Indian Affairs' mismanagement. Representatives of the Red Lake Chippewas testified that the bureau had responded to their requests for a full accounting of their trust fund by sending a single sheet of paper with indecipherable balances, scribbled by hand. A court-mandated audit later discovered nearly $811,500 missing from their account. Rather than restore what it owed, officials secretly—and inexplicably—withdrew $1,231,000 in certificates of deposit from the Red Lake trust fund. Other Native nations tried to withdraw funds from federal trusteeship, only to have the government tighten its grip. In one instance, the bureau flatly refused to permit the Saginaw Chippewas to receive money awarded by a court judgment without placing it in trust, forcing the nation to lobby Congress for two years, at significant legal costs, in order to secure a special statute granting them control over their own money. Native nations were, evidently, captive clients: They not only had no say in *how* their funds were handled but also *who* would handle them. "If we were Rockefeller," one critic of the trust funds told Congress, "we would definitely have changed our asset manager by now."[7]

The testimony brought by Cobell and others revealed a litany of abuses and prompted fruitless efforts at legislative remedies. Throughout, commentators frequently referred to the Indian trust funds as a "broken system." It was a term that implied a devolution, as if the trust funds had once worked in an ideal form. Yet almost every issue that afflicted the Blackfeet, Red Lake Chippewa, and Saginaw Chippewa funds—dubious investments, specious accounting, a preference for the interests of non-Native enterprise—had arisen before. What if the system was not broken, but working as intended?

So consistent were the government's violations that neither the misconduct of individual bureaucrats, the laxity of regulations, nor the indifference of Congress alone could serve as an explanation. All were aggravating factors but inessential to the core injustice at hand: that trusteeship had been designed from its inception to benefit the trustee, not the beneficiary. To take a continent from its original inhabitants, the United States warped trusteeship into what I call *fiduciary colonialism*: a regime in which federal officials gained control over Native lands, resources, and people by maintaining control over Native finances. A late twentieth-century trusteeship that privileged settler banks and treated beneficiaries as an afterthought was consistent with its roots in Native land dispossession. But as Cobell and others reiterated before Congress, the path forward lay not in abandoning trusteeship but in honoring the diplomacy in which it had originated. In treaties signed generations before, the federal government had committed to offer Native nations protection from enemies—both foreign and domestic—and to steward their wealth. These were promises in which many Native negotiators had found some measure of hope, until they witnessed the government's idea of protection veer wildly from their own. Even still, many had chosen trusteeship and fought tirelessly to preserve it—not as it was, but for what it always should have been and could one day become.

❦

This book tells the story of how—and why—the federal government assumed trusteeship over Indigenous peoples' wealth. Between its founding and the Civil War, the United States acquired 581 million acres of land by negotiating more than four hundred treaties with Native nations.

By the time the United States ended the practice of treaty making with Indigenous peoples, Native territories had dwindled from nearly two billion acres before European arrival to a mere 111,761,558 acres. Acquisitions were framed by federal officials as purchases, albeit ones without a market, since the federal government prohibited any competing bids. Offering compensation to Native peoples for cessions advanced the United States' aim to preempt rival empires and formed the first link in a chain of titles, allowing settlers to trade, convey, and collateralize Native land.[8]

But the nature of compensation offered meant treaties also did much more than ground a system of private property. In theory, the United States could have simply taken land by force, or bought it with a clean lump sum. Both options were tested but rather quickly set aside. Instead, officials made the fateful choice to prolong payment into yearly increments, called annuities.[9] What might have been a punctual event, a blood-stained land grab or a quick real estate transaction, became an enduring and asymmetrical relationship between a trustee and the nations it dispossessed.

Architects of federal Indian policy knew and stated explicitly that future annuities could serve as lure and ransom. Projected into the future, annuities disciplined their recipients: Funds held in trust today could be withheld, redirected, pilfered, or deliberately misapplied tomorrow. Although they shared connotations with life annuities, a form of insurance that supplied annual income to widows, the elderly, and other persons considered unable to support themselves—an impairment equally attributed to Native people by settler ideology—annuities in the context of Indian affairs referred simply to an annual payment. At first, annuities arrived primarily in the form of goods—including cloth, ornaments, firearms, powder, or agricultural implements—echoing the gifts dispensed by previous generations of colonial administrators to authenticate diplomatic goodwill toward Indigenous hosts. Starting in the late 1810s, money composed an increasing share. More important than annuities' composition, however, was their division into annual installments. Leverage over wealth, conferred by the simple fact of deferred payment, tilted the project of continental dispossession in the United States' favor. In short, if land was the *why* of colonialism, money was the *how*.[10]

Annuities' financing also changed over time. At first, annual congressional appropriations funded almost all annuity payments, whether delivered as goods or in cash. Under President Andrew Jackson, however, officials chose to fund more and more annuities by interest raised on financial investments, referred to within the federal bureaucracy as the Indian trust funds. Treaties that created trust funds promised to set aside for Native nations a principal, and bound officials to vest that principal in "safe and productive stocks" that earned a minimum rate of interest—usually 5 percent. Depending on the circumstances precipitating treaties and the whims of negotiators, the trust principal originated either in a one-time congressional appropriation, or built up gradually from the proceeds of selling the ceded lands themselves. Officials in the Treasury and War Departments then invested this principal in an array of securities more or less of their choosing. Each year, usually in the fall, Indian agents distributed the interest earned as an annuity.

Even if the government had not chosen to invest Native funds at all, annuities' incremental nature alone would have conferred the kind of grip on future revenue needed to keep federal trusteeship in place. When officials began investing the wealth they controlled, however, trusteeship became at once more literal, since officials now purported to manage Native wealth rather than simply suspend its full delivery, and practically immortal, since this wealth became encased in legal devices designed to outlast their creators.

Federal officials first embraced deferred compensation as conquest on the cheap, holding the pen to economize on the use of the sword. After the American Revolution, the federal government surged westward with plans to exterminate Native peoples and seize their lands by force. Yet tight constraints on fiscal and military capacity reined in these attempts and swung officials toward a policy of compensated dispossession that would endure for over a century. Treaty by treaty, dollar by dollar, a colonial regime that routinely stumbled in its attempts to subdue Native peoples became nevertheless hegemonic, affecting even those nations that chose to defend their land by arms rather than cede it for annuities. Fiduciary colonialism functioned only because the United States was willing to use as a mechanism of enforcement violence in many forms, from mere threats of annihilation, to the slow attrition of famine and exposure, to military campaigns that routinely tipped into genocide. But it was also a strategy of dispossession forged to conserve meager resources. At the dawn of its continental empire, the United States recognized that it could neither afford to eliminate Native peoples altogether nor deny that they were sovereign nations.[11]

Of course, the United States would fill its coffers, stock its arsenals, and build capacity overall over the course of the nineteenth century. Trust investments conscripted Native wealth into this project. Early Indian trust fund investments supported the First Bank of the United States, a cornerstone of Treasury Secretary Alexander Hamilton's construction of a creditworthy nation-state. When the federal government issued bonds or interest-bearing Treasury notes to fund wars against Britain, Mexico, and the Confederacy, these securities found their way into the Indian trust funds, which meant that Indigenous peoples lent sustenance to the same military that treated such major conflicts as pretexts to claim vast new territories, enforce Indian removals, and prosecute near perpetual if undeclared wars on any nation that mounted resistance.[12]

For much of the period under study, however, officials invested Indian trust fund money in bonds issued by the several states. State governments borrowed to build infrastructure, a prerequisite not only for capitalist accumulation but for states' very ability to assert borders and govern the spaces between them. Colonialism made states reliant on debt financing, since frontier states lacked sizable settler populations and taxable property: Borrowing made available in the present the anticipated value of Native lands once "improved," in the language of the period, by the construction of transportation routes and the capitalization of banks. That Indian trust funds were so heavily invested in the very financial instruments that made settler economies viable was a bitter irony, one that officials were more than happy to sustain. By the late 1830s, more than $3.8 million in Indian trust fund investment supported banks, canals, railways, and other state-financed carriers of westward expansion. Three decades later, the figure neared $4.8 million (or almost $3 billion in today's dollars).[13] Trust funds marked a moment in which Native nations were at once severed from their lands and tethered to a federal trustee—and, through their trustee, to the fate of the state banks, canals, roadways, and wars in which their funds were invested.[14]

Some caveats are necessary to grasp the quantitative significance of trust investments. Native dispossession and infrastructural construction— processes linked by Indian trust fund investments—were preconditions for capital accumulation in the United States.[15] Yet Indian trust funds did not secretly finance the rise of American capitalism. In 1841, Indian trust funds held 1 percent of states' roughly $207,895,000 in bonds; by contrast, foreign capitalists held at least half this sum, according to the best estimates. Canals would have been dug and banks founded, in other words, without Native money (but not without taking Native land). Like other investors, Indian trust fund beneficiaries were not always contributors to economic growth because the projects their wealth capitalized were not reliably profitable. Many canals financed by Native money grew muddied and stagnant as construction stalled, and many banks financed by Native money failed soon after their founding. State-funded infrastructure helped usher in a transition to capitalism that, unfortunately for state boosters, displayed a structural tendency toward crisis.[16] But too narrow a focus on trust funds' contributions to economic growth misses the point: Even in its failures, the infrastructure that trust funds financed succeeded in advancing Native dispossession.

For specific states and infrastructural projects, the proportion of Indian trust fund investments appears far more significant, and their timing decisive. After the first surge of state borrowing and trust investment in the late 1830s, Indian trust funds held 11 percent of Alabama's debt, 12 percent of Kentucky's debt, and a remarkable 17 percent of Tennessee's debt, including the entire $500,000 bond issuance that the state used to capitalize the Union Bank of Tennessee. These investments came at critical moments for states desperate for capital. Federal officials invested Native wealth liberally after a banking panic in 1837, when states began borrowing at unprecedented rates in a struggle to finance incomplete projects as an economic depression took hold. Indian trust funds were also invested in state bonds that no other creditor would touch, and in the bonds of slave states that brokers advised were riskier than their free-state counterparts.[17]

Another aspect of proportionality merits emphasis. Trust funds may have been modest when compared to the stock of settler investments, but they represented the entirety of Native nations' financial capital; annuities, by the same token, their primary source of public revenue. An untrustworthy fiduciary risked wiping out nations' collective wealth when lending it to shaky state governments. Herein lies a dynamic both familiar and strange. That agents of an empire held financial control over nations struggling against histories of colonialism is far from unique to the nineteenth-century United States. From France's crushing indemnity of 150 million francs, imposed on the new republic of Haiti to compensate former slaveholders, to the overwhelming debts Latin American countries owed to the British and French creditors who had financed their wars for independence (and who would deploy gunboats, if needed, to ensure they were repaid), to the apostles of a creditor-favoring gold standard who fanned out from New York City to an overseas empire strung from the Dominican Republic to the Philippines— all evidenced the mutable and enduring utility of finance to colonialism. What *is* remarkable, in light of all these examples, is that the United States took a continent not by compelling Native nations to borrow, but to invest.[18]

Native people did not passively submit to a world of finance beyond their grasp or influence. Indigenous treaty negotiators were compelled to invest in the sense that none ceded land of their free volition, even when signatories nominally granted their consent. Only after reckoning with unviable alternatives—subjection to settler jurisdictions; bare survival on depleted game and crops; exposure to settler vigilantes, state militias, and the US military; and the continued theft of their timber, property, and homes—only then did Native leaders agree to part with their territories and meet with treaty commissioners.[19] Once gathered in council, however, Native delegates had a small but critical space in which to maneuver and push for terms of compensation that would best ensure an uncertain survival. With clear eyes and their gaze fixed on a distant horizon, many chose to place wealth in federal hands, and some explicitly requested trust investments. They did so with the recognition that annuities' renewal across time—the very quality that made them powerful levers for the federal government—could also be to their advantage.

Many Native treaty negotiators had witnessed how rapidly windfall payments for land cessions could disappear. Thinking less of their own futures than those of coming generations, leaders recognized that lump sums were ephemeral forms of compensation. To provide for yet-unknown heirs, leaders sought a source of revenue that would outlast their lifetimes and replenish each year, even after their bones were put to rest. Investment could enhance annuities' benefits. Indigenous peoples long enmeshed in credit-fueled fur trades grasped readily that loaning out their funds would incur interest and enlarge financial legacies, an outcome early treaty negotiators compared to swelling harvests or to the multiplied offspring of a single hen. Years of living as trust beneficiaries only sharpened Native financial proficiency. Over time, speakers shed analogies, requesting specific securities by name and with reference to their yields.

As Native leaders grew more assertive in their dealings with the federal government, they also reconfigured their political economies to better capitalize on compensation. Treaties that laid out the terms of trusts and annuities became framing documents for Native fiscal states. Guided by commitments to social welfare, national preservation, and the ambitions of political classes, Native leaders assigned streams of annuities toward the costs of caring for the poor, infirm, and orphaned; set aside funds for council houses and public salaries; covered trade debts; bought farming implements and hired blacksmiths; or financed what many leaders wanted most of all—schools, which they correctly anticipated would equip a rising generation of leaders with the skills needed to defend their land in councils and before Congress. An exquisite ambivalence came to define fiduciary colonialism as annuities helped preserve nations while conferring power to the federal agents who administered them.[20]

Annuities also conferred power *within* nations. Deciding who, exactly, would wield that power provoked contention. Competition across bands, towns, or districts arose, and plans devised around treaties favored certain constituencies as they displeased others. Annuity-funded development could steepen inequalities. Grain mills, cotton gins, blacksmiths' shops, schools, and civic buildings sprung up in Native towns, funded by national annuities, but merchant and slaveholding classes often stood most to gain. Still, conditions changed, and people too. The very fact of annuities' recurrence meant that the disagreement they sowed could be resolved differently with each generation.

Federal officials tended to improvise when it came to their work as fiduciaries, but they did not invent trusteeship out of thin air. Trusts descended from two lineages of legal doctrine, one drawn from the prosaic traditions of probate and inheritance, the other from lofty legal debates over the virtues of empire. Trusts date at least to the Middle Ages, when Franciscans circumvented religious prohibitions against owning wealth by occupying land to which trustees held title on their behalf. Trusts evolved alongside property law, taking on new guises as instruments of conveyance. In the nineteenth century—as today—the bulk of wealth was not earned on land or as income but inherited in a cascade across generations. Trusts' ability to shield assets from creditors or spendthrifts and to dictate investments in perpetuity—or at least for a lifetime—meant they could act as silos of wealth for widows, minors, and other beneficiaries presumed financially incompetent, or simply host an ever-accumulating dynasty. As mercantile, manufacturing, and industrial enterprises blossomed alongside philanthropic associations, all employed trusts to channel the funds that flowed within and across their economic arenas. By the close of the nineteenth century, trusts were used to securitize assets and combine corporations, becoming emblems of Gilded Age inequality and in particular of the power of firms to consolidate monopolies that overpowered competitors, workers, and even democracy itself. Today, trusts remain firmly embedded in the legal "code" that configures capitalism, insulating patrimonial and corporate wealth from creditors, taxes, and the peering eyes of regulators.[21]

Indian trust funds were the progeny of mundane devices inserted to wills, contracts, and deeds, but the principle of federal trusteeship descended from a rarified discourse of imperial legal thought.[22] Most scholars trace the emergence of federal trusteeship to Supreme Court Chief Justice John Marshall's 1831 opinion in *Cherokee Nation v. Georgia,* in which Marshall argued that the Cherokees were a "domestic dependent nation," bearing a relationship to the government that "resembles that of a ward to his guardian."[23] Yet pronouncements of trusteeship over purportedly inferior and idle Indigenous peoples are as old as European settlement in the Americas, and were fashioned from even older doctrines of Roman law.[24] Within this roving tradition, empires justified their claims on land, labor, and resources by their ability to provide *protection*, a protean term that broadly signified a duty to shield a more vulnerable ally from an array of threats, be they a competing empire's invasion or the protector's own unruly subjects.[25] On the North American continent, British officials deployed the rhetoric of protection in the Proclamation of 1763, in which the Crown pledged military support to Native allies, restrained settlers from moving west of the Appalachian Mountains, and, in the same breath, asserted an exclusive right to purchase Native lands.[26]

After a brief and chastening experiment in taking Native land by unmitigated military force, the United States largely reverted to British policy and embraced the diplomacy of protection. Emissaries from a nascent republic desperate to edge out the competing European empires that lingered on the continent staked claims to Native lands by committing to protect their current possessors. It was this double-edged diplomacy that had set the Cherokees on their winding path to Marshall's Supreme Court, where they asserted their own interpretation of trusteeship. As the Cherokees well knew, accepting the United States' protection—which they first did in 1785—had placed conditions on their sovereignty: namely, their submission to federal protection constrained them from drawing alliances with—or ceding lands to—other European powers. Yet as they argued before Justice Marshall nearly half a century later, living under the protection of the United States did not grant any intrusions into their "internal affairs," nor did it make them wards. The Cherokees' attorney quoted Emerich de Vattel, an eighteenth-century progenitor of international law, who insisted that even a weaker state that "places itself under the protection of a more powerful one" does so without "divesting itself of the right of government and sovereignty."[27]

Native people were willing to affirm the idea of protection because they saw resonances between their own legal theories and the law of nations that they cited before settler courts. Long before the arrival of Europeans, Native emissaries had acknowledged the kinds of imbalances of power Vattel identified in their own diplomatic exchanges. Speakers often referred to stronger parties using paternal language, a practice that carried over into their dealings with newcomer empires. The fathers Native people invoked were not commanding Anglo-American patriarchs vested with arbitrary power, however. A father—or the Great Father, as the United States' president was often called—could only live up to his title by delivering protection and sustenance, obligations that grew in proportion to his means. These commitments, solemnly inscribed and reaffirmed in a canon of treaties, still exert legal force today. What we now call the federal "trust responsibility" compels the government to steward Native wealth and to shield Native nations from attempts by states, courts, and corporations seeking to divest them of land, resources, and self-governance. It is the quintessential colonial entanglement, a product at once of imperial power and its resistance, of Indigenous choices made within a world imposed upon them.[28]

⊰═══◈═══⊱

This book begins with the rise of fiduciary colonialism in the late eighteenth and early nineteenth centuries. It explains how trusts used to structure family and corporate wealth made their way into treaty negotiations, and why Native people accepted payments kept in federal possession for their land. It then shifts from the coalescence of fiduciary power to its sudden expansion during the period of massive and lethal dislocation conventionally referred to as the era of Indian removal, when trusts became, simultaneously, instruments to manipulate Native people and essential components of Native nation-building.[29] The book follows Native nations west in the decades after removal, and explains how the federal government managed to ratchet its grip on Native wealth. A series of crises—a collapse in the state bond market, a surge in monetary claims levied against the government as trustee, and the South's secession—all threatened but ultimately strengthened fiduciary power. No convulsion could match the Civil War, however, which necessitated a swift expansion of military and fiscal capacity that altered permanently the financial calculus of Indian affairs. On the heels of mobilizing an army of two million, a system of compensated dispossession once considered conservative no longer seemed necessary, at least in its current form. In 1871, Congress abandoned the practice of treaty making that had built fiduciary colonialism piece by piece, but federal control over Native wealth endured. By the century's close, most Indigenous peoples had abandoned defending

Elouise Cobell in Montana, 1999. Oil lease proceeds on trust lands accrued in Individual Indian Money accounts, which Cobell found were gravely mismanaged. *Source:* AP Photo / Ray Ozman.

homelands by force, accepted diminished territories, and received inevitably inadequate financial compensation held in trust. A struggle for the right to decide how that compensation would be spent began in earnest, and has yet to end.

When a new wave of land dispossession took hold in the wake of the 1887 Dawes Severalty Act, which broke apart collective landholdings into individual parcels subject to sale, trusteeship shaped every step of the process. Many land allotments were placed in trust with the Department of the Interior—some permanently. If the department approved leases for oil and gas companies to drill the land, it kept the proceeds of those leases in trust as well. Without the authority to do so, Indian agents pocketed funds belonging to Native individuals and opened accounts on their behalf in local banks, skimming a cut in the process if the temptation struck. Once numbering only in the dozens and held on behalf of nations, trust funds now proliferated wildly, with thousands of individuals collecting pittances from personal funds. Heirs multiplied with each generation, inheriting a dwindling fraction of trust assets. Decades passed. Through the churn of enterprise on Native allotments, money was earned, invested, and then seemingly evaporated, from Elouise Cobell's account and so many others.[30]

In Cobell's time and in its formative period, federal trusteeship fell short of the standards of protection Native people held. Yet nations survived by working within trusteeship's confines, configuring their compensation to their own advantage and holding their trustee to account through narrowing legal channels. That Indigenous peoples survived what they did is astonishing, but it is difficult not to wonder how much they could have thrived without the constraints of fiduciary control. Trusteeship, nominally intended to safeguard future prosperity, instead subjected Native nations to a compounding chain of diminished inheritances that widened the gap between the economies they could have had and what they instead lived with. Whatever endowments Native nations conveyed to their descendants were hard-won and fragile, the result of pulling wealth from the maw of the same trusteeship that was supposed to protect it. This had been plain to Indigenous leaders since the earliest decades of federal trusteeship. In 1826, one Miami *akima*, or hereditary leader, gestured to how much his people had lost on account of the government failing to fulfill its treaty obligations. "Who is to pay the damage which has accrued to my nation in consequence of this failure?" he asked, knowing the answer.[31]

The pages that follow will make clear that there was no golden age from which the system of trusteeship had devolved by the late twentieth century. But in this history we can also see traces of an ideal trusteeship yet to come, in which the federal government upholds long-standing treaty obligations while allowing Native nations to flourish on their own terms. It was this potential that motivated Elouise Cobell. Amid the torrent of revelations about trust mismanagement that her work brought to light, more than a century after the end of formal diplomacy with the United States, she still referred to trust funds as "sacred."[32] What this language implied was a not a bid for the abolition of trusteeship but for the federal government to recognize its sacredness too.

# CHAPTER ONE

# Strategies of Succession

IN THE WINTER of 1811 the Seneca Nation summoned US Indian agent Erastus Granger to the Buffalo Creek reservation in western New York. Granger was welcomed by Farmer's Brother, a Seneca military leader who had, as a young man, fought against the emerging American republic during the Revolutionary War. Tensions between the United States and Britain were again on the rise, and Granger had reason to fear that the Senecas and the larger Haudenosaunee Confederacy to which they belonged might once more join enemy forces. But the Senecas led with a far more mundane concern: money. As Farmer's Brother reminded Granger, years ago their "Great Father, the President of the United States" had promised to "take care of our Money, and plant it in a field" so that "it would bear seed forever, as long as trees grew, or water ran."[1] Senecas were beneficiaries of a trust fund that contained $100,000 in stocks issued by the First Bank of the United States. Each year since, the Senecas had received the interest earned on this investment from their Indian agent, a $6,000 installment referred to by all sides as an annuity.

But then the payments stopped. Almost a year before Granger's visit, the Senate—riven by partisan conflicts over the constitutionality of a federally chartered corporation—had allowed the bank's charter to expire. The bank retired its stock as its wound up its operations. Federal officials redeemed the Seneca's principal and then neglected to reinvest it. With their funds idling on Treasury ledgers—and without any precedent to guide the War Department's policy—their agent had no annuity to deliver. "We are told the field where our Money was planted is become barren," Farmer's Brother acknowledged. But their "Great Father" had made a promise, he warned, and the Senecas wanted their annuity, in full, as soon as it could be delivered.[2]

Farmer's Brother referred to a promise that the government had made within a complicated but consequential treaty. In 1797, the Senecas had ceded millions of acres of land in exchange for a $6,000 annuity. Their treaty conformed in many respects with a strategy of compensated dispossession federal officials had honed in the years prior, in which they offered to purchase Native lands with annuities, annual payments of goods or money. Yet in the case of the Seneca treaty, the United States had made this promise to deliver annuities on behalf of a land speculator, Robert Morris, who took advantage of the still-inchoate status of federal land law to execute what amounted to a private purchase of Native land. For entirely self-serving reasons Morris introduced a striking twist into a coalescing policy of compensated dispossession: paying for Native lands with financial assets held in trust. Because of Morris, the Senecas were unique among their contemporaries in receiving an annual payment funded not by Congress but by interest earned on shares in the First Bank of the United States. They were the first beneficiaries of a trust fund, but would not be the last.

Rogue speculators like Morris disrupted a federal government still struggling to solidify its authority over Indian affairs and assert an exclusive prerogative to acquire Native land. States posed another challenge. Like the national government, states were born heavily indebted and at a loss for revenue. Many turned west, rushing to claim Native lands that they might sell to service debts or, at the least, offer as payment in kind to creditors. As federal and state governments competed to convert Native homelands into a fiscal asset, they fashioned a new form of "proto-property" called preemptive title, or the exclusive right to purchase a given tract of Native land. Because preemptions allowed investors to trade in as-yet uncommodified Native territories, they spurred a stunning boom in land speculation, which in turn placed pressure on Native people to cede the lands settlers had staked as theirs to buy.[3]

The United States' political economy, it seemed, leaned headlong into a future in which Native lands were in settler possession. Yet a nation limping under the weight of its war debts could not easily launch a westward campaign. Federal officials soon realized that taking Native lands by force alone would simply cost more than an insolvent country could afford. Instead, they embraced a strategy of compensated dispossession that would counterintuitively save money through regular spending. Yearly outlays on annuities would economize, the rationale went, by avoiding the far more extravagant wars that uncompensated seizures could trigger. For this to work, the trick was to buy land incrementally—a kind of imperial installment plan. Offering annual payments instead of lump sums granted the government greater leverage over Indigenous peoples by incentivizing peace. Were Native nations to defend land by arms, or even cede lands to the competing European powers that remained on the continent, they would forfeit future annuity payments from the United States as their self-appointed trustee.

By protracting compensation across time, annuities set fiduciary control into motion. But Seneca negotiators at Big Tree had seen with clear eyes a potential upside to annuities. Having witnessed firsthand how quickly lump sums could be depleted, Senecas realized that the same extended timeline for payment that served federal interests could also ensure the longevity of their national revenue. This ambivalence of financialized trusteeship—its power to control and yet provide—would come to define fiduciary colonialism.

At the meeting with Granger, Farmer's Brother closed with an indirect threat. He reminded the agent that to the west of Seneca territories followers of the Shawnee prophet Tenskwatawa escalated their raids on American settlements, fueled by British supplies of arms, powder, and provisions. Farmer's Brother insisted that the Senecas "have had no hand in this bad Business."[4] But Granger did not misunderstand the implication. The Senecas soon received their full annuity. And when war broke out between Britain and the United States that summer, the Senecas fought alongside the nation in which their funds were invested.[5]

In January 1790, newly installed Treasury Secretary Alexander Hamilton submitted to Congress his plan to rescue the newly constituted United States from its stifling debts and establish a creditworthy fiscal state. Funding wars by printing money, a method that had functioned perfectly well for the British colonies, had placed the revolutionary Continental Congress on the brink of financial collapse. Under the Articles of Confederation, the federal government could neither obstruct states from issuing competing currencies nor effectively tax its own out of circulation, causing the value of federal money to plummet to near zero. Tallying up wartime obligations and overdue interest, and adding in sums owed by individual states, Hamilton found that the United States owed nearly $80 million, a sum almost thirty times greater than its anticipated annual revenue.[6]

Debt hobbled the national government. Civil servants and the entire military awaited years of back pay. Worse, the United States owed more than $1.65 million in interest alone to France and Spain. Alongside its war debts, the federal government owed British creditors and loyalists for indemnities under the 1783 Treaty of Paris. Britain had refused to vacate a line of posts in the Northwest Territory that stood well within the stated bounds of the United States so long as these obligations remained outstanding. The forts might have been tolerable were it not for their role in shoring up a constellation of powerful Indigenous polities, many of whom had fought with the Crown during the Revolutionary War. Creditors had begun to doubt the republic's viability, and insolvency only made the United States more vulnerable to its enemies.[7]

Hamilton's report outlined a series of linked fiscal proposals that would restore the nation's credit. States' debts would be assumed by the national government. All debts would be refinanced at a lower interest rate, a hit to creditors Hamilton offset by committing to pay them interest in specie. Finally, a national bank would service the newly consolidated public debt and, by building capital, keep the federal government afloat "in sudden emergencies."[8] Critics like Thomas Jefferson accused Hamilton of prolonging the nation's misery and burdening its future citizens with an ineradicable debt. But Hamilton had a plan to gradually repay creditors. It hinged on a critical source of prospective income that he called "western lands."[9]

When they ratified the Constitution, states had already ceded more than 220 million acres of land to the federal government, and a vast expanse lay uncharted beyond the states' borders. Calling these latter lands "western," as Hamilton did throughout his report, elided the fact that they remained firmly in Native possession. With rather unwarranted optimism, Congress soon after passed a funding act that assigned annual proceeds from future land sales toward the retirement of federal debt.[10] In order to free future generations from the cost of independence—and to ensure that these successors could borrow again, if needed, to *maintain* that independence—Hamilton earmarked for creditors the projected revenue from lands that the United States would need to build an empire to acquire.

Hamilton's "western" lands included the fertile soils located along the Maumee, Ohio, and Wabash Rivers. Spread across this region were prosperous Illinois, Lenape, Miami, Potawatomi, Odawa, Ojibwe, Shawnee, and Wyandot villages, subsisted by prolific matrilocal agriculture, the fecund hunting grounds of the Great Black Swamp, and a long history of profitable exchange with British and French fur traders. British settlers had made incursions to the region in the 1750s—causing skirmishes with the French that escalated rapidly into the Seven Years' War—but the American Revolution ushered in a new phase of dispossession. During

Lord Dunmore's War of 1774, Virginians swept westward, eventually establishing Kentucky. In their wake, federal officials claimed the region by conquest, ramming through sham treaties with the Haudenosaunee at Fort Stanwix, the Lenapes and Wyandots at Fort McIntosh, and the Shawnees at Fort Finney. In another act of hubris, the 1787 Northwest Ordinance projected incipient settler states across unceded Native lands north of the Ohio River and east of the Mississippi. To encourage settlement on this apparent domain, Congress then sold 1.5 million acres of it to the Ohio Company, a joint-stock venture founded by former Continental Army officers to speculate in the region. By way of payment, the Ohio Company handed over $1 million in federal debt certificates—a welcome reduction to the nation's towering war debts.[11]

Federal determination to make a fiscal resource of Ohio nations' lands triggered a war that would test the financial mettle of the new republic and force federal officials to realize the limits of their capacity to simply seize Native lands by force. In 1786, Haudenosaunee, Lenape, Miami, Odawa, Ojibwe, Potawatomi, Shawnee, and Wyandot delegates gathered to formally repudiate the illegitimate treaties by which the United States had claimed the Ohio River Valley region. By then most Indigenous peoples living in the Ohio Country had fled north from settler incursions to establish towns in the more sheltered Maumee River Valley. A message to Congress drafted by the council warned that its member nations would "prefer continual war" to any further submission to a "doctrine of conquest."[12]

While the more distant Haudenosaunee would not make good on this threat, Ohio nations forged a military alliance known as the Northwest Confederacy. Newly coordinated war parties set about defending their land from mounting intrusions, ambushing travelers on the Ohio River and picking off wayward US soldiers. In response to these outrages, General Arthur St. Clair, who also served as governor of the Northwest Territory, ordered an invasion into the heart of the Maumee Valley villages in November 1791. It was a humbling campaign. The Northwest Confederacy's decentralized command structure and familiarity with the terrain allowed them to outfox an undisciplined and largely inexperienced rival. St. Clair's forces met a crushing defeat, suffering nearly a thousand casualties in a matter of hours. Such catastrophic losses revealed the superiority of the region's Native military powers and cast doubt on Hamilton's vision to lift the republic's credit with the swift seizure and sale of Native land.[13]

Hamilton was, at first, an enthusiastic proponent of the war in the Ohio Country, assuring President George Washington that the Treasury could handle the costs. Writing to a friend, he reported cheerfully that

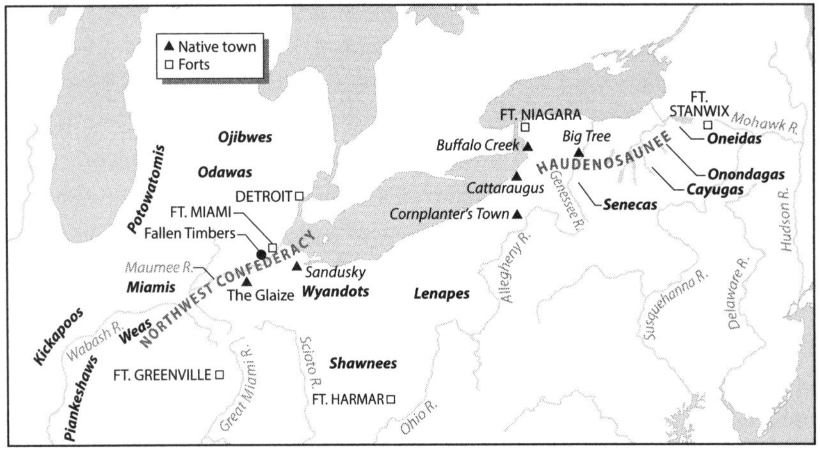


Territories of the Northwest Confederacy and the Haudenosaunee, circa 1790.
*Source:* Map created by Shane Kelley.

St. Clair's troops were "on their route to demolish every savage man, woman and Child."[14] Hamilton's mood darkened, however, when the Northwest Confederacy's resistance thwarted his progress on fiscal reforms. Congress had already authorized over $312,000 to enlarge the militia, which had proven disastrously ill-matched to the Confederacy's focus, coordination, and commitment. After its humiliation in 1791, the military clearly demanded reinforcement as well, and Congress was forced to appropriate another $1 million to bulk up the regular army. As alarming for Hamilton's fiscal outlook was the fact that the outbreak of hostilities had brought land sales to a standstill. In December, Hamilton warned legislators that "during the continuance of the present Indian war," expenditures were "likely to exhaust the product of the existing revenues."[15] Congress shelved plans to market the western territories. Native military power had compounded the very federal debt that Hamilton had hoped to redeem with Native lands.

St. Clair's defeat threw into question a widespread faith among settlers that the continent's changing demographics would automatically shift Native land into the United States' possession. The population of settlers in British North America had increased steadily in the second half of the eighteenth century, reaching 2.5 million by 1775. By the time Hamilton delivered his report, the first federal census counted over 3.9 million persons. Population increase became a point of pride, a source of confidence in the nation's future, and an economic indicator that encouraged land speculation. While they boasted of their own numbers, settlers also mythologized the collapse of Indigenous populations after European contact and interpreted Native mortality as an expression of inherent differentials in the civility and vigor of each society. Many men involved in the formation of early Indian affairs policy presumed Native peoples would vanish steadily as game animals disappeared, chased away by the United States' advance.[16]

For nations like the Senecas, who experienced firsthand the United States' obliterative force, shifts in population appeared anything but natural. The American Revolution had been cataclysmic for the westernmost member nation of the Haudenosaunee Confederacy, also known as the Iroquois, the Six Nations, or, in a reference to the structures that housed multiple families within their villages, the People of the Longhouse. Along with their sibling nations, the Cayugas, Mohawks, Oneidas, Onondagas, and Tuscaroras, the Senecas had at first resolved to sit out the conflict brewing among neighboring colonists and their empire. Unified neutrality toward neighboring powers had oriented Haudenosaunee diplomacy since the early eighteenth century, a period in which the confederacy held its ground between belligerent British and French empires. As a result of their careful diplomacy, on the eve of the Revolution the Haudenosaunee maintained a vast, arable territory that spread from the eastern tip of Lake Erie to the Unadilla River, scraped by narrow lakes and river valleys.[17]

When the war rumbled north from British-occupied New York City, however, the Haudenosaunee commitment to neutrality became more difficult to maintain. Within a month, the confederacy fractured, with the Cayugas, Mohawks, and Senecas siding with the British, the Oneidas and Tuscaroras siding with the rebels, and the Onondagas split by factions. Among Britain's Haudenosaunee allies, the Senecas would suffer the most for their involvement in the war. In the fall of 1779, after Haudenosaunee forces supported the British in battles in the Wyoming Valley, General John Sullivan launched a meticulously planned campaign to ruin Seneca country. Timing their expedition to coincide with harvests, Continental soldiers destroyed acres of corn, beans, potatoes, squash, pumpkins, cucumbers, and watermelons, took women hostage from fields as they worked, and torched the log houses, lodges, and larger frame buildings clustered in each town. Hundreds fled westward to Niagara, where they found the British Army scarcely able to provision the gathering refugees. For generations after the atrocities, the Haudenosaunee would refer to Washington, the man who ordered the campaign, as Town Destroyer.[18]

The Revolution's aftermath proved as difficult for the Senecas as the war itself. States cast their borders well into Haudenosaunee territory, citing fictive colonial grants that had extended colonial dominion indefinitely into an unknown interior. With Hamilton's fiscal revolution still years away, legislatures struggling to service their wartime obligations sought ways to raise revenue on the basis of flimsy paper possessions. States were well aware they had neither the legal authority nor military heft to sell off unceded Native land directly. They instead sold the right to a private purchase of Native land within their proclaimed borders—a kind of anticipatory property, or a land cession once removed. Preemptions, as preemptive titles were also known, allowed indebted states to sell a claim to Native land without assuming the risk or expense of actually persuading Native people to part with it.[19] This task fell on the preemption holder, who would only gain title to the tract in question once purchased from its Native possessors. Investors in preemptions felt sufficiently confident in their predictions of Native decline to believe that nations would cede their lands for a price rather than defend them by force.

Haudenosaunee lands—fertile, well irrigated, and within reach of existing settlements—became a quick target for purchase, both direct and preemptive. After the Treaty of Paris, speculators, state agents, and federal officials—sometimes working in concert, at other times at odds with one another—negotiated treaties that consumed almost the entirety of neighboring Cayuga, Oneida, Onondaga, and Tuscarora lands, employing combinations of trickery and threat. The Senecas were targeted as well. In 1784, at a treaty negotiation held with competing New York State and federal commissioners at Fort Stanwix, the Senecas ceded a strategically critical tract abutting the Niagara River, as well as vast acres in present-day Pennsylvania. In exchange, the treaty promised nothing more than an unspecified payment of goods. Meanwhile, Massachusetts staked its own claims to Seneca territory on the basis of its rather capacious colonial charter and in 1786 persuaded New York to concede to it all rights of preemption. Two years later, Massachusetts offloaded preemptive title to six million acres of Seneca land to speculators Nathaniel Gorham and Oliver Phelps, who committed to pay the state $1 million in its own heavily depreciated securities, in three planned installments. At a treaty signed soon after at Fort Harmar, Gorham and Phelps managed to purchase 2.6 million acres of eastern land from the Senecas by offering a deceptive payment of deflated New York currency, although Seneca negotiators refused to relinquish their prized lands west of the Genesee River. Then, before Gorham and Phelps had a chance to pay off their final installment to Massachusetts, Hamilton's financial revolution drove up the value of the depreciated securities the men still owed the state. With the real price of the purchase now far beyond their means, Gorham and Phelps were forced to forfeit their remaining preemptive titles.[20]

Massachusetts promptly resold these preemptions to another contender. Robert Morris had begun his career as a merchant, importing fine goods from Europe and shipping provisions to the slave plantations of Antigua, Barbados, and Jamaica. During the Revolution, Morris served as superintendent of finance and sat on Congress's Secret Committee of Trade, which afforded him access to privileged information and to the hulls of government ships. His wartime shipping trade grew so lucrative as to anoint Morris the richest man in the young republic: when he founded the first national bank, the Bank of North America, he personally guaranteed each banknote. After the war, Morris invested heavily in an assortment of state-issued claims to land in the nation's interior, ranging from Georgia to New York. The Seneca preemptions, which encompassed the arable Genesee River Valley, stood as the most promising of Morris's often unlikely speculations. Morris bought a large tract of "Genesee lands" directly from Gorham and Phelps, snapped up the preemptions that had reverted to Massachusetts, and then quickly resold most of his preemptive claims to a conglomerate of Dutch financiers that would eventually become known as the Holland Land Company. As a condition of the sale, Morris was responsible for extinguishing Seneca title. If Morris failed in this regard, the Holland Land Company would consider part of their payment a loan for which Morris would be liable.[21] With this leveraged purchase of an asset—preemptive title—that carried no certainty of realized value, Morris leapt over and above his unusually high risk threshold. Yet like Gorham and Phelps before him, Morris had assumed that the Senecas would offer little resistance to his venture—an assumption he began to doubt when the Northwest Confederacy brought the United States' westward advance to an abrupt halt.

St. Clair's humiliating retreat prompted officials in the Washington administration to reconsider their imperial strategy. Since his appointment as secretary of war in 1789, Henry Knox had warned that the costs of seizing Native lands by brute force far exceeded the republic's means. Knox estimated the war in the Ohio Country to cost $200,000 per year. If a similar conflict broke out with the restive Creeks, he added, it would likely cost

Congress an annual sum of \$1.5 million. Knox recommended that the government try a "a conciliatory system" of offering gifts—much as the British had done a generation before—to minimize Native use of force, which would in turn reduce the costs of frontier defense. Knox expected such an approach to cost a mere \$15,000 per year, a far more viable estimate than his eye-watering estimates for an Indian war. Purchasing peace from "barbarous nations" was the convention of "those more civilized," Knox would later explain to Congress, referring to the tributary payments European countries paid to the Barbary States of Algiers, Tripoli, and Tunis to protect their commercial fleets (the United States would soon adopt this same practice to control skyrocketing rates of marine insurance).[22] After the debacle in the Ohio Country, Washington agreed, advising Congress that Native nations should be taught "to expect annual presents, conditioned on the evidence of their attachment to the interests of the United States." Gifts would not preclude belligerence, but by inducing an "attachment" to the government, they might conserve the use of force, producing an expansion more orderly and achievable. Since gifts were intended not merely to pacify but also to displace Native peoples, they were not really gifts at all. Goods offered to Native nations would soon shed their charitable guises and become annuities, the instruments of compensated dispossession.[23]

In March 1792, Timothy Pickering, appointed commissioner to the Six Nations, invited Haudenosaunee leaders to a council in Philadelphia that would test the administration's reforms. Asking for neutrality in the Ohio war, he offered a yearly sum of \$1,500, pledged toward useful tools and agricultural instruction. As a commitment to pay an explicitly fixed value of goods each year, Pickering's agreement essentially extended retroactive compensation for prior treaties in which Haudenosaunee nations had ceded lands for a pittance. Pickering was not motivated by fairness. He hoped that annuities would not only deter the Haudenosaunee from joining the war but also enlist them in his efforts to neutralize the Northwest Confederacy by convincing the nations to accept compensated dispossession. Although they had not taken up arms in the confederation's defense, Haudenosaunee leaders like Mohawk statesman Joseph Brant had encouraged its creation and maintained diplomatic ties with the insurgents. As the Senecas were the westernmost nation of the Haudenosaunee Confederacy, it fell to them to convince Ohio nations to lay down their weapons, cede their lands, and accept annuities from the government.[24]

That fall, Cornplanter, Farmer's Brother, and Red Jacket traveled to the confluence of the Auglaize and Maumee Rivers to meet representatives of the Northwest Confederacy. The Senecas explained that they had accepted annuities from Pickering "hereafter for our protection."[25] But the Ohio nations saw no use in subjecting themselves to federal protection if it meant giving up homelands, vowing they would "stand firmly protected— for our lands and Rights."[26] A Shawnee orator flung the Senecas' wampum to the ground, leaving a humiliated Farmer's Brother to pick up the belt and retreat. At another council that summer, Wyandot runners again refused to sell their lands, proposing that the government instead pay the penniless settlers who squatted among them to leave. In a dig at the United States' fiscal strain, the confederation remarked that expelling settlers might save "the great sums you must expend in raising and paying armies, with a view to force us to yield you our country."[27]

After rejecting Pickering's offer by Seneca proxies, the Northwest Confederacy steeled for battle, but they would lose their war. In August 1794, General Anthony Wayne marched into their territories, leading an army transformed by its earlier defeat. Congress had expended considerable sums to bolster the military after St. Clair's losses, adding battalions of artillery, infantry, and additional regiments while improving soldier training and provisions. Wayne led a far better-equipped and disciplined force into a final, victorious battle against the Northwest Confederacy. Such a decisive blow prepared the ground for a treaty in which the United States could hold the upper hand. That fall, Wayne gathered with representatives of the Illinois, Kickapoos, Lenapes, Miamis, Odawas, Ojibwes, Potawatomis, Shawnees, and Wyandots at Fort Greenville, one of the recently built outposts meant to assert federal claims to lands north of the Ohio River. Adhering closely to instructions given him by Pickering, Wayne procured a combined territorial cession of roughly 11.8 million acres by offering each nation annuities in goods ranging from $500 to $1,000.[28] A policy of compensated dispossession, applied crookedly and after the fact in the case of the Haudenosaunee, reached its full fruition at Fort Greenville, when nations of the Northwest Confederacy were forced to cede lands in exchange for a payment spread across time.

Annuities served at once as payment and as incentive to disarmament. Compensation would not only ease territorial acquisitions, officials hoped, but also weaken the bonds among confederation members, splintering the unity that had fortified their resistance. While severing military ties between Native nations, annuities would also tether each nation to the United States. As Pickering argued, annuities' most important characteristic was not their degree of generosity but their recurrence. No "quantity of goods that could be named, if delivered at once . . . would create an obligation of which they would feel the force, beyond the moment of enjoying them," he explained.[29] Newly beholden to future installments of goods, nations would be more likely to comply with the United States' demands for their land. Such annuity-forged "attachments," as Washington had referred to them, were explicit in the Greenville treaty's fifth article, which specified plans for any future cessions. While the signatory nations were nominally assured the quiet enjoyment of their reservations, if at any point they were "disposed to sell their lands," they could do so "only to the United States." Such contradictory language indicated that the government had little respect for Native nations' rights to remain on their homelands.[30]

Much like the speculators who snapped up preemptive titles, the United States now claimed an exclusive right to purchase unceded Native territories. The treaty legitimated this presumption by invoking the language of protection, noting that "the said Indian tribes . . . acknowledge themselves to be under the protection of the said United States, and no other power whatever." The federal government would prevent its own citizens from disturbing the signatory nations, remove squatters, and even allow Native governments to punish violators "as they shall think proper."[31] As a condition of this protection, nations submitted to an unequal but binding relationship with the United States. They could no longer make or break alliances on an international stage with the freedom they had before, nor could they convey land to any rival power. These terms placed constraints on their sovereignty but did not extinguish their right to govern their internal affairs. They would preside over much smaller domains and receive goods that stood as mere tokens of the landed wealth they once had. Yet they remained nations, not subjects of a growing empire.

Morris kept a close eye on the Ohio Country. The Northwest Confederacy's early military successes—and widespread fears among land speculators that the Haudenosaunee might align with them—had scuttled his hopes of quickly clearing his sale of Seneca preemptions to the Holland Land Company. While praying for order to be imposed on the Northwest Territory, Morris had continued to invest in lands scattered from New York to Georgia, growing increasingly overleveraged. Using a trust, Morris combined his capital with that of James Greenleaf and John Nicholson to form the North American Land Company, which became the largest land speculation venture in the United States by far. The company took advantage of the era's still coalescing federalism, playing off state and national officials, shopping across jurisdictions to find the most favorable legal environment for their investments, and courting Native nations.[32]

By late 1794, it seemed Morris's stars had begun to align. Haudenosaunee diplomats agreed to continued neutrality in a November summit with Pickering in Canandaigua, New York, accepting an increase in their annuity from $1,500 to $4,500 in exchange for staying out of the northwestern war. A week later, the Jay Treaty settled lingering disputes between the United States and Britain, which agreed on a two-year deadline to shutter borderland military posts used to funnel provisions to the Northwest Confederacy. With the war quieted and the Haudenosaunee on more favorable terms with the United States, negotiations with the Senecas appeared far more likely to succeed. Then, in October 1795, the United States negotiated the Treaty of San Lorenzo with Spain, which opened the Mississippi River to American navigation and immediately buoyed the value of western lands, including those across the Northwest Territory. Delighted, Morris wrote a personal note thanking Wayne for the "check which you have given to the savages."[33]

There was a catch, however. Although Morris and his Dutch backers supplied the capital to purchase Seneca territories, they were now forced to do so under the auspices of the federal government. In line with Hamilton's aims to capture the revenue of ceded Native lands for Congress, Washington's administration had more broadly sought to establish the supremacy of the federal government over the interrelated fields of Indian affairs, territorial governance, and the public domain.[34] Under the 1790 Trade and Intercourse Acts—an as-yet skeletal body of Indian affairs regulations—Morris was required to secure executive approval and enlist a federal treaty commissioner to oversee negotiations. For the first time, only a federal treaty could acquire Native land.[35]

Morris's transaction now hinged on not only the Senecas' cooperation but also that of the War Department, making an uncertain investment even riskier. Worse, Morris was officially broke. Each of the partners in the North American Land Company had borrowed far more than their acres were worth and resorted to backing one another's debts to conceal their insolvency. The Seneca preemptions, Morris's personal venture, stood as his last opportunity to salvage some part of his once considerable fortune. As he prepared for the treaty, Morris shut himself up in his Philadelphia estate, the Hills—recently foreclosed on and already sold at auction— in order to avoid being served with one of the numerous writs that had accumulated against him. In a republic that had yet to pass general bank-ruptcy laws, any one writ would send him to prison if delivered.[36]

Fortunately for Morris, the United States had its own reasons for sup-porting the speculator's push into Seneca homelands. The War Department planned to cut a road between the Genesee and Niagara Rivers, and Mor-ris's purchase would spare it the trouble of negotiating rights of way. In the fall of 1796, Captain James Bruff, a veteran of the Continental Army, vis-ited the Senecas to encourage a sale to Morris. Bruff began by informing them that New York State held jurisdiction over their lands, a statement that the Senecas received with skepticism. Speaker Red Jacket rejected a sale to Morris, "the great Eater with a big Belly" who intended "to devour our Lands," and ordered that "Congress will not license nor suffer him to pur-chase our Lands."[37] Yet blocking Morris's acquisition would have absorbed more energy and expense than the skeletal War Department was willing—or able—to devote. With federal permission, that spring Morris invited key Seneca leaders to his lavish home in Philadelphia, launching a charm offen-sive that he prayed would clinch the treaty he desperately needed.[38]

Morris's most important guest was Cornplanter, a military leader born to a Seneca mother of the Wolf clan and a Dutch fur trader father. Cornplanter's role vested him with the duty to represent warriors' sen-timents in councils. He had reluctantly signed the Haudenosaunee land cession treaties of the late 1780s, including the sale to Gorham and Phelps, which had enraged his fellow Senecas, stoked rivalries with other leaders, and earned him a reputation for self-interested deceit. Cornplanter had, in fact, accepted the occasional bribe, but his motives were not entirely mercenary. The village where he and his kin lived abutted the Allegheny River, once a corridor of Indigenous trade and diplomacy that had more recently become a settlement frontier. Pennsylvanians repeatedly raided Cornplanter's community, and he hoped to bring an end to the assaults by strengthening his alliance with the United States.[39] Morris's overtures presented an opportunity for Cornplanter to secure protection for his enclave by sacrificing a part of his nation's broader territory.

Cornplanter visited Morris's home in late winter 1797 and listened care-fully to the speculator's proposal. Morris insisted a sale would enrich the Senecas and offered compensation in the form of bank stock, a medium of payment unfamiliar to Cornplanter. With Morris's words still fresh in his memory, he traveled across the capital city to seek counsel from President Washington. "Father," Cornplanter began, "I wish whilst I am able to do business to provide for the rising generation." He explained that Morris had told him of "a strong place" where people's money was not only safe but "produces them each and every year an increase without lessening the stock." The prospect of perpetual wealth appealed to Cornplanter, but he worried about the risk. "If we should dispose of part of our Country and put our money with yours," he asked, "will it be safe?"[40] Washington's response has not survived, but he evidently quieted Cornplanter's fears and encouraged the Seneca Nation to accept Morris's proposal. Writing to his son Thomas weeks later, Morris reported that Cornplanter seemed convinced that "it will promote the happiness of his Nation to sell at least a part of their Land + place the purchase money in the Public funds so as to derive an Annual income therefore."[41]

Negotiations began that August, at the settler town of Big Tree, just south of Buffalo Creek. Federal treaty commissioner Jeremiah Wadsworth was in attendance. Indian agent Israel Chapin had recently lost his daughter, so the Senecas performed rites of condolence meant to clear their eyes of tears, ears of blockages, and throats of obstructions. Wadsworth distributed presents before the council began, a gesture that lent a federal imprimatur to the proceedings. With the elder Morris under effective house arrest in Philadelphia, negotiations were led by his son Thomas, who held aspirations of his own to capitalize on "the Genesee Lands." Morris knew from his father's consultations with leaders like Cornplanter that the imperiled survival of their nation weighed heavily on their minds. A few days after the opening rites, Thomas laid out an offer. Vowing that the Senecas would receive the largest sum ever paid for Native land, Morris added that the fact of its investment would assure "that not only you but your children and your children's children can derive from it a lasting benefit."[42]

Red Jacket, a leader from the town of Buffalo Creek who, like Cornplanter, had survived the battlefields of the Revolutionary War, spoke next. Known as Sagoyewatha, or He Who Keeps Them Awake, Red Jacket had for the past decade served his people as a skilled if controversial speaker. He was far from convinced by Morris's financial reasoning. As Red Jacket explained, prior to the war between America and Britain the Haudenosaunee Confederacy "were a great People." Yet decisions made by other Haudenosaunee polities since then had eroded the confederacy's political integrity and weakened its power. Red Jacket pointed to the example of the Oneidas, who in 1785 had ceded 460,000 acres to the state of New York for a single payment of $11,500. The sale broke with the Oneidas' yearslong practice of leasing lands to non-Native settlers, an arrangement that had garnered the nation a reliable annual income without compromising its domain. Ceding land for a windfall payment had made the Oneidas "Rich in Money" at the cost of losing "their consequence as a nation," in Red Jacket's view.[43] Worse, the Oneidas' affluence had proven temporary. Money coursed through the Oneida economy, dissipated outward through market exchange, and left no trace of lasting benefit to the dispossessed nation.

If it was the ephemerality of a lump sum that held back the Senecas from a sale, Thomas Morris hoped that offering a form of payment that replenished yearly would convince them. Drawing on his prior observation of Haudenosaunee treaty conventions, Morris built his case by appealing directly to Seneca women. Women did not customarily participate directly in treaty negotiations. But since land was considered the communal possession of the women who tended it, their views on territorial matters carried significant weight.[44] Speaking to the elder women in council, Morris explained that yearly annuities financed by bank stock could be spent on hiring agricultural labor and on purchasing clothes, two objects that would primarily benefit Seneca women and children. To sweeten the deal, he promised a liberal distribution of stock animals immediately upon signing.[45]

One can only imagine how Seneca women received Morris's proposal. Memories were still fresh of General Sullivan's campaign, which had destroyed the literal fruits of their labor and weakened their children with famine. Safeguarding agriculture by gaining a regular stream of revenue designated for its support may have appealed to women as a means of recovering from the Revolutionary War's enduring devastation, especially if this revenue came from a treaty that further cemented their reconciliation with the United States. At least, Morris believed so. As he reported in his journal, his arguments "had an excellent effect" and the women "at once declared themselves for selling."[46]

With negotiations successfully rekindled, Morris delved into the specifics of the financial arrangement. If the Senecas agreed to cede the bulk of their territory—excluding modest reservations squared on their current villages—Morris would offer $100,000 in stock in the First Bank of the United States. To convey the scale of this principal, Morris boasted that at least thirty-five horses would be needed were he to ship the amount in a single delivery of specie. But he reiterated the wisdom of investment over a lump sum. By purchasing stock in the First Bank, Morris explained, the Senecas would receive an annual income of at least $6,000, or 6 percent interest on $100,000 in bank stock.[47] Pickering and Washington had argued that annuities' power to "attach" Native polities lay in their recurrence. Here, Morris argued for the recurrence of interest as a feature that would grant stability and longevity to the Seneca economy.

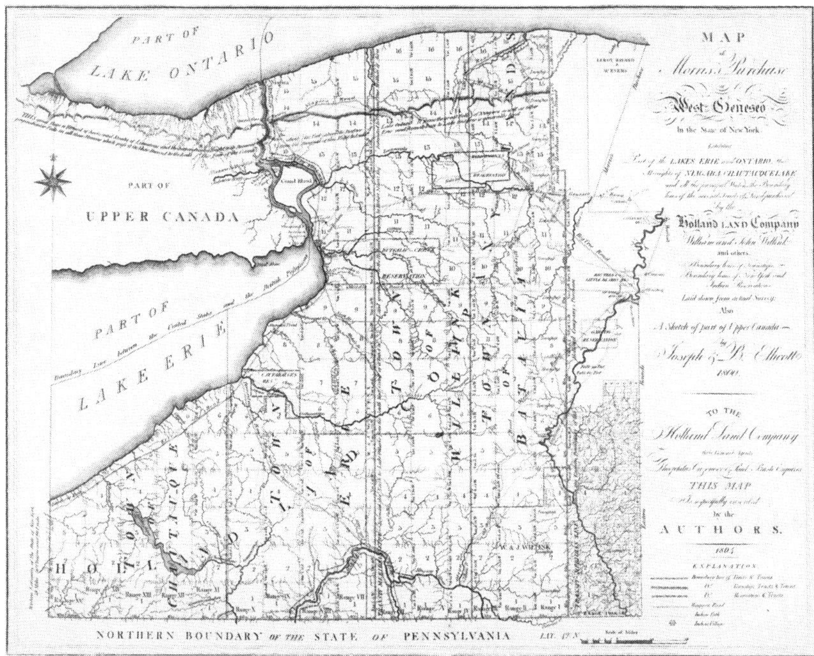

Map of Robert Morris's purchase. Joseph B. Ellicott began surveying Morris's purchase for the Holland Land Company soon after the 1797 Treaty of Big Tree. *Source:* Joseph B. Ellicott, *Map of Morris's Purchase or West Geneseo in the State of New York* [. . .], 1800. David Rumsey Map Collection.

By mid-September, after nearly two months of negotiation, the Senecas signed the finished treaty. Within a week, the Holland Land Company's surveyor began marking out the perimeter of the purchase.[48]

Morris had prided himself on a savvy appeal to women in council but quietly relied on underhanded tactics. Prior to the council, to ensure his son's success, Robert Morris had promised individual annuities to a number of influential Seneca leaders. In secretive negotiations held in the shadows of the council, Thomas rewarded Cornplanter, Red Jacket, and a handful of other prominent leaders for their cooperation. These private annuities would be drawn from interest raised by a second, smaller trust fund of $24,000, to be invested in federal 3 percent bonds and overseen by a board of trustees that included Morris the younger. Of these beneficiaries, Cornplanter had taken the most care in negotiating the size and terms of his personal trust. His was the only annuity to name heirs: Cornplanter's wife, Skawainau, along with his sons and daughter, would inherit the annuity in equally drawn portions after his death.[49] By accepting a wrenching territorial loss and embracing an unfamiliar form of wealth, Cornplanter had settled on a strategy to provide for his successors on both a national and personal scale.

Shortly before resigning as Treasury secretary in early 1795, Hamilton gave a parting update to Congress on the republic's public credit and the redemption of its debts. Progress had been slow, but Hamilton estimated that twenty-one million acres of "western lands" could eventually deliver $4.2 million in revenue. Ominously, though, he reminded Congress that "the boundary line between the United States and the Indians" remained "unsettled."[50]

Shortly thereafter Hamilton retired to a private legal practice in New York City. The most lucrative of Hamilton's clients was the Holland Land Company, which retained him for nearly a decade after he retired from public office. Many members of the conglomerate had invested in federal securities and so knew Hamilton from his years at the Treasury. When the investors shifted from American bonds to American lands, they sought Hamilton's services as an attorney. Most of Hamilton's attention was absorbed by the construction of byzantine legal agreements necessitated by New York's laws barring foreigners from holding real property in the state. But Hamilton also assisted with the technical details of Morris's unprecedented transaction. As Treasury secretary, Hamilton had presided over a financial revolution predicated on treating Native land as a fiscal asset. In his work for the Holland Land Company, Hamilton executed a purchase of Native land with the stock of an institution that his own revolution had ushered into existence: the First Bank of the United States.[51]

Under the Constitution, treaties with foreign powers were the sole prerogative of the executive and subject to ratification solely by the Senate. This provision assured coherent international diplomacy—including with Indigenous nations—by insulating foreign relations from the influence of states and the House, as the more democratic lower chamber. But the precise legalities of treaty agreements, including the role of private purchasers, remained inchoate. In order to ensure the validity of its title, the Holland Land Company solicited Hamilton's advice on precisely how to purchase shares in the First Bank of the United States on behalf of the Seneca Nation, and the exact wording by which this purchase should be recorded and certified by President John Adams. Hamilton outlined the best language to be used and advised on where the constellation of documents surrounding the land cession should be recorded. In doing so, Hamilton helped introduce legal devices drawn from the law of equity—an often idiosyncratic corpus that covered matters like divorces, foreclosures, probate, and trusts—to treaties between sovereign nations that were, ostensibly, artifacts of international law and diplomacy alone.[52] In a detail that indicated the multiple legal registers on which the treaty operated, the document was both ratified by the Senate and recorded as a deed in the office of New York's secretary of state.[53]

As a merchant and speculator, Robert Morris was intimately familiar with trusts and other instruments that Euro-American propertied classes employed to immortalize their wealth. Since the British Parliament had eased restrictions on mortgage foreclosure and debt reclamation in 1732, American subjects operated within a distinctive property regime that rendered real estate more liquid and privileged creditors over heirs. This meant that, in contrast to a British legal context that erected safeguards around family estates, in early America real (and chattel) property could be swept away by failure. In this precarious environment, Anglo-American elites embraced trusts in order to ensure an inheritance for their successors. Established in vivo, in wills, or later, as charitable endowments, trust funds became legal pockets in which figures like Morris could squirrel away stocks, land, or funds for their heirs.[54] Employed in this manner, trust funds can be imagined as the figurative "dead hands" of the testator, slapping away creditors from beyond the grave.

In this case, however, the graves Morris imagined were those of the Senecas. Just as Cornplanter had planned for his wife, children, and nation, Morris too held a strategy to provide for his successors, one that could succeed only if the Senecas had no successors of their own. Believing that he and his heirs would outlast the Seneca Nation itself, he planned to stake a future claim on the bank stock. Specifically, he intended to position himself as trustee to the Seneca fund and limit the nation's entitlement to the $100,000 in First Bank of the United States stock to their own lifetimes. Once the Senecas were gone, he (or his heirs) would take possession of the fund. As Morris explained to Holland Land Company agent Theophile Cazenove, he believed "that there would be nothing improper in having this so managed that the principal should revert to me or my heirs in case the Seneca nation shall become extinct."[55] It was a far-fetched scheme, as Cazenove warned him, and Morris would not live to see any of the principal reclaimed for his dynasty. But after his death, his heirs and creditors would, in fact, carry out a protracted legal battle in New York State's Chancery Court over rights to reclaim the Senecas' financial wealth, acting on a steady and unwarranted belief that the nation teetered on the brink of extinction.[56]

Federal officials were willing to authorize private investors like Morris to purchase Native lands in the name of expanding the republic's empire and stabilizing its fiscal base, but allowing these men to assume trusteeship over Native polities was another matter. Morris had expected to install himself as trustee, managing the investment and disbursing the annuities through his own agents. He was shocked to learn on the eve of the treaty council that Secretary of War James McHenry had instead insisted that title to the stock would reside with the president of the United States and his successors. Writing to Wadsworth, Morris expressed indignation "that Mr McHenry should conceive himself authorized to give any positive instruction on that head at all."[57] But from McHenry's vantage, allowing a private citizen to claim trusteeship over the economic affairs of an Indigenous nation—a status that would have come perilously close to rivaling federal preemption—was out of the question. Morris grudgingly conceded to have the stock bought in his name and subsequently assigned to the president and his successors, a proposal that the administration accepted.[58]

Following Senate ratification of the treaty that December, Cazenove carried out the investment according to Hamilton's instructions. Since Morris was hopelessly illiquid, and the success of the transaction hinged on fulfilling the terms of the treaty, the Dutch syndicate covered the costs of the stock purchase. The following March, Cazenove purchased 205 of the $400 shares in the First Bank of the United States at an eighty-seven-dollar premium—consistent with market prices—and deposited the remaining $126.94 in an account created for the Seneca trust at the bank.[59] With these loose ends tied, the first Indian trust fund had been established, and the federal government for the first time—but not the last—assumed fiduciary powers over the wealth of a dispossessed nation.

In accepting bank stock as compensation for their land, the Senecas had taken on an unprecedented risk, placing faith not only in Morris and the federal officials who had assumed the trust but in the integrity of the First Bank of the United States. As they waited for their first annuity to arrive, the reality of a payment deferred rather than delivered up front settled in. Cornplanter especially worried about the possibility of Morris's dishonesty, and asked visitors from Philadelphia to share any news they might hear about "the lot of our inheritance."[60] In order to maintain leverage during these anxious early days, Senecas from the Allegany and Buffalo Creek communities obstructed the work of Holland Land Company surveyor Joseph Ellicott. The Senecas' disruptions ceased only when Ellicott explicitly confirmed that their funds had been invested, and he reiterated that they would receive dividends equal to the sum discussed in council— nothing less.[61]

And yet the Senecas soon found their skepticism validated. In early September, with the customary season for annuity payments approaching, Indian agent Israel Chapin informed the nation that their first dividend would fall far short of the $6,000 annual sum discussed at the treaty. The bank released dividends to shareholders biannually, in July and January. The Seneca investment had only been made the previous March— meaning only half a dividend payment had accrued. Chapin warned Secretary of War James McHenry that this shortfall would anger the Senecas, yet the secretary responded with irritation, calling the expectation of a full $6,000 payment in the first year "extravagant."[62] When they learned of the shortfall, the Senecas were indeed upset. "We expect," they warned Chapin, "that an annuity of $6,000 will be ready for us at the falling of the leaves."[63]

Once briefed on the exchange, McHenry assumed that the Senecas had simply failed to grasp the terms of investment generally accepted by the bank's shareholders. But as Chapin informed him, this explanation for the shortfall "has been told them often and they understand it."[64] It was not that the Senecas failed to understand biannual dividends, as McHenry expected, but that they did not care. According to the Senecas, the amount that they had been promised in council was $6,000 per annum. It was an amount not only repeated by Morris but, as the Senecas had reminded Chapin, pledged by federal treaty commissioner Jeremiah Wadsworth. Regardless of Morris's involvement, to the Senecas the 1797 Treaty of Big Tree embodied a commitment from one nation to another, and the obligation to fulfill its terms rested with the United States itself, not a bank that happened to operate within its borders and under its charter.

McHenry persisted, and the Senecas ultimately conceded to a deferred full payment in January 1799.[65] Yet this detente failed to settle who, exactly, should shoulder responsibility for any deficits in the Seneca annuity. As the product of a treaty devised to facilitate a private trust, the Seneca annuity was neither solely an obligation of Congress nor a regular financial transaction. Were the Senecas owed by the United States under the terms of international law, such that the federal government should fulfill its obligations regardless of the state of its national bank? Or were the Senecas simply one body of foreign investors among others, subject to the vicissitudes of a financial institution operating beyond their jurisdiction? Annuities funded by interest made a commitment between nations difficult to delineate from a quotidian risk-bearing investment.

These questions remained unanswered when the Senecas received their first dividend at Buffalo, New York, a town established on their recently ceded lands. Planned as an entrepôt by the Holland Land Company, Buffalo remained but a satellite of the adjacent Buffalo Creek reservation, now the bustling political center of the Haudenosaunee Confederacy. Annuity disbursements brought crowds of Seneca to Buffalo for weeks as councils progressed, agents tabulated accounts and audited claims, and Seneca men battled in games of lacrosse. As a result of treaties signed between the Six Nations and the United States in 1792 and 1794, the Senecas had for several years received annuities in the form of goods: typically, supplies of Mackinaw blankets, calicoes, yarn, thread, needles, and ribbons, as well as farming implements and the services of a blacksmith. After Big Tree, however, the Senecas demanded the dividends on their stock in the First Bank of the United States paid as a cash annuity, delivered in silver dollars. Seneca preferences forced Indian agent Israel Chapin to travel east to the Bank of Albany, procure two sums in specie—$6,000 for the national annuity, and $780 for the private annuities promised by Morris—which he floated up the Mohawk River and hauled back to Seneca reservations.[66]

All national annuities were first apportioned to each reservation by making use of sticks carried by each sachem from the Allegany, Buffalo Creek, Cattaragus, and Tonawanda communities. Each stick bore a series of notches, representing the number of families in each reservation, figures that were carefully reconciled with a census carried out by Chapin months earlier. After this first-round distribution, Seneca policy treated material and monetary annuities distinctly: goods were distributed according to need, while specie was allocated to mothers, as heads of families, and to the single adults who remained. Annuities provided support, in Farmer's Brother's words, for "our old people, and our Women and children."[67]

Within a matter of years, the Senecas' early aversions to risk had sufficiently abated for them to request an expansion of their investment. At an 1801 council in Geneseo, New York, Red Jacket asked that Chapin "bring forward the use or interest of our money . . . to be deposited in the Bank of the US under the direction of the President" and to consolidate the interest earned to enlarge their existing annuity.[68] Recently elected President Thomas Jefferson agreed, promising that "so long as your Nation shall conduct themselves peaceably" he would "continue to be their friend, and to treat them as his Children."[69] McHenry had presumed Native peoples incapable of understanding the mechanics of investment. But once introduced to it, the Senecas had no difficulty grasping the concept of interest, which they described in their language using the term *ëwödönia:k*, or "it will continue to be to make, create, or establish itself."[70] It was a term that encapsulated what the Senecas sought for their people by placing their money in federal hands.

As indirect investors in the First Bank of the United States, the Senecas helped underwrite Hamilton's efforts to rectify the republic's credit, a program that kept the country viable while it was still striving for recognition within a community of European empires. Hamilton had intended the bank to act both as a fiscal safety net that could sustain the federal government with short-term loans during emergencies and as a financial engine that could generate credit, expand and improve the money supply, and create a nationwide banking system. To accomplish these aims, the First Bank of the United States was capitalized at an astounding $10 million. (By comparison, its only predecessor, Morris's Bank of North America, was founded with a mere $400,000 in capital.) Throughout its existence, the bank stood as the largest private enterprise in the United States. When its securities were first publicly offered on July 4, 1791, they sold out within an hour, a sign of optimism among the affluent merchants who could afford its $400 shares. With securities that regularly traded at a premium of 120–150 percent, the First Bank even lured in investment from across the Atlantic.[71]

The First Bank also catalyzed the formation of a national capital market. Public confidence and the bank's innovative branch structure ensured that its notes circulated widely without depreciating in value, a welcome contrast to the wildly depreciated Continental currency that had fueled the Revolution and to the myriad and often ersatz paper currencies emitted by state-chartered banks. By cooperating with customs officers and the US Mint, the First Bank also streamlined and lubricated revenue collection, kept specie from draining overseas, and made reserves available when needed.[72] Senecas were not major patrons, holding 1 percent of the First Bank's equity, yet they were patrons nonetheless. The arrangement revealed the doubled advantage of fiduciary colonialism: having first gained access to Seneca lands on the back of Morris's speculations, the United States now absorbed the imputed value of these lands as capital that its pillar fiscal institution could deploy to support its expanding economy.

The financial conditions established by Hamilton's reforms permitted successive administrations to pursue a bolder program of territorial dispossession. Shortly after Thomas Jefferson assumed office as president in 1801, he learned that Spain had secretly ceded Louisiana back to France.

Because Louis Napoleon had little interest in populating the North American colony—he intended to use it as a breadbasket for far more lucrative colonies in the Caribbean—he arranged for Spain to continue administering Louisiana. The following year it became clear that Spain would no longer permit citizens of the United States to engage in commerce through the Mississippi River, a key provision of the Treaty of San Lorenzo that was essential to sustaining settlements in the continental interior.[73] Rather than pursue warfare against France, Jefferson opted for a strategy that closely imitated how his predecessors had approached the dispossession of Native peoples: purchase.

Dispatching James Monroe to assist the United States' minister to France, Robert R. Livingston, Jefferson instructed the men to offer no more than $10 million for the purchase of New Orleans and, if possible, East and West Florida. Instead, Napoleon offered the entire territory of Louisiana, an expanse that would almost double the United States' alleged dominion. Jefferson owed his success to self-emancipated armies in Saint Domingue, whose war for liberation so drained Napoleon's resources that he abandoned the island colony altogether, obviating any need for Louisiana. But Jefferson also relied on the United States' sterling creditworthiness. The purchase itself was mainly financed through an issue of bonds, valued at $11,250,000, floated in Amsterdam, London, and Paris by the British House of Baring. A decade earlier Jefferson had bitterly opposed Hamilton's restructuring of the federal debt and his establishment of the First Bank. Now he reaped the benefits of Hamilton's financial revolution.[74]

The empire that took shape along the Upper Mississippi River shared little resemblance to the uniformly settled yeoman republic associated with Jefferson's political thought, however. Apart from settler outposts like Detroit, where half of the Michigan Territory's non-Native population resided, the territories carved from the Northwest Ordinance beyond Ohio remained Indian country. Annuities flowed out to Native nations through the "factory" system, a straggling web of fur-trading posts created by Congress in 1796 with the aim of eroding British dominance over commerce with Native peoples. Factories like the one at Fort Michilimackinac—located along the Straits of Mackinac, far north in Ojibwe territories—became founts of annuities and presents, payments of tribute intended to rival British offerings of trade goods to these same Native powers in the region. By 1811 the War Department disbursed roughly $37,950 in annuities to twenty-three different Native polities, at sites spread from Detroit to Ocmulgee.[75]

The War of 1812 presented the first serious challenge to the United States' viability as a military power since the resistance mounted by the

Northwest Confederacy a decade earlier. Resumed conflict with Britain was precisely the sort of calamity that Hamilton had in mind when founding the First Bank of the United States as a lifeline for the federal government. But by now too many of his Jeffersonian successors saw the institution as more of a peril to democracy than a safeguard. In 1811, Congress voted to allow the federal charter of the First Bank of the United States to expire. Among those investors impacted by the liquidation of the bank's obligations was the Seneca Nation.

Secretary of War William Eustis took pains to ensure that the Seneca trust fund's bank stock was promptly placed on the market, but depreciation meant that the sale yielded a new principal of merely $77,440. In the months before the United States declared war, Treasury Secretary Albert Gallatin issued the first federal war loan, setting a pattern for debt-fueled war financing that would become characteristic of military interventions for two centuries to come. In November 1812, Secretary of War Eustis reinvested the Senecas' funds in these newly issued bonds.[76] As trust beneficiaries, Senecas became indirect financiers for a war in which they held no direct stake but that would soon rage across their homelands.

By the summer of 1813, the United States' military flagged against its British opponents, and the War Department decided to recruit Haudenosaunee warriors. Well aware that annuities were one of the few means his administration had to retain Haudenosaunee loyalty, Secretary of War John Armstrong pledged to the Senecas that their interest would be "punctually paid," despite the Treasury's dismal outlook.[77] Soon after, hundreds of Seneca warriors enlisted to support US forces, including Cornplanter, Farmer's Brother, and Red Jacket. On the battlefields of Niagara, they would face their own kin from Grand River, a reservation founded by Joseph Brant, the Mohawk leader, in Upper Canada.[78]

When neutrality became untenable, the Senecas sided with their trustee. Yet Congress strained to maintain its economic obligations to Indigenous allies, including the Senecas. In 1813, the federal government failed to deliver interest payments to the Senecas as promised, offering yet another inadequate shipment of annuity goods for the Six Nations. Military wages owed Seneca warriors had yet to be paid in full. The Senecas continued to serve, but their resentments accumulated.[79] After Britain and the United States ended their war—in a peace treaty that once again excluded Native nations from negotiations—the Senecas did not wait before demanding their due.

In March 1815, a delegation of Haudenosaunee diplomats confronted President James Monroe with their grievances. Monroe promised the Senecas "an annual amount equal to what they have theretofore received."[80] Upon Monroe's urging, Congress supplemented the interest earned on the Senecas' stock—now drawing only 3 percent—to maintain their $6,000 annuity.[81] From the outset, the Senecas had interpreted their interest payments as obligations from one sovereign to another. After proving their fidelity during a war that nearly toppled the young republic, the Senecas had managed to compel the United States to see the fund this way as well.

Settlers' determination to break free of imperial constraints and claim Native territories west of the Appalachian Mountains had propelled the thirteen colonies toward revolt. Once they were independent, however, Native military power humbled the United States' aspirations to an easy conquest by arms. The Northwest Confederacy forced federal officials to prolong their imperial time horizon, supplementing a shortsighted belligerence with a policy of paying for land in annual installments. By meting out payments across time, federal officials held nations' future prosperity captive. Yet, as the Senecas demonstrated, even within these confines Native leaders could exercise measures of authority over annuities. Promises to maintain financial obligations, made by the government in treaties of dispossession, counted for something, Cornplanter and his peers argued. Implied in the Senecas' successful bids for the full value of their compensation was a theory of trusteeship as a reciprocal relationship, if an uneven one.

Treaties that conferred the first annuities declared the United States at once the protector of Native nations and the sole legitimate purchaser of their land, an assertion that slipped an underlying land claim beneath Native peoples' feet. With this combination of compensation, preemption, protection, and control, the fundamentals of fiduciary colonialism were in place. Thanks to the meddling of land speculators—and Robert Morris in particular—a precocious form of financialized trusteeship germinated in the 1797 Treaty of Big Tree. The Seneca trust fund would stand alone for several decades, in retrospect an outlier within the history of fiduciary colonialism. It took another group—missionaries—to reawaken the financial trust as an instrument of dispossession.

# CHAPTER TWO

# Inheriting the Earth

WRITING IN 1819 to his friend, the missionary Elias Cornelius, Choctaw captain David Folsom explained that his nation needed schools "so that our childrens may be wiser than we are."[1] Folsom's wish hinted at the challenges his people faced as a result of the United States' continental ambitions. Four years earlier, Folsom and hundreds of his fellow Choctaws had fought alongside General Andrew Jackson in an 1813 invasion of the Upper Town Creeks and, later, against the British in New Orleans. Yet Jackson now rewarded his Choctaw allies by demanding they cede their homelands in present-day Mississippi and relocate west, to a reservation nestled against the newly created Arkansas Territory. The impending treaty, to be negotiated in the fall of 1820, loomed in Folsom's mind as he wrote to Cornelius. He had no interest in leaving his ranch or his homelands—Nanih Waiya, in the Choctaw language—for a region the Choctaws knew to be arid and inhospitable. But Folsom wondered if Jackson's determination to acquire Choctaw land might be leveraged to some positive use.

For months, Folsom had been helping Cornelius establish a school for the Choctaws by locating grounds and lending out enslaved laborers. With this assistance, missionaries had erected several log buildings as part of a planned thirty-five-acre mission, including a dining hall, a mill, and a stable, which the Choctaws filled with donated livestock. This work was still underway, but proceeding slowly, since, as Folsom noted, "the means are wanting." As both Cornelius and Folsom knew, treaties that ceded land were the primary mechanism by which the Choctaws could secure income for any national project, schools included. Done well, a treaty could sacrifice only a section of territory in order to endow the nation with well-resourced education. In Folsom's thinking, the Choctaws had "a plenty of good land to get means with," and he had "no doubt but the Nation would be more than willing to support the school."[2]

Cornelius and Folsom's preparations embodied a kind of collaboration increasingly common in the years after the War of 1812, a period in which the United States moved aggressively into the Native South. When Jackson invaded Creek territories in 1813—in a war that soon swung east into Seminole country—other southern nations had begun to reconcile to the futility of armed confrontation with the United States. For the Choctaws, Chickasaws, and Cherokees, the 1810s and 1820s were spent shifting capacity away from making war and toward forms of nation building that engaged carefully with institutions rooted in the United States—institutions like missionary-run schools. At a series of councils with General Jackson during his protracted postwar military occupation of the Gulf South, leaders like Folsom weighed how they might offer limited cessions of their primary asset—land—in order to prepare their children for a struggle against a colonial assault that showed no sign of abating.

When Folsom and fellow Choctaw negotiators did cede limited tracts of homelands in the 1820 Treaty of Doaks Stand, they chose to structure the compensation they received as an investment that would finance education. After 1797, no new Indian trust funds appeared until a quarter of a century later, when missionaries began nosing their way into treaty negotiations and promoting a variant of financial planning distinct from the dynastic trusts that had served as a template for the Seneca fund. Endowments, bequests, and other philanthropic trusts had become common vehicles for wealth management in New England as a class of affluent merchants and manufacturers sought to sanctify their wealth and imprint their name on public institutions. Northeastern missionaries were steeped in this institutional context, and when they ventured south to Indian Country, they carried with them expertise in charitable wealth management alongside their Bibles, slates, and prayer books. Where dynastic trusts encased wealth to ensure it would outlast the conveyor's decease, philanthropic trusts attached a public good to this protected money. Much like the Senecas, who had embraced investment in the First Bank of the United States to weather the aftermath of the American Revolution, the Choctaws and their neighbors adopted trusts with an eye to the survival of coming generations. Native leaders realized they could do more than merely spread their wealth across time; they could assign this wealth to a specific purpose, and the purpose nations prioritized most was education.

Folsom's push for expanded schooling was in part a response to Indian agents' and missionaries' campaign to bring "civilization" to Native peoples. Civilization policy held the ostensibly humble aims of encouraging agriculture and domestic arts, of converting souls and instructing children. Yet since Secretary of War Henry Knox first espoused the policy in the 1790s, civilization intended not to uplift Native peoples but to cheapen their expropriation. Federal Indian agents sought through civilization to upturn Indigenous peoples' ways of living on their land, condensing their settlements by compelling them to abandon the hunt for husbandry. By engineering a new economic geography, the policy aimed to make swaths of territory superfluous to Native peoples, who would then—the plan went—part with them willingly and without excessive demands. Dispossession through civilization, like dispossession by purchase more broadly, was an option pursued not for its charity or gentleness but because it was expected to be less expensive than uncompensated conquest. Missionaries were far less concerned with advancing dispossession—in fact, as tenants on Native land, they feared removal for their own reasons. But their work nonetheless served colonial ends: By preaching civilization reforms intended to demilitarize and contain Native societies, missionaries acted as proxies for a federal program to compact Native landholdings and eventually seize what officials deemed a surplus. At a time when the War Department lacked the personnel needed to promote civilization policy on its own, missionaries extended the state's reach.[3]

Indigenous leaders subjected to civilization programs were by no means unaware that missionaries' gifts formed the tip of the spear. Native leaders were nonetheless willing to accept missionaries because these intruders could educate their children in an array of subjects, including the English language, which would place them on par with the United States' ruling classes. Expanding schools held immense importance for Native leaders who recognized that increasing pressure from the federal government to remove them west meant that the burden of defending homelands through strained negotiations would fall on rising generations. In Folsom's own words, teaching their children "to read and write the talk of our white brethren" would ensure that "they would be a great useful men to their nation."[4]

Education according to settler standards would, these leaders hoped, equip youth with the skills needed to confront officials as recognized equals. Yet schools required means, as Folsom put it. Building a resilient education system, one that could serve countless classes of leaders to come, demanded that these means recur and even grow over time. By working closely with missionaries who managed their own philanthropic trusts, men like Folsom could create an endowment for education—and by extension, ensure the perpetuity of their nation.

⊹⟩⟨⊹

Federal civilization programs were a recent permutation of a very old line of thinking. The idea that Native people were in need of civilizing threads through centuries of imperial justifications, liberal political theory, and Christian evangelism and is difficult to disentangle from the very colonization of the Americas.[5] Drawing on Protestant theology and teleological theories of history popularized by the Scottish Enlightenment, federal and missionary proponents of civilization imagined themselves ushering Native peoples through progressively more virtuous and advanced economic stages, not only by abandoning putatively backward practices, like hunting, but also by reorganizing their domestic lives, altering their gendered division of labor, and adopting written public law. Early civilization efforts were channeled through the dispensation of annuities, such as the annual deliveries of farm implements and merchandise promised to the Haudenosaunee by Indian agent Thomas Pickering in 1794. These goods served at once to deter the Haudenosaunee from joining the Northwest Confederacy and to compact their land use by replacing seasonal hunts with a brand of agrarian husbandry that ignored the matrilocal agriculture already in practice. In the South, Creek Indian agent Benjamin Reynolds took to his civilizing mandate with enthusiasm, promoting a patriarchal family form in which Creek women moved from the fields to work within the home, a system of criminal law that would replace clan-dictated forms of justice, and Anglo-style enclosed and exclusionary property, a paradigm disseminated visibly across the nation in the form of newly installed fences and locks.[6]

Civilization efforts supported a rising class of propertied elites across the Native South. Families endowed with merchant and political capital formed as non-Native traders married into their wives' valuable kinship networks. Many ascended to a small but significant slaveholding class and welcomed agricultural and manufacturing aid delivered under the auspices of civilization. Civilization found a cooler reception among Native peoples who disapproved, in whole or in part, of the complex of class inequality, slavery, and property that Indian agents' efforts seemed to encourage.

A burgeoning spiritual movement sweeping through nations gave voice to rising anticivilization sentiment and doubled as a revolt against assimilation. After a terrifying vision in 1804, the Shawnee prophet Tenskwatawa had begun preaching against the adoption of metal tools and weapons, stock animals, and noncustomary clothing, in a rejection of the civilization programs that Quaker missionaries had promoted in the wake of the 1795 Treaty of Greenville. Tenskwatawa and his brother, Tecumseh, gathered a growing army of disciples by criticizing northwestern Native leaders who had ceded lands in exchange for annuities and the appurtenances of civilization, deriding them as "medal chiefs" in a reference to the symbolic adornments doled out by federal treaty negotiators.[7]

In 1811, Tecumseh toured southern nations to drum up support for his brother's movement. A large council of Chickasaw and Choctaw warriors convened in the Choctaw Nation's Lower Town District to consider joining the prophet's war, but Tecumseh was ultimately rebuffed, condemned as dangerous by Choctaw *minko* Pushmataha, and escorted out of the Choctaw Nation by a group of warriors led by David Folsom. Tenskwatawa's divinations found a far warmer reception among the less prosperous Upper Town villages of the Creek, with whom the Shawnees had long enjoyed a close alliance. Tecumseh's visit inspired Upper Town warriors to take up arms—red clubs, for which they named themselves Redsticks—and carry out raids that targeted forms of wealth, like livestock, that symbolized civilization policy. General Andrew Jackson, who was still occupying the South even after a British retreat, took the Creek Civil War as a pretext to invade their country. More than fifteen hundred Redstick warriors fell to Jackson's forces in the winter of 1813–14 at Horseshoe Bend, earning the general the moniker Sharp Knife. By the war's end, between 11 and 14 percent of the entire Creek population had perished, making the conflict the bloodiest in Native peoples' recent memories.[8]

The war's aftermath brought another form of destruction. Even though many Lower Town Creeks had fought as allies of the United States—and many vanquished militants had fled east to join Seminole kin in Florida—Jackson forced a group of mainly loyal Creeks to cede over twenty-three million acres in present-day Alabama and Georgia at a treaty signed that summer. The Treaty of Fort Jackson claimed more than half of the Creek homeland. It also spilled over Creek borders to claim land belonging to the Choctaws and Cherokees, who would challenge the illegitimate sale of their lands for years to come.[9] Witnessing the consequences of the Redstick Creeks' crushing defeat only confirmed for many leaders that defending territories by arms could no longer protect homelands and carried a human cost far too heavy to bear.

Lands seized from the Creeks became the frontier of an expanding kingdom of cotton cultivated by enslaved labor. The war's interruption of Anglo-American trade and a glutted domestic market had caused cotton prices to slump to historic lows, only to soar once the prospects of overseas exports returned. Southern planters committed to cotton cultivation with abandon, and the southern United States became the largest exporter of raw materials to Britain's proliferating textile factories. Prices for cotton soared over thirty cents per pound, pulling up the closely entwined prices of land and slaves, and cotton production roughly doubled in the years after 1815.[10]

Chickasaws, Choctaws, and Creeks participated in the boom. Drawing on the tools and annuities supplied by civilization-minded Indian agents, Native women grew cotton and spun their harvests into domestically produced cloth. The wealthiest families purchased slaves to carry out this work in women's stead. Settlers seeking to enter the lucrative business of cotton slavery or to acquire larger plantations eyed the fertile lands Indigenous households were tending and applied consistent political pressure for the government to negotiate treaties of dispossession. Slavery shaped the pace and geography of displacement that ensued. Northern farmers moved steadily west, but at a tempo dictated by the gradual construction of transportation improvements—like canals—that enabled shipments to Eastern markets, slowed further by a dearth of free labor to establish farms. In the South, rivers sufficed to bring cotton to Atlantic shipping routes, and slaves could be forced to accompany their owners and to clear and plant fields on command. This meant slaveholders could be more dynamic and ambitious as colonizers.[11]

Nations across the Native South had succeeded in preserving considerable homelands until the cotton fields spread to their borders. At the time, between three and four thousand Chickasaws lived in present-day northwestern Alabama, northern Mississippi, and western Tennessee; fifteen thousand Choctaws lived in present-day Alabama and central Mississippi; fifteen thousand Creeks lived in southern Alabama and western Georgia; and roughly fifteen thousand Cherokees lived in present-day northern Alabama, northern Georgia, and southeastern Tennessee. A chain of ruthless and deceptive treaty negotiations, conducted in the shadow of wars with the Creeks and, after 1818, with the Seminoles, steadily compressed these four nations onto diminishing homelands. Between 1816 and 1818 alone they were forced to cede millions of acres of land in nine separate treaties, half of which were personally negotiated by Jackson, whose preferred method coupled threats of annihilation with secretively tendered bribes to primary leaders and headmen.[12]

Choctaw cotton press. Undated. *Source:* Gilcrease Museum, Tulsa, Oklahoma.

Had Jackson had his way, these treaties would also have compelled their Native signatories to abandon homelands altogether and move to western territories. Apart from small groups of Cherokees and Choctaws that made the difficult choice to explore life on land further sheltered from settler aggressions, Jackson failed to impose removal on Southeastern nations. But he did succeed in seizing millions of acres that would be surveyed and auctioned off as cotton prices surged. In 1815, federal land offices in Alabama and Mississippi sold around 27,300 acres of public land. In 1816, that number skyrocketed to almost 491,000 and continued to soar, cresting just short of an astounding 2.3 million acres in 1819. As land speculators and prospective planters snapped up tracts at public auctions, a massive forced migration began. More than 875,000 enslaved people from the Upper South would be pushed and prodded toward a rolling cotton frontier in the forty years before the Civil War.[13]

Federal officials highlighted the agricultural and economic aspects of civilization, but missionaries saw in the policy a chance to save Indians' souls. Starting in the 1790s, a broadening print culture and growing counterecclesiastical fervor swept up believers of all classes into a movement historians refer to as the Second Great Awakening. As this movement matured, a network of Bible, tract, Sunday school, social reform, and missionary organizations coalesced. Contemporaries called it the Benevolent Empire, an apt term given missionaries' utility for the federal government's colonial project.[14]

The earliest missionary organization devoted to proselytizing Native people was the Society for Propagating the Gospel Among Indians and Others in North America, modeled on a Scottish sister organization and chartered in Boston in 1787. Drawing on bequests and donations from Boston area elites, the society sent missionaries to convert the Mashpees, Narragansetts, Nantuckets, Passamquoddys, and Penobscots in New England and the Munsees, Oneidas, Senecas, and Wyandots in New York and Ohio. Religious associations like the Society grew as disestablishment took hold and severed religious institutions from direct access to public funds. As a result, much of missionary organizations' quotidian labors involved cobbling together funds needed for their ambitious projects. To manage a growing pool of donated wealth, benevolent associations often chose to create trusts rather than submit to the far more tedious special incorporation process. After 1814, as the nation's economy recovered from the shock of war, such associations saw rising donations and growing enthusiasm for further expansion, particularly to the lesser-known Indigenous nations living beyond the Appalachian Mountains. It was their prudent financial management of small donations and larger bequests that fueled New England missionaries' venture into Indian Country.[15]

The particular form of benevolent trust favored by missionary organizations reflected a regionally specific legal and financial culture. New England's upper classes certainly used trusts—as Robert Morris had—to shield assets from creditors and spendthrift heirs. But they also embraced trusts as vehicles for public-facing legacies. Capital and property became more fluid as merchant families incorporated stocks and other securities into their portfolios, founded banks that could collectivize and augment investments, and embraced partnerships and corporate charters that allowed wealth to accumulate independently of family lineages. With a transition from family to proprietary capitalism underway, trusts allowed an elite set to socialize part of their wealth in the form of endowments that would curry influence and attach prestige to their names. Public charity promised to cleanse generations of wealth reaped from slave-produced sugar and rum, or, more recently, from cloth woven by young women amid the deafening clatter of the mill. Accustomed to pooling their money using chartered corporations, Boston's capitalists pooled their gifts, too, funding public institutions like the Boston Athenaeum and Massachusetts General Hospital. In 1817, Massachusetts granted equity powers to the state's Supreme Court, creating a legal environment in which trusteeship thrived. Boston became a leading site for private and charitable investment, creating a demand for wealth management eventually met by the professional fiduciary—a career so closely associated with the city that "Boston trustee" became a generic term.[16]

From the outset, missionary organizations took a keen interest in how they might finance Native conversion. In 1812, the Society for Propagating the Gospel commissioned two ministers, Samuel J. Mills and John F. Schermerhorn, to undertake a survey of "Western Indians." In addition to providing clarity on Native social organizations and diplomacy, the society requested that Mills and Schermerhorn assess the size and nature of their annuities, which could indicate to missionaries which nations possessed streams of revenue that might supplement their own donations and endowments. Although the outbreak of war thwarted their tour, by 1814 Mills and Schermerhorn had produced a survey that estimated the size, state, and openness to conversion of Native peoples from Ohio to Utah. Of these diverse polities, the report concluded, the Cherokees, Chickasaws, and Choctaws appeared the most likely to benefit from a mission. "Here is a door opened for the spread of the gospel," the men announced.[17]

The Society for Propagating the Gospel may have found this door, but another New England organization charged through it. By far the most important missionary association unleashed by the fervor of postwar evangelism was the American Board of Commissions for Foreign Missions, an interdenominational organization founded in 1810. In its first decade of operation, the board grew from a small gathering of New England pastors to a network spanning the Middle East, the Indian subcontinent, and eventually, North America's Indian Country. Although the board itself operated as a corporation, rather than a trust—it had procured a charter from

Massachusetts in 1812—it adhered to fiduciary principles in managing charitable bequests, as indicated in the term used for its central governing body, the "prudential committee." Larger donations to the board were typically invested in bank stock, especially stock issued by the Second Bank of the United States, an institution favored by voluntary associations for its conservative management.[18] When American Board missionaries ventured to the Native South, they carried with them a model of charitable investments that would inspire Indigenous leaders to finance education through treaties.

Northeastern missionaries understood little about the people they planned to convert, and were largely ignorant of the crisis that nations like the Cherokees had faced in recent years. Still, they knew enough to recognize that treaty negotiations presented a ripe opportunity to offer their assistance. In 1816, Cyrus Kingsbury, an enterprising missionary from the American Board of Commissions for Foreign Missions, set out to intercept a Cherokee delegation on its way to Washington. Cherokee leaders had refused to accept the fraudulent cession of a part of their territories in the 1814 Treaty of Fort Jackson with the Creeks, and they hoped to recover these lands through a treaty of their own. When Kingsbury tracked them down in the capital, he found an especially receptive audience in one delegate, a young merchant named John Ross. Ross's father was a Scottish American trader, and his mother the daughter of a prominent interpreter within the Cherokee Nation. As a child, Ross had studied at a mission operated by the Moravians, and he continued his education at a private academy in Tennessee, where he acquired the commercial training that would launch his career. By the time he served as a treaty delegate, Ross had become a significant slaveholder, owning nineteen slaves and presiding over an expansive plantation appointed with a large two-story house.[19]

Education had proven instrumental to Ross's wealth and privilege, and in the decades to come he would work closely with Kingsbury and his peers to expand his nation's schools. Like many other Cherokee planters, Ross considered education critical to the future of his nation, not least because it would ensure that men with similar upbringing to his would remain in power. Ross helped Kingsbury locate grounds for the mission when he arrived in the Cherokee Nation that fall, offering up a plantation belonging to his own grandfather. Christened Brainerd Mission, the school welcomed in March 1817 an inaugural class of twenty-six Cherokee youths, ages four to eighteen.[20]

Federal Indian agencies offered only meager funds for civilization efforts before 1819, when Congress created a $10,000 fund for this purpose. Instead of giving unrestricted aid, the federal government preferred to

Brainerd Mission (woodcut, undated). *Source:* Penelope Johnson Allen
Brainerd Mission Correspondence and Photographs, University of Tennessee–
Chattanooga Special Collections.

subsidize construction and salaries for skilled laborers, encouraging missionaries to establish settlements and accumulate personnel to a degree that never occurred overseas. Yet since the civilization fund operated on a reimbursement basis, and since the grinding wheels of Congress delayed the arrival of federal funds, missions demanded a large, up-front investment of labor and resources to plant and harvest crops, erect buildings, and procure supplies. Missions often sank into debt during their earliest days, and Brainerd Mission was no different: In its first month of operation, the mission was forced to borrow one hundred dollars from John Ross to cover its expenses. By summer of that year its debts were considerable. So too did Brainerd missionaries rely on—and struggle to retain—Cherokee labor. In February 1817, for example, a Cherokee couple who had been cooking and helping with construction abruptly left, leaving one missionary to complain, "I know not what to do—am in great difficulty about help."[21]

Missionaries believed they were introducing education to Native societies, but, in fact, children's education was already central to societies across the Native South. Grandparents served as primary instructors, conveying oral histories, botanical knowledge, and ceremonial practice, among other lessons. But some Indigenous elites thought it worthwhile to include a layer of civilization-style schooling over the kind of knowledge transmitted between generations of kin. Many Native elites evoked an ideal of universal education that would confirm Native peoples' equality to nations across Europe and America. Since "natural man is in every country and in every age nearly the same," a Cherokee delegation explained to President James Monroe in 1818, it "is to the Lights of education to which every nation owes their distinction excepting in colour."[22] Others preferred the lights of their own spiritual guidance, with Tenskwatawa's movement only the most prominent example. Educating children American-style risked marginalizing lessons transmitted from elders to younger kin. Yet for a growing cohort of Native elites, failing to prepare their children for the challenges they were sure to inherit appeared far more reckless.

Calls for education reforms gathered strength as nations' political economies underwent dramatic transformation. Missions, branded as places of conversion and learning, served also as worksites that augmented the marketable value of homelands. Indigenous and enslaved labor helped erect buildings, carve out roads, and cut systems of irrigation. Missionaries' assistance in agriculture also held an economic impact beyond an grounds. In the Cherokee Nation, women embraced cotton spinning and weaving, demanding wheels and looms from their Indian agents and producing hundreds of thousands of yards of cloth per year. After decades of relying on outsider tradesmen, the Cherokees started to train their own as blacksmiths, mechanics, saddlers, and silversmiths and planned an iron ore works, where they could produce tools and repair their own guns. Within this broader push to diversify their economy and encourage domestic industry, the Cherokees also sought to more closely control their annuities. In 1816, they successfully petitioned to handle their annuity's national distribution on their own, and the following year, Cherokee headman Charles Hicks began operating a treasury from his home in present-day eastern Tennessee.[23] By working with missionaries, the Cherokees created institutional safeguards for their annuity wealth, sheltering money from misappropriation while demonstrating the nation's capacity to meet standards of civilization set by the United States.

News of the Brainerd Mission's success soon traveled southwest to the Choctaw Nation. The Choctaws, like the Cherokees, were suffering from crushing pressure to cede homelands. And, as was the case with their Cherokee neighbors, it was the Choctaws' rising planter elite that argued most fervently for a rising generation of missionary-educated leaders to stave off land dispossession. Among the most eager of these Choctaw elites was David Folsom. Folsom had learned English from his father, Nathaniel Folsom, a trader from North Carolina, and inherited his captaincy through the esteemed clan lineage of his mother, Aiahnichih Ohoyoh. Folsom's scant six months at a boarding school in Tennessee had left him with inconsistent spelling, for which he often apologized in his correspondence. Perhaps motivated by a desire to spare younger Choctaws his shame, in 1818 Folsom requested from the American Board of Commissions for Foreign Missions a mission for his own nation.[24]

Upon Folsom's invitation, Cyrus Kingsbury left Brainerd that spring for Choctaw territory. With fresh reinforcements sent by the American Board from the Northeast, he founded a new mission, named Elliot, in June. Like Brainerd, Elliot proved an ordeal to establish, with missionaries struggling to erect mills and log houses and bring acreage into cultivation. Once again the missionaries relied on the generosity of their Native hosts. Choctaw *minko* Apukshunnubbee, who presided over one of the Choctaw Nation's three districts, pledged $200 from his share of the annuities to the mission. Apukshunnubbee also arranged a kind of subscription model in which Choctaw families could stake claim to future enrollment by gifting the mission stock animals, an effort that generated eighty-five cows and calves, a $700 donation, and a promise of $500 to be delivered each year. While these contributions were more than welcome, both Choctaw and missionary leadership recognized a need for a more efficient method of financing, one that might avoid wrangling dozens of cattle across the nation's territory each year. Choctaws used a single word, *chelichi*, to describe the increase of breeding animals and the growth of interest on money. It was time to turn from one valence of *chelichi* to the other.[25]

Across Cherokee and Choctaw nations, Native leaders and their missionary counterparts contemplated how they might place education on better footing. An early plan outlined by a delegation of Cherokee leaders would have adopted benevolent organizations' solicitation through the written word. By founding a printing press in their nation that could serve, in their words, as "a repository of Indian law & History," the Cherokees hoped to raise subscriptions from interested citizens of the United States and to devote the profits solely "to the education of the Indian youths."[26] A decade later the Cherokee nation would, in fact, acquire a printing press and publish a national organ, the *Cherokee Phoenix*. Articles appeared in English and in the Cherokee language, using Sequoyah's syllabary, a tidy analogy for how the newspaper combined missionary-imported technologies with a deepened commitment to Cherokee culture.[27] Less visible than newsprint, however, were the legal instruments of wealth succession that missionaries introduced and that many leaders considered just as vital to their nation-building efforts.

◦────────◦

A new treaty provided a chance for Cherokees to make use of their missionary guests' facility with philanthropic trusts. The 1817 negotiations that Kingsbury had attended had failed to resolve Cherokee grievances with Creeks' illegitimate cession of their land at Fort Jackson, and in 1819 the nation lobbied successfully for a new agreement. Believing a lack of education the root of "nearly all of our evils," in the words of one Cherokee petition, delegates consulted with Brainerd missionaries before heading to Washington. John Ross visited Ard Hoyt, who had taken over after Cyrus Kingsbury had relocated to Elliot, and asked his advice on how the delegation might use the treaty to better finance Cherokee education. Delegates had steeled themselves for a land cession in some form, and Ross was in search of a silver lining. As Hoyt recalled, Ross envisioned offering "a large tract of good land at some place where it could sell high," with funds subsequently "secured in the hands of some white people . . . so that the nation should hereafter have the benefit of it for the support of schools." The funds should be kept in the hands of non-Natives, in Ross's view, since the Cherokees "had no law by which it could be secured among themselves." Hoyt responded by affirming Ross's interest in securing funds "for the benefit of the nation" and outlined "the standing & powers" of the American Board of Commissions for Foreign Missions.[28]

Ross traveled to Washington with the financial advice of American Board missionaries fresh in his mind. In a treaty signed at the capital in February 1819, the Cherokees ceded a tract of land that would become part of Alabama Territory, with the proceeds to be "vested, under the direction of the President of the United States, in the stock of the United States, or such other stock as he may deem most advantageous." The proceeds raised would flow into an education fund to be dispensed at the discretion of the president and his subordinates.[29]

Taking inspiration from missionaries' philanthropic trusts allowed the Cherokees to approach land cessions strategically. Donations of cattle, like those subscribed by the Choctaws to the Elliot Mission, could be bred to replenish over time. But unlike herds of livestock, the

Cherokee education trust fund converted value held in physical assets—land or cattle—into an immortal and presumably far more secure form. It also appointed an adviser—nominally, the president of the United States—whom the Cherokee chose to trust as a fiduciary, and it constrained this fiduciary to act prudently to the benefit of Cherokee education. In its use of land sales to fund schools, the arrangement resembled the Land Ordinance of 1785, which set aside the proceeds of the sixteenth section of every township to finance common schools in the new Western states.[30] But in its financial aspects the Cherokee school fund more closely emulated the trusts that benevolent associations used to manage their donations and endowments. By collaborating with missionaries to craft an education trust fund, the Cherokees had availed themselves of legal instruments that could securely structure a socialized succession of wealth.

Placing the value of ceded lands in trust with the federal government, a practice steeped in an Anglo-American legal regime predicated on privately held property and patrilineal inheritance, marked a significant break with Cherokee customary laws governing wealth. These customary laws flowed from the seven clans that composed the Cherokee polity and shaped every aspect of town life, from the organization of ceremony to the pairing of marriages to the work they performed and what they did with the fruits of their labor. Esteemed elder women granted outsiders entry into a clan—and thereby full membership in the Cherokee nation—or denied it to them, a fate that left captives in a state of slavery without kin, protection, or social legibility. Clans also dictated the distribution of wealth. Clan law recognized property rights, but did not abstract property from the possessor or their kin; through ceremonies and feasts clans allocated prestige goods among elites and surpluses to those in need. Most important, the elder women who headed clans protected the nation's wealth in land. In one 1818 petition to the Cherokee National Council, elder women reminded the nation their territory "was given to us by the Great Spirit above as our common right, to raise our children upon, & to make support for our rising generations."[31]

By the time American Board missionaries arrived in Cherokee territories, a hybrid legal system had emerged within the nation. Under the influence of civilization policy, political elites had adopted the rudiments of a private and patrilineal property regime. In a pair of resolutions passed in 1808 by the Cherokee National Council, the Cherokees approved a new police force, with salaries drawn from their national annuity, and affirmed the rights of heirs to "their father's property," including a widow's right to her "share."[32] The

ascent of common-law-inspired legal protections for property also reshaped
Cherokee slavery: where once clan membership—or its denial—determined
the status of captives, Cherokee society increasingly treated the enslaved as
chattel. But Cherokee property law was only spottily enforced, suggesting
that practices ordered by clan structures continued quietly to restore justice. Principles that had guided clan law also persisted, including the distinctive Cherokee tenet of social welfare, or *gadugi*, translated by historian
Julie Reed as "coordinated work for the social good."[33] In one 1817 petition
Cherokees explained that their annuities served "to educate our children &
support our old men & women & poor people."[34] While the institutional
mechanisms Cherokees used to preserve and allocate wealth were new, then,
the ideas that guided their nascent fiscal regime were not.

When missionary Samuel Worcester reported on the Cherokees' 1819
treaty to the membership of the American Board of Commissions for Foreign Missions, he rejoiced that it would provide "funds which eventually
will not be small" for promoting benevolent causes. Since this method of
securing funds could be reproduced in subsequent treaties with the Cherokees—or those of any other cooperative nations—Worcester declared that
the benevolent empire had entered "a new and propitious era."[35] Just as
Worcester hoped, the model of assigning compensation to an education
fund kept under federal control would be replicated in treaties signed
across the Native South.

In August 1820, the Choctaws gathered at Doaks Stand to confer with
General Andrew Jackson and their Indian agent, John McKee. For over a
year, Jackson had pushed for the Choctaws to relinquish their homelands
and relocate to western territories on the Red River. While a few Choctaw elites were in favor of this plan, seeing a short-term opportunity to
raise cash through a land sale, the majority of the nation was not. District
*minkos* Mushulatubbee and Pushmataha opened the council by explaining that the Choctaws had no land left to spare—in Pushmataha's words,
if one were to "take two fingers from the hand, the remainder would be of
little use." After four days of stalled negotiations, Jackson grew impatient,
cast off any veneer of goodwill, and resorted to outright threats. Allowing
room for the imagination, Jackson warned the Choctaws that were they
to refuse to cede lands "no foresight could calculate your distresses." To
offer reward alongside punishment, Jackson and McKee snuck twenty-six
Choctaw statesmen and warriors individual "donations" of up to $500.[36]

Choctaw negotiators recognized that parting with a portion of their lands could protect their nation by staving off removal, a much graver prospect. To salvage the treaty they focused on realizing the plan contemplated by David Folsom: a limited cession that could supply critical funds to the nation's school. The final treaty, signed in October 1820, ceded 4.5 million acres and granted the Choctaw Nation western lands that the War Department hoped would become their eventual home. The treaty's seventh article also pledged to set aside the revenue from fifty-four sections of "good land . . . to the support of the Choctaw schools." Unlike the 1819 Cherokee treaty, the Choctaw agreement did not stipulate an investment, but still placed education funds "in the hands of the President of the United States . . . to be applied by him, expressly and exclusively, to this valuable object." Secretary of War John C. Calhoun approved, calling education funds "a very great improvement" on annuities, which could carry "a pernicious effect" of encouraging "idleness and dissipation." He recommended that the model be replicated and adopted in subsequent treaties. Within a decade, the Kansas, Odawas, and Osages had also agreed to education funds drawn from land cessions, and many other nations had signed treaties that set aside a portion of their annuities for schooling.[37]

Education trust funds were uncontroversial but quietly pivotal introductions to the repertoire of treaty making. They invited federal oversight of the spending of Native annuities at a time when nations had yet to reach a consensus on civilization policy. By the same token, education funds allowed nations to dedicate portions of bitterly earned compensation toward the long-term project of self-preservation. This was, at least, how Native leaders wanted the funds to function. Education funds were supposed to express trusteeship as they understood it: a relationship of mutual obligation between sovereign polities, each bound to the other but free to govern their internal affairs, their duties commensurate to the circumstances, resources, and vulnerabilities of each party.[38]

To federal officials, however, trusteeship meant something very different. When the Cherokee's Indian agent Return J. Meigs learned of their plan to create an education fund, he wrote to Calhoun to suggest that the fund be placed "under the control of the Government, so as to secure a proper application."[39] Calhoun agreed. Education funds confirmed federal officials' predisposed notion that Native money was best kept in federal hands, and that federal officials could—*should*, even—have a hand in dictating how it would be spent. Where Indigenous conceptions of trusteeship preserved the sovereignty of each party, Calhoun denied that Native nations were "independent people . . . nor ought they to be so considered."

Instead, as he advised the Senate, "they should be taken under our guardianship; and our opinion, and not theirs, ought to prevail, in measures intended for their civilization and happiness."[40]

Despite federal officials' pretensions to financial superiority, a panic produced in part by fiscal immaturity prevented the government from fulfilling its fiduciary duties to the Cherokees. For a decade, the General Land Office's liberal credit policies, coupled with the liquidity created by a rapidly growing banking sector, had driven rampant speculation in western lands—until a financial panic caused land values to plummet. In the summer of 1818, in an effort to protect its own balance sheet, the Second Bank of the United States began to curtail and call in loans, siphoning specie eastward and triggering a wave of commercial failures that spread west along the Ohio River. By year's end, prices for wheat and cotton had plunged by half, ruining farmers and planters who had purchased lands on credit. The Panic of 1819, as it would become known, left investors in public lands owing over $21 million to the federal government—a sum roughly one and a half times larger than the entire federal budget for that year. Inundated by the sheer volume of Native land commodified in the years before the panic, the Land Office was now doubly burdened with the clerical labor of pursuing overdue installments. In the crush of business, lands set aside for Cherokee schools were neither sold nor the proceeds invested until 1833, when an incensed John Ross discovered the oversight.[41]

The Cherokee school fund's disarray did not deter federal interest in trusteeship. To the contrary, in the context of the economic crisis that followed the panic of 1819, trust funds took on a new allure. During Monroe's second inaugural address the president recommended ending Native territorial sovereignty, partitioning homelands into allotments, and seizing surplus lands, the proceeds of which should "be vested in permanent funds for the support of civil government over them and for the education of their children."[42] By converting the value of ceded homelands into an income for Native polities that would be meted out by federal officials over time, Monroe's vision of trusteeship promised to mitigate the costs of administering civilization policy.

Trust funds also appealed to a Congress mired in a post-panic period of retrenchment. In April 1820, the Senate requested that Calhoun calculate the principal sums needed to fund annuities if invested at an annual interest rate of 6 percent. Instead of authorizing expenditures each year, as

Congress did for all annuities that were not funded by a trust, the Senate considered whether a large initial expenditure—creating principals for trust investment—might be worthwhile. When Calhoun delivered his tabulations to Congress later that year, they showed that converting all annuities into trust funds would certainly spare the public purse over the longer term— since interest payments would lessen the amount Congress would have to appropriate directly—but that the plan would require a principal of almost $1.4 million. Daunted by the scale of investment needed, Congress never followed through. One official later reported that no bonds could be found with sufficient yield to fully fund annuities, a problem that also diminished returns on Seneca trust fund investments throughout this period.[43]

While Congress reckoned with the financial strain imposed by its obligations to Native polities, missionaries reeled. Donations in cash, still the most significant stream of income for the American Board of Commissions for Foreign Missions, had not kept up with the frenetic pace of expansion, and revenue from investments had flatlined. As a result, the board had run at a deficit since the panic, eventually depleting its entire cash reserves and forcing budget cuts of $10,000 in 1821. That spring, board treasurer Jeremiah Evarts faced a choice between sending funds to overseas missions—which were necessarily transmitted in direly scarce specie—or continuing to finance an expanding network of missions across Indian Country. By April, missionaries in Cherokee and Choctaw territories received word from headquarters that if they could not support themselves, they were to suspend any new construction, dismiss hired help, and halt instruction, in that order.[44]

Choctaws bore the brunt of missionaries' fiscal crisis, since the American Board was midway through expanding its schools at Mayhew and in the Six Towns district. By the summer of 1821, board missionary Cyrus Kingsbury was touring the Choctaw districts, hat in hand, in an effort to scrape by on the nation's collective resources. David Folsom observed the missionaries' efforts with pity and wrote to reassure them that "I am shure means will come where we have no expectation off."[45]

⁂

Indigenous peoples' commitments to expanding their education systems would only deepen as pressure to cede their territories increased. In the winter of 1824–25, the Choctaws negotiated a treaty that revealed how important education trusts had become to their plans for economic development and the political defense of their homelands. Months before, the federal government had discovered settlers from the United States on lands between the Arkansas and Red Rivers, which had been set aside in the 1820 Treaty of Doaks Stand as an eventual western territory for the Choctaws. With squatters having derailed his plan for Choctaw removal, Calhoun called for a renegotiation. He intended to extinguish Indian title to the western tract and, for good measure, purchase another tract of lands in the eastern section of Choctaw homelands on the Tombigbee River.[46]

A Choctaw delegation headed for Washington that November. Among them was James McDonald. His mother, Molly, was an affluent rancher and slaveholder in the Choctaw Nation, and she had insisted on her son's education among Quaker missionaries in Baltimore. In 1818, after completing his Quaker schooling, McDonald was adopted into the Georgetown household of Thomas McKenney, then the superintendent of Indian trade. McDonald trained as McKenney's clerk before moving on to read law under the Ohio attorney John McLean, who would later serve on the Supreme Court. McDonald's formative years—which placed him under the quite literal guardianship of federal bureaucrats, while introducing him to a corpus of knowledge that would drastically improve his nation's diplomatic standing—seemed to encapsulate at a human scale the tensions and promises of the Choctaws' selective embrace of civilization policy. This background would also render McDonald's role on the treaty delegation a personal trial. Earlier that year, McKenney had taken a new position as commissioner of Indian Affairs (after Calhoun, impatient with Congress's frugality, had created the Office of Indian Affairs by executive fiat).[47] When McDonald arrived in Washington along with his fellow delegates, he faced his former guardian as a diplomatic adversary.

McDonald, along with fellow delegate David Folsom, represented a rising cadre of statesmen who believed that only settler-style education could prepare leaders to contend with their counterparts in the United States. Both men were determined to domesticate this experience by cultivating schools within the Choctaw Nation. Also represented in the delegation was the older cohort of district *minkos* who had witnessed firsthand the waning days of the deerskin trade and armed struggle against the United States. Apukshunnubbee, Mushulatubbee, and Pushmataha were as persuaded of the need for a new strategy to defend against the United States, but resisted the impulse to channel change through centralized governance at the expense of districts' autonomy. All delegates wanted to minimize losses of territory, even of a western tract remote from their homelands. But they were equally determined to finance schooling, however much they disagreed on the form this schooling should take.[48]

Younger delegates demonstrated the benefits of their education by driving hard negotiations in Washington. McKenney, representing the War Department, opened discussions by asking the Choctaws to cede their western lands for a onetime payment of $65,000. David Folsom and James McDonald responded that this sum was *entirely inadequate*," demanding instead a financial package totaling $450,000, spread into annual installments that would last decades, and that included three separate education funds, designated for a mechanical institute, a national school system, and additional funding for any Choctaws who resettled in the West.[49] Just as the Senecas had a generation before, the Choctaws refused a lump sum that might be spent haphazardly and impatiently, without lasting impact. Instead, the Choctaws approached the treaty as an opportunity to create fiscal silos that would store wealth and finance education for many years to come.

Choctaws also raised the matter of their earlier school fund, created as part of the Treaty of Doaks Stand to help finance the Elliot Mission. The Choctaw school fund, like that of the Cherokees, had suffered from the postpanic downturn, with sluggish land sales failing to generate the wealth expected. Only one-third of the lands had been sold, raising just under $12,800. Rather than wait indefinitely for revenue from future land sales, the delegates offered to forfeit the proceeds and receive instead a onetime payment, calculated by valuing their remaining lands at the federal minimum price of $1.25 an acre. These funds could then be placed "at interest (under the direction of the President) to go to the education of our children."[50] By seeking to place a principal at interest as soon as possible while tying gains to education, the delegation's proposal balanced long-term security with a pressing social need. David Folsom, who also attended the treaty negotiations as a delegate, noted with some pride that the "payment for that land will all go to the support of education of the Choctaws children."[51]

Federal negotiators balked at the scale of compensation demanded by the Choctaws, especially since the nation had refused to part with their most coveted land on the Tombigbee River. In a private letter, McKenney chastised his former adoptee for the extravagance of his nation's proposal, which he characterized as "beyond everything we have heard of before." Trying in vain to pressure the Choctaw delegates to cede the Tombigbee tract, McKenney ordered McDonald to consider "the dead and profitless relation which those lands bear to you, and compare it with a principle, producing nearly $4,000 per annum interest."[52] But the delegates had already decided that only their less-valued western lands would be worth relinquishing to finance education.

Ultimately the Choctaws ceded no homelands in 1825, selling only the Arkansas lands that had been assigned them as a prospective postremoval territory. The final treaty granted the Choctaws recurring payments and education funding, albeit in more modest sums than they had hoped. As the Choctaws had requested, they would receive an annuity of $6,000, effective immediately, instead of land proceeds that could take years to arrive. A separate perpetual $6,000 annuity was earmarked for education for the first twenty years. After that date, the sum would be "vested in stocks, or otherwise disposed of . . . at the option of the Choctaw nation." Thanks in part to the erudite contributions of younger delegates like Folsom and McDonald, the Choctaws had succeeded in securing a treaty far more in line with their priorities than the one signed five years before at Doaks Stand. Were the provisions for education to have their anticipated effect, the Choctaws would reproduce this success on an expanded scale as a rising generation of educated leaders emerged even better prepared to defend their nation.[53]

A new set of challenges confronted the Choctaws once they began the difficult work of implementing the treaty within their own nation, however. They did so in mourning, since two *minkos*, Apukshunnubbee and Pushmataha, had died during the trip to Washington in unfortunate and unrelated accidents. Amid the chaos, the third *minko*, Mushulatubbee, had raced ahead of fellow delegates to the Choctaw Nation, where he quietly struck a bargain with Senator Richard Mentor Johnson that changed the course of Choctaw education for more than two decades. Hailing from one of Kentucky's richest families, and alleged to have slayed Tecumseh at the Battle of the Thames, Johnson owned a plantation named Great Crossings where dozens of slaves toiled under the management of his enslaved wife, Julia Chinn. Johnson was broke, having failed to fulfill a contract to provision military posts during the War Department's aborted push into Arikara and Mandan territories on the Missouri River.[54] When Johnson's brother-in-law, the Indian agent William Ward, alerted him of the Choctaw treaty negotiations and proposed school fund, Johnson lunged at the opportunity to stabilize his finances.

Johnson had begun courting Mushulatubbee in the months before treaty negotiations began. By then, the Choctaws' relationship with the American Board of Commissions for Foreign Missions had soured: without their donation base, the missionaries began to strike some as parasitic on their Native hosts. Choctaws cared little for the conversion that missionaries considered tantamount and resented corporal punishment of their children. American Board missionaries also insisted on putting children to labor in fields, work that was feminized within Choctaw culture and more recently associated with the degradation of chattel slavery. Before heading to Washington, Mushulatubbee had indicated to Ward his desire to redirect Choctaw annuities toward a secular academy situated outside the nation that could emulate the prestigious residential academies that reproduced the United States' upper classes. Learning of Mushulatubbee's interest through his brother-in-law Ward, Johnson had persuaded the *minko* that he should receive the $6,000 education annuity to finance a boarding school on his Kentucky plantation. By the time the Choctaw National Council met to discuss the result of treaty negotiations in August 1825, Mushulatubbee had already made a gentleman's agreement with Johnson: the *minko* offered him the entirety of the Choctaw fund were Johnson to reserve the majority of spots in the academy for boys from Mushulatubbee's district.[55]

Mushulatubbee's monopolization of education funds dismayed Folsom and McDonald, who had intended for the Choctaw National Council to oversee a more representative domestic school system conducted in partnership with American Board missionaries. Within a few years, Mushulatubbee's betrayal would force him from his position as *minko*, with Folsom elected in his stead. Folsom and other Choctaw allies worked with the American Board to lobby the Office of Indian Affairs and attempt to block Johnson's receipt of their education funds. "It is of immense importance to these poor people," Kingsbury wrote, "that they feel *here* the exercise of the parental care and authority of their great father the President of the United States."[56] McKenney, a devout Quaker and firm believer in missionaries' salutary influence in Indian Country, was inclined to agree, but he was no match for Johnson, whose political clout assured his success. In late 1825, McKenney capitulated and agreed to honor Johnson and Mushulatubbee's agreement. In a subsequent meeting at the War Department, Johnson negotiated aggressively, requesting salaries for Thomas Henderson and other tutors, building expenses, and books, with McKenney pushing back against some of his more exorbitant estimates. Breaking with precedent, Johnson requested to be paid "per scholar per annum," explaining that this would allow him to cover any "contingencies" that might arise. Privately Johnson explained to Henderson, "The more scholars I have, the more profit."[57]

Missionaries had drawn on Native wealth and federal funds to carry out their civilizing mission, but the new Choctaw Academy twisted the model to serve Johnson's private gain. Aware that his position as a senator might lead some critics to view the arrangement as corrupt, Johnson arranged to have Henderson installed as the public manager of the academy's finances.

Yet, Johnson had quietly procured a power of attorney from the minister that allowed him to control a steady stream of Choctaw annuities. By the end of 1825, Johnson had set his sights on claiming the pot of money raised by land sales under the Treaty of Doaks Stand. While Choctaw negotiators at the 1825 treaty council had forfeited the proceeds of future land sales, the $12,800 raised up to that point remained unspent. When Johnson learned that McKenney planned to invest the amount in 6 percent bonds, as the treaty of 1820 had prescribed, he urged the War Department to spend the interest raised on additional scholars for the Choctaw Academy. In a perverse mirroring of Folsom and McDonald's aims in negotiating for the school annuity, Johnson was especially appreciative of its recurrence—even to perpetuity, noting to Henderson that the school fund's investment "would make with 6% stock $3,000 per annum *for ever*."[58]

Observing Johnson's maneuvers, McDonald was dismayed by the prospect of financing a boarding school he had never intended to support with a fund that would now "be totally exhausted in less than four years," as he complained to McKenney. Despite dissent from McDonald and others, Johnson triumphed. By the spring of 1826, twenty-five Choctaw youth had enrolled at the academy, some as young as eight years old.[59] In Johnson's hands, educating Native children had gone from philanthropic calling to business.

Nations across the Native South selectively adopted techniques and ideas that missionaries carried with them. They did so to shield their territories from the spear of militarized invasion and to prepare their children for the coercive treaties that they knew would come anyway. Having deemed war an untenable defensive strategy, Native leaders embraced education as the brightest hope for their nations' futures. By educating their children, they promised to endow their successors with the skills to develop diversified and therefore resilient economies and to negotiate effectively despite the forked tongues of federal negotiators. Native leaders made a paradoxical choice, selling pieces of territory to create an enduring legacy in the form of annuities earmarked for education. Trusteeship offered a vessel for this legacy. In accordance with their understanding of trusteeship as protection, Native leaders considered it among the government's duties to provide a reliable fiscal structure to endow education.

While Native nations weighed distant possibilities when investing in education, many missionaries and their federal collaborators embraced a narrative in which Indigenous people lacked any future at all. In 1822, Connecticut preacher Jedidiah Morse completed the first census in Indian Country, commissioned by Calhoun two years earlier. It depicted a distorted reality that had become commonplace. Morse projected that Native populations were on the decline, a belief that historians have since demonstrated as empirically untrue. Whether oblivious to or willfully ignorant of the population growth among the Indigenous societies he visited, the minister's report offered a severely misguided solution to this nonproblem: the mass relocation of Native nations to territories far from American settlements, where their isolation would, Morse believed, protect them from extinction.[60] The kind of comprehensive expulsion and territorial compression Morse recommended would soon become a policy enacted with far more force than Calhoun's piecemeal efforts. As nation after nation was forced to abandon their homelands east of the Mississippi River, Native leaders would continue to negotiate as best they could for long-term revenue and to earmark financial streams for education. But the same tools that allowed them to endow and uplift future generations—trust funds—became in the age of removal a weapon in the hands of their trustee.

# CHAPTER THREE

# Banking on Removal

IN 1832, Principal Chief Levi Colbert sent a petition to President Andrew Jackson, signed by dozens of his fellow Chickasaw statesmen. The petition concerned a recent treaty in which his nation had ceded the entirety of its remaining homelands, which spread in rolling hills and fertile prairie across present-day northwestern Alabama and northern Mississippi. Chickasaws would far rather have stayed with the bones of their dead. Yet remaining on their homelands was simply no longer viable. Settlers emboldened by the 1830 Indian Removal Act had begun squatting on their land, and soon after, Mississippi proclaimed its jurisdiction over their remaining territory in an effort to undermine their sovereignty. Once Chickasaws had reconciled themselves to removal, a debate arose within the nation over the kind of compensation they should receive. The removal treaty failed to satisfy all sides, and Colbert's petition emerged from renewed deliberations over money.

The treaty had promised Chickasaws yearly annuities financed by the interest raised on a trust fund. In a tidy circle, the sale of Chickasaw land would finance the trust fund: Money would flow in as lands sold, the Treasury secretary would invest the growing balance, and the interest accumulated would flow out to the Chickasaw Nation as an annuity. Colbert's petition listed several concerns, but clarified that investment itself was not among them. As he explained, it had been his "intention to vest largely, through the President in bank Stock," to "let the old corn stand and my generations—feed on the new, year by year."[1] Yet Chickasaws worried that placing too much wealth in trust would deprive the nation of direly needed resources in the shorter term. The treaty had assigned nearly all their compensation for investment, including the proceeds of tracts allotted to individual Chickasaws. "We wanted *this* money in our power," Colbert explained.[2] What the Chickasaws sought, in other words, was the correct balance between security, or storing wealth at a consistent value, and liquidity, or the ability to convert wealth into cash without losing value.[3]

By comparing financial investments to the preservation of corn, Colbert offered a distinctively Chickasaw frame of reference for how his nation planned to survive the ordeal of Indian removal. Communal maize cultivation bore deep roots in Chickasaw history, tracing back to their precursor chiefdoms of the Mississippian era. Non-Native observers had since the sixteenth century misunderstood Southeastern Native agriculture as merely subsistence-oriented, even as intruders relied on the plunder of Native corn stores to sustain their expeditions. In fact, across centuries of warfare and adaptation Chickasaw women had deliberately produced large surpluses to carry the nation through famine, war, and other crises. Collecting and storing grain had provided security to the Chickasaw economy and embodied principles of social obligation by allowing elders, orphans, and others in need to be fed from a common reserve. By invoking the storage of grain, Colbert and the petition's cosigners signaled their commitment to investment as a hedge against uncertainty and as a form of protection for their most vulnerable members as the nation entered a dark stage of its history.[4]

Colbert and his fellow Chickasaw statesmen knew the dangers ahead. They had already witnessed how Indian removal campaigns advanced by Jackson and his appointees wracked Native economies, fractured their politics, and afflicted their peoples with disease. A euphemism that conjured a simple change of place, *removal* in fact encompassed months of settler terror and plunder in the lead-up to departure; the severing of a people from spiritual and subsistence relationships bound to homelands and the living beings that they hosted; the interruption of multiple season-dependent cycles of planting, cultivation, and food preservation; the compelled abandonment of personal property, including livestock and buildings like houses, churches, farms, mills, taverns, schoolhouses, and council houses; the forced exodus of entire populations on highly lethal journeys, spanning hundreds of miles; and the unlikely reconstruction of an economy and polity from fragments carried on the trail west. Amid this turmoil, storing funds in trust, like grain held in a corncrib, could bring a measure of confidence by keeping money stashed away, at a safe distance from the present crisis.[5]

A reproduction of a Chickasaw corncrib, exhibited at the Chickasaw Nation Cultural Center, Sulphur, Oklahoma. *Source:* Photograph by the author.

For Chickasaws and other nations who had cautiously agreed to place wealth in trust, investment promised longevity: it allowed them to salvage wealth from sacrificed land and dedicate it to future generations. For federal officials, however, trust investments enabled removal on a shoestring. After their relatively spotty appearances as education funds in treaties signed in the 1810s and 1820s, trust funds proliferated rapidly across the many treaties signed under Jackson. Trust funds became such a prevalent mode of annuity financing because they granted officials broadened discretion over large portions of treaty compensation that they now retained as an investment principal. In their capacity as trustees officials could decide precisely how much of the earnings on an investment would be released to the intended beneficiary. As the Chickasaws would learn, officials could avoid disbursement altogether, adhering to an unfounded belief that cash would be wasted in Native hands. Annuities became subject to the same miserly spirit that plagued the larger project of removal, as officials pursued efficiency and produced chaos and death instead.[6]

Rather than ensure that the Chickasaws had access to the cash they needed to survive removal, officials invested as much of their wealth as possible. Chickasaws became major holders of Alabama bonds, in particular, which capitalized the state's blossoming network of publicly owned banks. By emitting generous quantities of paper notes, state banks like Alabama's supplied settlers with the liquidity they needed to purchase Native land. Their paper money was of a greater quantity but lower quality than the notes produced by the more conservative Second Bank of the United States, which prioritized stability and retention of specie reserves. Chickasaws were entangled in this hierarchical monetary system at both levels, drawing in federal money through annuities and investing in state-backed money through their sizable trust fund.[7]

As Colbert's petition indicated, the Chickasaw Nation had its own monetary policy, which it adjusted to meet the challenges of dispossession and displacement. In the decades before their removal, Chickasaw diplomats deliberately negotiated for annuities in specie or federal banknotes and took care to configure how this currency would circulate within their diminished territory. When their removal crisis arrived, the Chickasaws applied their monetary practices to a terrifying new context, embracing trusteeship to strike a balance between cash in hand and wealth in storage. Yet federal trusteeship took on new prerogatives as it stretched to accommodate the many concurrent removals underway and the many states suddenly eager to borrow. Removal treaties multiplied funds under federal management, and officials eagerly bought up favored bonds—all under the guise of offering compensation and protection to Native peoples stripped of their homelands. With this conflict of interest lodged at the heart of fiduciary colonialism, the Chickasaws suffered through a forced migration that played out exactly how they feared.

⊱━◈━⊰

Chickasaws entered into their removal crisis with centuries of practice responding creatively to the economic destruction of colonialism. After coalescing from prior Mississippian groups, including the Chickaza and Summerville cultures, by 1715 the Chickasaws had emerged as a relatively small nation of around twenty-eight hundred persons. Organized into four major districts, each divided into towns bound together by matrilineal relationships, Chickasaw homelands spanned the Tallahatchie, Tennessee, and Tombigbee Rivers. Slight in numbers, the Chickasaws acted inventively to contend with the many competing European and Indigenous powers seeking to trade in the highly coveted Lower Mississippi Valley. They established themselves as intermediaries for the early eighteenth-century's burgeoning slave trade, delivering to Carolinian settlers roughly two thousand Native captives from the Lower Mississippi Valley. These alliances secured the Chickasaws protection from colonists, even at the cost of predation on neighbors, and their success in slaving bolstered their military power amid the interimperial tumult of the mid-eighteenth century. Maintaining martial capacity on an outsized scale kept the Chickasaws supplied with the fruits of a violent trade in people and deerskins, as British, French, and Spanish emissaries courted the nation with gifts and goods in hopes of gaining their services. Diplomatic prestige backed by near-continuous military engagement came at a human cost, however, as the Chickasaws lost almost one-third of their population by 1760.[8]

Chickasaws adapted their economy after the détente that followed the Seven Years' War. In their homes and nearby fields, Chickasaw women grew corn, beans, and squash, cultivars that rounded out a diet of game, fish, berries, hickory nuts, walnuts, pecans, persimmons, wild plums, and grapes. In the nineteenth century, Chickasaw men moved into the previously feminized sphere of agriculture, freeing women to work on the nation's nascent ventures in cotton processing and cloth manufacturing. Grain and lumber mills sprouted up alongside manufacturing workshops, while farms expanded, acquired a widened array of stock animals, and fanned out from once fortified and densely clustered towns. The Chickasaws entered the nineteenth century no longer reliant on war, at peace with their neighbors, and with a rising population.[9] Lessons learned from these adaptations would directly inform their leaders' decisions in the removal era.

When the United States sought to gain footing in the Gulf South after acquiring New Orleans from Spain in 1795, the Chickasaws pivoted from war to entrepreneurship. Leading the charge were members of the Colbert family, descendants of a Scottish trader and his Chickasaw wife. Brothers George and Levi Colbert acted as civil statesmen and diplomats for their nation and businessmen on their own accounts. The Colberts opened a ferry at the mouth of Bear Creek, where federal officials had planned but failed to establish a trading post. After the US military extended the Natchez Trace, a Native thoroughfare to the Gulf of Mexico, travelers came in a thickening stream, with the road serving as a route home for vendors who had rafted their produce down the Mississippi River. To capitalize on the increased traffic, the Colberts relocated their ferriage and tavern to the juncture of the Natchez Trace and the Tennessee River. There, the family's post enriched its owners while facilitating the United States' logistics across the region.[10]

By ushering foreigners through their territories, Chickasaws like the Colberts were seeking more than friendship. By planting commercial nodes in the United States' budding fiscal-military frontier, Chickasaws were in pursuit of the federal government's higher-quality money. Money meant many things in the early United States, and a hierarchy of value structured the many forms of money in circulation. At the top sat silver or gold coin—specie—that flowed into the United States from Cuba, Mexico, and the West Indies or was acquired as bullion, assayed, and coined into dollars by the US Mint. Specie's embodiment of the dollar unit of account and bimetallic standards, its association with the mint's federal authority, and its parallel life as a commodity—its potential to be melted down and resold as silver or gold—meant it carried relatively consistent value across the nation and, uniquely, between nations. Specie served as a monetary standard, and all other forms of money in circulation bore value that hinged on their convertibility to it. Put otherwise, specie was the only form of money that was not also a form of debt: Banknotes were effectively IOUs for redemption in silver or gold. The fact that the United States suffered a chronic specie scarcity only appreciated its value: In 1820, the country held roughly $20 million in specie, with only $4.5 million in circulation.[11] Well aware of specie's preciousness, the Chickasaws, like many other nations, insisted on receiving annuities in coin.

Ranking below specie were notes of the Second Bank of the United States, a publicly chartered but privately owned institution that handled federal funds and, by holding the lion's share of the nation's specie, issued notes that often traded at par with silver or gold. Scattered below the Second Bank's notes were more than ten thousand different notes issued by hundreds of state-chartered banks. Paper money held value to the extent it could be converted into specie—an attribute captured by the Choctaw term for dollars, *tvli holisso*, or "metal paper." Whether state banknotes could successfully be redeemed in silver or gold was often uncertain—or infeasible, depending on the distance of the bank from the note bearer. Some notes came from ailing or fraudulent banks, and some of them were outright fakes. Yet notes issued by state banks were far more convenient than hauling boxes of coin, and remained essential to ordinary people. In an era in which quality money was rare, what mattered was convincing someone that the cash they held should be accepted.[12]

Chickasaws held a monetary advantage that most settlers did not: a privileged relationship with the federal government, the most important source of high-quality money. In lands claimed but thinly occupied by the United States, banks were few and their paper currencies unreliable. On this fiscal frontier, Second Bank branches and federal sites like military forts, post offices, land offices, and Indian agencies received and expended reliable currency in a locale where money was otherwise scarce and discounted. Chickasaw men and women procured money from federal outposts by peddling meat and produce or by working for wages as couriers, guards, interpreters, cooks, or manual laborers. Only treaties could bring in money on a national scale, however. Chickasaws had received annuities since 1795 and within a decade were receiving a share in specie. When the federal government began pursuing land cessions more aggressively in the late 1810s, the Chickasaws pushed to receive the entirety of their treaty payments in hard money.[13]

Specie annuities represented an alternative not only to questionable state banknotes but also to payment in goods. Like many Native nations, the Chickasaws were often frustrated by the quality and selection of merchandise that the government occasionally offered in lieu of money. In 1811 an Indian agent warned the secretary of war that the Chickasaws "complain very much of their blankets in their last annuity not being Good, two small and some of them very ratten" and noted that "they wish you to send them more blankets and less calico, less thread and no more scissors nor cotton balls."[14] Rather than engage in a tedious back-and-forth over their consumer preferences, the Chickasaws demanded annuities in cash during an 1816 treaty negotiation. When Indian agent Robert Nicholas pushed to implement the treaty's terms by purchasing livestock and merchandise on the Chickasaws' behalf—in line with the aims of civilization policy—George and Levi Colbert refused, insisting that "the money belongs to individuals & they have a right to do with it as they please."[15] Over $35,000 in specie was delivered to the nation the following year.[16]

Aside from their inadequacies as consumer items, annuities in goods also thwarted effective internal redistribution according to the laws, customs, and political geography of Native nations. In an 1807 Cherokee annuity disbursement, towns each received a small bundle containing goods of widely varying quality, including strips of flannel, blankets, combs, scarves, brass kettles, and knives. Although each town brought a census recorded on notched staffs of wood, the idiosyncratic value of goods prevented an equitable apportionment, and many Cherokee individuals received items that did not meet their wants. After the distribution, one Cherokee woman "cried bitterly that she did not receive a blanket," a missionary recalled.[17] As a nation composed of four districts, dispersed towns, and diverse households with their unique material needs, the Chickasaws were, much like the Cherokees, eager to receive cash in order to properly allocate annuities' value.

For the federal agents charged with delivering annuities, procuring tens of thousands of dollars in specie in a region with scant banking capital posed a challenge even in the best of times. A financial panic that tore across the country in 1819 made it impossible: When the Chickasaws' Indian agent arrived at the federal land office in Natchez, Mississippi, to obtain the more than $35,000 owed to the Chickasaws, the receiver promptly informed him that he could not possibly withdraw specie in that amount. But the Chickasaws continued to refuse goods, and specie payments eventually resumed. In 1824, for instance, the nation received $70,000 in specie, a payment for two years' worth of annuities.[18]

The Chickasaw National Council developed a fiscal regime to ensure that highly prized specie remained within their territory, to their nation's benefit. A council house built at Pontotoc, the nation's center, hosted annuity distributions in which national leaders decided who could—and could not—attend these important transactions. Controls on money

Coins can be seen on the table at this 1875 annuity distribution in Wisconsin.
*Source:* Charles Zimmerman, *Annuity Payment*, Miriam and Ira D. Wallach
Division of Art, Prints and Photographs, New York Public Library.

annuities reinforced older regulations that banned unauthorized traders,
tavernkeepers, and ferry operators who might compete with Chickasaw
entrepreneurs and capture the nation's higher-quality money. In case of
violations, the Chickasaw impounded and auctioned off offenders' goods,
with the proceeds divided between the nation and the federal government.[19] Spearheaded by the Colberts, these fiscal strategies regulated the
circulation of annuity money to the Chickasaws' advantage.

While the Chickasaws were unusually proactive in their pursuit and
management of specie annuities, they were not alone in pushing for a
shift from annuities in merchandise to high-quality money. After a pivotal
treaty with Lenape, Potawatomi, Shawnee, and Wyandot negotiators in

1817, Michigan territorial governor Lewis Cass oversaw a shift away from goods annuities to annuities paid in money. Specie rapidly became standard for annuities disbursed along the river villages and lake ports of the Northwest. By 1830, "frequent complaints" from Native annuity recipients prompted the secretary of war to direct all Indian agents to issue payments "in specie or United States notes, and not in goods."[20] That year federally negotiated treaties promised specie payments totaling $93,900. But since nations that had not negotiated for specie by treaty nonetheless requested their annuities in that format, nearly half of all annuity payments were doled out in coin, amounting to $119,000, or in present-day terms, over $129 million. Even more common by the mid-1830s was the delivery of annuities in "money," which regulations defined as notes bearing value equivalent to specie—in effect, notes of the Second Bank of the United States (until Jackson's removal of federal deposits in 1833) and of authorized federal depositories. In 1834, an unusually granular statement counted 46 percent of annuities as deliverable in money, 29 percent in specie, and only 25 percent in goods.[21]

⁊⸱⸱⸱⸱⸱

Cash annuities' impact reverberated beyond the nations that received them. Underbanked settler economies that surrounded points of distribution gained much-needed liquidity through trade with Native annuity recipients. Concentrations of customs revenue, mercantile activity, and financial capital caused higher-quality money to collect in Northeastern cities like Boston, New York, and Philadelphia. Settlers pressing onto freshly ceded Native homelands borrowed from better-capitalized Eastern banks, and Western merchants imported Northeastern goods and wares to frontier zones. Both transactions entailed settling payments with notes or bills on Eastern banks or businesses, which could only be procured from specialized brokers at a premium. For merchants, one way to avoid this premium was to market goods (or services) to the federal government in exchange for Treasury drafts or notes of the Second Bank.[22] As one of the most prominent federal agencies in the West, dispensing tens of thousands of gold or silver coin, the Office of Indian Affairs became an indispensable source for Westerners seeking to settle their accounts with Eastern creditors. Annuities were a major—sometimes *the* major—source of higher-quality money on the fiscal frontier.

Like mineral strikes, cash annuities could attract rushes that brought disreputable traders and liquor peddlers to Native payments. In 1827

Isaac McCoy, a Baptist missionary stationed among the Potawatomis at Carey Mission on the Joseph River in present-day Michigan, published his *Remarks on the Practicability of Indian Reform*, which included a proposed remedy for ills the missionary attributed to cash annuities. McCoy served on behalf of the American Board of Commissions for Foreign Missions, the same organization that had sent missionaries to the Cherokee and Choctaw Nations in the late 1810s. At Carey Mission, McCoy had observed with dismay as traders quickly collected tens of thousands of dollars in annuities, offering goods in exchange at enormously inflated prices. Oblivious to Potawatomi political economy, McCoy attributed any resistance to his civilizing mission to the influence of annuities and the trade they fueled. In his *Remarks*, McCoy recommended that the federal government abandon compensating Native land cessions with cash annuities funded each year by Congress. He proposed instead that the federal government sell off lands acquired by treaty, place the proceeds of the ceded lands in trust, and apply the interest toward financing missionary-led civilization programs in perpetuity.[23]

McCoy's proposal combined missionary and fiscal arguments for expanded trusteeship. On the one hand, he cast depriving Native people of their own wealth as a benevolent act, one that protected them from traders that preyed on their high-quality money. On the other hand, he posited that investing the proceeds of ceded lands, and releasing the interest alone as services, not cash—a practice already tested on a limited scale with education funds—could considerably alleviate the costs of dispossession. With its timely publication on the eve of an enormous scaling up of federal forced migrations, McCoy's *Remarks* sketched out a blueprint for sparing settlers the financial burden of removal.

McCoy's *Remarks* also contributed to a growing campaign in support of Indian removal. In 1830, Governor Cass published a watershed pro-removal treatise in the *North American Review*. The piece became a rallying cry for the rapid expulsion of Native peoples east of the Mississippi River and for the expanded control over the compensation offered to dispossessed peoples. Citing McCoy's *Remarks*, Cass included long digressions on the maladies of cash annuities, even as their prevalence could be credited to his own record as a treaty negotiator. He drew on doctrines of equity to recommend guardianship and praised French and Spanish empires for their professed commitment to principles of "pupilage." A strong hand was needed, Cass argued, because Indigenous peoples were inherently incapable of managing their own wealth. Cass found it "difficult to conceive," he informed his readers, "that any branch of the human family can be less provident in arrangement, less frugal in enjoyment, less industrious in acquiring, more implacable in their resentments, more ungovernable in their passions, with fewer principles to guide them, with fewer obligations to restrain them, and with less knowledge to improve and instruct them."[24]

Enacted the following May, the Indian Removal Act enshrined a policy of mass dispossession and forced relocation espoused by Cass, Jackson, and McCoy. The law hardly inaugurated the displacement of Indigenous peoples, present since before the founding of the United States, but rather endowed the executive with the requisite funding and discretion over the disposition of public lands needed to carry out removals and redraw territories. Although removals would formally hinge on the consent of removing nations, the act included a telling clause, worded in language that evoked precisely the fantasy of Native disappearance and preemptive entitlement to Native wealth that Robert Morris had employed in his claims to the Seneca trust fund. Lands to which Native peoples were removed would be secured to those nations, the law explained, provided that "such lands shall revert to the United States, if the Indians become extinct."[25]

The year after Cass's article appeared in print, Jackson appointed him secretary of war. As he presided over removal treaties, Cass put into practice McCoy's theories, approving trust investments that would minimize the amount of cash in Native hands and thereby leaven Indian removal's fiscal burden. When Cass assumed office, his short-lived predecessor, John Eaton, had already begun to implement the Indian Removal Act. The Choctaws were unfortunate pioneers, submitting to removal in an 1830 treaty council after Eaton threatened to imprison anyone who failed to comply with his orders. Cass inherited the task of carrying out the first of many removals under Jackson's administration. In late 1831, roughly fifteen thousand Choctaws traveled west in the dead of an especially punishing winter. The journey cost hundreds of Choctaws their lives. It also quickly cost the federal government double the estimated sums, stoking congressional ire and prompting Cass to tighten regulations and transfer oversight over subsequent removals to the military.[26]

The dizzying costs of the Choctaw expulsion only burnished the appeal of McCoy's ideas. A treaty in which Odawa, Seneca, and Shawnee villages agreed to part with their winnowed-down homelands in Ohio (promised them since the Treaty of Fort Meigs in 1817) served as a trial for the missionary's scheme. Lands ceded in the treaty would be sold and the proceeds placed in a fund that would finance saw- and gristmills, blacksmith shops, and other improvements in the nations' new home. Federal officials took McCoy's model even further by deducting the cost of surveying the cession from the amount the Odawas, Senecas, and Shawnees received—essentially using the federally ascribed value of Native homelands to fund the administrative costs of dispossession. The balance would be invested for their "use and general benefit" in securities generating at least 5 percent interest.[27]

With preparations for Chickasaw removal beginning soon after, President Jackson urged federal negotiators to replicate the Ohio treaty, albeit on a far bigger scale: Chickasaws possessed over 6.4 million acres of homeland, much of it prime for cotton cultivation. Drawing the costs of removal—including treaty compensation—from the proceeds of land sales shifted the financial burdens onto dispossessed nations themselves. It would, Jackson hoped, allow the president to pursue a personal obsession: the destruction of the Second Bank of the United States. Jackson publicly criticized the Second Bank as unconstitutional, aristocratic, and subject to the influence of foreign creditors, but quietly aspired for government control and looser credit than the privately managed bank allowed. As the federal government's fiscal agent, the Second Bank serviced its debts to creditors, including overseas financiers. Once that debt was eliminated, Jackson hoped, the path toward destroying the Second Bank would be clear. Jackson made explicit the significance of self-financing removal in instructions to his friend John Coffee, who he appointed commissioner to negotiate the Chickasaw treaty. As Jackson explained, he wished for the costs of removal to be "raised out of the sales of the chikisaw lands" since "I keep in view steadily, the full discharge of the public debt on the 3rd of March 1833."[28]

Paying the Chickasaws with the money raised from their own lands would avoid a large congressional outlay, and trust funds only sweetened the deal for Jackson by keeping the bulk of compensation out of Chickasaw hands. As Eaton remarked to his successor Cass, allowing the Chickasaws too great a proportion of their wealth in cash seemed to be "a questionable course of policy" since it would tend "to throw the Indians upon the Government for support and protection" were funds "wasted through any improvident management."[29] By holding the full proportion of Chickasaw funds in trust and thereby preemptively mitigating future claims for aid, Cass could carry out removal without slowing progress toward eliminating the national debt.

❦

The Chickasaws negotiated their first removal treaty in the fall of 1832. Coffee, a seasoned land surveyor and speculator, represented the United States. To assure a robust attendance from the Chickasaws, he timed his arrival in their territory to coincide with Indian agent Benjamin Reynolds's payment of the yearly annuity. After Reynolds completed his work, Coffee outlined a proposed agreement that would relocate Chickasaw families immediately onto allotments carved from the northeastern corner of their territory, allowing the bulk of their land to be surveyed and marketed as soon as possible. Once the nation had located a suitable home west of the Mississippi, Chickasaws would sell off their allotments to interested settlers. Taking their experiment with the Ohio nations even further, the Jackson administration modified McCoy's model by stipulating that the *entire* costs of Chickasaw removal—from purchasing rations to remunerating the clerical labor needed to process their land sales—would be covered by their national fund. Federal officials would then invest whatever remained of the land proceeds after deducting the costs of removal and deliver the interest accrued to the nation as an annuity.[30]

After requesting Coffee's treaty in writing, the Chickasaws convened in a council at Pontotoc to "have the proposals read again, and again, and interpreted until it was well understood by the whole nation," in the words of interpreter Benjamin Love. By avoiding a need to rely on congressional expenditures for compensation or removal costs, the treaty's fiscally lightweight design clearly suited Jackson's interests. But the proposal appealed to the Chickasaws too: They knew their land would fetch a handsome price at auction given its fertility and the buoyant state of cotton markets. Having observed speculation in their own previous cessions, and having witnessed a more recent manic investment in neighboring Choctaw and Creek lands, the Chickasaws correctly anticipated that their own lands would fetch far more than whatever set sum they could have negotiated for by treaty. Controversy arose over how exactly these sales should proceed, however. Certain affluent mixed-ancestry Chickasaws, including Levi Colbert and his sons, preferred to receive individual allotments that would be sold for their personal benefit; other members of the Chickasaw Nation wanted lands conveyed to the United States and the proceeds given to the nation as a whole. To please both parties Coffee suggested carving out a portion of the cession as allotments that could be sold on an individual basis, with the remaining lands sold for the collective gain of the Chickasaws.[31]

Notably, Coffee's proposed treaty did not address investing funds raised by the Chickasaw land cession. The Chickasaws may have suggested the revision themselves, given that they had made similar requests in the past. Like the Cherokees and Choctaws, the Chickasaws had entertained missionaries and appropriated their prudential models with an eye toward grooming a rising generation of statesmen. In 1824, the nation had approached Secretary of War John C. Calhoun with a plan to put their $35,000 annuity "into a Bank so as to be Drawing interest, and the interest to be put to the support of our schools."[32] This fund met the same fate as the Cherokee education fund: A lack of appropriate securities for investment prevented the Office of Indian Affairs from abiding by the Chickasaw's wishes.[33] By the 1830s, no such dearth in the bond market existed, and officials would have no trouble investing Chickasaw wealth.

In order to ensure that his fellow Chickasaws all understood the mechanics of investment, Love translated interest using a metaphor of a "hen laying eggs" to illustrate interest, according to one observer. "That one hundred dollars would lay six dollars in twelve months," he recalled, "they at once fully understood." Weeks of tedious deliberation followed. After slightly less than a month of negotiations, Coffee lost patience, reminding the Chickasaws that Mississippi would soon extend its jurisdiction over their territories. "Sign it, or regret it," Coffee ordered.[34] Chickasaws faced a choice between two evils: parting with homelands or allowing their sovereignty to be undermined to a degree that might cause their nation to disintegrate. After somber discussion, Colbert and his fellow Chickasaw representatives signed a final draft of the treaty on October 20, 1832.

Soon after the treaty council dispersed, however, many Chickasaws started to regret the terms of their compensation, which they feared may not have struck the optimal balance between longer-term security and liquidity for the journey to come. The Chickasaws clearly desired to build national wealth through the mechanism of investment. The problem, as Levi Colbert and others understood it, was that the treaty in its current shape stored too much of their wealth in federal hands. Proceeds from the allotment sales were to be invested alongside proceeds of the national cession. Considering that a $20,000 annuity the Chickasaws had received since 1818 was scheduled to expire in 1833, the nation would likely run out of cash on the eve of their journey west. Levi Colbert drafted his petition demanding a renegotiated treaty. Suggesting that the nation would refuse removal until their objections were addressed, Colbert noted that among other purposes, the Chickasaws required cash to repay their debts, which "must be done before we go."[35]

Slaveholding elites like Colbert were poised to capture prime allotment lands and were preoccupied with liquidating these lands for business reasons. Resuming large-scale cotton planting, ranching, tavernkeeping, and cloth production on resettling in the West would demand cash up front. Chickasaw planters G. M. Long, Sloan Love, Joseph A. Perry, and James Wolf predicted that a failure to place the profit from reserves in household hands would impede Chickasaw economic recovery, warning "that for the ensuing twenty years there would not be found within the limits of our nation twenty looms," and "a total prostration of industry and improvement would be the result."[36] But even less affluent Chickasaws were indebted and in need of seed money to establish themselves in Indian Territory. As Colbert's petition explained, only cash could "feed and sustain my people on their new homes until they can again build houses clear farms and get stock about them."[37] Without cash these purchases would inevitably be made on credit, skimming off a growing share of future annuity payments toward servicing avoidable debts.

Chickasaws also faced a collective need to "meet expenses in the search and payment for a country west," as Colbert noted.[38] A suitable country to replace their homelands had so far eluded the Chickasaws despite their venturing west twice to scout out a new territory. Soon after the 1827 publication of his *Remarks*, none other than Isaac McCoy had accompanied a delegation of Chickasaws, Choctaws, and Creeks on a federally funded expedition to Arkansas Territory. Counting interpreters, advisers, servants, and Levi Colbert's Black slave, forty-two men and over sixty horses set out from St. Louis with the mission of locating suitable homes in the West. No location satisfied the Chickasaw delegates, however, and another attempt followed an 1830 treaty negotiation. This time, Colbert's party found the only suitable region to be significantly farther south and west, in lands claimed by Mexico between the Red and Sabine Rivers, where the Caddo and Osage peoples lived. But the idea of permitting an embittered Native nation to decamp to a competing republic—or, worse, to the Comanche empire expanding into northern Mexico—was simply too much of a risk to the United States' security. Reynolds abandoned the delegation in protest, the Office of Indian Affairs refused to approve the Chickasaws' wishes, and the treaty lapsed before the Senate could ratify it.

Undaunted, Chickasaw negotiators continued to explore emigrating from the United States. At their next round of negotiations two years later, they requested payment for any land cession in specie, a currency that retained value across borders. Cherokees also contemplated an exit to Mexico when their removal crisis came to a head in 1835, demanding from Jackson a $20 million lump sum specie payment for their remaining homelands, but Jackson refused, and Mexican officials rejected their overtures.[39] Neither the Chickasaws nor Cherokees succeeded in defecting to Mexico. Nevertheless, their efforts reveal how specie—in ample sums—struck Indigenous leaders as a ticket to a wider geography, one that could allow dispossessed nations to escape the United States' bounds.

Despite the Chickasaws' vocal protests, the Senate ratified the Treaty of Pontotoc Creek in 1833. The following spring, a Chickasaw delegation left for Washington to demand amendments, even though Jackson had personally forbade it. In a stroke of misfortune, Levi Colbert died on the journey, leaving the remaining delegates to carry on in his stead. After days of negotiation in the capital, the Chickasaws won several concessions, including one that allowed individuals to keep the proceeds of their allotment sales rather than have them placed in trust. Reflecting delegates' concerns about post-removal economic recovery, a portion of the national land proceeds would also be withheld from investment in order to provide immediate funds for schools, mills, and blacksmith shops and "for any other needful purpose." Finally, the Chickasaws placed a twenty-year cap on the maturities of the bonds federal officials could invest in. This shorter investment horizon would enable the nation to withdraw their funds in case of crisis or disagreement with federal trust management.[40]

The Chickasaws' revised treaty demonstrated the care and deliberation with which their negotiators planned for life after removal. But there were limits on what the federal government would concede. Prior to signing, the Chickasaws had demanded that the "United States will save the nation from any loss of any part of the principal, or interest of their money."[41] But despite the delegates' prescience, the revised treaty offered no protections against loss on investments. The risk would be borne by the Chickasaws themselves.

Removal enthusiasts applauded the financial innovation of the Treaty of Pontotoc Creek and were invigorated by its ratification. When he received his copy, Jackson singled out the "stipulation" that the Chickasaw "remove at their own expense and on their own means" as "an excellent feature."[42] McCoy, for his part, proudly recognized his ideas in its unique clauses.[43] Treasury Secretary Amos Kendall eagerly volunteered himself to President Jackson for the duty of investing the "large sum of money . . . about to accrue to the Chickasaws."[44] Jackson obliged. Kendall secured a promotion to postmaster general soon after, but his maneuver ensured that his successors at the Treasury would play a pivotal role in directing the flow of Indian trust fund investment. Kendall's replacement, Levi Woodbury, found himself charged with investing a growing pool of Indian trust fund money. He gained control over a set of trust funds created for the Cherokee

Nation—$200,000 in trust for the nation as a whole, $50,000 for orphans, and $150,000 for education—after a proremoval faction broke with the Cherokee National Council and signed a treaty that ceded the remaining homelands. Woodbury also began investing the proceeds accrued on the sale of lands ceded by the Senecas and Shawnees. By late 1836 Woodbury had invested over $1,054,000 of Indian trust fund money.[45]

In the 1810s and 1820s lagging land sales and a paucity of government-issued securities with sufficient yields had prevented the Office of Indian Affairs from investing education trust funds. As recently as 1830, a lack of viable outlets for investment had led Congress to shift the Seneca trust fund's principal into the Treasury and to imitate a 6 percent rate of interest with annual appropriations of $6,000, as the Senecas demanded. Much had changed over the course of a decade. As Indian removal campaigns accelerated, state governments began issuing millions of dollars in debt, embarking on a borrowing boom without precedent since the Revolutionary War. Some established states increased their debts, but more pronounced was a trend toward first-time borrowing among newer states and territories. As Michigan's governor, Stevens T. Mason, informed his legislature in 1836, "the heavy expenses of the state, in the completion of important and essential state improvements, must be sustained and accomplished by loans on the credit of the state." "Immediate taxation," he explained, would only be viable "as our population and wealth increases."[46]

Secretary Woodbury catered to these capital-deficient states. Just months after Mason's comments, Woodbury purchased $64,000 in Michigan Territory bonds from New York City broker Joseph D. Beers on behalf of the Cherokees. This meant the nation's trust now held nearly two-thirds of the territory's entire debt. Among the biggest beneficiaries of Woodbury's trust management was Tennessee, whose internal improvement program keenly interested its native son, Andrew Jackson. In spring 1836, Woodbury purchased for the Cherokee trust fund $250,000 in state bonds issued to capitalize the Union Bank of Tennessee in Nashville, which sat on land ceded by the Cherokee Nation in 1785 after a disastrous settler invasion spurred by the Revolutionary War. The Cherokee trust now possessed nearly half of the $530,000 in bonds Tennessee had issued to finance railroads, turnpikes, and the Union Bank. Of the seven states Woodbury selected as recipients of Indian trust fund investment, only one—Maryland—had not voted in favor of Jackson in the 1828 election, and that state had split its electors. In exercising partisan preference for banks in the newer states in the Midwest and South, Woodbury disproportionately supplied capital to infrastructural projects that would anchor settlement on recently acquired Native land.[47]

As the first direct fiduciary for the Indian trust funds, Woodbury coordinated investment of Chickasaw wealth in one such project: the State Bank of Alabama. From its birth on the eve of the Panic of 1819, Alabama's state banking system served to supply settlers the money needed to acquire Chickasaw lands. Territories ceded by the Chickasaws in 1816 and 1818 had become a focal point of speculation amid surging cotton prices. More than a million acres in the western Tennessee River Valley sold at public auction in 1818 alone. So frenetic was the land market that money grew scarce across the region; local interest rates rose as high as 40 percent. Federal land law had established a two-dollar minimum price for public lands at auction, but permitted purchasers to deliver payments in four annual installments at a charge of 6 percent interest. According to regulations, only banknotes that traded at par with federally designated deposit banks would be accepted—hence the vernacular category of "land office money." One exception came in the form of "Mississippi stock," a non-interest-bearing bond issued by the federal government to settle claims by an earlier generation of land speculators in the Yazoo River Valley. This boutique form of federal money contributed 45 percent of payments for Alabama lands between 1816 and 1820. To procure cash that would meet land office receivers' standards, affluent investors collateralized land, slaves, or both to secure loans from Southern banks, which were increasingly willing to underwrite speculation. Whether drawing on state-chartered banks or federal scrip, bidders at auction had by 1818 committed to purchase $7 million in newly acquired Native lands in the Tennessee River Valley—although more than three-fourths of that sum remained to be paid.[48]

In early 1819, the bubble burst, and a dazed crowd of investors in Alabama land owed half the entire federal land debt. As a full-blown financial panic set in, speculators scrambled to make installments and meet their interest payments. The Tennessee River Valley was particularly hard hit. In 1820, the only bank in northern Alabama suspended specie payments, setting off a monetary contraction that caused thousands of purchasers to default on their land payments and drained the region of any money that traded closely enough to specie to be accepted by federal land offices.

Three years later, the Alabama legislature chartered the State Bank of Alabama with the explicit purpose of providing land office money to debtors. A state bank was necessary, according to Alabama Governor Israel Pickens, because ceded Native lands "must not only be paid in cash, but in such kind as will answer the expenditures of the United States."[49] To supply the bank's initial capital, the state issued $100,000 in bonds. Under the US Constitution, no state could issue paper money of its own. But by debt financing a state bank, Alabama could create land office money by proxy.

Alabama's decision to borrow to fund a banking system conformed to a larger pattern of infrastructural development in newer and capital-poorer states. Investing in bank stock, requiring banks to subscribe to turnpike or canal companies, eliciting charter fees and bonuses, or taxing banks in more straightforward ways allowed state governments to extract public revenue without imposing onerous taxes on their recently settled citizens. Bank-fueled public finance especially appealed to the Southern slaveholders who dominated state legislatures and believed excessive taxation could undermine their rights to human property. Just as planters hoped, by 1836 Alabama's state banking system had sufficiently flourished for the state to abolish direct taxes on landed property and slaves.[50]

Towering over the State Bank of Alabama's branches was the Second Bank of the United States, which rose to the height of its powers in the years after the Panic of 1819. As the federal government's chief depositary, the Second Bank was especially prominent on the fiscal frontier, where its branches handled funds related to Indian diplomacy, military campaigns, and public land sales. While penetrating the interior, the Second Bank also reached across the Atlantic, paying the federal government's international creditors and carrying accounts for overseas merchants. To fulfill these functions the Second Bank required sizable specie reserves—since only specie held value across borders—and it procured much of this stock by demanding that state banks settle their accounts in hard money rather than their own notes. Specie obligations to the Second Bank constrained state-chartered banks from issuing more notes than they could honor and thereby contracted the supply of money in surrounding communities. Meanwhile, Second Bank branches in the Cotton South monopolized the most lucrative commercial accounts. Together these factors pitted state banks and their stakeholders against the Second Bank. Jackson capitalized on these resentments when he vetoed the renewal of the Second Bank's federal charter in 1832. The following year he withdrew the federal government's deposits, scattering them among dozens of favored state-chartered banks.[51]

In 1835, the Jackson administration repaid the final installment of the federal debt. Stripped of federal deposits, demoted to a Pennsylvania charter, and now devoid of one of its original purposes, the Second Bank branch system atrophied. States legislatures eagerly filled the vacuum, planning ambitious expansions to their banking systems. Many would eventually be anointed as federal depositories, inheriting the Second Bank's privileges. By the end of Jackson's second term, the number of banks in operation had more than doubled. Most of these banks, like Alabama's, were capitalized by state-issued securities backed by legislatures' power to tax. By borrowing from creditors and then investing that borrowed money in banks, states succeeded in swelling bank credit by $337 million between 1830 and 1836, with the money supply growing at a stunning average rate of 30 percent for the last two years of that period. Banks multiplied fastest on the fiscal frontier, where the Second Bank was forced to close its once sprawling network of branches and where settlers' purchases of Native lands created the greatest demand for an expanding money supply. In the newer states of the South, like Alabama, the number of banks grew more than three-and-a-half times between 1832 and 1837.[52]

Alabama had founded its state banking system in the aftermath of treaties negotiated by then-General Jackson, and began borrowing in earnest to expand this system amid a removal Jackson helmed as president. By December 1832, Alabama had issued $3.9 million in bonds to found new branches of its fledgling banking system, with all but $500,000 remaining unsold.[53] Unlike more established Eastern states, Alabama relied on the promise of future prosperity to market its bonds. Yet this prosperity was projected onto tracts that settlers could scarcely purchase until the banks had accumulated the capital from bond investors needed to open their doors.

In November 1832, newly minted president of the State Bank's Mobile branch, George S. Gaines, confronted this dilemma head-on with his first official duty: marketing $3.5 million in Alabama state bonds, issued to finance the Decatur and Mobile branches. Gaines had recently concluded a stint as removal agent for the Choctaws, shepherding the nation's lethal expulsion from central Mississippi to Indian Territory. As he prepared for his trip to court New York City financiers, Gaines compiled a prospectus that included the bank's charters, favorable correspondence from New York City brokers, and a description of recent treaties that had transferred vast acres of Choctaw and Creek land to the United States. In his own pen Gaines explained that, once settled, these prime lands promised to increase his state's cotton crop by 20 percent, an increased output that would undoubtedly swell bank profits. After several rejections, he finally struck an agreement with the same broker who had sold Michigan bonds to the Treasury, Joseph D. Beers.[54]

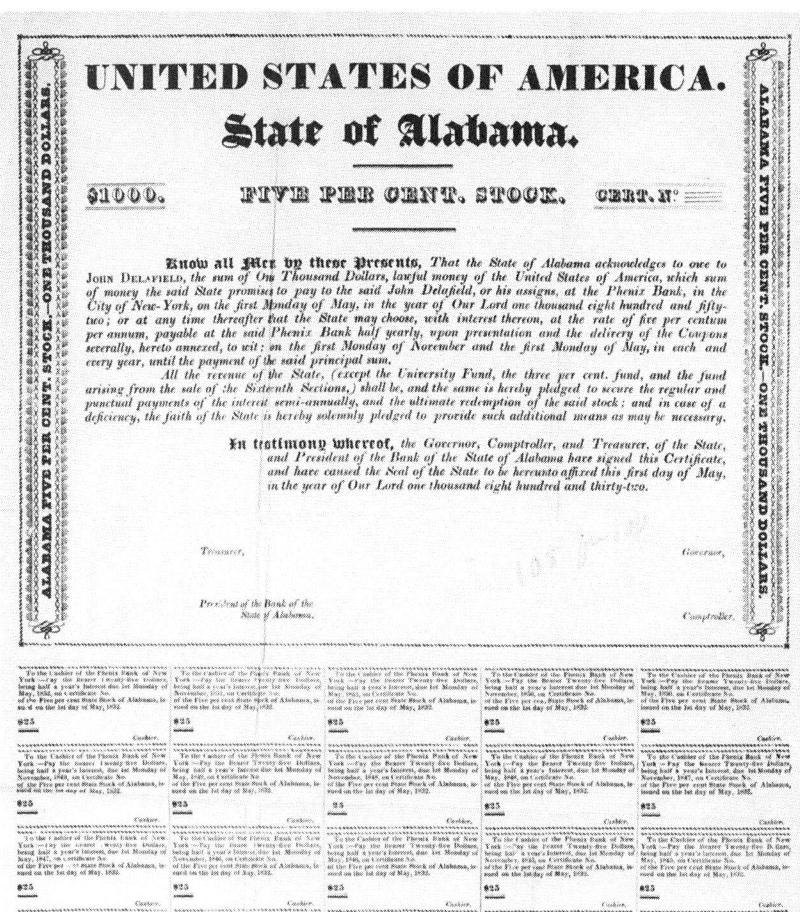

Five percent bond issued by the State Bank of Alabama. Each coupon would be torn off and submitted to the Phenix Bank of New York for redemption of biannual interest payments. *Source:* LROIA 853 [23].

Four years later, in early 1836, Treasury Secretary Levi Woodbury sent out a circular to financial houses soliciting proposals to invest the first wave of proceeds from the Chickasaw cession. Philadelphia broker Charles Macalester responded with an offer of Alabama state bonds. He admitted that no market had been found for the bonds in London or Philadelphia, since the reputations of slaveholding states "do not stand as high either abroad or at home." If Woodbury was willing to tolerate the risk, the broker suggested, a deal could be struck.[55] That March, Woodbury purchased a whopping $500,000 in Alabama bonds directly from the Decatur branch of the State Bank. (Macalester, incensed, demanded and ultimately received a commission for his role in the transaction.) Even though the state had struggled to find creditors, Woodbury did not exactly drive a hard bargain. The bank's president asked for a 4.5 percent premium, enclosing assurances from a "mutual friend," Alabama Senator William R. King, that "a better stock is not to be found in our country." Woodbury accepted, paying above face value for bonds that one might have expected would sell at a discount.[56] A week later, Woodbury bought another $65,000 in Alabama state bonds for the Chickasaw trust at a 4.5 percent premium, this time from Beers. As revenue streamed in from Chickasaw land sales at the Pontotoc Land Office, Woodbury invested in two more rounds of Alabama securities, bringing the nation's investment in the state to $1,295,000. By 1837, in aggregate, the Chickasaw owned roughly 11 percent of the state's debt—16 percent if one counted only long-term issuances. Even more striking, the Chickasaw trust held a quarter of the Decatur Bank branch's $2,000,000 capital stock.[57]

By investing in bonds that backed the State Bank of Alabama, Woodbury also channeled Chickasaw wealth toward the armed enforcement of removals. When Governor Clement Comer Clay called in militias to suppress Creek militants in 1836, the Alabama State Bank lent the legislature $70,000 to pay soldiers' wages and furnish supplies. Banks also provided credit to traders who supplied rations and transportation services to migrants. The Huntsville branch of the State Bank, to give one example, extended loans to the land speculator John W. Sanford's Alabama Emigrating Company.[58]

By investing in the Decatur branch of the State Bank of Alabama in particular, Woodbury channeled Chickasaw funds toward an institution several speculators in the Chickasaw cession relied on for loans, banknotes, and the transfer of funds with their Northeastern counterparts. These state banks adopted more accommodating lending practices

The State Bank of Alabama's Decatur branch, as photographed in 1934. *Source:* W. N. Manning, Historic American Buildings Survey, Prints and Photographs Division, Library of Congress.

than the Second Bank to enable the territorial expansion of slavery. The Second Bank had adhered to a more conservative "real bills" doctrine, primarily accepting collateral attached to merchant transactions. In order to cater to an expanding cotton kingdom, however, rural state-chartered Southern banks took on riskier loans secured by land and enslaved people. Banks permissively renewed credit in the form of short-term notes, providing liquidity to borrowers purchasing and planting on lands so recently in Native possession.[59]

Prospective speculators had begun forming land companies targeting Chickasaw lands shortly after the 1834 treaty the Chickasaw signed in Washington. One firm, the Chickasaw Land Company, was headed by Alabama Representative David Hubbard and John Tindall, the president of the State Bank of Alabama's Tuscaloosa branch. Hubbard quickly realized that their modest capitalization was a hindrance and set out to secure additional financing. He wrote to Joseph D. Beers, the same broker who had sold Woodbury bonds from Alabama and Michigan, boasting that he and his associates had staked claims to "the most valuable cotton lands in the U.S.," which he estimated would sell for ten to twenty dollars per acre. Convinced by Hubbard's pitch, Beers formed the New York and Mississippi Land Company, an outfit dedicated to financing speculation in the Chickasaw cession. Another founder was John Delafield, president of the Phenix Bank of New York, which would soon serve as the Office of Indian Affairs' primary deposit bank.[60]

The Decatur branch of the State Bank opened shortly after Gaines's successful bond sale in New York City. Located on the southern bank of the Tennessee River, the Decatur bank was easily accessible from Pontotoc by following Chickasaw roads to the recently completed Tuscumbia, Courtland, and Decatur Railroad. In a testament to its importance as a physical conduit for capital in the Chickasaw cession, the railroad counted both the Decatur branch and shareholders in the New York and Mississippi Land Company among its investors. While land companies preparing to speculate in the Chickasaw region drew on northern capital, they needed local intermediaries like the State Bank's Decatur branch to conduct their business in the South. In April 1835, for example, Chickasaw Land Company agent Robert Bolton borrowed $150,000 from the Decatur bank. With competitors rushing to the scene, the capacity to convert large sums of capital into cash at hand proved essential to capturing as much of the Chickasaw cession as possible. Alabama's banks helped the New York and Mississippi Land Company acquire nearly thirty-one thousand acres of the Chickasaw cession, and they were far from unique in their success. One estimate found that at least 80 percent of Chickasaw lands were purchased as an investment rather than for settlement.[61]

Woodbury bought Alabama bank bonds on the Chickasaws' behalf at a moment when liquidity gained heightened importance. Only a few short months after Woodbury bought Alabama bonds, Jackson ordered him to issue the Specie Circular, an executive order that stipulated receivers at federal land offices could accept only hard money, rather than banknotes or other paper, for payments on land. Jackson's order intended to dampen rampant land speculation but managed only to constrict the frontier South's monetary supply. Settlers and speculators scrambled for specie to buy new lands and cover payments due. Specie was already scarce in the region; at the time, the entire United States contained a mere $70 million in specie, much of it concentrated in New York City and other Atlantic ports, where it could be used to balance international accounts. Within Alabama, specie pooled in the commercial hub of Mobile, where the state's strongest private bank, the Bank of Mobile, served cotton factors and a mercantile clientele.[62] The Specie Circular only worsened this drought of

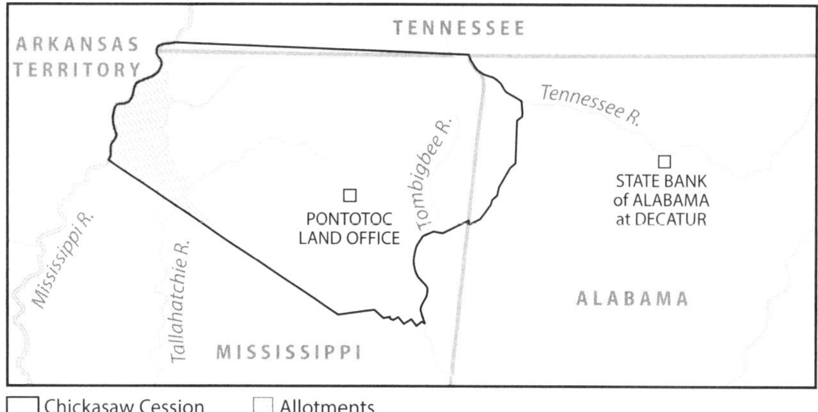


Chickasaw land cession, 1834. The Federal Land Office sat at Pontotoc, once the capital of the Chickasaw Nation. The Decatur branch of the State Bank of Alabama, founded to provide "land office money," was one of Pontotoc's closest banks. *Source:* Map created by Shane Kelley.

liquidity at a time when speculators were more desperate to purchase land than ever.

Some state-chartered banks engaged in fraud to circumvent the Specie Circular. Pontotoc's Agricultural Bank of Mississippi, for instance, issued certificates claiming specie had been deposited when only banknotes or bills of exchange had been accepted. Other banks, including the State Bank of Alabama, simply leveraged relationships they had forged to federal officials via trust investments. By coincidence, when the Specie Circular came into force, the Pontotoc Land Office, which collected funds for the Chickasaw trust, had yet to actually hand over payment for the state bonds Woodbury had purchased on the Chickasaws' behalf. Two weeks after Jackson issued the order, James Durno, the cashier of the State Bank's Decatur branch, wrote to Woodbury to ask if the land office might be allowed to accept payment for Chickasaw lands in notes of the Decatur bank instead of the specie Jackson's circular demanded. Every dollar in Decatur notes that the land office received would cancel out a dollar owed in specie by the Chickasaw trust fund to the Decatur bank. Woodbury agreed, creating a paper loophole in an otherwise ironclad policy.[63]

More than a mere collusion between bankers and bureaucrats, Durno and Woodbury's arrangement took to a clarifying extreme a dynamic operative throughout the financial infrastructure that sustained colonization: State banks paid out money in order to allow settlers or land company agents to purchase land, but it was federal officials who ensured that this money held value by choosing whether or not to accept it as payment. Notably, Woodbury invested trust funds at precisely the moment—after the Specie Circular—when monetary constraints might have choked the market in ceded Indian territories. Instead, a collaboration between the State Bank of Alabama and the Office of Indian Affairs made possible by trust investments kept the land market liquid enough for speculators to continue their frenetic acquisitions.

With their political class of entrepreneurial planters, broad experience in trade, and keen awareness of the market value of their lands, the Chickasaws had fully anticipated a rapacious land sales process that would devolve into fraud and exploitation. Levi Colbert and other Chickasaw leaders had tried to erect guardrails to keep land sales from veering toward corruption. In 1832 they formed a land commission of seven Chickasaws—Isaac Alberson, brothers George and Levi Colbert, Levi's son Martin Colbert, the *minko* Ishtehotopa, Benjamin Love, and Henry Love—to oversee the process of selling the allotments. Commissioners would first decide whether a given Chickasaw allottee could handle a sale on their own. If not, commissioners branded the individual "incompetent," a vague and subjective term that connoted an inability to consent due to immaturity, old age, disability, drunkenness, or lack of education. So-called incompetents would need to secure approval of the land commission before selling, and the proceeds would be kept in the Indian agent's hands for safekeeping rather than handed over to the allottee. Similar provisions extended to allotments set aside for Chickasaw orphans. Conceived as a protective check on the market, the land commission would emerge from the tumult of dispossession as a governing body charged with Chickasaw finances, gradually displacing a dual system of an inherited, clan-derived council headed by the *minko* and elected leaders at town and district levels.[64]

Despite their precautions, the Chickasaws suffered from precisely the exploitation they had anticipated. Speculators offered enticements to public officials, and the Chickasaws' Indian agent, Benjamin Reynolds, was easily swayed. When allotted lands went up for sale in March 1836, Reynolds, charged with overseeing the process, protected the claims of companies in which he had a financial interest against competing offers that often doubled, tripled, or quadrupled the price. In the words of one observer, Reynolds refused to acknowledge any but the original preemptive agreements. If a Chickasaw allotment holder tried to accept higher bids at the auction block, Reynolds would deny the claim and order them "to 'sweat awhile.'" Ultimately, the Chickasaw allottee "would at length be brought to sell" at the depressed price.[65] Levi Colbert's own grandson, Robinson James, petitioned Andrew Jackson to protest a speculator's usurping of his own prime lands. "I am unaccustomed to the Laws & customs of the *whiteman*," James admitted, "but, having some of the benefits of education, I have some advantage over *many* of my country men." Yet this advantage had failed to safeguard James against fraud, and he demanded redress since his land was "of great value + would have made me rich."[66]

Even though Chickasaw allotments were being auctioned off to the best-connected bidder, the nation had yet to locate a new home west of the Mississippi. Only in January 1837 did a Chickasaw delegation finally broker an agreement to purchase their new territory from the Choctaw Nation. The Choctaws permitted the smaller Chickasaw Nation—which had a population roughly one-third the size of the Choctaws'—to create a fourth district within their territory. This land, however, would be located in the westernmost section of Choctaw territory, which the Chickasaws described as "sterile" and which was exposed to raiding from multiple groups: Caddos, who defended their homelands; refugee Cherokees, Kickapoos, Lenapes, and Shawnees, who raided north from their adopted home in the Red River Valley; and Comanches and their Wichita allies, who raided east from their vast empire across the Southern Plains. For these contested lands the Chickasaws would pay $30,000 in specie and $500,000 in bonds to the Choctaw Nation. The arrangement moreover subjected the Chickasaws to the laws and the overriding governance of the Choctaw National Council, carrying discomfiting parallels to Alabama and Mississippi's extension of state jurisdiction over their homelands years before. But even as they agreed to a partial integration with the Choctaws, Chickasaw negotiators carefully protected their nation's fiscal resources. As the 1837 compact stated, the Chickasaws reserved the "sole right and privilege of controlling and managing the residue of their funds."[67]

With their new territory secured, the Chickasaws now faced the long-dreaded journey west. Chickasaws were wary of the federal government's reliance on companies specializing in removals—many formed by land speculators—to provide transport and provisioning, an arrangement they knew would encourage fraud and degrade the quality of rations. Removal contractors' determination to widen profit margins had resulted in especially deadly forced migrations: the Alabama Emigrating Company's 1834 coordination of a Creek removal carried a 22 percent fatality rate. Aware of the Creek Nation's experience, Chickasaw leaders warned that contractors, "whose object it must generally be to make their contract profitable," would "stint the allowance and comforts of those under their charge."[68] Chickasaw protests went unheeded. Removal agents hired private contractors who were, according to the terms of the Chickasaw treaty, paid out directly from the nation's trust fund.

Chickasaw removal began in early July 1837, with the first emigrating parties moving at a crawl through Arkansas' swamps and bogs. Some were stricken with smallpox, and horse thieves and liquor vendors stalked the migrants, causing diversions and delays that drove up the cost of the operation. By the end of July, the summer heat threatened to spoil rations housed in depots across Arkansas. Commissioner of Indian Affairs Carey A. Harris made a halfhearted effort to cut Chickasaw losses, urging removal officers to sell off or swap out supplies of pork and corn on the cusp of rot.[69] Because of their self-financing removal, all waste, spoilage, and corruption would be paid by the Chickasaws themselves.

Chickasaw groups left in waves for more than a decade, with most traveling west between 1837 and 1839. Some better-off Chickasaws successfully navigated the land sales process, sold their lands for $5 to $10 per acre, and accumulated sizable fortunes. A number of Chickasaw planters sold allotted lands to investors who offered a combination of cash and slaves as payment. Enslaved migrants bore the brunt of deprivation during the Chickasaw trek west, and many perished before reaching the Choctaw district. Yet while select Chickasaws could deflect the burdens of dislocation onto their human property, most ordinary Chickasaws experienced removal as a crisis compounded by a lack of liquidity. As another Indian agent reported in the fall of 1837, the Chickasaws were arriving in Indian Territory "quite destitute."[70]

This was because Chickasaws were wealthy on paper, but cash poor. At the outset of their removal negotiations, Levi Colbert had pushed for a prohibition on federal investments of more than three-fourths of the Chickasaw land proceeds at one time. Yet as land sales boomed in the lead-up to removal, Woodbury had invested every last dollar collected by the Pontotoc receiver. A month before removal had even officially begun, Commissioner Harris realized that the Chickasaw national fund would not cover their costs of emigration, given that "the whole has been invested in stocks."[71] Woodbury assumed, as did many of his contemporaries, that land sales would continue at the same rate and would supply sufficient income to cover removal costs. He was wrong.

In March 1837, cotton brokerage firms in New York City went under one by one, dragged down by failing merchant houses in New Orleans. Pressure on cotton merchants had mounted after the Bank of England raised the discount rate on loans to American debtors, a factor compounded by Jackson's Specie Circular and the redistribution of the federal surplus to its multiplying constellation of depositories. Soon a commercial panic radiated to each corner of the transatlantic Cotton Kingdom. Prices for land, slaves, goods, and stocks plummeted. By the summer, the United States found itself in its first great depression. Once spirited, sales in the Chickasaw cession withered, falling from over 1.3 million acres in 1836 to less than 200,000 acres in 1837. Declining demand pulled down prices. While most elite Chickasaws had sold their coveted tracts early on, tracts that remained unsold slumped from an average price of around $1.70 per acre in 1837 to $0.69 in 1838.[72]

The Panic of 1837 arrived at a peak of removal activity, as multiple nations were winding their way west. Monetary scarcity caused by the panic heightened their suffering. Banks closest to removal routes across Tennessee and Mississippi suspended the conversion of their notes into specie, leaving military disbursement officers unable to procure rations. The panic also impacted the distribution of annuities at a time when nations needed them most. Transmitting annuities in money, especially specie, had always posed a challenge to the Office of Indian Affairs, even during periods of economic health. In 1833 one agent charged with distributing over $28,000 in specie to Northwestern nations complained that "the distance is great—the roads bad—and a part of it a wilderness country." Hauling boxes of coins through such conditions necessitated the employment of a guard and two teams of oxen. Along the route the Chickasaw were compelled to travel, fiscal networks were especially sparse: the nearest major node of Treasury draft and remittance was New Orleans. No federal deposit bank existed beyond Arkansas Territory, near the end of the Chickasaw's route to Indian Territory. By June, Indian agents reported to Harris that since federal depositaries across the West had received orders to ship specie surpluses to Washington and sales had plummeted at federal land offices where specie usually collected, it would be impossible to furnish that season's annuities.[73]

Because the vast majority of their wealth had been invested in state bonds against their wishes, the Chickasaws were ruined by the Panic of 1837. The nation's nearly $1.5 million in state bonds sank in value, mirroring the deflating prices of cotton, slaves, and land. This meant the Chickasaws' investments could only be liquidated at a deep discount, as the nation learned when they pled for cash to purchase direly needed provisions. In June 1837, Harris urged that President Martin Van Buren instead offer to the Chickasaw an "advance on a pledge of their Stocks." The following month, Van Buren approved a Treasury loan of $100,000 to the Chickasaw Nation, collateralized by their trust fund.[74] Because their federal fiduciary had chosen to sink so much of their wealth in investments without anticipating a collapse in the market, the Chickasaws became both creditors to several states and debtors to the federal government.

Worse, Chickasaws still lacked access to cash, leaving many poorer families unable to clear land and begin cultivating food for their own subsistence. In a petition sent to Van Buren in 1838, Isaac Alberson, James Colbert, Stone Love, and other Chickasaw headmen pled for provisions, explaining that "since our emigration we have suffered severely, by sickness many of our people have died," and that those who survived were suffering from hunger. They asked for a loan to cover their urgent needs, adding that "our situation so obviously requires further subsistence that we deem it unnecessary to say more."[75] That the removed nation richest in capital now ranked among the most impoverished did not strike federal officials as a sign of their own failures as trustees. Indian agent William Armstrong instead doubled down on a precept increasingly core to the administration of fiduciary colonialism: the notion that placing cash in Native hands, even when that cash belonged to them, only impeded orderly economy and drained the federal purse. "A large portion of the Chickasaws are disposed to be idle," Armstrong reported, "and if gratified in their wishes, would expose every dollar they had." Given the large sums of interest that would accrue on their securities held in trust, Armstrong recommended "to keep invested as much as possible," since "it is a waste of money to pay such large sums to Indians."[76]

⁂

Money had made Indian removal possible and worthwhile for the United States. A composite financial infrastructure that involved both federal and state institutions made settler property of Native homelands. The federal government's superior stores of specie and national banknotes flowed out as annuities, military spending, and remuneration for contractors, accomplishing the process of taking, surveying, and commodifying Native land—by force if necessary. State governments worked in the federal government's wake, borrowing to erect banks that provided the credit and means of payment needed to make a market for these lands.

Trust investments threaded these two processes together: Federal officials swayed by agents of upstart states invested Native wealth in state financial institutions. Within this perverse circuit, men acting as trustees habitually privileged borrowers over the prosperity of the peoples whose wealth they oversaw. Endowed with the largest trust fund, the Chickasaws were nonetheless investors without control over their portfolios.

The Chickasaws waited for years after their arrival in Indian Territory to receive their annuities. Sales of their cession flattened during the economic depression that set in after the Panic of 1837, and the federal government garnished any earnings as repayment for its emergency loan to the nation. Chickasaws did not acquiesce to the immiseration that removal caused and that they had so carefully tried to avoid. By the spring of 1840, Chickasaw leaders began petitioning the Office of Indian Affairs for "a statistical account of our sales, expenses, balances, stocks, &c."[77] It would be a struggle to gain access to information about their investments and to challenge the federal government's control on the basis of what they learned. But it was a struggle that the Chickasaw were willing to wage—and one that would only become more critical in the years to come.

# CHAPTER FOUR

# Money Flows

IN THE FALL OF 1845, a group of Odawa, Ojibwe, and Potawatomis traveled east toward Washington. The trip would culminate, they feared, in yet another treaty of dispossession. More than a decade earlier, their people had been forced to abandon their homelands on the western shores of Lake Michigan and undertake a torturous migration, first to a reservation in the Platte River region of present-day northwestern Missouri and then—after the government abruptly reversed its grant of these lands—to their current home near Council Bluffs, Iowa Territory. Floating south on the Missouri River years later, the delegates retraced this painful journey, passing by the Platte Country with its fields in full harvest. The group reached St. Louis by the end of September, boarded another steamer at the forks of the Ohio River, and wound their way toward the Allegheny Mountains, arriving in Harrisburg, Pennsylvania within two weeks. There they embarked on Pennsylvania's answer to the Erie Canal. The Portage Railroad was a futuristic water-to-railroad system that placed modestly sized canal boats on flatbed railroad cars to carry them over a thirty-six-mile stretch of the Alleghenies. The railroad employed a system of ropes, horses, and stationary steam engines to drag the vessels up a series of inclines and then ease them down the other side. Altogether the Portage drew the amphibious vehicles over 2,007 vertical feet of mountainous terrain.[1]

Feats of engineering like the Portage Railroad inspired the awe of local residents and travelers alike, epitomizing the sublime character of many nineteenth-century "internal improvements." Less visible were the currents of investment that allowed settlers to cross mountain ranges, cut through canals, and overcome the obstructions that inhibited interregional commerce. Marvels of the improvement era owed their existence to significant sums of debt taken on by states and marketed to creditors in London, New

The Allegheny Portage Railroad, financed in part by the United Nations of Odawa, Ojibwe, and Potawatomi's trust fund. *Source: Annual Report of the Secretary of Internal Affairs of the Commonwealth of Pennsylvania, 1899* (Wm. Stanley Ray, 1900), lxxxvi.

York, and Philadelphia, as well as Washington, where the Office of Indian Affairs bought up bonds for the Indian trust funds. Although they had no way of knowing it, the Odawa, Ojibwe, and Potawatomis were among this class of investors. Only three years prior, the commissioner of Indian affairs had invested $39,000 of their trust fund in Pennsylvania state bonds issued to finance, among dozens of projects, the Portage Railroad.[2]

After cresting the Alleghenies, the representatives of the United Nations of Odawa, Ojibwe, and Potawatomi, as they were known in treaties, boarded a southbound train on the Baltimore and Susquehanna Railroad, another beneficiary of their trust investments to the tune of $130,000. This railroad brought them to the Chesapeake Bay, and in late October the delegation finally arrived in Washington. President James K. Polk greeted them warmly and promptly referred them to two appointed treaty commissioners. After the usual preliminaries the commissioners proceeded to pressure the Odawa, Ojibwe, and Potawatomis to relinquish their current territory yet again and march south to a reservation awaiting them on the Osage River, in present-day Kansas. Were they to agree, it would be the third time since 1833 that the nations would be compelled to cede their entire territory and relocate to lands they had no desire to inhabit. To accomplish these repeated forced migrations the federal government had relied less on arms than on a tactic of financial warfare, one that deployed the same trust funds that had carved the canals and laid the rails that carried the delegates east. By denying annuities owed to the nations by treaty, federal officials had starved their economies and enforced a condition of temporariness that left them vulnerable to repeated displacement. Abtegizhek confronted Polk with this injustice, reminding him that "the government had owed them for twelve years," in the paraphrase of one observer. From the day the Odawa, Ojibwe, and Potawatomis had left their homelands "they had not been paid," Abtegizhek reiterated, leaving no room for ambiguity.[3]

Federal officials ostensibly created trust funds to benefit Native recipients. But in the case of the United Nations, the financialization of their wealth compounded the ordeal of removal. Commissioners made trusteeship into a mechanism of enforcement, withholding annuities in order to compel the United Nations to relocate to territory outside the margin of settler advance. Using the contingency of annuities as leverage worked particularly well to manipulate Native nations in the Northwest, where Indigenous political formations were decentralized and many nations were removed more than once. What the United Nations endured exemplified a principle that had animated fiduciary colonialism from its outset: Deferring full payment meant delivery of future installments could be contingent on Native compliance. Fiduciary leverage took on new significance, however, as federal officials undertook massive forced migrations across the 1830s. By spreading compensation across time, officials gained an upper hand in controlling Native peoples' movement across space.

In the Southeast, nations like the Chickasaws faced a removal process accelerated by the Southern banks in which their funds were invested. Native nations in the Northwest (a region that would become known as "the Midwest" as colonialism progressed) faced a more uneven pattern of dispossession, driven by state plans for large-scale transportation routes that would attract settlement, encourage commerce, and cement states' claims to Native land. Some nations inhabited key transportation corridors and were thus targeted for early and aggressive removal. Others were able to remain, into the present, on territories considered marginal to an emergent agrarian capitalism.[4] Much like their Southern counterparts, state governments in the Northwest relied on federal officials to extinguish Indian title to land before they could realize their often wild ambitions for a transportation revolution. Money flowing out of trust funds assigned to the United Nations and to a dozen other nations fed this revolution, and

Native wealth became capital for the very state-financed infrastructural boom that propelled their dispossession.

{⚜}

For centuries before the United States' intrusions, the Lower Great Lakes region hosted a bustling network of Indigenous travel and transportation carried across water. The Great Lakes spanned nearly one hundred thousand square miles, a vast interior sea that connected sites spread across the continent. The Saint Lawrence River drained the Great Lakes' waters past Montreal and into the Atlantic Ocean; travelers could by tributaries, portages, and trails reach the Mississippi and Ohio Rivers that in turn flowed south toward the Gulf of Mexico. Altogether these fluid corridors and their land bridges connected diverse peoples, from the Dakotas and Ojibwes, rooted northwest of frigid Lake Superior, to the Ho-Chunks, Kickapoos, Menominees, Odawas, and Potawatomis, who clustered around Lake Michigan's northern forests, swampy lower basin, and adjacent prairies, to the Haudenosaunees, Mississaugas, and Wyandots, who tended to the fertile lands and smaller lakes surrounding Lakes Erie and Ontario, and finally to the Innus and Wabanakis, who inhabited the rocky bluffs and tundra abutting the St. Lawrence River.[5]

Controlling the heart of this varied region were the Anishinaabeg, a group composed of three closely interrelated peoples: the Odawas, Ojibwes, and Potawatomis. Long before the arrival of Europeans the Anishinaabeg undertook a storied westward migration and converged on Michilimackinac, a site overseeing the straits between Lakes Michigan and Huron. Remaining tied to Michilimackinac, the Odawas became renowned for trade as they presided over the rise of a canoe-borne commerce in fur pelts. Their Anishinaabe kin took on different roles defined by a continued movement to new territories. Ojibwes migrated northwest toward Lake Superior, carrying sacred birchbark scrolls inscribed with the teachings of Midewiwin, an Anishinaabe religion, which anointed them as keepers of this faith. The Potawatomis, for their part, migrated south along Lake Michigan, keeping lit the council fires that anchored the alliance among all three Anishinaabe peoples. As the Anishinaabeg dispersed along their homelands' intricate waterways, fire represented a regular pattern of regrouping, alliance, and lawmaking. Over time some villages from each of the three nations formed the tightly knit unit known as the United Nations of Odawa, Ojibwe, and Potawatomi. In a reference to the councils that cohered their polity, the Anishinaabeg were also known (and are still known today) as the People of the Three Fires.[6]

Harsh winters and limited growing seasons across their homelands, or Anishinaabewaki, necessitated a yearly circuit of site-specific labor. In response to the severity of the climate, communities engaged in a seasonal rotation that began at summer villages nested among rice swamps or corn fields, bifurcated into hunting parties of men and winter camps of women and children, and converged on sugar bushes and trade posts in the spring. The pathways and labor of seasonal rounds were tailored to variations in resources and climate. Across the Lower Great Lakes, the Anishinaabeg and their neighbors, especially the Wyandots, produced enough corn to trade with kin in other regions or to keep enormous stores that could sustain villages through years of famine. Farther north, Ojibwe women cultivated wild rice.[7]

Anishinaabe mobility relied on two interlocking infrastructures: kinship and carrying places. Council fires hosted a process of collective governance carried out by the patrilineal clans, or *doodemag*, that composed Anishinaabe society. Defined by reciprocal obligations and spread across geographic communities through exogamous marriage, *doodemag* radiated out from council fires, stretching across Anishinaabe homelands and guiding the incorporation of outsiders at its margins. *Doodem* affiliation acted as insurance and passport, with Anishinaabe voyagers receiving shelter, protection, and nourishment from kin of the same *doodem* when away from their home. In a world of predominantly waterborne travel, power could be best wielded at bottlenecks: places of narrow passage within or across bodies of water. For this reason council fires were frequently situated at portages, or "carrying places," where banks connected adjacent bodies of water. Marked by trees shorn of their lower boughs, portages tethered kinship relationships to sites of lawmaking and economic power, as *doodemag* collected rents from the travelers who lifted their watercrafts and hauled their cargo between bodies of water.[8]

Control over the region's waterlogged transportation network gave Native people in the region an upper hand. In the summer of 1812, a multinational Indigenous alliance assembled by Shawnee military leader Tecumseh and Potawatomi leader Main Poc seized the opportunity created by the outbreak of an Anglo-American war to decimate the United States' forts along the Mississippi, Ohio, and Wabash Rivers. With their nimble birchbark canoes Native military forces could easily navigate the war zone's shallow waters. When combat ended and the muck settled, military officials realized that inadequate logistics had forced their retreat from a region that the United States putatively governed. In the wake of these defeats, Congress considered a concerted, federally funded transportation improvement plan. In an apt turn of phrase, proponent John C. Calhoun, then senator of South Carolina, dared Congress to "let us conquer space."[9]

Debates over the constitutionality of federal infrastructure financing scuttled the bill, but the Department of War nonetheless targeted an array of Native transportation corridors for seizure. Among them was a carrying place controlled by the Odawa, Ojibwe, and Potawatomis on the southwestern shore of Lake Michigan, a marshy seven-mile strip that connected the Chicago and Des Plaines Rivers. Federal officials eyed the corridor as a potential route for a canal that could shuttle materiel and information between Eastern command centers and Detroit. In 1816, federal negotiators persuaded the United Nations to cede the portage. Twenty years later, construction began on the Illinois and Michigan Canal, a project that helped launch Chicago on its trajectory from Northwestern outpost to Midwestern entrepôt.[10]

The United States' acquisition of the Chicago portage initiated a pattern of dispossession that would turn carrying places across Anishinaabe homelands into canals, a form of infrastructure designed for a specific form of agricultural development and commercial transportation. In the early nineteenth century the Appalachian Mountains posed a formidable barrier to commerce: the range hemmed in the Eastern Seaboard from Maine to Alabama, dividing Northwestern prairie from Eastern port. The large volume of corn, wheat, and other grains sales made overland shipment impractical and often impossible given the terrain. With steam travel still a prohibitive expense, most farmers and country merchants selling surpluses built rudimentary flatboats and floated their modest supplies of pork, corn, whiskey, or flour down the Mississippi River to New Orleans. The Mississippi trade brought challenges, exposing perishable cargoes to the vicissitudes of climate and seasonal gluts. Return trips often required an aching march over the Natchez Trace, a Chickasaw and Choctaw road that connected the Cumberland and Ohio Rivers. It was a slog, and an expensive one at that: grain-vending settlers spent up to three-quarters of their earnings on the cost of transportation. After the Panic of 1819 lowered freight rates, a multiplying fleet of steamships made reverse trips up the Mississippi possible and the overall experience far easier—though no less dependent on access to waterways. As a result, newcomers concentrated in the Illinois, Ohio, and Wabash River Valleys. To push settlement inland and upward, toward the northern reaches of Illinois and Indiana, both fledgling states planned ambitious canals that would connect these rivers to the Great Lakes.[11]

Canals became even more alluring after 1825. That year, New York State successfully completed the Erie Canal, a product of a half century of Native dispossession and roughly $7 million in state bonds. Carving west from the Hudson River through Haudenosaunee territory, the canal poured out into Lake Erie at Buffalo, a settler town that encroached on the Senecas' largest reservation. An evolving cast of politician-entrepreneurs had laid the groundwork for the canal for decades, many with ties to speculation in Seneca lands. The Ogden Land Company, which had purchased preemptive title to Seneca reservations created by the 1797 Treaty of Big Tree, used the prospect of a canal as a pretext to push both New York and the federal government for new land cession treaties. The Holland Land Company and other speculators formed a venture to build the canal, but failed to raise sufficient capital. After the federal government declined to lend its support, New York set about financing the canal itself, through repeated issuances of bonds. It was a gamble worth taking. Even before its completion, the Erie Canal brought in revenue for the state, and officials boasted of their capacity to service its large debts with toll receipts. The canal dropped toll rates from Buffalo to New York City from $100 to $9 per ton, ensuring that the city's port would dominate Atlantic-facing trade while demonstrating canals' suitability for shipments of voluminous, low-yielding goods like wheat, flour, and corn.[12]

New York State's success in financing the Erie Canal inspired an array of less developed Northwestern states. Ohio began a debt-financed system of improvements, stirring Illinois and Indiana lawmakers to draft plans for their own artificial rivers. Boosters in the two states promised that their canals—the Illinois and Michigan and the Wabash and Erie, respectively—would draw in settlers, encourage export-directed grain farming, appreciate land values, and ultimately repay state coffers with increased property taxes. But to realize this vision, states depended on the federal government, the only authority that could force out the Native peoples that stood in their way.

{⚬⚬⚬⚬⚬}

War aligned federal and state priorities to clear the Northwest of its Native possessors and make way for a transportation revolution. In April 1832, a group of Sauk and Meskwakis followed Sauk war leader Black Hawk to their summer village on their homelands in Illinois, in defiance of federal efforts to permanently remove them to Indian Territory. State militias attacked a party of Sauk envoys, and four months of brutal fighting ensued, with neighboring Dakota, Ho-Chunk, and Menominee bands drawn into the fray. The Black Hawk War clouded the Great Lakes region's isolated settlers in a fog of paranoia and amplified calls for denser settlements to achieve safety in numbers. Although the Odawa, Ojibwe, and Potawatomis had remained neutral, Michigan territorial governor George Porter complained that their presence still deterred settlers, depressing the value of public lands recently acquired from the Sauk and Meskwakis. In July 1832 Congress approved a $20,000 expenditure to extinguish Indian title to lands coveted by Illinois, Indiana, and Wisconsin.[13]

The following spring, Secretary of War Lewis Cass set treaty preparations into motion, appointing as commissioners Indian agent Thomas V. Owen, Michigan's George Porter, and Colonel William B. Weatherford. The council opened at Chicago on September 12, 1833, with thousands of Odawa, Ojibwe, and Potawatomis in attendance. Chicago, a remote federal outpost populated by little more than a hundred non-Native settlers, swelled into a bustling metropolis of over six thousand people. Encampments spread across prairie, forests, and sandy hills for a five-mile radius from the city.[14]

Owen and Porter opened the council by demanding a cession of all remaining homelands and promising to relocate the United Nations on land equivalent in quantity and quality beyond the Mississippi. Following a prolonged discussion among the United Nations, Potawatomi speaker Abtegizhek delivered an outright refusal, explaining that they feared "some great evil might happen to us" if severed from their homelands. After the commissioners expressed their displeasure, the council broke to give time for the Odawa, Ojibwe, and Potawatomis to deliberate.[15]

Anishinaabe governance consisted of an assiduous deliberative process carried out at an intimate scale, with consensus transmitted by outward-facing representatives. Historically, diplomacy had been conducted by hereditary leaders, or *ogimaag*, who were authorized only to voice positions crafted within *doodemag* and village councils. In the decade preceding the treaty the United Nations had begun to make use of a different kind of leadership in their negotiations with the United States. As pressure to cede lands grew, Anishinaabe groups living in the Lower Great Lakes began appointing nonhereditary leaders whose merits rested on their pragmatism and intercultural fluency. Most prominent among these ascendant leaders was Billy Caldwell, the Catholic-educated son of a British Army captain and a Mohawk woman. After serving with the British during the War of 1812, Caldwell had relocated from Upper Canada to the Wabash River Valley with mercantile aspirations. He began his career clerking for influential Illinois fur traders Thomas Forsyth and John Kinzie. After marrying the daughter of a prominent Potawatomi leader, Caldwell became a particularly effective mediator for his chosen people, ably negotiating with local traders and government agents alike. After earning their respect, Caldwell had committed to representing the United Nations for the rest of his life.[16]

When negotiations dragged into late September, the commissioners grew frustrated. John T. Schermerhorn, one of three removal commissioners appointed by President Andrew Jackson, arrived at the council determined to hasten the process by any means necessary. Schermerhorn would go on to sign some of the most contested agreements of the era, including the 1835 Treaty of New Echota, signed by an unauthorized faction of Cherokees, which consigned the Cherokee Nation to removal. With Schermerhorn in the wings, Porter began to threaten the United Nations, declaring that Jackson was "the greatest War chief that any of you have ever seen," and that he would take up arms against his "red children" if they "refused to hearken to the words of his council."[17] Porter's threats conjured a specter of war that had yet to dissipate from the region, and the United Nations knew to fear settler vengeance, however unjustified it might be. The treaty was signed two days later.

The 1833 Treaty of Chicago extinguished the United Nations' claims to their remaining homelands. The nations ceded five million acres, a tract spanning present-day northern Illinois and southern Wisconsin, with additional reservations in Michigan. In exchange the nations received $100,000 in goods and presents, yearly annuities amounting to $14,000 for twenty years, the repayment of numerous large debts to regional traders, a $150,000 fund to finance agricultural improvement, and a $70,000 fund designated for the purpose of founding a school. While the agriculture fund was not designated for investment, the education fund was. Conspicuously, the treaty noted it was "the wish of the Indians" for the education funds to be invested "in some safe stock" by the president, with the interest only applied toward education.[18]

It was not the first time that the Odawa, Ojibwe, and Potawatomis had earmarked portions of treaty compensation to the support of farming and schools. A treaty signed in 1821 had provided $1,500 annually for Odawa villages to receive agricultural instruction, livestock, and farming implements and $1,000 for Potawatomi villages to receive a blacksmith and teacher. Isaac McCoy, the Baptist missionary who had promoted the idea of financing civilization policy through land cessions and funds held in trust, took credit for these provisions, calling the funds an "accomplishment" for which he "had felt much solicitude and put up many prayers."[19] While McCoy did not attend the Chicago council in 1833, the treaty signed

there certainly conformed to his recommendations (short of financing the
agriculture and education funds by the proceeds of ceded lands, as in the
Chickasaws' removal treaty). Missionary influence aside, the treaty's language suggested that the United Nations pursued their own aims.

Like most nations facing the prospect of removal, the United Nations
negotiated a cession of homelands amid settler encroachments, resource
depletion, and the menacing threat of genocide. Treaties offered a means
to salvage some wealth from the wreckage. By the 1830s peoples across
Anishinaabe homelands had already learned that some forms of compensation proved longer lasting than others. Starting in the late 1810s, federal officials had paid out annuities to the Anishinaabeg and their neighbors in specie. As in the far South, cash of any kind was scarce on the
encroaching northwestern edge of the United States' continental empire,
let alone hard money that could serve as a relatively reliable store of value
and avoid the discounts of bank notes. In 1833 alone, Indian agents distributed $56,000 in specie at the Chicago treaty council, or more than
thirty-seven times their own annual salaries. Specie carried a premium
above all other currencies, but it could also bring challenges to its recipients. Once annuities arrived in precious metal, whisky peddlers and traders crowded in, offering their wares or demanding repayment of debts in
hard money. Cordoning off wealth into federally managed funds withheld
money from often predatory traders in favor of financing schools, mills,
and blacksmith shops, the rudiments of an economy adaptive to colonial
pressures.[20] Put otherwise, placing compensation in federal hands would
allow nations like the Odawa, Ojibwe, and Potawatomis to build infrastructure of their own.

After concluding the treaty at Chicago, Porter wrote to debrief the commissioner of Indian affairs on his success in securing a major land cession.
He closed his report by confiding that he anticipated "confidently a favorable result to my intended effort with the Miamis."[21] Porter referred to his
next assignment: extinguishing Indian title to a cluster of reservations that
abutted the southern shore of the Wabash River. These were the remaining homelands of the Miamis, a nation that held close ties to Potawatomi
villages north of the river and that had signed several of the same treaties
with the federal government as the United Nations, including the 1795
Treaty of Greenville. Porter's optimism would prove misguided. Reporting on his progress nearly a month later, he admitted that the Miamis, led

by their powerful head *akima* Pinšiwa, or Jean Richardville, had rebuffed him without hesitation. Since the lands sat at the "intersection by the line of the canal, now in progress," the Miamis "had derived impressions of its importance better suited to its prospective than its present value."[22]

Miamis managed to stave off removal in 1833, but Indiana was undeterred. The state would spend the better part of the next decade raising money to cut the Wabash and Erie Canal through the Miamis' reservations. Indiana found one of its earliest investors in the United Nations of Odawa, Ojibwe, and Potawatomis. Through a set of transactions that involved federal officials in Washington, brokers in New York City, and canal fund commissioners in Indianapolis, the United Nations' education fund became capital for a canal that the Miamis recognized would raise the value of their lands but that would eventually force many of them to abandon their home.

Like Chicago's Illinois and Michigan Canal, Indiana's Wabash and Erie Canal carved through a portage—in this case, one that had belonged to Richardville's family for generations. Richardville's mother, Tahkamwah, and her kin in the Crane clan had for generations controlled the shortest land route between the Maumee and Wabash river systems, a central corridor in Myaamionki, as the Miamis referred to their own homeland. From the mid-eighteenth century onward the portage had served as a hub for communication between allies, and in the 1790s it became a logistical channel for the Northwest Confederacy's armed defense of its homelands. Tahkamwah governed trade and travel through the portage until the defeat of the confederacy in 1794 and the subsequent intrusion of the United States into the Wabash River Valley. After the establishment of Fort Wayne and land cessions north of the Ohio River under the 1795 Treaty of Greenville, settlers rushed into the region. But Tahkamwah and her son held on to their home at the crux of the rivers. When annuities granted the Miamis and other signatory nations began flowing through Fort Wayne, Richardville and Tahkamwah adapted their family business, exchanging federal annuity goods and specie with local traders.[23]

The coming of canals posed the greatest challenge yet to the Crane clan's possessions. In an 1826 treaty the Miamis granted the United States rights of way for a canal through their remaining reservations—a path eventually assumed by the Wabash and Erie. The following year, Indiana successfully petitioned the federal government for donations of public land that the state could liquidate to finance the canal. Yet hundreds of thousands of acres that the government promised to Indiana to support its

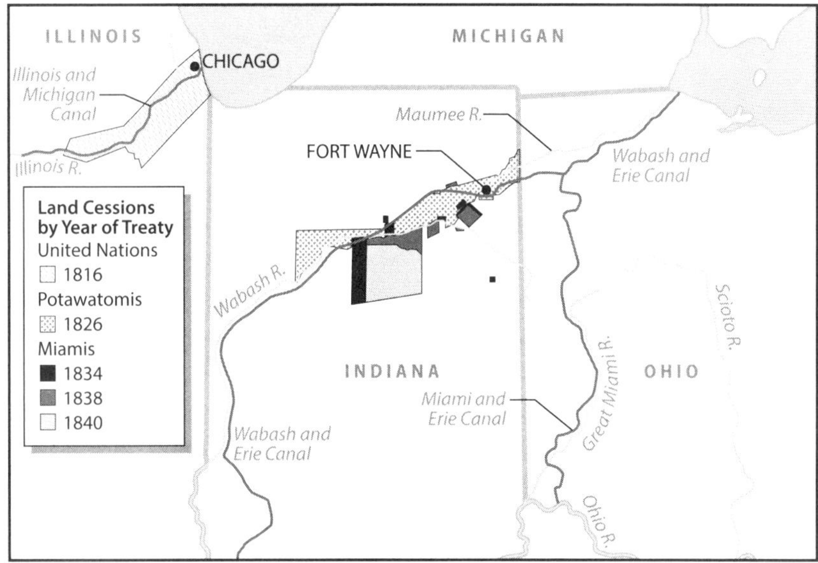


Canal-related land cessions, by nation and year of treaty. Treaties acquired land along existing Native transportation corridors, including portages at Chicago and between the Maumee and Wabash Rivers, in order to allow states to build canals. *Source:* Map created by Shane Kelley.

canal were, in fact, swaths of unceded Miami land, a fact that would come to haunt the state as the project's construction progressed.[24]

Although its canal land grants were rather encumbered, Indiana was lucky to have them. Once President Andrew Jackson entered office, he changed the course of federal support for state-led internal improvements. In May 1830, Jackson vetoed a proposed road running through Kentucky from Ohio's Cumberland Road to the Tennessee River. The Maysville Road veto scuttled the possibility of a nationally coordinated system of internal improvements that many had imagined as federally financed trunk lines and state-built branches. Jackson especially opposed federal aid for state-chartered public works in the form of donated public land. With no further grants forthcoming, Indiana, Illinois, Michigan, and Ohio all turned to New York's model of debt financing, borrowing heavily to convert an Indigenous transportation network into one that could ship grain eastward and encourage settler immigration. In a pattern that echoed state bank financing, by 1838 states across the country had borrowed almost $110 million for transportation improvements, amounting to two-thirds of states' overall debts at the time. Much of this debt concentrated in the capital-poor Northwest, where states legislatures expected to service their debts by drawing on a future tax base that would swell as canals began to flow. Indiana entered the fray in January 1832, with a $200,000 bond issuance assigned to finance the Wabash and Erie Canal.[25]

Bonds of American states were relatively new, as was Indiana, and the state's canal fund commissioners struggled entice investors. New York brokers snubbed Indiana's first bond issuance because of its low printing quality and vulnerability to counterfeiters. Canal fund commissioners were forced to hire printers in New York, haul the certificates back to Indiana for the treasurer to sign, and then double back to peddle the loan in New York City. Commissioners attempted to save face by extolling their state's freedom from slave labor and its "most fertile and productive" soil in letters to brokers, bankers, and newspaper editors. The state's yields, they promised, would only increase once roads and canals lowered shipping costs and encouraged cultivation for the market.[26]

In March 1835, Indiana canal fund commissioners received a timely letter from Elbert Herring, the commissioner of Indian affairs. That spring, the canal fund had barely covered monthly expenses, and Indiana had been forced to issue another $627,000 in bonds to cover the costs of construction. Herring announced his interest in purchasing bonds from their state for a trust fund belonging to the United Nations of Odawa, Ojibwe, and Potawatomi. The directors responded immediately, offering Wabash and Erie Canal bonds at a premium of 7 percent. They admitted this rate exceeded previous sales, but gestured to expectations of continued national prosperity as a justification. Herring agreed, making his office the third major purchaser of Wabash and Erie bonds, along with land speculator and bond broker Joseph Beers, and the prominent New York City merchant banking house of Prime, Ward, & King. A few months later, a canal boat loaded with revelers would slide through the canal's first completed segment, between Fort Wayne and Huntington. A short detour brought the maiden voyage down the St. Mary's River, where Jean Richardville might have seen the boat slip by from his riverfront estate. The celebration would have been ominous to the Miamis, but it was rather premature, given that only thirty-two of the canal's projected 468 miles had been excavated.[27]

Herring's purchase of Indiana's canal stock represented an early trickle of what would soon become an outpouring of investment from the Office of Indian Affairs. On July 4, 1836, Jackson appointed his close friend and fellow Tennessean Carey A. Harris to replace Herring as commissioner of Indian affairs. Harris took full advantage of the mercenary opportunities his office afforded him. Days after assuming his post, he maneuvered to gain control over the investment of the trust funds from his superior,

Secretary of War Benjamin Butler. By the end of the year, the Treasury had transferred all but the Chickasaw trust fund to the War Department, where Harris now oversaw over a dozen separate Indian trust funds.[28]

Endowed with broad discretion, Harris expanded the number of trusts and the proportion of funds under investment. He personally created several trust funds while serving as a treaty commissioner and also added several more without authorization, purchasing bonds with funds that were not stipulated for investment by any treaty. Within a year of entering office, he had bought nearly $1.5 million in bonds from seven states for the Indian trust funds. Opportunities for illicit gain likely motivated Harris; he would resign in disgrace in late 1838 when a clerk uncovered his speculations in Creek lands, acquired by the United States through a treaty Harris himself had overseen. But Harris also responded to mounting demand and political pressure from states in search of capital.[29]

As the credit crunch of late 1836 devolved into a general bank suspension in March 1837, states struggled to complete the ambitious improvement programs their legislatures had already borrowed heavily to finance. Amid a general collapse across a relatively consolidated transatlantic sovereign debt market, states could not secure private investment without selling bonds far below their face value. Yet they needed to borrow more than ever to cover the costs of projects already underway, and to service debts already contracted.[30] Desperate, state officials started to lean on personal connections to federal officials in the Office of Indian Affairs. Where once the commissioner of Indian affairs had sent out circulars inquiring about bonds available for purchase, now the solicitations rushed in the opposite direction, as states clamored for trust investment.

As Harris conferred with bankers and brokers to select bonds for the trust funds, he regularly referred to their "market value." The term was somewhat misleading. With newspapers yet to regularly publish data on the state bond market, officials could not easily measure bonds' worth. Makeshift valuations served in place of centrally listed prices ostensibly equilibrated by supply and demand. Brokers, canal commissioners, and bank cashiers enclosed corporate charters, state statutes, bond prospectuses, professions of confidence from prominent politicians, or letters from third parties praising a given bond's merit for Harris's consideration. When Congress later asked the Office of Indian Affairs to prepare a statement of the Indian trust funds that included bonds' current value, a clerk left the column blank save for an annotation: "There are no means within the dep't by which the present value of the stock can be ascertained."[31]

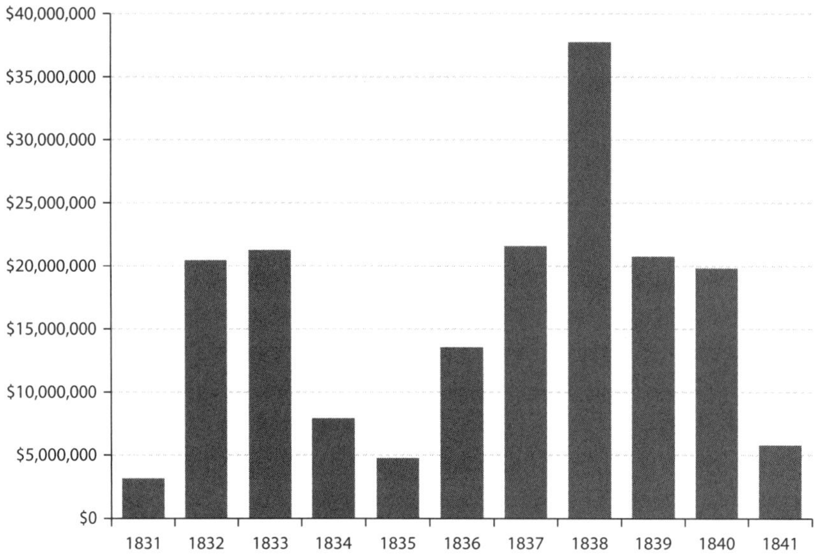

State debt issued, by year, 1831–1841. *Source:* John Joseph Wallis, Richard Sylla, and Arthur Grinath III, "Sovereign Debt and Repudiation: The Emerging-Market Debt Crisis in the U.S. States, 1839–1843," Working Paper No. 10753 (National Bureau of Economic Research, September 2004), table 3.

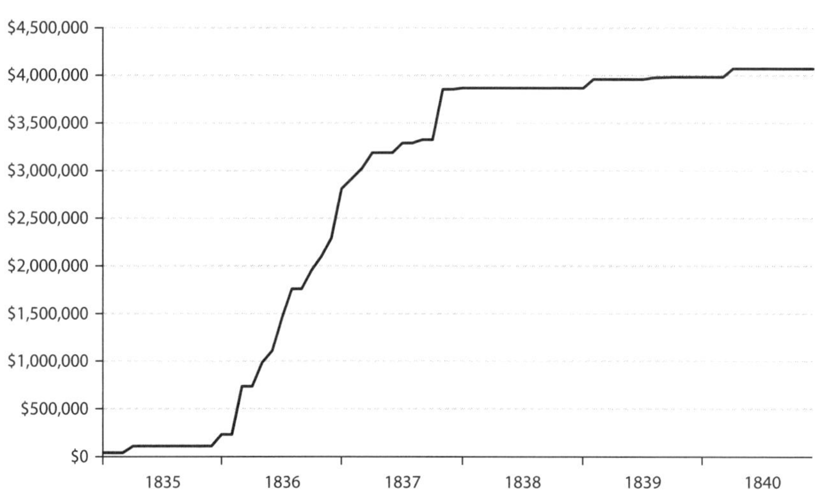

Nominal value of Indian trust fund investments, 1835–1840. *Sources:* H.R. Rep. No. 25-892 (1838); Exhibit Showing the Description of Stocks Held by the United States in Trust for the Chickasaw Indians, Vol. 1, TTFC, 416; Trust Fund Ledger, Vol. 1, Journals and Ledgers for Indian Trust Funds, Records Concerning Indian Trust Funds, BIA, NARA, 11; Trust Fund Journal, Vol. 1, Journals and Ledgers for Indian Trust Funds, Records Concerning Indian Trust Funds, BIA, NARA, 48–49, 57.

The notion that state bonds held an objective, market-determined value assumed that these bonds were already on the market. Often the bonds that the Office of Indian Affairs purchased had yet to clear that hurdle. States needed to convince a bank, broker, or other major creditor to "float" their bond issuances, essentially buying bonds wholesale to then sell to retail investors. In the spring of 1837, as the economic panic intensified, many states found themselves unable to float their debt. For these ailing states, the Indian trust funds became a creditor of last resort.

On March 28, 1837, as cotton brokerages began failing in New Orleans and New York City, Harris agreed to purchase $250,000 in Missouri state bonds at a generous 8 percent premium. (That very day, President Martin Van Buren declared the Platte Country a part of Missouri, consigning the Odawas, Ojibwes, and Potawatomis to a second removal that would take place months later.) The premium Harris paid was particularly remarkable since, at the time, no creditor was willing to float the nearly $965,000 in bonds that the state had issued to finance the State Bank of Missouri. Harris had, it turns out, promised too much. As the money market contracted, land sales slowed, bringing the stream of new funds flowing into trusts for potential investment to a trickle. Unable to honor promptly his original commitment of $250,000, Harris instead chipped away at the purchase, buying smaller increments that fall when he had Creek, Seneca, and Shawnee money at his disposal, each time paying a premium for bonds that the state had yet to float on the market. Missouri Senator Thomas Hart Benton nonetheless complained that the initial $250,000 purchase had yet to be honored, and demanded more Indian trust fund investment in his state. After a rejection from the House of Barings in London, two failed campaigns in Eastern cities, and an aborted deal with John Jacob Astor, the state only managed to float around half of its bonds in August 1838, nearly a year after the Office of Indian Affairs first bought them at a premium.[32]

Harris offered a similar lifeline to Kentucky. The state's internal improvement bonds languished without a single buyer until the intervention of Vice President Richard Mentor Johnson, whose Kentucky plantation boarding school, the Choctaw Academy, was financed by Choctaw education funds and the annuities of several nations. In a letter marked "unofficial," Johnson urged Harris to invest trust fund money in Kentucky bonds, promising to "ever recollect" the favor. Harris promised to invest an impressive $415,000 but managed only to purchase $165,000 before the Panic of 1837 halted the flow of available cash. Like Missouri, Kentucky entered the panic without a single creditor to float its issuance, making the Office of Indian Affairs its sole major investor.[33]

By the spring of 1837, Harris had so overcommitted the trust funds to state investment that he was forced to refuse one especially notable solicitation. Recently retired President Andrew Jackson inquired that May if there might be "any of the Chickasaw fund" to invest in stocks that would support the Nashville and Lebanon Turnpike, a road planned to run alongside his Tennessee plantation. Jackson's inquiry was particularly ironic given his repeated vetoes of infrastructure bills as president.[34] And, as he was certainly aware, War Department regulations in fact limited trust investments to federal and state securities, excluding private or municipal bonds like those of the Nashville and Lebanon Turnpike. Considering his track record, Harris would have likely bent or broken the rules if he could have, but as he explained to the former president, all available trust fund money had already been invested. A few states were, like Jackson, too late in their appeals for trust fund capital. When the Illinois canal fund commissioner John Reynolds—who as governor had overseen the invasions of Sauk and Meskwakis lands during the Black Hawk War—wrote to Commissioner Harris with a request for Indian trust investment in the state's "most splendid scheme of Internal Improvement," Harris regretfully declined his request.[35] Years later, Illinois representatives would continue to complain that "not one dollar of Illinois stocks have been accepted" by the Office of Indian Affairs as trustee.[36]

Harris's last bargain was his most unethical. In May 1837, with the panic in full swing, Harris welcomed to his office Jacob Brown, president of the Bank of Arkansas. By the end of their conversation Harris had promised to purchase $300,000 of the bank's state bonds. It was, in more than one sense, an investment in Indian removal. Located in Little Rock, a way station for many forced relocations of Southeastern Natives, the Bank of Arkansas received federal funds sent to agents for rations, transportation contracts, and other expenses associated with removal. In an impressive instance of self-dealing, Brown served simultaneously as the bank's president and, in his capacity as the federal disbursement agent for Indian removal west of the Mississippi, as one of its major clients. His dual role undoubtedly factored into the unlikely bargain he struck with Harris. Reporting on the importance of Brown's bond sale for the Bank of Arkansas, one newspaper commented on the "lucky hit for our young sister" given that "it must be difficult, if not impracticable to sell State bonds in the Atlantic under present circumstances."[37]

What seemed a lucky hit missed the mark. With advance purchases of Kentucky, Missouri, and other state bonds pending, Harris could only buy $115,000 of Arkansas bonds for the Ojibwe trust fund before he left office

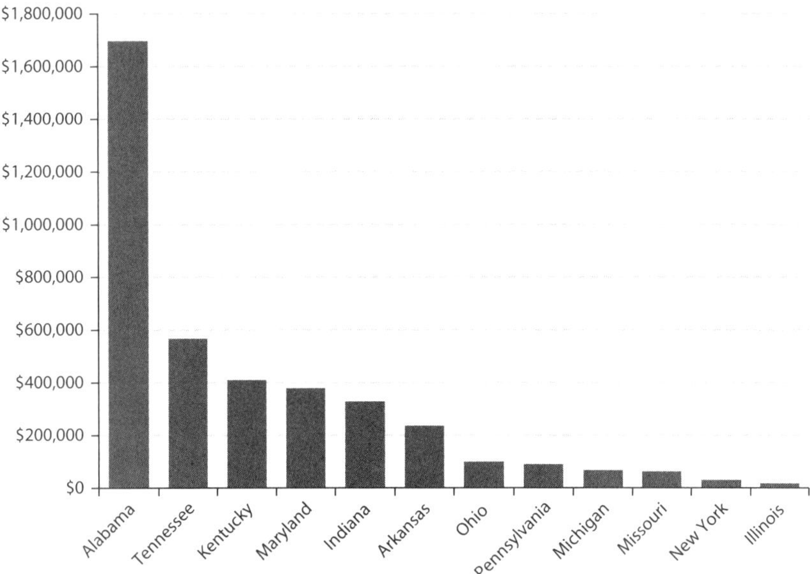

Indian trust fund investments in state bonds, 1840. *Sources: ARCIA* 1840, 276–77; H.R. Doc. No. 26-19 (1840).

disgraced in October 1838. Secretary of War Joel Poinsett was appalled once he learned of Harris' contract with Arkansas, but felt compelled to honor it nonetheless. This was fortunate for the Bank of Arkansas, since the Indian trust funds were the bank's sole source of capital. Unable to secure any other investors, officials at the Bank of Arkansas for years pestered the Office of Indian Affairs to buy up the remaining $185,000 committed by Harris, even though the value of Arkansas bonds had plummeted after the panic. Such was Harris's parting accomplishment as a public servant—and the beginning of his next chapter. After his resignation, the Real Estate Bank of Arkansas, a rival to the Bank of Arkansas, recruited Harris with the hope that the former commissioner of Indian affairs could finagle an investment from the Chickasaw trust fund. He became the bank's cashier and in 1842 was promoted to president, receiving the highest salary of any bank official in the state.[38]

Over the course of his brief tenure, Harris accomplished a breathtaking expansion of the Indian trust fund system. At the time of his appointment, the Office of Indian Affairs managed seven trust funds containing just over $1.1 million in state bonds. By the end of his truncated term in office Harris had overseen the creation of thirty-five new trust funds and filled them with nearly $2.8 million in state bonds.[39] The Indian trust funds may not have been the largest investor in states' borrowing boom on the aggregate. But because they were managed by such a pliable and risk-tolerant trustee, they became a lifeline for many states, and significant creditors to specific projects.

⁕

States had borrowed—and Harris had invested—amid an era of exuberance. A decade-long upswing in land values had convinced Northwestern legislatures that they could follow New York's model, accumulating transportation debt that could be repaid in a presumed context of even higher land value and settlement, and thus higher tax revenue. Indiana epitomized this approach. On January 27, 1836, its state assembly passed the Mammoth Internal Improvement Act, which authorized a staggering array of simultaneous works: an extension of the Wabash and Erie canal, an improvement of the Wabash River, two additional canals, a railroad, a turnpike, and two additional surveys for potential routes. Altogether, the bill authorized the state to borrow $10,000,000 to cover the jumble of transportation improvements. This figure is even more astounding when compared to the roughly $50,000 in annual tax revenue Indiana collected at the time.[40]

Indiana's fiscal plan for a transportation revolution hinged on projections of continued growth in the land market. When legislators approved the Mammoth Act, public land sales were booming in Indiana, with sales for the year 1835 totaling more than the previous two years' sales combined. Northwestern states also expected a fiscal windfall in the early 1840s due to the expiry of a five-year moratorium on taxing lands purchased from the public domain, a clause that originated in the Northwest Ordinance. But the inflationary conditions that had heated the land market had also caused the cost of constructing improvements to soar: Prices for materials and wages exceeded initial canal commission estimates by 20 percent. Even after the bubble burst, legislators continued to authorize debt, hoping that the trickle of revenue from land sales might buoy the state through the five-year lapse before freshly purchased lands became taxable.[41]

These predictions presumed not only a steady influx of settlers on Native land but also the steady increase in the taxable value of this land once made into settler property. Preoccupied as they were with celebrating incomplete canals, few settlers imagined that a financial panic would soon bring their transportation revolution to a crashing halt. Public land sales across Indiana roughly halved in a single year, from 1,250,000 acres in 1837 to 602,000 acres in 1838. Land values also plummeted, winnowing tax revenues to a fraction of estimates.[42]

The Panic of 1837 heightened the urgency of Miami removal for Indiana. Canal construction already infiltrated Miami territories, reaching Logansport by 1838. Traders' dependency on annuities had only increased after banks suspended specie payments, which made cash even scarcer in the Northwest. At an annuity disbursement at Logansport the year before, traders had crowded in as $13,050 in gold and silver coins was handed over to the nation. It was only half of their usual cash annuity, but the sum was nonetheless a stunning injection of hard money to the region amid banks' general suspension of specie payments. Annuities' ability to hedge against crisis was so vital to local markets that traders opposed removals for fear of losing such a lucrative customer base. Yet once traders used annuities to diversify into enterprises like mills, tanneries, taverns, and ferries, their opposition softened. Once canal-adjacent ventures became profitable, the value of their alliances with the Miamis began to depreciate, and traders started to collaborate with Indian agents and treaty commissioners.[43]

At a council held in the fall of 1838, the Miamis agreed to explore a potential home in the West and ceded 170,000 acres of their most desirable lands abutting the Wabash River. Canal commissioners eager to sell the next batch of Wabash and Erie Canal land grants were quickly disappointed to learn that many of the most valuable sections of the Miami cession were already spoken for. Before agreeing to remove, the Miamis had sold preemptive title to over twenty-four thousand acres of riverside tracts to local traders and boosters, including their former Indian agent John Tipton. Indiana's legislature petitioned Congress to challenge these private sales, complaining that the tracts they had lost were valued at $8.25 per acre, whereas available "back lands" located farther from the river were valued at $3.75 per acre. Congress refused to override the preemptive title, only authorizing Indiana to relocate its grants (without expanding the grant to compensate for its lesser value, as Indiana had hoped).[44] Having banked on a windfall from the Miami cession, Indiana's canal commissioners found their efforts to complete the project undermined by their own citizens, whose speculations countered the state's ability to gain revenue from ceded Native lands.

{⁂⁂⁂}

While the Miami used their commercial power to retain lands adjacent to their formerly central portage, the United Nations of Odawa, Ojibwe, and Potawatomi—along with many other Anishinaabe groups spread across lands now claimed by Illinois, Indiana, and Michigan—wound their way west. In 1838, Potawatomi bands with distant political ties to the United Nations began their notorious Trail of Death, overseen by now-Indiana Senator John Tipton. Tipton employed local militias to pry Potawatomis from their homelands just north of the Wabash River from the Miamis. Forty-two Potawatomis lost their lives on the journey to their new home on the Osage River. For the Anishinaabeg and other Northwestern nations, removal was as brutal as the better-known Southern removal campaigns but unfolded along diverging trajectories that expressed the decentralized nature of Anishinaabe politics. Some groups forked away from federally chosen routes, preferring to cope with the ordeal on their own terms; others fled to the woods of northern Michigan or across the border to Canada, evading removal through another path of migration.[45]

As Anishinaabeg dispersed, annuities and interest payments remained tagged to named treaty signatories. Treaties had consolidated Anishinaabe villages and *doodem* into polities like the United Nations, and their identities were further reified by the ritual of gathering to receive the annuities those treaties had promised. Unlike a lump-sum payment, annuities and trusts positioned specific Native leaders and their successors in an ongoing relationship with the federal government. As bearers of annuities, federal officials could twist this relationship to their own aims, conferring funds to preferred leaders and for purposes that aligned with their objectives. Annuities' tendency to consolidate and demarcate polities would be particularly consequential for Anishinaabe peoples who had always refused political centralization and instead forged interdependent ties, through *doodem* lineages, between locally governed villages. And as the United Nations would soon learn, the fact that they now had such significant funds in federal hands subjected them to new forms of control: Officials could now decide where, when, and *if* future annuities payments would be delivered.

After the 1833 Treaty of Chicago, the United Nations endured a decade of uncertainty, frustration, and hunger. In the treaty the United States had promised them a five-million-acre tract along the Missouri River, known as the Platte Country. Federal officials had envisioned it as a resettlement zone for Eastern Natives since the 1820s, but Missouri senators blocked the ratification of the Treaty of Chicago until a committee agreed to swap out the Platte Country assigned to the United Nations for a five-million-acre tract near present-day Council Bluffs, Iowa.[46]

When the United Nations learned of the land swap, they expressed dismay that Congress chose to rewrite terms of the Treaty of Chicago

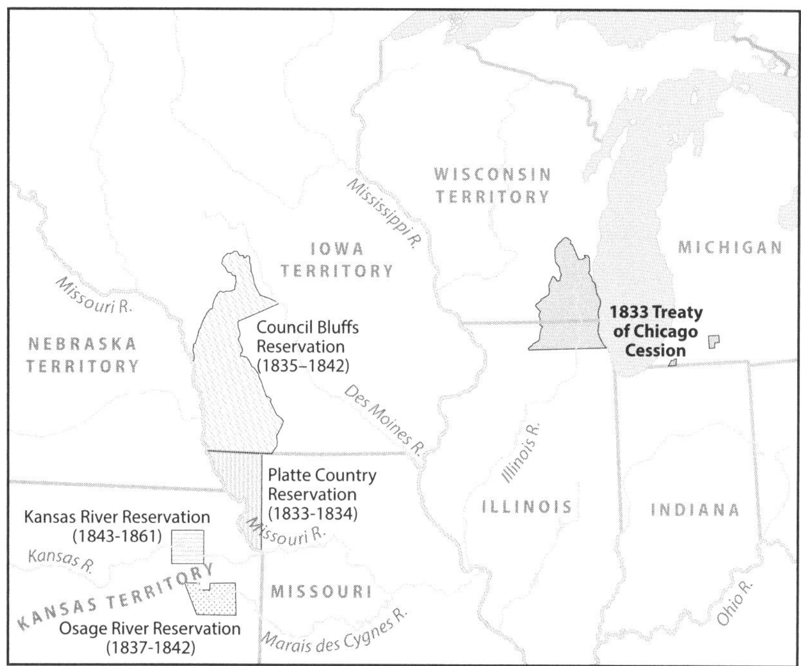


United Nations of Odawa, Ojibwe, and Potawatomi land cessions and reservations. Reservation periods overlap due to multiple and partial removals. After 1846, the United Nations were consolidated with Potawatomis removed from Indiana on the Kansas River, where they remain today on a diminished reservation. *Source:* Map created by Shane Kelley.

unilaterally. "It does seem to us," wrote the United Nations' representatives in response, "that *their* interpretation of a treaty and ours is very different."[47] After exchanging proposals and counterproposals through their agent Thomas V. Owen, in October 1834 Billy Caldwell and other representatives agreed to accept the large tract in Iowa Territory instead of the Platte Country, with an additional $10,000 annuity. This angered Potawatomis in Michigan, who had not been consulted about the change, but were nevertheless expected to cohabitate with the Odawas, Ojibwes, and Potawatomis in their new home west of the Mississippi.[48]

But before the army-escorted expedition of the United Nations could reach its destination, Harris changed his mind about Council Bluffs too. Citing an advancing tide of white settlement in Iowa, and the territory's imminent passage to statehood, Harris decided to relocate the United Nations once again—this time farther south, on a tract alongside the Osage River. But when a party of Odawa, Ojibwe, and Potawatomi *ogimaag* traveled south to explore the territory, the Osages advised them to remain in Council Bluffs, where the climate, lands, and game animals better suited their needs. (Osages may have had their own reasons to cast their homelands in a negative light.) Twenty-five hundred Odawa, Ojibwe, and Potawatomis had resettled at Council Bluffs by February 1838. Billy Caldwell, Padekoshek, Shambonee, and other United Nations leaders sent a petition to the military officer overseeing their removal warning that they would not leave. "We have now lit our council fires in this our new country," they wrote. Read in the context of Anishinaabe politics, in which councils anchored kinship networks and lawmaking to place, this was a statement of inextinguishable possession. Yet Harris refused to reevaluate, even as emigrating parties streamed onto the Council Bluffs reservation.[49]

Education and agricultural funds inserted to the Treaty of Chicago had formed the outline of a fiscal plan for the United Nations' post-removal reconstruction west of the Mississippi. But in the months to come, Harris and his successors held annuities ransom, refusing any spending on schools, farms, or any other improvements. The Office of Indian Affairs essentially thwarted the United Nations' capacity to erect their own infrastructure, keeping them in a state of economic purgatory that, they hoped, would be intolerable enough make another removal appear worthwhile.

The United Nations, like the Choctaws, had intended their education fund to finance schools in their own territory, and nearby missionaries were eager to volunteer their services. Yet the government opposed building a school at Council Bluffs since it would tether the United Nations to what they insisted was a temporary home. Commissioner Elbert Herring instead decided that by May 1836 sufficient interest had accrued on the education fund to finance the education of twelve Odawa, Ojibwe, and Potawatomi youth at a boarding school: the Choctaw Academy. In the years since Richard Mentor Johnson had established the academy with Choctaw funds from their 1825 land cession treaty, the senator had successfully turned mission education into a profitable enterprise. Because Johnson collected shares of annuity funds on a per-student basis, he fixated on maximizing enrollment and minimizing costs. "You must crowd many of the little Boys together," he ordered the academy's headmaster, "as it is no disadvantage & this makes room for the large Boys." Johnson also withheld older students from graduating, repeatedly pressured the Office of Indian Affairs to expand the allowed number of students, and kept a close eye on the progress of removal treaties, appealing for more scholars if any new education funds were created. Johnson even recruited additional students by appealing directly to Indian agents, without authorization from their superiors. When complaints reached his desk, the commissioner of Indian affairs found himself in the awkward position of reprimanding a senator for his misuse of federally managed Native funds.[50]

Enrollment continued to bloat as Johnson ascended in political rank, becoming vice president under Martin Van Buren in March 1837. By then the Odawas, Ojibwes, and Potawatomis were, in the words of their Indian agent, "violently opposed" to sending children to the Choctaw Academy.[51] Twelve of their children were in attendance—the maximum enrollment afforded by the education fund's interest. Conditions deteriorated within the crowded academy as Johnson's operation grew more extractive. Students were subjected to manual labor instruction in wagonmaking, cordwainery, tailoring, and blacksmithing, which became compulsory in 1838. Johnson sold the wagons, shoes, garments, and metalworks produced by the boys, pocketing the profit. As mandatory physical instruction supplanted the original model of a liberal education, both parents and students condemned the academy's degrading environment, which in their definition included a discomfiting proximity to Johnson's slaves. Wealthier families refused to send their sons to Kentucky, and so the commissioner directed Indian agents to select poorer children and "the most promising of the orphans."[52] What began as a school for elite Choctaw boys had become a compulsory residential school fueled by the very funds that nations had set aside in treaties to provide for their children at a moment of catastrophic dispossession.

In order to prevent the Odawas, Ojibwes, and Potawatomis from taking root in Council Bluffs, the Office of Indian Affairs also withheld interest accrued from the agricultural fund. As soon as they arrived at Council Bluffs, the United Nations set about splitting rails and clearing fields for farming as best they could. But the commissioner of Indian affairs withheld agricultural implements and refused to spend funds assigned for that very purpose, arguing this money would only be wasted on improving a temporary home. Without necessary plows, implements, and stock animals, the United Nations had been forced to depend on substandard provisions provided by federal contractors since leaving their homelands. During their stay in the Platte Country, one military official became so concerned with the United Nations' condition and the Office of Indian Affairs' refusal to provide agricultural support that he threatened to alert Congress. Harris acknowledged that some had become "indigent" over the course of their journey, but he refused to spend a dime of their agricultural fund to support their subsistence. In Harris's view, the nations planned to sit on their Council Bluffs lands for as long as they could, "that they may hereafter cede it to the United States at an enhanced rate, when its value shall have been increased by the fulfillment of the stipulation of the treaty of 1833."[53] Interpreting their petitions for equipment as an effort to hike up the value of their property, he treated the United Nations as speculators with an invalid title.

In January 1837, Harris decided that he might as well invest the United Nations' agricultural improvement fund. Despite the fact that the Treaty of Chicago had not stipulated its investment, Harris sunk the entire $150,000 fund into Maryland state bonds. A year later, Treasury auditors flagged Harris's purchase as unauthorized, noting that he had failed to secure the United Nations' consent to investing their fund. Harris defended his decision by protesting that the money had been "lying idle in the Treasury."[54] Nearly a decade later, one of Maryland's bond-financed canals would carry toward Washington a delegation of Odawas, Ojibwes, and Potawatomis steeled for a confrontation with a trustee who had for nearly a decade denied them their own money.

⟨⟩

Jean Richardville had anticipated the canal's significance for the Wabash River Valley. Acting as the nation's principal chief, Richardville had over the course of two decades applied skills accrued as a trader perched on the Crane clan's portage and negotiated treaties that reserved lands along the canal's banks for his nation. Using Miami possession of these coveted lands as leverage, Richardville had coaxed substantial annuities from federal treaty negotiators, securing $95,000 for a population of seven hundred persons in the 1838 treaty. But this strategy had run its course. In another treaty signed a mere two years later, Richardville finally agreed to cede remaining Miami lands along the Wabash River. The United States would purchase this 480,000-acre tract for slightly more than fifty cents per acre, or less than half the federal minimum price. Several affluent Miami elites, including Richardville, quietly negotiated clauses in the treaty that granted them privately held tracts of land, which enabled them and their heirs to remain in Indiana. For ordinary Miamis, however, the 1840 treaty prescribed removal west, to lands located in present-day Kansas.[55]

The Miamis would not easily acquiesce. After stalling for six years, the nation received word in the fall of 1846 that the Office of Indian Affairs had deployed military forces to Peru, Indiana, with orders to expel them. When soldiers arrived, they discovered that families had scattered into the woods and swamps rather than report for emigration. Troops circled the region, hunting for fugitives. Removal began on October 6, when emigrating agent and established fur trader Alexis Coquillard shepherded over three hundred Miamis onto three canal boats. Hundreds more embarked on another two boats the next day. As they boarded, many carried bundles of earth loosened from burial grounds. Among them was Mary Pesawah, a child of no more than twelve. In an oral history recorded decades later, she would remember mostly her own incomprehension of that day's events, describing a "strange journey" away from her home.[56]

Miami removal would begin on the Wabash and Erie Canal, the same project that had profited from the United Nations' trust fund and attracted settler investment in Myaamionki. But the Panic of 1837 had so undermined the state's capacity to maintain construction on its complex network of public works that the Wabash and Erie Canal remained unfinished, forcing a circuitous route. The party first floated east, taking the canal from Peru to Fort Wayne. From Fort Wayne the five boats were tugged south on the Miami and Erie Canal, reaching Cincinnati four days later. There the Miamis transferred to a steamship on the Ohio River and finally headed west, trailed by a handful of traders chasing the annuities that would resume in Indian Territory. For their contract to carry out the Miami removal, Coquillard and his business partners, all seasoned traders, collected more than $60,000.[57]

Indian trust funds encapsulated in a single narrative the formation of national markets and the compelled removal of Indigenous peoples across the wider Great Lakes region. Throughout the improvement era, state agents and federal officials collaborated on the displacement of thousands of Indigenous peoples in order to unlock a vision of canal-driven development. By building infrastructure, boosters aimed to spur immigration, enhance land values, encourage exports, and secure territory for non-Native settlers. Federal initiative in the form of treaties of dispossession, removal campaigns, and land grants laid the literal groundwork for states to pursue these visions.

Historians debate whether Indiana's pursuit of a canal-powered future repaid its dizzying costs. By the 1840s internal improvements, and particularly canals, had redrawn the geography of interregional trade in early America. Canals shuttled grain toward the Great Lakes and Erie Canal systems, entrenching commercial flows between the Northwest and the Northeast that would prove decisive as the nation marched toward fracture over the question of slavery. Yet Indiana's internal improvement

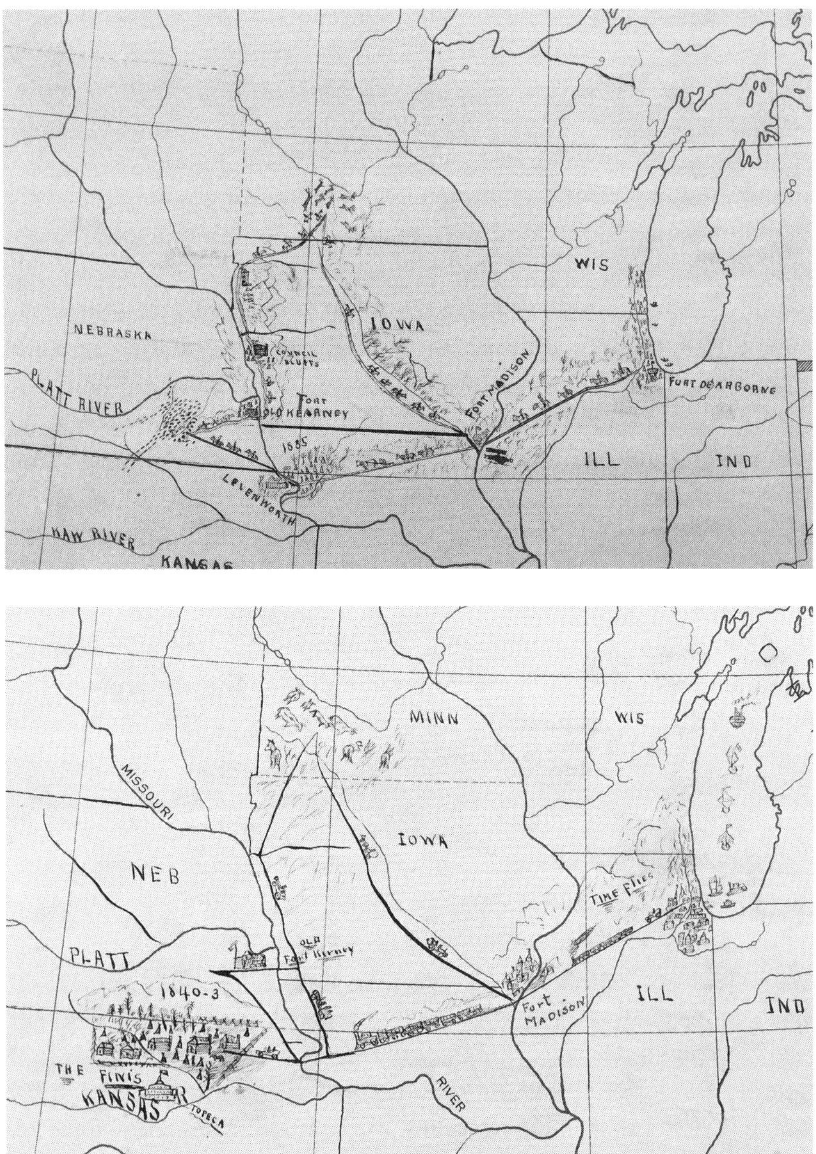



Time flies, parts 1 and 2. These hand-drawn maps illustrate military removal agent John W. Todd's recollections, dictated to his son, of accompanying the United Nations of Odawa, Ojibwe, and Potawatomi on their 1835 journey west. Both Council Bluffs and Kansas reservations are shown, as is Chicago, labeled Fort Dearborn. Most striking is that the maps closely relate removal to the progress of transportation improvements, including a shift from wagon travel to rails and steamships. A comment written on the second map reads "time flies." *Source:* Joseph Allen Todd Papers, Chicago History Museum.

An 1872 wedding party on the Wabash and Erie Canal. The canal would close to traffic two years after this photo was taken. *Source:* Indiana Historical Society.

program, advertised as the spadework needed for a yeomen's republic, stimulated more land speculation than lasting agricultural development. Between 1835 and 1837, land values in Indiana counties adjacent to transportation routes rose by $4.55 an acre, only to plummet in value by $5.49 an acre by 1839. Once completed in 1848, the Illinois and Michigan Canal swept in grain from the prairies toward Chicago. But by then settlers had embraced a new mode of commercial transport, and competition from railroads under construction would eventually flatten canals' toll revenues.[58] All told, the Northwest's transportation revolution was a costly, ambivalent transition, yielding temporary profit and a statewide crisis. Regardless of canals' economic impact, though, they undeniably remade Indigenous routes of travel into settler commercial thoroughfares. Even a bankrupt transportation revolution succeeded in taking Native land.

# CHAPTER FIVE

# American Insecurities

ONE MORNING in early 1843, the Odawa, Ojibwe, and Potawatomis greeted a runner at their villages at Council Bluffs. The messenger carried news from the Cherokee Nation, inviting them to a grand council convening representatives from dozens of Native nations affected by Indian removal. Cherokees had planned the council in an effort to ease tensions among the many newcomer nations that had been compressed into Indian Territory as a result of their relocation. As they listened to their visitor, the Odawa, Ojibwe, and Potawatomis considered the deprivation they had withstood for years while resisting displacement to a new reservation on the Osage River. They had so far struggled alone, without progress. They accepted the invitation.[1]

That June, Potawatomi headman Wabaunsee and speaker Abtegizhek, accompanied by more than a dozen headmen from different Odawa, Ojibwe, and Potawatomi villages, headed south to Cherokee territory. The delegation arrived in Tahlequah, the Cherokee Nation's new capital, to find it bustling with activity. Several thousand attendees staked tents and built fires among the log cabins that lined each street. Larger cabins, which housed the Cherokee Nation's two legislative chambers—the National Committee and the National Council—framed the town's square. Within it the Cherokees had erected an enormous open-sided shelter outfitted with a podium, a table covered with strings of wampum and calumets, and rows of long benches that radiated outward in a semicircle. Cherokee women pounded hominy, prepared corn bread, and roasted beef to serve their guests in an adjacent area. In addition to the Odawa, Ojibwe, and Potawatomis, the Cherokees had dispatched runners to thirty-five Native nations, spread from the Upper Missouri to the Red River.[2]

Not every nation accepted the invitation. But representatives from the Chickasaws, Creeks, Lenapes, Osages, Quapaws, Seminoles, Senecas,

Shawnees, and at least ten other nations did. Altogether, 219 delegates crowded the benches at Tahlequah. Each carried unique, even conflicting experiences of the massive forced migrations of the previous decade. Among the notables present at the Grand Council were Roly McIntosh and John Ross, principal chiefs of the Creek and Cherokee nations, respectively. Much like Wabaunsee and Abtegizhek, these men governed nations struggling to recover from destructive and fatal westward removals. Others, like Seminole delegate Cooacoochee, arrived as refugees. Cooacoochee had fled west with other Seminoles after surrendering his homelands on the Florida Peninsula in 1841 to end a brutal war. Members of his nation now lived on Cherokee lands, with no country of their own. Other nations present at the gathering had lost their homelands to removed nations pushed onto Indian Territory. Tahlequah sat on land that once belonged to the Osage people, who had fought and lost a war to prevent the Cherokees from acquiring their home through the mediation of the United States. This made the entry of an Osage delegation, led by Shinkawassa, one of the conference's most poignant moments.[3]

When John Ross delivered his opening address to the assembled crowd, he spoke in a measured English, pausing regularly for interpreters to translate his words into more than a dozen languages. Because of federal removal policy, Ross observed, "tribes hitherto distant from each other have become neighbors." Some nations remained "strangers," he admitted, alluding to the fact that the Comanches and other Plains nations had declined to attend, to the great disappointment of many present in the audience. Forced to compress and cohabitate, Native nations needed to establish a system of "international laws," Ross argued, to address the regular raids, murders, and unauthorized commerce taking place across Indian Territory and its surrounding region. Removal campaigns had triggered this cascade of violence by packing unalike and distressed peoples into close quarters. Now they would make peace on their own terms.[4]

The tentative discussions that proceeded at Tahlequah were not unprecedented, but the 1843 Grand Council nonetheless rattled the federal Indian agents who monitored the conference from its outskirts. In the years since the 1830 Indian Removal Act accelerated and scaled up forced migrations, the United States had signed dozens of unequal or outright fraudulent treaties that sowed widespread resentment across dispossessed nations. Most of these treaties depended on annuity payments to disincentivize Native warfare and compel nations' loyalty to the United States. Many annuities depended, in turn, on states paying regular interest on bonds to the Office of Indian Affairs. That this system could fail had hardly

The 1843 Grand Council at Tahlequah. *Source:* John Mix Stanley, *International Indian Council (Held at Tallequah, Indian Territory, in 1843)*, 1843, Smithsonian American Art Museum.

occurred to the men who assumed federal trusteeship. But fail it did. When a major bond brokerage collapsed in 1839, many indebted states became insolvent, and Indian affairs officials were caught flat-footed. Within three years, eight states and one territory had defaulted on their creditors. Among those creditors were the Indian trust funds.[5]

States' defaults forced lawmakers, federal officials, and Indigenous leaders to confront contradictions latent in the federal government's choice to finance a significant portion of annuities by investing Native wealth in states' sovereign debts. Through its broad powers over land, internal revenue, commerce, treaties, and war, the government had, since the administration of President George Washington, deliberately excluded states from the field of Indian affairs. But by investing Native wealth in state bonds, the national government rendered its own relationships with Native peoples dependent on the solvency of states. When states failed, their losses undermined the peace that annuities purchased.[6] In this context, a coalescence of political and commercial alliances among Indigenous nations appropriately unnerved federal Indian affairs officials.

Advocates for Indian removal had argued that only distance from settlers could stave off Natives' disappearance. Far from preserving Native peoples, removal journeys were so lethal that they brought the myth of Indigenous extinction closer to reality. But Native nations outlived the disaster, and federal officials found themselves scrambling to pacify a population they had written off as a dying race. The federal government's response to states' financial collapse betrayed their persistent fears of Indigenous peoples, especially of their confederation against the United States. Since its inception, fiduciary colonialism had been designed to avert costly wars through the expenditure of recurring compensation, a format that permitted federal control over Native wealth. Now this delicate balance faltered. Encircled by conflicts of their own making, federal officials would go to surprising lengths to persuade Congress to step in when states failed to make Native creditors whole.

⟨⸺⚜⸺⟩

The nations gathered at Tahlequah had survived an apocalyptic period of their histories. Removal had transferred one hundred million acres of Native homelands to the United States and compressed displaced nations onto a scant three million acres. Despite the Indian Removal Act's promise to secure consent for removals, in practice the government refused to recognize Indigenous peoples' right to remain.[7] While certain nations conceded to removal in order to escape violence and legal assaults on their sovereignty, most had been divided internally, and still more refused to leave their homelands altogether.

Some Seminoles waged a war against the United States rather than accept relocation to Indian Territory. In 1823, the Seminoles had been coerced into the fraudulent Treaty of Moultrie Creek, in which they ostensibly ceded twenty-eight million acres to the United States for a mere $221,000, or less than one cent per acre. Confined to two reservations in western and central Florida after the treaty, Seminoles languished. Florida planters accused them of theft and of harboring runaway slaves and retaliated by committing raids on Seminole villages.[8] As non-Native settlements grew, Indian agents attempted repeatedly to force a treaty on the Seminoles that would remove them west to Indian Territory. Federal authorities thought they had succeeded at an 1834 council, but they were negotiating with only a narrow minority of Seminoles who had agreed to consider the prospect. Others prepared for battle.

In December 1835, Seminole forces ambushed their Indian agent and troops that had been deployed to support him. Next they struck at the plantation belt, driving most settlers out of central Florida. Their actions inspired the Lower Creeks in Georgia to take up arms against their own Indian agent and the settlers who squatted on their territory. Creek militants targeted the stagecoaches that shuttled banknotes and commercial paper between cotton ports and effectively halted traffic on the Federal Road, which sustained communications across the slaveholding South. The Second Seminole War would last through four presidential administrations, cost upwards of $20 million, and claim the lives of fifteen hundred US soldiers and as many as two thousand Seminoles.[9]

The war was only one eruption in the long catastrophe of removal. Taking into account the thousands pushed out of homelands to create Indian Territory, the roughly eighty-two thousand Indigenous peoples compacted onto it, and the tens of thousands more who perished on their journey westward, Indian removal upturned or ended the lives of well over a hundred thousand Native people.[10] For many migrants, the conditions that awaited them in Indian Territory were as difficult as the journeys themselves.

Indian Territory represented a colonial experiment and a novel political geography. The policy of Indian removal had begged the question of where, exactly, tens of thousands of displaced Natives would be removed to. Indian Territory was the answer. Unlike other territories, Indian Territory was never intended to achieve statehood, but rather to contain colonized peoples indefinitely. Isaac McCoy, the Baptist missionary whose proposal to purchase Indian land with trust funds had influenced the administration of President Andrew Jackson, played a central role in its creation. In 1828, McCoy set out twice from St. Louis with expeditions of Native delegates to scout the as-yet undesignated region for prospective relocation, first with a party of Odawas and Potawatomis and second with a group of Chickasaws, Choctaws, and Creeks. Even as its representatives urged Native people to move to the region, the War Department knew little of its geography. McCoy would go on to conduct surveys for the department, but he could only sketch out future reservations on an approximated and skeletal topography.[11]

On paper, the territory bordered Arkansas and Missouri and spanned two hundred miles between the Platte River, to the north, and the Red River, to the south. In this area of roughly one hundred thousand square miles, federal officials aspired to resettle and govern two dozen emigrant nations, or an estimated one hundred thousand people. Nations forced from far-flung and markedly different places, from New York to

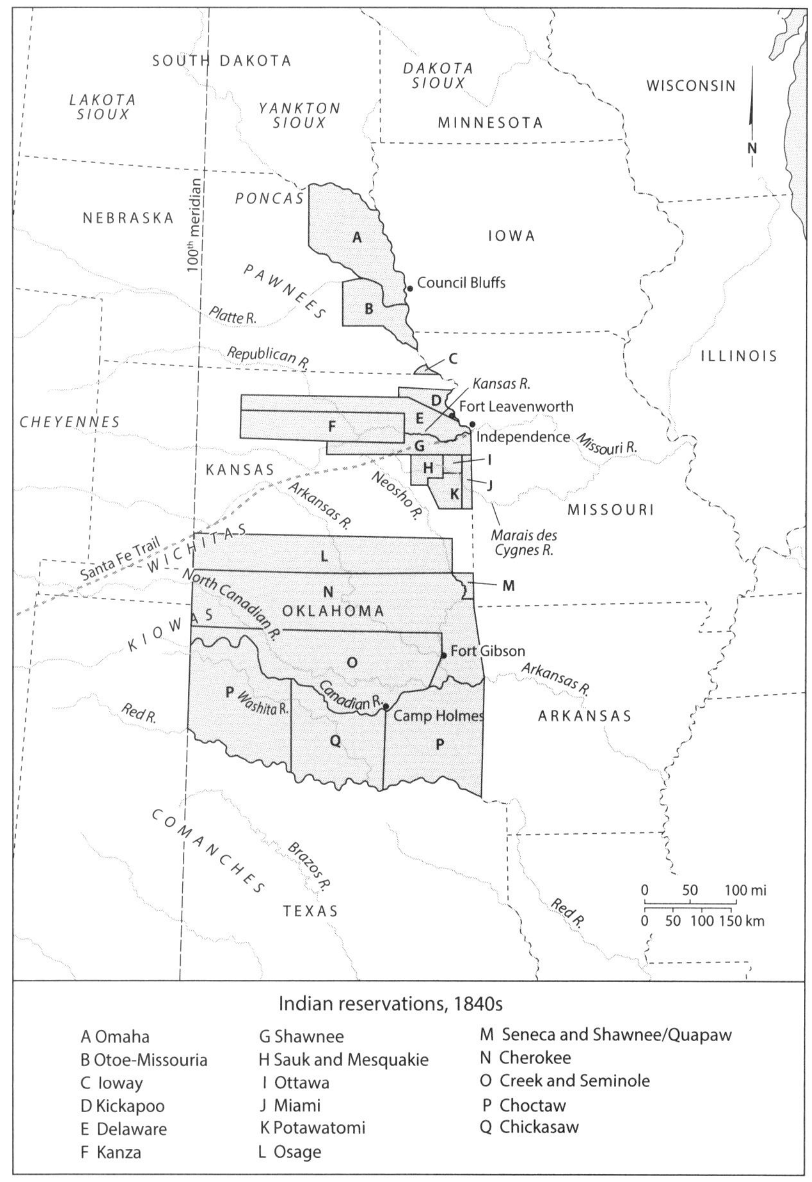


Indian Territory, circa 1840. *Source:* Reprinted from Jeffrey Ostler, *Surviving Genocide: Native Nations and the United States from the American Revolution to Bleeding Kansas* (Yale University Press, 2019); map created by Bill Nelson.

Michigan to Florida, all converged on this swath of relatively arid and mostly unwooded land. For smaller nations, the War Department created compact reservations clustered along the Kansas and Neosho Rivers to the east, where modest supplies of timber offered arrivals a more familiar environment. More populous nations like the Cherokees, Choctaws, and

Creeks received larger bands of territory that spread west toward buffalo ranges on which they were now expected to hunt to survive. Remarkably, removal—a policy framed as in service of "civilizing" Natives into adopting agriculture—instead stripped nations of established farms on eastern homelands and, by transplanting them onto less fertile land, forced them to compete for a thinning population of game.[12]

Buffalo ranges, like the rest of Indian Territory, were not unoccupied when the removed nations arrived. Newly created reservations overwrote Kanza, Osage, and Quapaw homelands. The United States staked its claim to these territories on treaties signed decades earlier, to clear a path for the Santa Fe Trail and carve out a space for peoples displaced from east of the Mississippi. The region appeared ripe for this purpose because it had previously served as a destination for Indigenous migrants. Sometimes under their own initiative, but always under duress, groups of Cherokees, Chickasaws, Choctaws, Kickapoos, Potawatomis, Sauk and Meskwakis, and many other small polities had migrated to the area with the hope that establishing distance from an advancing front of settlers would better protect their autonomy than staying in place.[13]

Taking advantage of this established migratory route, the United States started in 1808 to relocate Cherokees onto unceded Osage land. By 1817 the government estimated that between five and six thousand Cherokees had resettled in the west without invitation or sanction from the Osages of the Arkansas River Valley. Tit-for-tat raiding between unwilling hosts and newcomers grew especially bitter. Cherokees who left their homelands did so only to preserve their way of life, especially hunting and adherence to clan law. While the Osage were willing to accept payments to restore justice after killings, including confrontations over hunting grounds, Cherokees demanded blood revenge. As retaliatory attacks between the two nations escalated, the Cherokees assembled an alliance from Native nations with long-standing grudges against the once dominant Osages. In 1821, Cherokees formally declared war and appealed to the United States for assistance, portraying themselves as the civilized party fighting a savage enemy. Weakened and battered by the Cherokee coalition, the Osages capitulated in 1825, signing a treaty with the United States that made way for the Cherokees and consigned their nation to a reservation on the northern edge of their vastly reduced homelands. Another 1825 treaty seized most of the Kanzas' lands, creating northern Indian Territory. Soon after, the government forced the Quapaws out to the Red River Valley, creating the territory's southern border. These treaties cleared the ground for Indian Territory but did not quiet the violence. Skirmishes between Cherokees and Osages continued, driving up military expenses and leading the Office of Indian Affairs to threaten cutting off annuities to both sides. Coming waves of immigration from eastern nations would only intensify competition over land and resources.[14]

Indian Territory also displaced a group of Indigenous immigrants that had inhabited its southern borderlands since the late eighteenth century. To buffer settlements from the British, Osages, and, later, Americans, Spain had invited groups of Chickasaws, Choctaws, Illinois, Lenapes, Lower Town Cherokees, and Shawnees to settle on Caddo lands that would eventually become eastern Texas and western Louisiana. By the time Mexico declared its independence in 1820, roughly ten thousand displaced Biloxis, Cherokees, Choctaws, Coushattas, Kickapoos, Lenapes, and Shawnees inhabited the region in dozens of autonomous communities. When the newly founded Republic of Texas claimed the territory in 1836, Governor Samuel Houston at first courted migrant Natives in the hopes of shielding Texans from raids. But when attacks continued, the Texas Rangers responded indiscriminately, targeting migrant Natives alongside the Caddos, Comanches, and Wichitas who carried out most of the attacks. Texans forced out groups of Caddos, Cherokees, and Shawnees at gunpoint and then, as fears of impending retaliation set in, appealed to the US military for protection. The War Department stepped in reluctantly, recognizing that Indigenous powers in the Southwestern borderlands held little regard for federal diplomacy and posed genuine military threats to settlers.[15]

Surveying this landscape in 1837, Secretary of War Joel Poinsett begged Congress to authorize a line of frontier posts running south from Lake Superior through Texas to the Gulf of Mexico. Ostensibly intended to "protect the emigrant and feebler tribes," the forts would run along the eastern border of Indian Territory rather than its exposed western border, suggesting that their actual purpose lay in protecting settlers in Arkansas and Missouri from Native peoples. As Poinsett's report explained, Indian removal had added a population of more than thirty-one thousand individuals to the more than one hundred fifty thousand Natives living west of the United States' settlements, with another 62,700 to come in the coming years. Collectively this population could muster nearly 66,500 warriors. Only a fraction of this force would be needed to overcome the US Army, which at that that time numbered roughly ten thousand troops. Congress did grant Poinsett an additional twenty-five hundred regulars to fight the Seminoles and to deter Britain in a simmering conflict on the Canadian border. But the Panic of 1837 soured Congress on the expense of a line of military posts across Indian Territory, to the dismay of civilian Indian affairs officials.[16]

Removal had spurred ongoing conflicts that made the policy far more difficult to sustain than its champions had anticipated. Under the auspices of trusteeship, the federal government had committed to protect displaced Native nations from harms caused by the United States' own citizens as well as neighboring powers—including other Native nations and, now, the Republic of Texas. As was so often the case, treaty promises were poorly kept, if at all. The deployment of military personnel to Florida to fight Seminoles and to escort removal parties left Indian Territory and its adjacent zones thinly garrisoned and federal law unenforced.[17] Indian Territory, envisioned as a zone where Native people could be pacified and confined, now produced so much instability that it posed a barrier to further westward expansion.

It was a mess entirely of the United States' own making, but the consequences fell heaviest on nations weakened by displacement. Fractious removal negotiations east of the Mississippi had opened political rifts within nations that persisted after resettlement. Levels of alcohol consumption and addiction rose because prohibitions on trading liquor in Indian Country went unenforced, adding fuel to the fire. Native constitutions established criminal legal systems to resolve conflicts, but the lighthorsemen assigned to uphold the law were far from effective, and victims continued to avail themselves of clan-based forms of retributive justice. Insecurity within Indian Territory made specie annuities even more dangerous to distribute. In one instance, an Indian agent who had to leave suddenly to visit a dying brother enlisted missionaries to guard $60,000 in gold coins, weighing more than two tons, armed with only a worn-down axe and a shotgun.[18]

The Cherokees especially suffered from political strife, with three distinct groups at war for the power to govern: the earliest migrants, known as the Old Settlers or Western Cherokees; the Treaty Party, represented by John Ridge and Elias Boudinot, who had signed the Treaty of New Echota in 1835; and an opposing majority faction led by John Ross. With internecine violence flaring and promises of federal protection hollow, Ross depended on armed guards and military escorts whenever he traveled through Indian Territory. Disputes over how to partition annuities across factions added fuel to these conflicts: Western Cherokees, who had emigrated from their homelands decades before the 1835 Treaty of New Echota, now demanded a part of its compensation. A fight over annuities lasted over a decade, with both Western and Eastern Cherokees petitioning Congress for a bigger share.[19]

Displaced nations also suffered from the most intimate of invasions: disease. On average, removal journeys claimed the lives of as much as

The payment room. Treasurer E. E. Starr of the Cherokee Nation oversees a per capita payment at Fort Gibson, circa 1890s. Star is surrounded by clerks and guards, a necessity to protect the tens of thousands of dollars in specie that would be distributed. *Source:* Gilcrease Museum, Tulsa, Oklahoma.

19 percent of predeparture populations. The figure was higher still for southern nations. Malaria, cholera, and a blistering smallpox epidemic greeted the fortunate who had survived their travels west. An American Fur Company steamer carrying merchandise and annuities to the Arikaras created one smallpox vector. Fur trade officials and the crew aboard knew the ship was infected but continued anyway, fearing retribution from the Arikara and other Northern Plains peoples if they failed to deliver the annuities as expected. Pox rippled outward from the Great Plains, reaching Indian Territory by 1838. More than fifteen thousand Indigenous people would perish during the outbreak.[20]

Significant headwinds slowed resettled nations as they hurried to reestablish sources of nutrition and subsistence, compounding their poor health. Most nations had already fallen in debt to traders by the time they agreed to removal, which then forced them to abandon their homes, possessions, and crops. "We have expended with few exceptions our individual money," Chickasaw headmen wrote in an 1839 petition. Federal ineptitude ensured that many removal parties arrived in Indian Territory too late to sow for the next year's harvest, or with little ability to procure lumber or implements to erect needed shelter before winter. As lethal as journeys west had been, greater numbers of migrants succumbed to violence, disease, or famine after they arrived.[21]

All this devastation had been carried out under the auspices of federal trusteeship. Yet this same trusteeship had conferred to nations trust funds and annuities that, at least in theory, offered seeds for recovery as nations rebuilt their governments. Shortly after their arrival in Indian Territory, for example, the Choctaws drafted a constitution that reinstituted a republican government and began passing laws to allocate education funds across the nation's three districts. In their 1839 constitution, the Cherokees recomposed their tripartite political system under a central executive office of principal chief occupied by John Ross. Annuities also contributed to a salary revolution within several governments, in which elected officials were paid for their service a sum decided by law. In the Cherokee Nation, for example, lighthorsemen received ten to twenty dollars per month, depending on rank, and circuit judges received $200 per year. District clerks in the Choctaw Nation collected a modest salary of fifty dollars per year. The Chickasaw commissioners who oversaw the land sales process established under their 1834 treaty received a more generous annual income of $250. Salaries could raise controversy, especially since they flowed to a political class populated by affluent, often slaveholding, men. Some ordinary Chickasaws, for example, advocated for a return to leadership that was inherited and uncompensated.[22]

Although wealth concentrated at the top of social hierarchies, Native governments also applied annuities toward the general welfare of their citizens. Many removal treaties, including ones signed by the Cherokees and Creeks, had created funds for orphan care. The Cherokee Nation, guided by long-standing commitments to common work for social good, assigned nearly $50,000 of annuity wealth in the immediate aftermath of removal to their poorer classes. The Creek Nation, still split into the Lower Town and Upper Town constituencies, preferred a decentralized per capita distribution. They shared annuity wealth with naturalized outsiders, offering $120 of their annual payment to roughly 250 Piankashaws displaced from their Kaskaskia River homelands. Using annuities to subsist immigrants allowed the Creeks to supplement a population devastated by removal. In a tense Indian Territory, there was strength in numbers.[23]

Annuities were also the lifeblood of education systems, which nations rushed to revive after their arrival in the West. Missionary organizations that had for decades operated annuity-funded schools trailed Native nations to Indian Territory. Isaac McCoy founded a Baptist church in the Creek Nation where scholars—especially slaves, who leapt at the opportunity—learned to read and write. Others moved in once nations had resettled. In the Choctaw Nation, Baptists established the Armstrong Academy and Presbyterians the Spencer Academy. But familiar frustrations with missionaries' emphasis on conversion at the expense of secular education endured. "We want a school," Upper Creek *mikos* cautioned one prospective instructor, "but we don't want any preaching." When the missionary began his lessons, there were more "constant & urgent applications" from parents than he could accommodate.[24]

By forcing nations to start from scratch, removal gave them a chance to reconsider and revise previously entrenched systems. Many Native leaders demanded far more control over how their education funds would be spent. In 1841, after years of frustration with Richard Mentor Johnson's avaricious management of the Choctaw Academy, the Choctaw successfully deposed superintendent Thomas Henderson and installed a Choctaw citizen, Peter Pitchlynn, as his replacement. Commissioner of Indian Affairs Thomas Hartley Crawford called Pitchlynn's appointment "an experiment" in "the selection of a native Choctaw, at the insistence of the Nation, in the hope that from a better comprehension of the Indian character, he can judiciously manage the pupils at the Academy."[25] But students still complained under Pitchlynn's custody, and the Choctaws closed the academy within a few years. In its stead, the Choctaws created a system of domestic education that comprised common schools and long-awaited academies for both male *and* female students. A board of trustees composed of the *minko* and an additional trustee from each of the nation's three districts oversaw these annuity-financed schools. In the years to come, Choctaw success in self-determination would inspire other nations to seize control of schools from missionaries and Indian agents.[26]

Federal investment of Indian trust funds had for nearly a decade funneled Native wealth toward settler canals and banks. Native polities now applied the interest toward infrastructure of their own. In 1841, over $126,100 in annuities and trust fund interest went to nations within southern part of Indian Territory alone. Much of this sum was spent on gristmills, cotton gins, and mechanics shops that carried wider economic impact. Choctaws called the town where they received their annuities Iskvlli Kaunti, or "Money Town," an apt term for a pattern of spatial development underway across Indian Territory. When Native leaders had convened at Tahlequah in 1843, little more than a smattering of cabins had greeted them. A year later, the Cherokee capital had burst into a thriving town. Stately brick buildings housing two legislative chambers and a courthouse anchored the central square; handsome two-story houses and bustling stores lined gridded streets; and a spacious hotel was under construction. Among its many local businesses was the *Cherokee Advocate*, a newspaper financed entirely by annuities and published by John Ross's nephew William Potter Ross. Even the burgeoning internationalism that so alarmed federal officials made use of federally administered annuity payments. The Grand Council at Tahlequah had cost the Cherokees an estimated $250 per day, or over $5,000 in total, drawn entirely from their national annuities.[27]

Money became an object of political contention as nations debated how much wealth should be spent for the common good, and how much should be meted out to each citizen as a personal allowance. Even the most infrastructure-minded nations distributed a residuum of annuity wealth as per capita payments. More affluent recipients spent their share on enterprises like saltworks, steamboats, and taverns, or to expand their ranches and plantations. Yet thanks to annuities, "even the common Cherokees have comfortable houses," remarked Indian Superintendent William Armstrong.[28] Policies of distribution varied: one trader criticized the Creek system for excluding women, orphans, and the poor, whose shares were claimed by the town leaders who allocated the money. Chickasaw politicians disagreed on who should inherit the right to benefit from annuities, with some arguing for a matrilineal principle that would reflect their clan organization—and keep national funds from flowing into the hands of non-Chickasaw husbands.[29] Often coupled with censuses, annuity disbursements became moments of boundary drawing between citizens and outsiders. For those who counted as eligible recipients, how those distributions proceeded became a measure of how fair and functional their governments were.

Institution building gave nations more flexibility in the use of their funds, but not all nations were institution builders. Unlike the Cherokees, Chickasaws, and Choctaws, the United Nations of Odawa, Ojibwe, and Potawatomi had not developed republican states outfitted with auditors and treasuries, instead preserving decentralized councils represented by seasoned delegates like Billy Caldwell. Once settled on their reservation near Council Bluffs, in western Iowa Territory, the Odawa, Ojibwe, and Potawatomis requested funds to establish farms, blacksmiths shops, and a gristmill, pleading with Indian affairs superintendent William Clark for "the necessary tools" or else "his children will starve this winter."[30] Even though the 1833 Treaty of Chicago had reserved $150,000 precisely for these kinds of expenditures, Indian affairs officials refused on the premise that the United Nations were slated for removal. Funds would only be spent on their next destination, the Potawatomi reservation on the Osage River, Harris insisted, going so far as to send back oxen and wagons ordered by the well-intentioned Indian agent at Council Bluffs. While the United Nations subsisted on rations, the commissioner invested their entire agricultural fund in Maryland state bonds.[31]

Yet the United Nations nonetheless improvised means of applying annuities toward their economic priorities. In 1840, after years of futile pleading, Caldwell and fellow United Nations representative Joseph La Frambroise hired a local millwright directly, offering as payment for his services a $3,000 draft from the commissioner of Indian affairs, essentially pledging money from their own agricultural improvement fund and daring the commissioner not to honor the agreement. After some haggling, in August 1843, a few months after the Odawa, Ojibwe, and Potawatomi delegation returned from the Grand Council at Tahlequah, the commissioner of Indian affairs begrudgingly paid the millwright $3,000 from the interest raised on the Maryland bonds.[32]

The Office of Indian Affairs would replicate this approach in other cases, withholding annuities to inhibit the development of Native-initiated infrastructure. When the Menominees requested funds to erect a lumber mill in their territories, the office refused, instead reinvesting all the interest earned to date on the Menominees trust fund in federal Treasury notes. Financing a mill, according to the government's logic, would only have appreciated the value of homelands for the Menominees, making it more difficult for the federal government to take them away. Yet Commissioner of Indian Affairs William Medill also justified withholding funds for the opposite reason, predicting that the Menominees would so abuse their mill "that in a few years the lands would be stripped of their timber & thereby become valueless."[33] Medill's accusations were particularly ironic given that the Menominees carefully restricted harvests to protect their forests, resisted pressure to clear-cut for agriculture, and, in the early twentieth century, adapted their conservation techniques for an industrial timber operation that is today recognized as a model for sustainable forestry.[34]

Federal officials wielded their fiduciary discretion to deny Native requests to develop and thereby remain on their territories. They also intruded into the fiscal operations of Native governments. When the

Cherokee National Council tackled a deficit by reassigning surplus interest earned on its own education and orphan trust funds, the commissioner of Indian affairs suspended the payment of interest on both trusts until Ross supplied a report detailing how the Cherokees had spent their own annuities.[35] All told, nations like the Cherokee and the Odawa, Ojibwe, and Potawatomis accomplished economic development only in spite of their trustees.

Annuities could offer nations sustenance, even prosperity, or they could be used to impose crippling constraints. Often they did both at the same time. Federal officials wielded annuities as both carrot and stick, but no purpose became more relevant after removal than their ability to discourage Native peoples' armed resistance. Gazing out on a horizon riddled with borderland disputes, and watching Indigenous diplomats converge in a newly pressurized interior, federal officials relied on annuities to maintain goodwill. But these same officials had made the federal government's ability to deliver annuities contingent on the health of the bond market. Investing trust fund money in state bonds had tangled together two realms of tense international relations. On the one hand, a circle of dispossessed Native nations and the federal government they could no longer trust; on the other, a group of deeply indebted states tied to their powerful creditors. A financial crisis would drag down the whole web of debts that bound these groups together.

States' economic difficulties began in the summer of 1839, with the failure of one of the nation's largest investors in state bonds, the Morris Canal and Banking Company. The crisis that followed reverberated across the Atlantic. British financiers had invested eagerly in the Morris Bank and other like securities, purchasing, by most estimates, over half of the bonds American states issued during their borrowing boom. State bonds commanded confidence overseas because of a precedent for punctual specie payments on federal debt by the First and Second Banks of the United States. London's bankers, chastened by losses backing Latin American revolutions, had also appreciated that states' bonds supported theoretically productive and presumably uneventful infrastructural ventures. Most important, rates on American state bonds ran at an impressive 5 or 6 percent (compared to 3 percent for British consuls), and yields were often augmented by British agents' hardline negotiation. The resulting international capital transfer was significant enough to offset, for several years, the United States' chronic trade imbalance with Britain. But by mid-June 1839, when packet ships brought the dismal news of the Morris Bank failure to London, creditors' romance with American state securities started to sour.[36]

As the Morris Bank failure dragged down the international bond market, enraged creditors began pressuring Congress to step in and protect their investments. In a widely reprinted circular, the House of Baring, a prominent British merchant bank that had invested heavily in American state securities (and slave-produced cotton), called for the federal government to assume states' debts. For states' improvement schemes to survive and the crisis to abate, the House of Baring argued, "a more comprehensive guarantee than that of individual states will be required."[37] Some Whig politicians eager to salvage both state and federal creditworthiness supported the Baring proposal, including Massachusetts Senator Daniel Webster, who had—reasonably enough—criticized Indian trust investments under Jackson as evidence of Democratic cronyism.[38] Despite Webster's best efforts, however, he failed to convince Congress to step in and bail out failing states. In January 1840, a Senate select committee asserted that federal assumption of states' debts would violate the Constitution by effecting a disbursement of general funds for "local purposes," echoing the very arguments against concerted federal aid for internal improvements that had led state governments to borrow so heavily in the first place. States had risen to the occasion as economic sovereigns; so, too, would they fall on their own. And fall they did. In January 1841, both Florida Territory and Indiana defaulted on their debts. By July of that year, Arkansas, Michigan, and Mississippi had joined their ranks. What was once a panic—a crisis of confidence in states' abilities to meet obligations—had matured into a full-fledged financial collapse.[39]

States' bond crisis devastated the United States' standing among European creditors at a moment of intensified geopolitical uncertainty. Diplomatic relations between the United States and Britain strained as states' credit sunk, in part because of a political upheaval led by Canadian settlers. In December 1837 a group of rebels opposed to Upper Canada's oligarchic government drew a stalemate with British troops at Navy Island near Fort Niagara. When a privately commissioned American steamboat, the *Caroline*, delivered multiple rounds of supplies to the besieged rebels, Upper Canada's militias attacked the ship, killing one American, before setting the flaming vessel adrift over the falls. In response, Secretary of War Joel Poinsett called out the militia to northern New York and Vermont. For the next half decade, conflicts simmered across the

US-Canadian border. Settlers in the Aroostook Valley, a contested strip of the Maine–New Brunswick frontier, grew close to armed conflict in February 1839. The subsequent arrest of a Canadian sheriff in Buffalo, New York, on charges related to the *Caroline* attack pushed Britain and the United States to the brink of war. In 1840, residents of Michigan and Wisconsin stood by helplessly as British troops buttressed installations along the Detroit River and enlisted Ho-Chunk and Potawatomi warriors into their ranks. With the military still focused on extirpating Seminoles, one correspondent moaned that the Canadian border reinforcements went "unopposed by a single work or gun" from the American side.[40]

Anglo-American tensions compounded states' fiscal crisis, making it nearly impossible for the United States to find British backers for their bonds. One American emissary tasked with gauging interest among London financiers was instructed by Baron Rothschild to "tell your government, that you have seen the man who is at the head of the finances of Europe and that he has told you—that they cannot borrow a dollar, not a dollar."[41] And, sure enough, when agents arrived in London to market an 1842 Treasury loan issuance, not a single banker would touch the securities. Soon after, news reached London that the once highly esteemed Pennsylvania and Maryland had joined the four other states (and Florida Territory) in default, driving home the magnitude of the sovereign debt crisis. Embittered British creditors punished American states collectively, neglecting to discriminate between the solvent and insolvent. Even Canadian debentures suffered devaluation merely by geographic proximity to the United States. Brokers at London's Stock Exchange began referring to state bonds as "American insecurities," a phrase that inadvertently captured not only the financial crisis but its geopolitical consequences for the United States' settler empire.[42]

Turning from the Atlantic and the northern border to the continent's southwest interior, the United States found another set of challenges. Texas had become a serious liability. When Mirabeau Lamar ascended to the presidency of the Republic of Texas in 1838, he scuttled his predecessor Samuel Houston's peacekeeping measures and embraced instead an exterminationist Indian policy. Lamar launched a war against immigrant Kickapoos and their Biloxi, Caddo, Cherokee, and Coushatta allies, sent Texas Rangers to assault Comanche camps, and, the following year, unleashed another round of attacks on the Red River Valley. Suspecting Indigenous support for Mexico, which refused to recognize Texas's independence, the republic undertook a programmatic genocide within its claimed borders. Caddos were forced to abandon their homelands, and Lenapes,

Shawnees, and Western Cherokees fled to Indian Territory. Albeit formally independent, Texas expected US federal and state governments to back up its belligerent Indian policy and abet its chosen methods.[43]

Natives terrorized by Texas moved north at a highwater mark of removals, colliding with thousands of eastern Natives arriving on their reservations. Stripped of land and subsistence, refugees from Texas scavenged and stole from resettled Indian Territory nations, whose annuities and easier access to settler goods made them wealthy by comparison.[44] When the Choctaw National Council passed a law expelling intruders from their territory, an Indian agent warned of another Seminole War, one that "will not soon be ended" and that "might be the means of creating a War in the whole West."[45] Creeks volunteered to host the refugees, averting a crisis— but only temporarily. Mexico soon invaded Texas, and officials in both Texas and the United States feared that Indigenous polities who nursed grudges against Anglo-Americans would offer reinforcements. There was little evidence that Texans' provocations had actually driven Native people to join Mexico's war, yet the Office of Indian Affairs nonetheless prohibited the sale of gunpowder or ammunition to Natives in the Southwestern Plains.[46] Disarmament was the Indian agent's best hope for containment given that Congress, fed up with the spiraling costs of the Second Seminole War, had just slashed the military budget to a quarter of its allowance from the year before.[47]

Mirroring attacks on Indian Territory's southern border were Dakota raids sweeping down from the north. The United Nations' Council Bluffs reservation, situated just east of the Missouri River, sat squarely on hunting grounds belonging to the Santee and Yankton Dakotas. "The Sioux tell us that this is their Land, that you never bought it," a group of headmen and *ogimaag* from the United Nations wrote in a petition for military fortification to President John Tyler. "When you sent us to this Country," the petitioners wrote, "you promised us that we should be protected from the Wild Indians—but you do not send us that protection."[48] Exposure to nations defending their territories by force violated the terms of trusteeship as enshrined in the treaties the Odawa, Ojibwe, and Potawatomis had signed.

These prismatic conflicts forming in and around Indian Territory bore costs, both financial and military, that strained the United States' colonial project. Indian affairs officials attempted to coordinate peace between Native parties to minimize expenses and cement their governance of Indian Territory. But Native nations had their own aims, and they initiated a peacemaking process designed to achieve them. One of the most important diplomatic breakthroughs took place far west of Indian Territory. In 1840, at a council on the Arkansas River, Comanches and their Kiowa allies ended long-standing hostilities with Arapahoes, Cheyennes, and Naishan Apaches. What came to be called the Great Peace freed Comanche war parties to raid far deeper south than before. From Mexican ranches Comanches procured tens of thousands of horses and mules—a form of property many removed Natives had been forced to leave behind or that they had lost to disease, famine, or theft on their journeys to Indian Territory. A complementary trade emerged. Comanches could supply the herds Indian Territory nations needed, but Indian Territory nations had something that Comanches needed to plunder this livestock in the first place: weapons. Because they had signed treaties and received annuities, Indian Territory nations had access to lead, powder, and flintlock rifles, which were accurate for three times the distance of the muskets then in use on the Southern Plains. Their annuities also paid for on-reservation blacksmiths, who could repair guns worn out from heavy use.[49]

Gradually and unevenly, nations made enemies by the upheavals of Indian removal became commercial partners. A lively trade in bison robes, military goods, human captives, and ungulates coalesced, to the benefit of Indigenous peoples and at the expense of Mexico and, to a lesser extent, Texas, which continued to suffer occasional raids from Comanches and Kiowas. Autonomous groups of Kickapoos, Lenapes, and Shawnees living on the Canadian River in western Indian Territory acted as intermediaries, shuttling between Comanche camps on the Southern Plains and the plantations and towns of eastern Indian Territory. They carried goods and weapons west and returned east with packs of horses, mules, and slaves in tow. Commerce's pacific effect had its limits: Osages continued to raid Creek towns, as did autonomous groups of Natives living on the Canadian and Red Rivers. On more than one occasion, Chickasaw planters were forced to buy back their own escaped slaves, who had been harbored by the Lenapes and Shawnees, traded to the Comanches, and then marched back to Indian Territory for sale.[50] But trade fed by annuities created the incentive for cooperation among vastly different Indigenous peoples. At the very least, it supplied a rationale to gather in multinational councils.

Councils that assembled seemingly hostile polities to discuss matters beyond Indian agents' understanding raised alarm. Just as threatening to the United States as a war between Native nations was the prospect of peace brokered among them without federal agents' influence. One council hosted by the Cherokee Nation in 1838 convened Creek, Lenape,

Quapaw, Sauk, Seminole, and Shawnee delegates. An American military official stationed at St. Louis panicked, believing that a potential twenty thousand warriors planned an attack on Texas. In response, the military deployed ten thousand troops from nearby installations to Cherokee country, called on Arkansas and Tennessee to deploy volunteer militias to their borders, and accelerated the erection of forts along the Arkansas–Indian Territory border.[51] It was a false alarm—the council addressed trade and alliance, not war against the United States—but Indian affairs officials' fears were far from allayed.

Indian agents tried and failed to quash councils that they did not themselves initiate. As tensions between Mexico and Texas flared, Superintendent Armstrong caught wind of a council hosted by the Creeks. He eventually learned that it would address collective agreements around stolen property, but he still worried that with so much "combustible matter" on the frontier it could turn into "a great hostile meeting."[52] Contrary to Armstrong's expectations, the summit marked the first steps toward forging an international law of peaceable conflict resolution and extradition to settle disagreements produced by crowded hunting grounds, overlapping territories, and retaliatory raids. Despite their intent, such council proceedings continued to make federal officials nervous. Commissioner of Indian Affairs T. Hartley Crawford ordered Indian agents stationed in the Territory to prohibit multinational councils, urging that "too much caution and prudence cannot be exercised" in preventing "such conventions or large meetings."[53] The very next year, in defiance of Crawford's orders, Cherokee runners fanned out to thirty-six Indigenous polities with invitations to join the Grand Council at Tahlequah.

The conflicts raging at edges of the United States' continental empire escalated at precisely the moment that states slipped into insolvency, disabling the very instrument—annuities—that the federal government had long deployed to defuse tensions with Indigenous peoples. In the fall of 1841, as the Second Seminole War settled into a stalemate, unredeemed bond coupons piled up on the commissioner of Indian affairs' desk. States had begun to default on their interest payments, dwindling the dividends that flowed into the Indian trust funds and threatening the annuities that were paid from this revenue. By July 1842, eight states (and one territory) owed roughly $200,000 to nearly two dozen Indian trust funds, with little hope on the horizon that interest payments would resume.[54]

The prospect of interrupted annuity payments was far from abstract to federal officials: The Office of Indian Affairs had faced precisely the same conundrum five years before, during the height of the Panic of 1837. Banks' general suspension of specie payments in March of that year had occasioned the first large-scale interruption of the federal fiduciary system. Faced with a shortage of specie, then–Commissioner of Indian Affairs Carey A. Harris decided to cut the specie delivered to each polity in half and offer the remaining value owed in goods. Native leaders protested, demanding full payment in cash. In Michigan, rumors swirled of a frontier murder provoked by delays in an annuity payment to the Grand River Odawas. Harris himself feared that "Indian war . . . is probable if not inevitable" if peoples awaiting removal in Indiana did not soon receive their annuities.[55] When banks returned to specie payments in 1838, so too did the Office of Indian Affairs revert to fulfilling its obligations in hard money.[56] States' fiscal collapse five years later threatened to restage the annuity disruptions of 1837 at a moment when the United States faced military insecurity across multiple theaters.

Among the first polities to feel the impact of state defaults were the Choctaws. In 1837 the Chickasaws had purchased their western territory from the Choctaws in part by transferring $500,000 in Alabama state bonds, held thereafter in trust on behalf of the Choctaw by the Office of Indian Affairs. Alabama, which narrowly avoided a general default by resuming direct taxation (abolished in 1836 at the State Bank's peak profitability), nonetheless stopped interest payments on its debts to the Indian trust funds—presumably a creditor of lesser consequence in the state's estimation. By late 1842, Alabama owed $12,500 in interest to the newly created Choctaw national trust fund. Hearing of states' delinquencies that year, Choctaws refused to accept anything less than the entire sum owed them by the federal government. When delays stretched into June 1842, their agent reported "considerable feeling" was "beginning to show on the part of a number of the Choctaws."[57] The Chickasaws, meanwhile, castigated the Office of Indian Affairs for keeping them waiting "year after year with great anxiety for an annuity" until they had become "all but beggars."[58] Seneca and Shawnee groups displaced from the Maumee River to Indian Territory also awaited their annuities— smaller payments of between $300 and $1,800 per year—after Maryland and Missouri's defaults. Looking north, Odawas and Ojibwes in Michigan were owed interest by that very state, and by Pennsylvania too. For the second time in recent memory, annuities had been delayed or outright denied amid a financial crisis.[59]

Assessing the accumulating damage, Commissioner Crawford first retraced his predecessor's steps. He sent out a memo to agents ordering them to offer annuities paid partially in government-purchased goods. As expected, however, nearly every nation insisted on full delivery in specie. Many protested the specific choice of annuity goods, noting that they failed to include liquor, ammunition, and weapons, items desired for use in exchange with other Native peoples. Heeding the lessons of 1837, Crawford realized that resentments toward goods could tip easily into organized retribution; only by paying annuities immediately and in cash could such a scenario be definitively avoided. He sent an urgent request for Congress to cover the delinquent payments that July. George Evans, the chair of the Senate Finance Committee, responded with irritation. With the nation in the midst of a depression, a Whig-controlled Congress was preoccupied with trimming the excesses of the Jacksonian patronage machine, of which the Office of Indian Affairs had formed one of the squeakiest components. In a quick note, Evans asked whether "the appropriation" to cover delinquent states' interest payments was "important at this time, and if so, for what particular reasons? Is it wanted for immediate use? Will the want of it be likely to be attended with inconvenience to the Indian tribes?"[60] Alarmed at Evans's naivete, Secretary of War John C. Spencer responded by outlining the threat to the United States. "If we shall fail to pay to various Indian tribes their cash annuities," Spencer warned, echoing Harris's assessment five years earlier, "an Indian War, and probably a general one, will be the consequence."[61] A month later, Congress authorized expenditures to cover the overdue interest owed by states to the Indian trust funds.[62]

No single Native nation registered as a significant enough military threat to merit a bailout of ailing states: The fear was of a confederation in the tradition of multinational alliances forged in the Ohio River Valley in the 1790s and by Tecumseh in the 1810s. The Chickasaws' experience of the crisis was an exception that proved the rule. Since the Chickasaw fund was managed by the Treasury Department instead of the Department of War, their annuities were not included in the legislation that replaced states' overdue bond interest. Fraudulent contracts, waste, and outright theft over the course of their removal had drained the Chickasaw fund, but a particularly acute exposure to states' failures kept interest from replenishing it. Roughly two-thirds of the bonds held in the Chickasaw trust had been issued by states that defaulted during the crisis. By 1845 Arkansas, Illinois, Indiana, and Maryland owed more than $37,700 to the Chickasaw fund, with another payment of more than $15,000 due the following

January.[63] Despite receiving the largest package of compensation in absolute terms of any nation removed during the 1830s, it would take a decade after their removal treaty for the Chickasaws to receive a single annuity payment, thanks to their fiduciary's questionable performance.

With their location at the crux of Plains raiding circuits, the Chickasaws resettlement to Indian Territory had been especially difficult. Most Chickasaw families were too fearful to claim land in their new territory, which sat closest to groups on the Red River and Southern Plains. Instead, Chickasaws interspersed themselves among the Choctaw towns and plantations to the east. Prevented from farming and buffeted by raids, Chickasaws relied disproportionately on trade, and many became heavily indebted to local dealers for their basic subsistence. Most vulnerable were the so-called incompetent Chickasaws, who had no cash at all, since they had not been permitted to sell their own reservations. They became dependent on traders like Felix Lewis and Daniel Saffarans, who had speculated in Choctaw land, secured contracts to conduct Chickasaw removals, and then sold hundreds of thousands of dollars of goods to "incompetent" Chickasaws on credit, at inflated prices and under questionable terms.[64]

Conditions improved in 1842, when the federal government erected Fort Washita in response to Native demands for protection against Plains Natives. The establishment of the fort satisfied the Cherokees, Choctaws, and Creeks, who primarily saw the fort as a commercial opportunity. But the Chickasaws, who had earnestly hoped for federal protection, found Fort Washita's impact disappointing. Raids continued and discouraged most Chickasaws from moving west onto their own territory. An annuity could have bought measures of defense, but none came. Chickasaws still gathered in hope when the disbursement agent arrived each fall, but only the Choctaws had an annuity to collect. Impoverished even as land, state bonds, and federal money changed hands in great quantities all around them, the Chickasaws felt, according to one witness, "as if they had purchased themselves into degradation."[65]

❦

The state bond crisis also forced the federal government to reckon with the inherent risks of fiduciary investment. Once considered a safe haven, state bonds became the object of striking new regulations. Midway through the collapse, with five states in default, Congress had prohibited officials from investing federally managed trusts in state bonds. Indian trust funds, along with the much smaller Smithsonian and Navy pension trust funds, could now be invested in federally issued securities alone. As some lawmakers pointed out, no such securities existed at the moment: the Jackson administration had retired federal bonds when it eliminated the national debt in 1835. Only short-term Treasury notes came close enough to serving the purpose. First passed in the House of Representatives, the bill met vehement objections from senators concerned that federal disinvestment in states would cast doubt on their creditworthiness at the most critical juncture in their history as borrowers. Missouri Democratic Senator Louis Linn protested the bill as "the most outrageous, treacherous, and fatal stab to the State stock credit system, that ever was attempted by any representatives of the people or the States."[66] But Whigs in the Senate argued that federal investment in state debts simply entailed too much risk, since states could not be compelled to repay, even to a federal government acting as trustee for Native nations. The Whigs prevailed, and the law took effect in September 1841.[67] Earlier in the crisis, Congress had ignored foreign creditors' pleas for assumption. Now, it acted to honor trusteeship, even at the cost of downgrading the creditworthiness of its constituent political units. It did so not from a sense of decency, but because federal officials had repeatedly warned of multinational Indigenous warfare as a costlier alternative.

States' debt-financed infrastructural boom—and bust—altered their political economies as much as it irreversibly remade states' physical and demographic terrains. Florida, Louisiana, and Mississippi repudiated their debts altogether, a decision that European financiers would not soon forget and that would haunt a future Confederate Congress desperate to sell bonds overseas. Having once led the way in issuing bonds to carve its canal, New York State again set a fiscal precedent after the crisis by passing legislation that abruptly halted all construction on public works and implemented a property tax earmarked specifically for its improvement debts. Indiana went even further by abolishing the kinds of special charters, secured only by the politically connected, that had incorporated banks and canal companies. An era of general incorporation began in which states stepped back from directing infrastructural development and acted instead as regulators of the proliferating enterprises that forged ahead on development frontiers. Across the subsequent decade, lawmakers eager to protect these reforms from successive legislatures enshrined restrictions on borrowing and special charters within revised state constitutions.[68] At a time when states' proclaimed rights grounded legal arguments for slavery and Indian removal, legislatures largely ceded their mantles as creditworthy agents of economic development.

A number of states carried out these fiscal reforms at the behest of foreign creditors. After abandoning their campaign for federal assumption, British financial houses began intimidating states directly. Midwestern states like Indiana endured the humiliation of creditors orchestrating legislation to refinance their debt and, ultimately, seizing the very assets that the state had fallen so deeply in debt to construct. In July 1847, a group of foreign creditors led by the House of Baring formally accepted title to the Wabash and Erie Canal from Indiana Governor James Whitcomb, marking the transfer to European creditors of the nation's longest artificial waterway. In the South, meanwhile, British creditors forced state banks to accept their own worthless state bonds as payment for cotton.[69]

Only the contingency of revolution would reopen the flow of British capital toward US states' sovereign debts. With the outbreak of the Mexican-American War in 1846, the federal government began borrowing again in earnest, initially by soliciting domestic capital. This included the Indian trust funds, of which more than $83,500 would be invested in an 1847 Treasury loan issued to finance the conflict. But by 1848 the domestic market had been more or less tapped, casting doubt on the federal government's capacity to make good on promised salary increases for the military and to carry out obligations to Mexico incurred in the Treaty of Guadalupe Hidalgo. Reluctantly, in March 1848 Treasury Secretary Robert J. Walker authorized the marketing in London of the latest loan, a $16 million issuance of 6 percent Treasury bonds. The securities entered a financial market profoundly destabilized by a chain of revolutions that had erupted across the European continent in the spring of 1848. In an era when bond markets were particularly sensitive to political strife, Europe's newfound radicalism cast erstwhile unfavorable American securities as comparatively stable. The Rothschilds became the most significant investors to return to investing in US states, brokering their bonds to French, German, and British clients.[70]

War against Mexico marked a watershed in expansionists' decadeslong dream of stretching the United States' continental empire to the Pacific Ocean. California, with its valuable San Francisco Bay harbor, had been the target for President James K. Polk, who steered the nation toward an offensive war in its pursuit. When stores of gold were discovered in the territory shortly after its formal transfer from Mexico to the United States, California became a magnet for a global immigration rush, transformed the Isthmus of Panama into a nexus of American trade, and inspired Congress to begin scouting routes for a transcontinental railroad.[71] The United States' continental ambitions stretched farther than ever before, setting the stage for a new front of conflict with Indigenous powers on the Great Plains and beyond.

The Cherokee's Grand Council at Tahlequah concluded with modest success. Only the Cherokee, Creek, and Osage delegations signed a collectively drafted compact that outlined policies for extradition and reciprocal naturalization. Most significantly, the council established a coordinated policy to resist colonial dispossession: The agreement prohibited any future territorial cessions to the United States unless approved by all signatories—a prohibition that would hold until the Civil War two decades later. The Tahlequah compact also established the groundwork for shared governance of the overlapping hunting grounds and inter-Native trade corridors formed through the rocky creation of Indian Territory. Progress was not steady. In 1845, the Comanches nearly killed Creek messengers inviting them to a council in retaliation for an earlier attack by the Pawnees. But Indian Territory leaders managed in this case to broker peace, sending Caddos with a peace offering of tobacco to the Comanches, and dispatching Osages to do the same with the Pawnees.[72]

These painstaking efforts paid off. By 1847, the Great Salt Plains served as a neutral trading zone between Plains and Indian Territory peoples. Comanches hosted an enormous trade fair on the site, offering bison, mules, horses, and human captives. The Osages brought their entire year's annuity to the fair, carting $24,000 in guns, gunpowder, lead, blankets, and other goods to the Great Salt Plains and returning home with fifteen hundred horses.[73] Indian Territory leaders had managed to steady a turbulent region by using annuities to establish trade relationships with hostile neighbors.

Annuities threaded together a Native world whose geography the federal government had in some sense created but that carried consequences that far exceeded its control. Violence between Indigenous powers and the even more daunting prospect of an alliance of once enemy nations against the United States compelled the government to continue paying annuities when states defaulted. Removal, presented as an act of charity to an ailing race, instead laid bare how even weakened Native peoples could recover power. In an exquisite irony, annuities paid out to avoid a multinational offensive funded a traffic in weapons and materiel that kept Native militaries stocked for war. Most Indian agents on the ground knew annuities fed this trade. But they were far more afraid of a world without them.[74]

# CHAPTER SIX

# Unsettled Claims

IN 1844, the Chickasaw Nation submitted a petition to Congress protesting the government's failure to fulfill its duties as their fiduciary. The nation complained of "large sums . . . drawn from the Chickasaw fund" without their authority and in violation of the "letter and spirit" of their treaties with the United States. Bonds in which their trust fund had been invested were "not safe and valuable," as the treaty had stipulated, but "greatly depreciated below par value" and had earned no interest "for some time past." The United States was doubly liable, the petition argued, given that officials had loaned out Chickasaw funds "not to third persons, but to a portion of themselves"—to state governments.[1] To seek remedy for these abuses the Chickasaws could have pled for a council with Indian agents, or sent a delegation to visit heads of the administration in Washington, methods that had waned in efficacy over the course of their lifetimes.[2] Instead, the Chickasaws adopted an approach increasingly common among their peers: They hired an attorney to assist them in bringing a claim to Congress for monetary restitution against their trustee, the federal government.

Two years later, a pair of Indian traders pressed a claim of their own, seeking resolution not in the halls of Congress but at the council fire where a treaty negotiation was to take place. George and William Ewing, brothers who had sold goods to the United Nations of Odawa, Ojibwe, and Potawatomi on credit for years, presented themselves at a gathering where the assembled leaders of the United Nations agreed to negotiate another removal treaty. This latest treaty would see the nations displaced farther south, to a new reservation on the Kansas River, where they would be consolidated with Potawatomis removed from Indiana years before. In the weeks before the negotiations began, the Ewings campaigned for the treaty to devote a $100,000 fund to repaying outstanding trade debts with the aim of capturing as much of this fund as possible for themselves. George had even taken the opportunity to specify the quality of specie currency that creditor-traders like himself should receive as payment, insisting that the United Nations "should have *Dollars*—Eagle, half dollars, and American quarters—But no 5 Franks—no Dutch Thalers—nor no ten cent pieces."[3] The treaty commissioners ignored the most presumptuous of Ewing's wishes, but the brothers' debt claims succeeded. As part of their compensation for ceding their Council Bluffs lands, the Odawa, Ojibwe, and Potawatomis received a $50,000 fund earmarked for the expenses of relocation, reimbursing improvements, and—inauspiciously—for clearing debts allegedly owed to Indian traders.[4] The Ewings ultimately collected $40,277 of this fund, leaving hardly anything to compensate families forced to leave behind farms and other improvements.[5]

In the decades after removal, the federal government contended with a rapid proliferation of financial claims against related to Indian affairs. Claims ran the gamut, but two distinct classes emerged: those brought forward by Native nations (and their legal agents) to hold their federal trustee accountable for financial losses, and those brought forward by Indian traders for debts allegedly owed them by Native peoples. The Chickasaws and the Ewings were very different kinds of stakeholders in funds managed by the government for Native peoples. Yet their bids for indemnification shared root causes in removal's chaotic and sweeping conversion of Native land into money and converged on a single addressee: the federal government in its role as a fiduciary to Native nations.

Claims mushroomed after removal because there was, quite simply, more money to be claimed. Indigenous peoples had borrowed from traders since the dawn of the North American fur trade. But by the 1830s, outfits in former fur-trading regions like the Lower Great Lakes or along the Missouri and Wabash River valleys increasingly focused their ventures on capturing the greatest share of Native annuities rather than on profits from a global trade in Native-trapped pelts. When alleged debts to traders exceeded the available amount, or if nations refused certain debts as illegitimate, traders submitted claims to the federal government—a recourse they pursued more often and with more ambition in the wake of removals. Trade debts clung to nations forced west, resurfacing in the form of claims submitted to treaty councils, the Office of Indian Affairs, and Congress.[6]

As treaties exchanged vast acres of land for annuities and trusts, money became an object of colonial struggle and, claimants hoped, a means of redress. Countless grievances attended removals during the administration of President Andrew Jackson, many of which came at a literal cost to Native peoples. Rushed mass expulsions converted homelands into haphazardly marketed public land and poured considerable sums of cash into politically destabilized Native societies. A profusion of frauds stripped Native people of property, starved them of rations, and aggravated the immiseration of forced relocations. Relief was elusive, especially since the entity to which Native people were expected to appeal, the Office of Indian Affairs, was usually the source of their grievances. Unenfranchised and limited in their leverage, Native people had one last resort: petitioning Congress directly. To navigate the bureaucratic intricacies, Indigenous leaders partnered with claims agents, proto-lobbyists who specialized in expediting bids for compensation in Congress in exchange for a hefty cut of the anticipated award. Indian claims became a business for agents and their bankers, to the detriment of Native peoples already in economic distress. That non-Native people could profit from their bids for justice compromised the process but made it no less necessary. In an era of waning diplomacy, claims were one of the few means by which Indigenous peoples could contest abuses, hold their trustees accountable, and recover even a fraction of what they were owed.[7]

From the United States' vantage, Indian claims were a fiscal problem and an administrative headache. They overwhelmed Congress, stoking resentment toward the treaty system and prompting intrusive regulations of Indigenous economies. To officials mired in tedious evaluations, claims indicated that Native nations possessed excessive wealth and far too much latitude over how to dispose of it. Cash annuities certainly attracted unsavory outsiders who, through a variety of contracts, sought to tap funds held in trust with the federal government. Yet rather than hold the traders and attorneys who exploited Native wealth culpable, federal reforms set out to smother the relative autonomy Native people possessed over their internal affairs. Native and trader claims were distinct, but to the federal government they both stemmed from the same predicament: Treaties signed long ago to minimize the costs of conquest were not buried but instead resurrected, time and again, to impose fiscal burdens on the present.

❦

Large influxes of annuities in specie or reputable banknotes changed the tenor of Native nations' relationships with their commercial partners.

Credit had facilitated the inherently seasonal business of American furs since the seventeenth century. Traders lent goods, arms, ammunition, and subsistence to Native hunters in the fall. Debts were cleared in the spring, after hunters had harvested pelts and brought them to the post for trading. In the late 1820s and 1830s, however, Native peoples' acquisition of sizable annuity payments monetized these debts: Traders demanded repayment in cash rather than furs, a trend reinforced by a slackening demand for beaver and other skins. Fur traders became Indian traders. The more forthright among them called their business the "money trade."[8]

When borrowing, Indigenous people adhered to an ethic distinct from settler economic traditions. While Native customers generally incurred debts in good faith and saw repayment as a matter of honor, many considered debts nullified if owed for longer than a year. For profit-dependent traders accustomed to prompt repayment, Native peoples' frequent defaults and high debt loads were a risk to be factored into the price of their wares. Yet risk was also a pretext to gouge, and traders openly charged exorbitant markups of 100 percent or more. One Office of Indian Affairs correspondent estimated that a pound of gunpowder worth twenty cents had cost the Sauk and Meskwakis four dollars. Records from an 1832 treaty show that traders charged Potawatomis five dollars for fur-trimmed hats bought at $1.60 apiece in New York City. Claims further padded profit margins. Traders charged high prices under the guise of offsetting the risk of Native defaults, only to submit claims to cover defaults when they occurred.[9]

Traders operated in a favorable business environment. Many Indian agents cheerfully colluded with traders, favoring certain claims in exchange for a kickback in cash or merchandise. More to the point, many Indian agents *were* traders. William Clark, the first superintendent of Indian affairs in St. Louis, was an associate of Manuel Lisa's Missouri Fur Company, as was his successor, Joshua Pilcher. When they were not plucked directly from merchant ranks, Indian agents often owed their appointments to the influence of fur-trade-boosting politicians. Missouri Senator Thomas Hart Benton, who had advocated for the end of the government-run factory trading system on behalf of the American Fur Company, regularly recommended sympathetic agents to the Office of Indian Affairs. Regardless of their backgrounds, agents were lone figures attempting to govern communities in which traders had spun a dense web of alliances. For generations, traders had gained access to choice pelts and recruited laborers to process them by marrying Native women from powerful clans. Families of mixed ancestry produced via trading marriages became a powerful caste in states like Michigan and Indiana, where the Indian trade predominated and where "mixed-bloods" enjoyed a privileged legal status denied their "full-blood" counterparts.[10]

Even relatively honest Indian agents struggled to resist the sway of traders in their midst. When agent Joseph M. Street attempted to distribute a specie annuity to the Sauk and Meskwakis in 1837, more than a hundred traders crowded into the council house to jockey for their share. Street managed to expel the men and bring the Sauk and Meskwakis inside, but the traders lurked around the hewn-log council house, pulled out strips of insulation, and peered in as Street doled out coin to the families gathered. By the day's end, traders had collected over $12,000 in specie. One agent assigned to the Cherokees begged for an iron chest to protect the cartons of specie he used to settle claims, complaining of a country "filled with a white population from almost every state in the Union, who have sought here a refuge from the laws of the states, and in whose honesty and virtue, t'would be imprudent to place much confidence."[11]

Indian agents occasionally criticized traders' extravagant charges for merchandise, inflated debt claims, and demands for repayment in cash annuities. Some recommended price controls and fixed tariffs on goods imported from Eastern cities and sold at Western outposts, while others espoused a return to the factory system that had prevailed until 1824, in which federal agents sold merchandise to Native peoples directly. Despite perennial calls for reform, however, federal facilitating of debt repayments continued throughout the 1830s and early 1840s because the practice could be instrumentalized by officials working to pry Native people from their land. Under the presidency of Thomas Jefferson, the War Department had deliberately encouraged Native people to take on considerable commercial debts, only to demand that they repay those debts in the form of land cessions. Thirty years later, when federal treaty negotiators intent on territorial acquisitions strode into councils, they too promised to assume Native debts. Conveniently, this financial leverage also brought around traders to supporting a policy—removal—that many had resisted for fear of losing their captive market.[12]

Funds designated for trader-creditors became a trope in the canon of treaties that advanced Jacksonian removal. Observing an 1836 treaty negotiation with the Odawas of the Grand River, in southwest Michigan, Baptist missionary Isaac McCoy described the "many hangers-on" who saw treaties "as times when large sums of money could be obtained under the title of *claims*, or something else."[13] By that time, treaty councils had functioned as ad hoc debt clearinghouses for more than a decade. Starting

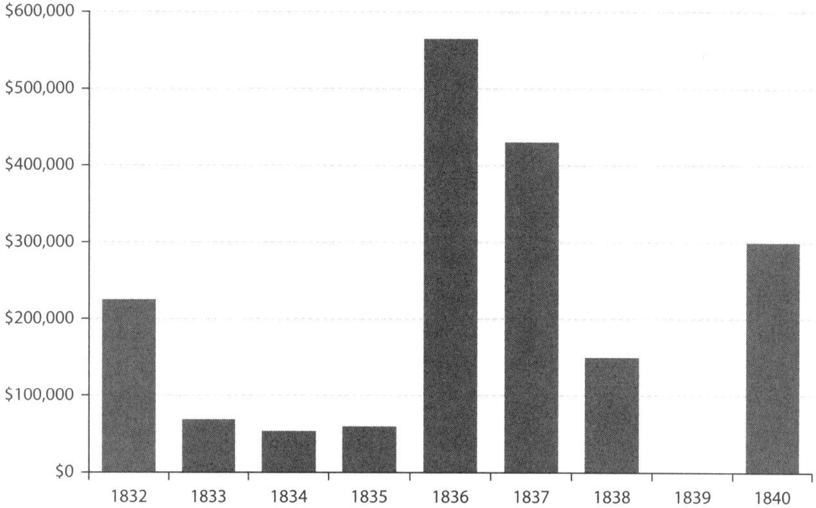

Total trader debt claims included in treaties, by year, 1832–1840. *Source:* Compiled from Charles J. Kappler, *Indian Affairs: Laws and Treaties*, Vol. 2 (GPO, 1903).

in 1825, explicit provisions for the repayment of traders' debts appeared in an increasing number of treaties, particularly those signed with nations in the Lower Great Lakes and Missouri River regions where the fur trade had once thrived. Funds for debts created by treaties ranged in size from a few hundred to hundreds of thousands of dollars. Debt claims exploded after the passage of the 1830 Indian Removal Act. In 1829, just over $35,133 had been reserved in treaties for traders' debts. In 1836, the year McCoy witnessed traders operating on the Odawa firsthand, treaties set aside a staggering $549,858 for traders' debts. By comparison, in the same year, Congress appropriated $495,400 to subsist every soldier in the US Army.[14]

Soaring debt claim totals in 1836 and 1837 spurred a backlash in Congress against including provisions for traders' debts in treaties, resulting in a sharp decline in allowances. Rebuffed traders could simply change venues, however, and appeal to the commissioner of Indian affairs. To meet growing demand, the Office of Indian Affairs assigned a clerk to do nothing more than process claims. Claims were either dismissed upon review or, if determined fair and legitimate, referred to the Treasury Department's second auditor for payment. If rejected, especially persistent traders could directly petition Congress. One way or another, traders foisted their claims on the federal government in its capacity as a trustee. As a result, by 1842 Congress was spending more than $2 million per year on Native peoples' alleged debts.[15]

George and William Ewing were among the traders most successful at lodging debt claims of this sort. The Ewings had begun their career trading furs along the Wabash River corridor. By the 1830s, they commanded a large trading empire, importing dry goods from merchants in New York for resale to Native customers across the Midwest. In addition to the Odawa, Ojibwe, and Potawatomis, the Ewings had close relationships with groups of Sauk and Meskwakis, Miamis, and Wabash River Potawatomis. They sold goods on credit to all and received specie in turn. Ewings dominated the trade but faced fierce competition nonetheless. On at least one occasion, the brothers brought armed guards to cash in on their debt claims at a treaty negotiation.[16]

The Ewings reinvested their earnings from the annuity trade in an array of enterprises that, fittingly enough, hinged on Native dispossession. William purchased six thousand acres of land along the projected routes of the Wabash and Erie Canal and the Michigan Road, carved from Miami and Potawatomi homelands, respectively. Both Ewings invested in Wabash and Erie Canal bonds—the same bonds in which $70,000 of the United Nations' trust fund was invested—and in the construction of canal-adjacent mills, tanneries, hotels, and other enterprises. Yet even as the Ewings integrated new ventures into their core trading operations, they remained dependent on annuities as a more liquid form of capital. In 1839, as their investments in Indiana's Wabash and Erie Canal bonds depreciated and the prospects for the canal's completion darkened, George Ewing cursed the brothers' forays beyond the Indian trade. "I will have nothing to do with white people," he swore. "I go for Indian skins—Indian Specie, Lands, and Treaty allowances in future."[17] Indian agents habitually portrayed Native peoples as dependent on traders, but as George's outburst indicated, traders had become just as dependent on annuities.[18]

❦

In 1842, as Jacksonian removal wound down, the new Whig-controlled Congress carried out a probe of alleged frauds within the three preceding Democratic Party administrations. Its final report indicted the Departments of the Treasury and War with "gross and wholesale injustice to the Indian tribes." Entries had been ineptly tabulated by pencil in the margins of ledger books, which also contained chronic lapses. Trust fund moneys were spent with "great prodigality" and invested in dubious bonds at prices that were inexplicably above par. Some funds due to nations since 1831 had yet to be paid at all. Finally, the Chickasaws, who were by treaty responsible for the costs associated with their own removal, had been charged more than $10,500 in fees for surplus clerical labor in the Office of Indian Affairs, despite the fact that clerks had written only thirty-five brief letters on the subject in the year their land sales began.[19]

Whigs blamed Democratic appointees, but violations were too widespread to be ascribed to bad apples. Corruption and fraud flourished because men acting as trustees enjoyed the impunity to pursue their own interests at the expense of unenfranchised beneficiaries. Federal officials used their trusteeship as a pretext to withhold information and obstruct challenges to misconduct. Native people could gauge their trustee's performance only through indirect observation, when Indian agents came to reservations to survey and sell off land allotments, mete out rations, or disburse annuities. Yet even by these indirect measures it was obvious to Native nations that their funds were diminished by a contorted and self-serving trusteeship. When the humiliation and poverty became too much to bear, they chose the difficult path of pursuing claims for monetary restitution.

Most Indian claims fell under three broad categories. First, Native nations submitted claims for a lack of fair compensation for land cessions—especially allotments. Treaties with the Chickasaws, Choctaws, and Creeks, among others, divided ceded lands into tracts allotted to heads of households (and to orphans). For Southern nations, this approach helped treaty commissioners secure the consent of the planter class, since recipients might be permitted to remain on land they owned in fee simple and could, in any case, sell that land for personal gain—during a cotton boom, no less. But while some affluent families successfully marketed their allotments, most ordinary Natives fell prey to land companies formed by Northeastern capitalists to invest in Indian land cessions. Traders, state politicians, and bankers present on the ground all joined in on land speculation, forming a circle of settler collusion that surrounded allotment holders before sales even began.[20]

Land companies succeeded in diminishing Native compensation for their homelands in several ways. Conniving speculators could significantly depress prices. In the case of Choctaw lands in Mississippi, coordination among speculators reduced bids by an estimated 30 percent.[21] At the Chickasaw land sale, speculators bribed the Indian agent to gain favor at the auction block, and then paid for allotments in depreciated state banknotes—an especially offensive arrangement given the Chickasaws' historical insistence on specie payments for their annuities. Speculators could also engage in the more intimate fraud of coerced purchases. Chickasaws entitled to an allotment received scrip, which in a painful irony conferred to the bearer ownership of a piece of homelands for the sole purpose of selling it away. A Chickasaw woman named Shompaka sold hers to traders at Boggy Depot in Indian Territory. It was a sale in name only, as in her words she "never touched a pen" and received only "goods at enormously high prices" for her tract of prime cotton-growing land.[22] Complaints from devastated Native allottees and settlers excluded from speculative combinations led Congress to convene a series of byzantine claims commissions to adjudicate thousands of poorly documented sales. By 1835, an inundation of individual land claims forced the government to abandon offering allotments as incentives.[23]

Another category of claims concerned inadequate compensation for property destroyed by settlers or left behind as nations were forced west. While Native lands were typically held in common, most nations recognized immovable personal property. Many removal treaties accordingly promised compensation for "improvements," either by assigning a sum to be allocated internally by nations to affected households or by appointing a commissioner who would assess properties and decide on the compensation owed.[24] Provisions consistently undervalued Native possessions—and underestimated the lengths Native property owners would go to collect what they were rightly owed. In the 1835 Treaty of New Echota, for example, Cherokees had been promised $240,000 as compensation for improvements. Much of their property had been seized or destroyed by settlers from Georgia, who had mounted a yearslong terror campaign to force the nation to abandon its homelands. Principal Chief John Ross, who had opposed the 1835 treaty and believed the Cherokees were due far more for their lands than the government had granted, ultimately collected over four thousand separate claims totaling more than $4 million.[25] Claims submitted regularly exceeded the amount set aside, and Congress balked at covering the difference.

Finally, Native nations submitted claims to recover funds lost to government malfeasance or, more generously, to official incompetence. Many frauds occurred because the government relied on contractors to carry out removal, an admittedly enormous and logistically complex undertaking. Regulations stipulated that Indian agents select these contractors through an open and competitive bid process. Some agents broke these rules, failed to advertise competitions, and accepted uncontested bids from contractors for a kickback. Even when agents did hold open calls for bids, contractors could form combinations to inflate bids and share the excess profit. Contractors complemented price gouging by delivering the lowest-quality goods possible, maximizing their returns.

From his home a mile from the Arkansas River, an east-west artery used for several Southeastern removals, Samuel Smith, a Creek man, saw his share of chicanery. In 1837, contractors delivered to Creeks gathered on his fields an emaciated calf, swaying from weakness, whose estimated weight the contractors' agent put at an unlikely five hundred pounds. Smith also saw barrels packed with corn on the ear passed off as if they were filled with grains alone. Sloan Love, a Chickasaw man, saw rations of corn so mildewed "that the horses would not eat it" and pork so rotten that those forced to consume it fell ill with diarrhea. "It was always my opinion," Love would later recall, "that poor people died in consequence of it."[26] A poem written by a Choctaw migrant in 1831 commemorated the experience:

> The salted pork & damn poor beef
> Enough to make the Devil a thief
> This is hard times I do say
> This is hard times I do say.[27]

Contracting frauds especially impacted the Chickasaws because, according to the terms of their 1834 treaty, the nation bore financial responsibility for the expense of their own removal. The costs of land surveys and sale, as well as transportation and rations during the journey west, were all deducted from the funds raised from selling their land. Whatever sum remained after these deductions would form the principal of their trust fund. The lower the costs of their removal, the more land revenue would flow toward their trust fund principal. The larger the principal, the higher their earnings, the more substantial the Chickasaws' annuities would be—and, unfortunately, vice versa.

Chickasaws waited nearly a decade to receive their first postremoval annuity, and with each passing year of nonpayment their suspicions increased. The Chickasaws correctly inferred that trustee had spent lavishly and failed to protect them from fraud, and they repeatedly demanded to see a full accounting of their funds. The statement the Chickasaws received from a reluctant commissioner of Indian affairs included several alarming items. With roughly two-thirds of their money sunk into bonds issued by defaulting states, the bond market crisis of 1841–1842 withered earnings. But the fund's balance also suffered from excessive outflows. There were large and unwarranted payments to contractors and to creditors, who, once the Chickasaw trust was depleted of cash, demanded payment in the few interest-paying bonds left in the account. Most frustrating was the fact that the Chickasaws had anticipated this kind of wastage and warned federal officials ahead of their removal against contracting with local merchants for provisions. Indian affairs officials had evidently ignored the Chickasaws' instructions.[28]

Chickasaw leaders escalated their confrontation with the Office of Indian Affairs by enlisting the services of an attorney, William M. Gwin. Originally from Tennessee, Gwin would later become a senator from California, known for his expansionist fervor and promotion of railroad development. But Gwin's career had begun in Mississippi, where, thanks to President Andrew Jackson's patronage, he served as a US marshal during the Chickasaw and Choctaw land sales. Along with future Treasury Secretary Robert J. Walker and a small cohort of other Mississippi statesmen, Gwin had founded the Choctaw Company, a joint-stock venture formed to speculate in the million acres of ceded Choctaw territory offered in the Cocchuma district. By working to eliminate or combine with competitors, and by collaborating with Gwin's brother Samuel, who served as register at the Cocchuma land office, the Choctaw Company acquired a stunning 70 percent of the land offered in the district, yielding a profit of $301 on each $1,000 share. On the side, Gwin offered to assist Indigenous allottees in the pursuit of their scrip for a share of the proceeds.[29]

Often (but not always) trained attorneys, claims agents like Gwin brought petitions for redress before Congress and ensured that these petitions received favorable hearings. A revolving door separated the world of claims agents and that of federal personnel, and agents made heavy use of insider knowledge and connections. One agent for the Cherokee, Samuel Stambaugh, had recently served as an agent at the Green Bay Indian agency; his partner Amos Kendall had served as postmaster general under President Andrew Jackson. One career Office of Indian Affairs clerk, Charles Mix, who eventually gained sufficient seniority to serve as interim commissioner of Indian affairs, shared privileged documents with claims agents for a fee. Eventually Mix would retire from public service to undertake claims lobbying on his own. Standard string pulling could be complemented by shadier tactics. Claims agents bribed clerks to access correspondence and to receive favorable reporting to the commissioner of Indian affairs. At least one claims agent posed as a press reporter to gain access to the House floor, where his claim competed for attention with the thousands of petitions each Congress received.[30]

Gwin's relationship with the Chickasaws began in November 1844. He met with the Chickasaw land commission, a body originally convened to oversee the assignment of land allotments within the nation during removal but which had since taken on a disproportionate and contested role in Chickasaw politics. A cohort of planters led by Isaac Alberson had seized the commission's reins and vastly expanded its powers, forming a de facto national council. A rival faction led by Pitman Colbert, nephew of Levi Colbert, opposed the commission and called for restoration of the *minko*-led system of heritable leadership. Eager to take advantage of these political divisions, Gwin proceeded to negotiate a power of attorney with the Chickasaw land commission that allowed him to act as an agent for the nation as an apparently unified whole. Gwin acted on a tip from his friend, William Armstrong, head of the Southern Superintendency of the Office of Indian Affairs. Armstrong suggested that Gwin focus his efforts on recovering a suspicious payment of $20,000 to the Agricultural Bank of Mississippi and funds spent nearly $113,000 on enormous supplies of superfluous rations, some solicited without open bids. Thousands of rations had been damaged or were never even delivered. The Chickasaws would later estimate that the Office of Indian Affairs had purchased an excess of 1,360,000 rations, at a cost of nearly $177,000 to the Chickasaw, and spent almost $318,000 on illegitimate expenses associated with their removal. Alberson and the land commission gave Gwin power of attorney to bring a claim to Congress for funds rightly owed to their trust fund. For his labors, Gwin would collect 50 percent of any recovered funds. His fee was hefty but not unheard of: fees ranged from 5 percent to Gwin's 50 percent, with most falling somewhere in between.[31]

Gwin began by assisting the Chickasaw land commission in crafting a petition to Congress that outlined the basis for their claim. The petition identified two violations of fiduciary duty. First, the government had evidently failed to invest in securities that were "safe and valuable," as the treaty had stipulated, and that matured in less than twenty years, as the Chickasaws had specifically requested. Second, the government had withdrawn funds from the Chickasaw trust fund for purposes not authorized by their treaty—namely, fraudulent payments to contractors and clerks. In their demand for remedy the Chickasaws went further than most claimants in that they requested to sue the federal government, or in the words of their petition, to submit their trustees' record "to the scrutiny of the judicial tribunals of the country." In essence, the Chickasaws called for the suspension of sovereign immunity, a legal doctrine derived from the unquestioned authority of the monarch and so ingrained in Anglophone legal traditions that the US Constitution fails to explicitly address it.[32]

It might be tempting to focus here on Gwin's hand and his pecuniary interests. Gwin certainly exercised a strong influence on the petition's construction, and he would later take credit for the idea to sue the federal government. Yet the petition's argument clearly relied on the historical knowledge and legal rationales of its Chickasaw signatories, which included land commission members Isaac Alberson, James Colbert, James Wolf, and the *minko* Ishtehotopa (although Alberson later admitted to forging Ishtehotopa's signature). Reminding Congress of their service as military allies during the War of 1812, the petitioners cast the Chickasaw Nation as "one to whom the Government is indebted for kind and friendly treatment, in war and in peace."[33] This history of diplomatic and military friendship demanded reciprocity. As the Chickasaw petition argued, if "any portion of the Chickasaws had failed to discharge any of their duties to the Government of the United States, the fulfilment of the same would have been required from the Chickasaw nation."[34] The argument emphasized the mutual, if unequal, obligations codified within the canon of treaties Chickasaws had signed with the United States. Put otherwise, the petition insisted on the Chickasaws' interpretation of trusteeship as a mode of protection.[35]

Other Native claimants similarly emphasized federal trusteeship as the obligation of a stronger nation to shield a weaker but nonetheless sovereign nation from harm. In 1843, a group of Cherokees protesting the federal government's failure to compensate them for property lost as a result of removal reminded Congress that the Cherokees "have complied with their part" of the treaty, "by an entire relinquishment of every foot of their lands, embracing millions of acres of the choicest soil in four sovereign States." And yet by withholding compensation, the petitioners asked, had "the stronger party, the Government of the United States, complied with its part of it?"[36] Even as bringing claims to Congress forced Native nations to sacrifice a large proportion of the money they might receive to mercenary agents, the process still allowed petitioners to testify to the failures of trusteeship, and more consequentially, to assert their own interpretation of the legal duties trusteeship carried. A trustee held a duty to protect its beneficiary from enemy nations and violent settlers. But as claimants implicitly argued, their federal trustee also held a duty to protect Native nations from itself.

After a strong rebuke by Mississippi Representative Jacob Thompson, Congress rebuffed Gwin's petition on behalf of the Chickasaws, refusing the nation's request to sue.[37] Yet their claim for restitution was far from settled. By that point, Gwin had already transferred his interest in the claim to Corcoran & Riggs, a Washington merchant bank that had helped underwrite his speculation in Choctaw land. Founded in 1840 by

William W. Corcoran and George Riggs, Corcoran & Riggs maintained close ties with Democratic lawmakers and acted as a major federal depositary. Alongside their services to the government, Corcoran & Riggs cultivated a thriving business processing claims lobbied by men like Gwin. In addition to collecting and transmitting awarded funds, the firm also extended advances to claimants or their agents. By 1843, the standard discount rate for advances—that is, the fee claims agents would pay to cash in an unresolved claim, and the profit the bankers would likely collect were the claim to succeed—ran at 12 percent for "undoubtedly safe" claims. After Corcoran & Riggs purchased Gwin's claim in 1850, the bankers' attorneys stepped in to handle its resolution. If the claim proved successful, Gwin's share of the sum awarded to the Chickasaws would be immediately transferred to Corcoran & Riggs.[38] Indian claims had become an asset that agents could liquidate and an object of speculation for specialist bankers.

In 1850, after years of languishing, the Chickasaw claim finally received favorable attention from the Office of Indian Affairs. Secretary of War Thomas Ewing—a distant relative of George and William Ewing—submitted the claim for an opinion to Attorney General Reverdy Johnson, who agreed that the funds spent on extraneous rations should have been covered by federal, rather than Chickasaw, funds. After purchasing the claim from Gwin, Corcoran & Riggs had furnished Ewing with generous loans and cash presents to incentivize his cooperation, and the firm appeared on the cusp of claiming 50 percent of the funds paid out to the Chickasaws. Yet before Ewing could finalize approval of the claim, the department received notice of objections to the fee from Jacob Thompson, the same congressman who had challenged the Chickasaw petition Gwin brought to Congress. Thompson, it turned out, served as an agent for another group of Chickasaws led by Pitman Colbert, who opposed the land commission's increasingly centralized powers. Thompson submitted to the Office of Indian Affairs a petition from this rival faction, signed by Chickasaw headmen Jackson Frazier, Maxwell Frazier, Davis James, and Gabriel Love, which demanded an investigation to the "arrangement" with Gwin since it had been made "privately, without the knowledge of our people."[39] Rather than authorize a review, however, Ewing simply resubmitted the case to Attorney General Johnson, who upheld his prior decision. The following year, Corcoran & Riggs and the Chickasaw land commission split the award in accordance with Gwin's contract, each receiving over $56,000 from the Treasury.[40]

The Chickasaws' dueling claims were but one among a growing number of petitions pressed by Native governments and their agents. In the mid-1840s, Kendall and Stambaugh formed a partnership to lobby on behalf of a group of Cherokees known as the Old Settlers who had migrated westward prior to the 1835 Treaty of New Echota and had therefore been excluded from the $5 million fund accorded by that treaty as compensation for ceded lands. The attorneys pushed for a claim of more than $500,000 for their clients. In 1849 Richard W. Thompson pursued claims full-time after leaving the House of Representatives. Thompson's most promising case, coordinated through the Ewings, was brought on behalf of the Menominees, who had received a mere fraction of the compensation they were promised for nearly 10 million acres ceded two years earlier. Working with allies in Congress, Thompson pushed for a claim of $221,840, one-third of which would redound to him as a fee—although he sold this claim at a discount to Corcoran & Riggs before any restitution was awarded.[41] Several claims agents drew up contracts with nations familiar to them from previous experience as traders, speculators, or removal contractors. This career path meant, of course, that agents had profited from the very exploitation that they now petitioned Congress to redress and charged nations onerous fees to pursue.

With Congress buffeted by demands from traders, Native nations, and their agents, Indian affairs officials targeted what they considered to be the root of the problem: the excessive proportions of wealth at Native disposal. Acting on Commissioner William Medill's recommendation, Congress passed a law in March 1847 that would undermine nations' ability to use annuities as collective revenue. Agents were directed to carry out annuity distributions biannually, to diminish the sums of money Native nations had on hand at a given time, and to mete out annuities to "heads of families" rather than to designated Native leaders, as had been standard for most nations. The law essentially individuated Native money a generation before the Dawes Act of 1884 mandated the widespread individuation of Native lands. In a further blow to nations' economic sovereignty, the law also voided any future contracts drawn by nations with non-Native outsiders, including attorneys, agents, or traders, unless specifically exempted by the commissioner of Indian affairs.[42]

Lawmakers and other federal authorities explicitly framed these new regulations as trusteeship's prerogative. When instructing Indian superintendents of the changes, Commissioner Medill attributed them to "the President" as "the responsible guardian of the interests and welfare of the Indians."[43] Foreshadowing many of the arguments that would be deployed forty years later during the widespread allotment of communal landholdings, Medill praised the law as an instrument of economic discipline: "Where each individual goes to the pay table and gets his due proportion," he reasoned, "each knows exactly what he has to rely upon, and that beyond it the support & maintenance of himself and family depends upon his own exertions."[44] Implicit in Medill's reasoning was the idea that Native families disciplined into self-subsistence would be less likely to make future financial demands of their trustee.

The regulations enacted in 1847 were not as watertight as Medill hoped. Traders and claims agents were seasoned in circumventing policies related to Indian affairs, and the law provided a significant loophole in the form of a grace period for extant claims. By the deadline in April 1848, the Office of Indian Affairs had received thirty-three claims from traders totaling nearly $163,000, with the bulk of this sum allegedly owed by the Menominees, the Sauk and Meskwakis, and the Miamis. The regulations also preserved latitude for executive discretion to overrule the prohibition on contracts, with predictable consequences. In the spring of 1849, Interior Secretary Thomas Ewing overruled Medill and authorized payments to George and William Ewing (his distant relatives) for their trade debts, and to Corcoran & Riggs for the Chickasaw claim. Secretary Ewing's actions spurred a backlash from Congress, which further strengthened restrictions in 1852. The following year, Commissioner of Indian Affairs George Manypenny recommended further enforcing prohibitions on contracts with Native nations by declaring any violations "penal offences."[45]

Many nations had for years distributed a portion of their annuities per capita, often the amount remaining after covering the costs of government, schools, and other national expenses. But federal regulations now imposed an individuation of annuities from above. Per capita payments appealed to federal officials as instruments of social engineering, in which the government could discourage certain behaviors and promote others, all while calibrating annuities to the size of populations. Enforcing per capita distributions invited a new degree of surveillance and necessitated that agents collect finer-grained demographic information to tabulate sums due each person. The 1847 law dictating per capita payments coincided with the government's first attempt to gather comprehensive "statistical information" on Indigenous peoples, many of whom remained scarcely known to Indian agents.[46] Agents often used the lure of annuity distribution to carry out a head count: Such had been Office of Indian

Affairs policy since at least 1842, when Commissioner T. Hartley Craw-ford had called the "period of paying the annuities . . . the proper season for making this census."[47] Indian agents attempting to enumerate popu-lations met with resistance. Wary of seeing his nation's robust political economy undermined once again by the dissolution of annuity revenue into individual payments, John Ross refused to gather Cherokee citizens for a census held in the fall of 1847.[48]

Population statistics gathered at sites of payment encouraged authori-ties to apply an actuarial logic to annuities. Even before the legal mandate of per capita payments, federal negotiators had begun experimenting with treaty clauses that pegged annuities to presumptively declining populations. The 1846 treaty with the Odawa, Ojibwe, and Potawatomis promised the nations an $850,000 sum that, after deducting the costs of their removal and subsistence, would form the principal for a trust fund. Invested at a rate of 5 percent, the interest would furnish the nations' annuity for thirty years. After that point, the treaty specified in a forebod-ing clause, the annuity would be prorated if "the nation shall be reduced below one thousand souls."[49] No commentary from the Odawa, Ojibwe, and Potawatomis on their projected demise survives in treaty negotia-tion records. When commissioners attempted to insert a similar clause in a treaty with the Ho-Chunks, however, speaker Little Hill noted that it "might suit that tribe, but it don't suit us." As Little Hill argued, such a clause would only penalize the Ho-Chunks for their suffering at the hands of the United States, given that the nation had only "dwindled in conse-quence of our removals." If the government was genuinely concerned for the future of the nation, federal officials should "give us more annuities instead of taking away part of them from us, as we shall die off."[50] Unable to respond to Little Hill's arguments, the commissioners agreed to remove the provision from the treaty.

Per capita distributions also presumed that Native nations existed as fixed and unitary societies. The assumption was particularly ill-suited to Anishinaabe peoples, whose malleable and weblike kinship formations flouted territorial containment. Like other Northwestern nations, many Anishinaabe groups had revived time-tested strategies of migration along kinship networks to avoid involuntary relocations during Jacksonian removal. A party of Potawatomis from the Illinois River, led by Quiquito, had sought refuge in the mid-1830s with Kickapoos from the Wabash River. The multinational group had since resettled near present-day Fort Leavenworth, Kansas, where the Potawatomis received a portion of the annuities due under the 1833 Treaty of Chicago. After the 1847 shift to

*Statement designating the Indian tribes to whom per capita payments in money were made during the year 1854; the number of recipients; the amount per capita, respectively, and the total amount paid to each tribe or band.*

| Names of tribes. | Total number of Indians. | Payment per capita. | Total amount paid. |
|---|---|---|---|
| Menomonees | 1,930 | $9 75 | $18,817 00 |
| Sioux of Mississippi, viz : | | | |
| Seseetoan and Wahpaytoan band | 4,004 | 9 00 | 36,043 51 |
| Medawakantoan and Wahpakootah | 2,379 | 23 50 | 55,916 17 |
| Winnebagoes | 2,561 | 15 00 | 38,415 00 |
| Chippewas of Lake Superior— | | | |
| 3 bands | 606 | 3 89 | 2,362 94 |
| 20 bands | 2,479 | 2 14 | 5,323 21 |
| Chippewas of Mississippi | 2,206 | 4 25 | 9,375 50 |
| Pottawatomies | 3,440 | 18 50 | 63,862 50 |
| Sacs and Foxes of Mississippi | 1,626 | 24 50 | 40,000 00 |
| Chippewas and Ottawas, viz : | | | |
| 16 bands | 1,590 | 6 38 | 10,147 78 |
| 6 bands | 755 | 6 75 | 5,101 22 |
| 10 bands | 1,061 | 9 85 | 10,457 44 |
| 12 bands | 1,746 | 8 75 | 15,293 56 |
| Ottawas, 14 bands | 1,212 | 1 40 | 1,700 00 |
| Chippewas, Ottowas, and Pottawatomies | 236 | 6 72 | 1,587 50 |
| Pottawatomies of Huron | 45 | 8 88 | 400 00 |
| Chippewas of Swan Creek and Black River | 138 | 2 17 | 300 00 |
| Chippewas of Saginaw | 1,340 | 1 64 | 2,200 00 |
| Delawares | 902 | 42 50 | 38,335 00 |
| Wyandots | 554 | 36 00 | 19,944 00 |
| Shawnees | 851 | 67 50 | 54,067 50 |
| Stockbridges in the Territory of Kansas | 13 | 4 60 | 59 80 |
| Christian Indians | 44 | 9 00 | 402 80 |
| Kaskaskias, Peorias, Weas, and Piankeshaws | 220 | 38 00 | 8,360 00 |
| Miamies west | 207 | 206 00 | 42,642 00 |
| Miamies in Indiana | 276 | 154 92 | 42,758 98 |
| Miamies of Eel river | 12 | 183 00 | 2,196 00 |
| Senecas | 180 | 6 50 | 1,250 00 |
| Senecas and Shawnees | 271 | 4 00 | 1,940 37 |
| Osages | 4,098 | 2 50 | 10,245 00 |
| Chickasaws | 4,787 | 10 00 | 47,870 00 |
| Sacs and Foxes of Missouri | 180 | 83 00 | 15,000 00 |
| Iowas | 433 | 57 00 | 24,681 00 |
| Kickapoos | 344 | 72 50 | 25,000 00 |
| Omahas | 800 | 25 00 | 20,000 00 |
| Senecas of New York | 683 | 2 14 | 1,461 62 |
| | 2,146 | 3 48 | 7,468 08 |

Censuses and per capita annuities, 1854. Per capita annuities entailed the collection of detailed censuses, which led to proposals for pegging annuities to population size. *Source: ARCIA* 1855, 574.

per capita annuities, however, the commissioner of Indian affairs refused to allow payments to the Kickapoo Potawatomis, telling the Indian agent that the department's policy was "to have all the Indians of the same tribe live together," since permitting "tribes to scatter about among each other & to divide their annuities accordingly, would produce the greatest difficulty and confusion."[51] Per capita annuities at once laid bare the complex memberships of Indigenous communities brutalized by removal policy and acted as individuated incentives for Native people to comply with federal officials' efforts to demarcate political units—and to fix those units to assigned tracts of land. "When the Pottawatomies remove to and settle in their own country," wrote one commissioner of Indian affairs in 1850, "they will be paid."[52]

What was perhaps most disturbing to Native leaders about the new regulations around annuities, however, was that they accomplished precisely what the Office of Indian Affairs had intended: The policy abruptly divested Native nations of the power to collectively decide how their own national revenue should be spent. Nations could no longer invest their own annuities in larger, longer-term projects, nor could they use established political mechanisms to resolve disputes that emerged over annuity distribution and trade. Native nations had relied for generations on traders' credit, and even the Office of Indian Affairs acknowledged the legitimacy of certain "national debts"—that is, debts taken on by the nation in accordance with its political process. Fracturing annuities impeded such borrowing. From this angle, the enforcement of per capita annuities was particularly striking coming from a country—the United States—that had relied on borrowing to gain independence and indeed to build its empire on Native lands. Many nations expressed outraged that the government would impair their ability to borrow and spend as sovereigns. The Onondaga and Stockbridge Nations submitted petitions to Congress protesting per capita distributions, and Superintendent David D. Mitchell reported "great dissatisfaction" among Native people who demanded to "let *them* in their national or individual capacities settle with their creditors."[53]

Anti-claim laws allowed some exceptions for public initiatives like schools, or for salaries and other costs of governance. But nations now had to justify any collective expenditure in supplication to the Office of Indian Affairs. Nations without centralized, republican governments were more likely to have their request for exceptions rejected. In the spring of 1850, the Sauk and Meskwakis asked for portions of their annuities to be set aside to fund agricultural training and improvements. Commissioner of Indian Affairs Orestus Browning approved only part of the sum requested, and recommended "great caution . . . be observed in doing anything for these Indians."[54] When the United Nations requested that some annuities be reserved from per capita distribution to cover salaries for "interpreters, counsellors, secretaries" and other public offices, the commissioner outright refused, and warned that only when the nations had "formed a regularly organized government for the management of their affairs as a united tribe" would such spending be approved.[55] Officials justified the deprivation by referring to demography. When the Ho-Chunks applied for roughly $20,000 of their own annuities in the spring of 1850, Commissioner Browning rebuffed their request, arguing that "they are in no need of any more money than the very large amount, considering their numbers, they now receive annually. . . . They are the richest tribe in the northwest, and it would be far better for them if they were less so."[56]

⟨═══⟩

Congress's prohibitions on contracts and collective annuities after 1847 slowed but did not stop the rush of claims. Unable to lobby openly or collect payment legally, claims agents were forced to step aside, or at least recede into the shadows. In their stead arose a group to which this prohibition did not apply: Native claims agents. In 1850, the Choctaw Nation authorized two district chiefs, Forbis LeFlore and Thompson McKinney, to serve as claims agents. The men would represent a class of Choctaws who had, under the terms of the 1830 Treaty of Dancing Rabbit Creek, made the wrenching decision to disaffiliate with their nation and become citizens of the United States in order to receive allotments and remain on their homelands. An unscrupulous Indian agent had thwarted the majority of willing Choctaws from actually availing themselves of this provision by omitting names from the record, discouraging applications, and sometimes refusing them outright. On at least one occasion, when a group of Choctaws presented him with a collection of sticks representing a count of households seeking allotments, he dismissed them by throwing the bundle to the ground. Unwilling to remove but denied title to their land, thousands of Choctaws remained in Mississippi, many picking cotton on nearby plantations to survive.[57]

Choctaws who appealed for allotments eventually received scrip entitling them to land. Land speculators swept through Choctaw homesteads in Mississippi, offering advances of cash or goods to persuade scrip holders to relinquish their titles. Both Choctaws and speculators were thrown for a loop when federal authorities decided to incentivize removal by announcing that the scrip could no longer be traded for land but only redeemed in Indian Territory for a fund kept in the scrip holder's name. An amount equivalent to the price of the land for which the scrip could have been traded (valued at $1.25 an acre) would be placed on the Treasury's books and interest paid to the scrip holder. Denied both land and a cash substitute, Choctaws rejected the arrangement. LeFlore and McKinney were appointed by the Choctaw National Council to make scrip claimants whole by persuading Congress to pay out to each bearer the full value of the scrip they held in cash. The pair agreed to take on the case in exchange for a 5 percent fee for each partner. McKinney set out for Washington in January 1851, with LeFlore staying behind in Choctaw country.[58]

A graduate of the Choctaw Academy, McKinney embodied the success of nation building through education, which had prepared him for precisely the kind of challenges that claims seeking would pose. Apart from his schooling, McKinney's career had also familiarized him with his nation's treaties, annuities, and the various purposes to which federally controlled trust funds were assigned. He sat on the board of a girls' seminary in his district of Mushulatubbee, for example, which since its founding in 1844 received the interest on bonds transferred from the Chickasaw Nation as payment for their lands in Choctaw territory. Serving as a claims agent, however, demanded that McKinney develop fluency beyond the purview of Choctaw financial governance. By necessity, he mastered the intricacies of the United States' legislative procedures—whether an appropriation for his claim would require a simple majority rather than a two-thirds vote, for example.[59]

More important still was for McKinney to learn the delicate choreography of Washington influence: determining who possessed power over Indian affairs (or proximity to it), avoiding the pitfalls of misalignment, and placating the diverse, sometimes conflicting interests of key players. All were steps that could be taken only once he had drawn attention to the merits of the Choctaw case. On this front, McKinney warned LeFlore that "it is slow and up hill business here" since "a continual crowd of people" sought to have their business heard. McKinney persisted, drawing on government cachet accumulated from his work as an interpreter. He secured the cooperation of Charles Mix, the Office of Indian Affairs' chief clerk, who "assured" McKinney that he would "take great pleasure in putting me in right track," presumably for a price.[60] After gaining a toehold in the Office of Indian Affairs, McKinney courted Mississippi Representative Jacob Thompson and House Indian Affairs Chairman Robert Ward Johnson, a representative from Arkansas, who—like McKinney—had attended the Choctaw Academy in Kentucky (operated by his uncle Richard Mentor Johnson) as one of the academy's few non-Native students.[61]

McKinney also needed to lobby his claim without violating the terms of the 1847 law barring Native nations from hiring attorneys. Both Mix and Johnson had warned McKinney that working with an attorney or claim agent would be illegal and give the impression of "some under handed work going on."[62] As McKinney explained to LeFlore, the Indians "have been imposed upon by the white men so much that the members of congress are afraid to act, especially when any Lawyers [are] employed in this business."[63] McKinney denied it, but, in fact, he and Leflore *had* quietly hired an attorney. Before his departure for Washington, the men had contracted with Arkansas attorney John B. Luce, a former clerk within the Office of Indian Affairs and a subagent at the Neosho Indian Agency—a classic claims agent biography. McKinney considered Luce an essential adviser, and enough of a Washington outsider to avoid recognition.[64] Despite Luce's involvement, McKinney credited himself: "If I obtained the action of congress," he explained to LeFlore, "it will be because I attended to my business and employ no lawyer."[65]

After a hiatus forced by the close of the legislative session, McKinney returned to Washington the following year to continue to press the claim. In July 1852, Congress finally approved the distribution of $872,000 to scrip claimants, a sum that amounted to nearly three-fourths of the entire sum authorized for Indian affairs spending in the previous session. The Choctaw National Council ratified the settlement that November. McKinney's share of the award would amount to $43,600—if he succeeded in collecting it. Federal authorities decided to distribute the claims payment directly to each entitled person, but Leflore and McKinney had no legal relationship to individual claimants, only to the Choctaw National Council. With Congress's payment imminent, LeFlore and McKinney scrambled to collect signatures from all eligible claimants on a power of attorney drafted by Luce, using a clerk to speed up the process of collecting X marks. When the agent in charge of distributing the money arrived, LeFlore and McKinney shadowed him across the Choctaw Nation, painstakingly deducting their portion from individual claimants' shares. As McKinney reminded LeFlore during one of their many quibbles over fees, when it came to the delicate art of claims "of course it is a risk like all other business."[66]

Claims on Native money *were* a profitable business. It is doubtful that many of the Choctaws who had waited a decade for their compensation—already a paltry substitute for the land they had been promised in 1830—managed to keep whatever share remained of the cash distribution after Lefore and McKinney took their cut from the predating settlers in their midst. If anything, Congress's attempts to obstruct contracts between nations and attorneys had only submerged these relationships into secrecy while pulling prominent Native men into the claims agent role. Most Native claims agents acted as a delegation, an old diplomatic form altered by its novel application. Where delegates had once carefully relayed broad consensus to the government, they now operated at a troubling remove from the nations they represented. When Commissioner Manypenny assumed his office in late March 1853, he found waiting for him delegates from four separate nations—the Cherokees, Chickasaws, Choctaws, and Shawnees—each in the capital to lobby a claim rooted in removal-era treaties.[67] Claims cases required lengthy stays in Washington that spanned months (if not years), a close working relationship with political power brokers, and a speculative payment scheme. Under these circumstances, delegates could easily become more invested in the financial success of their claim than in the prosperity of the nations they ostensibly represented.

Some Native claims agents even took on cases beyond their own nations. John Armstrong, for instance, started his career bringing a successful claim for the value of improvements owned by his own Wyandot people. By the early 1850s Armstrong had taken on an Ohio Shawnee claim for land compensation and a complaint brought by the Munsees in Missouri over annuities they shared with Stockbridges and Munsees in Wisconsin.[68] Shared experiences of treaty violations and exploitation allowed Indigenous leaders to transcend their own contexts, connect with other nations, and build careers in the business of claims seeking.

McKinney and Thomson's success inspired a group led by Peter P. Pitchlynn to mount a titanic claim against the federal government. By the 1850s Pitchlynn had enjoyed a career not unlike the typical claims agent. During the heyday of Choctaw removal, he had speculated in his own nation's ceded land scrip, reinvested his profits in human chattel, and emerged in Indian Territory as his nation's largest slaveholder. Pitchlynn had first dabbled in claims in the early 1840s, pursuing the recovery of $5,000 owed to the Choctaws by the Chickasaw Nation, but he found that the amount of work involved barely justified the modest return. LeFlore and McKinney's sizable earnings changed his mind. With the assistance of attorney Joseph Bryan, Pitchlynn first pursued a claim for funds owed to Choctaw orphans. He then persuaded the Choctaws to allow him to take on a far larger claim—the largest Indian claim that Congress had seen to date.[69]

Under the 1830 Treaty of Dancing Rabbit Creek, the Choctaws had been promised the proceeds of their land cession minus the cost of Choctaw relocation and the purchase of their new territory in the West. Along with fellow delegates Israel Folsom, Samuel Garland, and Dickson W. Lewis,

Pitchlynn secured a contingency fee of 20 percent to pursue land proceeds owed under this clause that had never been paid to the Choctaws—what would become known as the net proceeds claim. In the spring of 1854 Pitchlynn traveled to Washington to take on what he considered "the hardest task . . . that ever was undertaken by a delegation from the Choctaws."[70] Once there, he spent long hours hounding the commissioner of Indian affairs, the secretary of war, congressional committee heads for Indian affairs, and any other men of influence who might grant him an audience. Along with fellow delegates, Pitchlynn reminded the Office of Indian Affairs that if the claim were paid as "one single national fund" it could provide for "education, necessary governmental expenses" and "roads, bridges, mills, mechanical establishments, and agriculture." Warning against per capita payments, he added that "distributive annuities . . . we consider a curse instead of a benefit."[71]

Pitchlynn did not gain traction, however, until an 1855 treaty negotiation between the Chickasaws, the Choctaws, and the federal government. The Chickasaws had moved onto Choctaw territory after removal, and the negotiations concerned the Chickasaws' level of independence from Choctaw authority. The Choctaws were willing to cooperate, but they also sought to use the negotiations to advance their own interests, including the net proceeds claim. Both nations hired several attorneys to advance their position, including War Department clerk John T. Cochrane, Choctaw Indian agent Douglas Cooper, former Commissioner of Indian Affairs Luke Lea, and Arkansas-based lawyer Albert Pike. Pitchlynn secured a clause provisionally acknowledging the net proceeds claim, as did the Chickasaws for their own outstanding claims. Five years later, the Interior Department assessed the net proceeds owed the Choctaws at a staggering $2,380,000. Were Congress to authorize payment, Pitchlynn and his collaborators would receive $480,000.[72] With such an enormous sum at stake, Pitchlynn would spend the rest of his life lobbying to redeem it.

Claims relating to Indian affairs flooded Congress at a moment when the United States' own colonial aspirations had imposed crushing demands on the public purse. President James K. Polk's campaign to stretch the United States' continental empire to the Pacific through war, purchase, and annexation enlarged the United States by more than 1.2 million square miles, increasing the country's size by 64 percent in a mere two years. Over the subsequent two decades, settler migration would outpace and overwhelm a federal government spread thin across a newly expansive territory. Demobilization after victory over Mexico contracted the military to between seven and eight thousand regulars, or roughly the same size as before the major territorial acquisitions of 1848. In an effort to better integrate governance over the West, the Office of Indian Affairs migrated from the Department of War to the newly created Department of the Interior, which also housed the Post Office and the General Land Office. Indian affairs administration underwent a reorganization that transposed and stretched out its web of agencies from the trans-Mississippi to the transmontane West. The number of agents roughly doubled, but these agents now presided over thousands of square miles, policed unfamiliar jurisdictions that spread across five distinct ecological zones, engaged Indigenous people almost entirely unknown to the office, and communicated with a headquarters whose labors had roughly doubled without any increase to its clerical workforce.[73]

Polk and his fellow Democrats had sought to avoid the accumulation of a burdensome national debt, which they bemoaned as a form of unproductive capital associated with monarchical decay and politically unpopular taxes. Despite these aversions, Polk's administration issued more than $83.5 million in Treasury notes, land scrip, indemnities, and bonds to fund the war. The peace negotiated in 1848 presented new financial burdens. To acquire Alta California and New Mexico, and to set Texas's southern border at the Rio Grande, the United States agreed to pay Mexico $15 million and relieve it of two classes of claims. First, the federal government agreed to assume $3 million in claims for unpaid debts and damages that US nationals held against Mexico. Far more expensive, however, would be claims detailed in article 11 of the Treaty of Guadelupe Hidalgo, in which the United States promised to cover the costs of claims from Mexican citizens for property destroyed during raids by Indigenous powers living within the claimed borders of the United States. Between 1848 and 1853 the US military spent $12 million trying—and failing—to stop Apache and Comanche raids across the southern border. In 1868, Mexico presented the federal government with a bill for article 11 claims that topped $31 million. Nonmilitary spending on Indian affairs also surged, rising from slightly more than $1,252,000 in 1848 to nearly $2,830,000 in 1852, as the United States confronted—and attempted to incorporate—new polities in its Western acquisitions. Two years later, in a bill passed as part of the tortured Compromise of 1850, Congress issued another $5 million in securities to cover land claims in Texas, assume the states' debt, and indemnify military and civil properties surrendered during annexation.[74]

Congress, riven by the sharpening tensions over the geographic extension of slavery, could scarcely handle the amassing pile of claims that attended the westward thrust of expansion. Claims sought recompense for a panoply of injustices: Artisans sought due payment for work on navy yards, widows sought military pensions, and owners of livestock sought damages for livestock felled by Indigenous hunting parties.[75] Native claims were but one category among the many that bombarded Congress at unprecedented rates, but they were an especially tricky class, one that the government was desperate to foreclose.

After years of failed legislative proposals to create a dedicated system for reviewing claims, in February 1855 Congress created the first Court of Claims. In its nascency, the court could only issue nonbinding recommendations to Congress for rendering compensation on claims it deemed valid. Claims agents attempted to bring Native cases, but the court declined to hear them in an apparent informal ban. In March 1856, for example, Albert Pike—who was still working with Pitchlynn on the Choctaw net proceeds case—filed two separate cases on behalf of the Creek Nation, but neither received a hearing. As the Court of Claims gained legitimacy, however, so too did its exclusion of Indigenous claimants take explicit form. In 1863, in response to a deluge of claims unleashed by the destruction of the Civil War, Congress strengthened the Court of Claims' authority in legislation that simultaneously closed its doors to claims emanating from treaties with foreign powers and Native nations. While non-Native claimants could now seek monetary redress for their grievances through a relatively expedited process, Indigenous polities were restricted to petitioning through the same system long maligned for its infestation with predatory agents. Only in 1881 would Congress reverse this section of the law and expand the court's jurisdiction to encompass Native polities' grievances—although their claims would still have to appeal to Congress first, rather than to the Court of Claims directly.[76]

Even as claims cast doubt on annuities' continued effectiveness in lowering the costs of dispossession, flares of violence after 1849 made Congress unwilling to abandon fiduciary colonialism. Treaties signed with the Apaches, Arapahoes, Cheyennes, Comanches, Dakotas, Kiowas, and

Lakotas across the 1850s offered annuities merely to secure corridors of travel and trade. Since these nations did not relinquish any land, their annuities struck officials as uncomfortably close to tribute. As one agent stationed on the Arkansas and Upper Platte Rivers warned, the policy "must be either an army or an annuity"—and all were miserably aware which would cost more.[77] In the words of Commissioner of Indian Affairs Luke Lea, "the system is fastened upon us, and its attendant evils must be endured."[78]

From the vantage of Lea and his subordinates, efforts to mitigate the "evils" of the fiduciary system by prohibiting contracts and collective annuities had succeeded primarily in making the administration of annuities more convoluted. Per capita annuity distributions entailed tedious censuses and closer monitoring of Native economies, even as they provoked disputes with Indigenous governments who resisted reforms to protect their own fiscal autonomy. Ostensibly hard prohibitions on contracts with non-Native outsiders softened when challenged by well-organized Indian traders, who had long cultivated close ties to Indigenous customers and local agents of the state. Efforts to bar contracts with attorneys invited a class of Native leaders to replace settler claims agents and deploy the skills they had gleaned from annuity-funded schools in the service of bringing claims to Congress. Indian affairs administrators haplessly stayed the course, with stipulations for per capita distributions continuing to appear in treaties signed across the 1850s and 1860s.[79]

Yet the postremoval claims crisis resonated far beyond shaping individual treaties. It stirred a profound antipathy to the treaty system among federal lawmakers, and to annuities in particular, that would only gain momentum in the coming decades. Annuities were supposed to sharpen federal control over Native economies. But claims made clear that the government could not dictate the fate of annuities once they left an Indian agent's hands, making annuities' origin points—treaties—the object of Congress's growing revulsion toward the escalating costs of conquest.

The evolution of claims into a system perpetuated in part by agents and bankers held its own legacy for Native peoples. Nations that had experienced removal no longer considered warfare a viable option to challenge the United States' domination, and the rash of secondary dispossessions— fraud, theft, and exploitation—that attended land cessions proved that the era of good-faith treaty diplomacy had long passed. Pursuing claims emerged as the only practicable recourse for nations to protect their remaining wealth and hold their fiduciary to account. But claims differed from previous modes of opposition between Native nations and the federal government. It forced Native peoples to occupy the narrowed role of legal adversaries rather than military foes or diplomatic counterparts. More disturbing still, Indigenous leaders adopted their adversarial posture before the courts of the United States. Petitions for redress could and did frame grievances within Native peoples' interpretations of trusteeship, but merit as claims would be adjudicated by the legal standards of the country that had dispossessed them. That claims could be so lucrative for well-positioned outsiders at the expense of nations only added to the compromises Native leaders were forced to make. One final legacy of the postremoval surge in claims was perhaps the most striking, if also inevitable. After decades of receiving the alleged value of their lands in annuities and trusts, Native people now aimed not at the recapture of territory but at a degree of justice measured in money.

# CHAPTER SEVEN

# The Fall and Rise of Fiduciary Colonialism

IN FEBRUARY 1861 banker George Riggs presented coupons worth $125,000 in South Carolina bonds for payment in Charleston. Riggs's banking house, Corcoran & Riggs, had since the 1840s dominated the speculative market in Indian claims and more recently had become a key bond broker for the Indian trust funds. It was in this latter capacity that Riggs had been dispatched to Charleston. South Carolina owed $7,500 in overdue interest payments to the federal government, which in turn owed this sum as annuities to the Cherokees, Lenapes, Iowas, and confederated Kaskaskias, Peorias, Piankashaws, and Weas. But instead of paying specie, as stipulated by the bond's prospectus, the state treasurer offered only state banknotes that would hold little value north of the emerging Confederacy's border. Since he was tasked with remitting the funds to Washington, Riggs understandably refused.[1]

With the majority of Indian trust fund wealth invested in Southern state bonds, the United States' Civil War broke apart financial ties that had bound together federal, state, and Native sovereigns. A war over the westward expansion of slavery set off a dramatic transformation of fiduciary colonialism that would unfold in three acts: a moment of crisis, a swift expansion of state capacity, and a reconfiguration of colonial power that would carry consequences for Indigenous peoples across the continent. Crisis erupted with secession, which forced the government to contend with a financial risk too calamitous for officials to have taken into consideration when investing Native money in the debts of American states: that these states would break away from the Union. Trusteeship's integrity had always rested on the premise that the United States would continue to exist as an intact and uncontested polity. Instead trust funds seemed to have outlasted the government that served as trustee. Congress now needed to decide whether it would honor Confederate debts to the trust funds—and, worse, whether it would honor debts to nations allegedly allied with the Confederacy. Not for the first time, trust funds proved more vexing than the government had anticipated because they were, at once, nation-to-nation obligations rooted in treaties and investments in a market subject to panics, downturns, and, most spectacularly, war.

Unable to secure deliveries of annuities in precious metals beyond enemy lines and unwilling to prioritize Indian affairs given the crisis of secession, the Union abruptly abandoned its treaty obligations. To leaders in Indian Territory these actions amounted to an abandonment of the federal government's role as a trustee, and specifically its obligations to offer protection—from its own rogue citizens and from the losses incurred by the Union's dissolution. Indigenous peoples who had dealt with a century of narrowing diplomatic alternatives to the United States now faced two warring republics where a single empire had once stood. Many Indigenous nations opted to break with a trustee who had failed them one time too many.

Slaveholders within Native nations' governing classes needed little convincing to ally with the rebelling South. Six months into the war, factions from each major Indian Territory nation had signed treaties pledging to take up arms for the Confederacy. Soon Native peoples faced civil wars within their own nations. Waves of refugees unwilling to join the Confederacy—or unable, given their status as slaves or freed Afro-Indigenous peoples—fled to Kansas in desperation, only to face another form of federal neglect in squalid Union encampments. Meanwhile, violence exploded in the West. Seeing opportunity in the crisis, formidable Great Plains nations either rejected the United States' diplomatic terms or, when the treaties they signed were swiftly broken by the federal government, seized the moment to raid into thinly garrisoned settlements and recover territory from a distracted empire.[2]

But after 1862, the Union regained its footing. Without the obstructions of Southerners—who had always feared federal power as a threat to slavery—the Republican Party could finally pursue its ambitions to incorporate the resource-rich West. In quantitative terms, the Civil War's immense human and economic destruction arguably outweighed any stimulus from war mobilization. Yet these indicators fail to capture how the war transformed the nation's political economy by producing a developmental state that held colonizing the West as its principal object. Amid a war that cost $1.8 billion—more than had been spent on all other purposes combined since 1789—the fiscal calculus underpinning fiduciary colonialism shifted. With its swiftly expanded fiscal and military capacity the government could, for the first time, conceive of maintaining its grip on territories seized from Indigenous peoples across the West by waging near-constant albeit largely undeclared wars. It chose to partner with industrial capital to carry out that invasion. Railroads, private corporations infused with federal debt, became powerful if crash-prone vehicles of economic integration. By plowing through Native homelands, railroad corporations and their military chaperones redrew the nation's political economy, linking extractive zones in the West to financial centers in the Northeast.[3]

As transcontinental construction collided with Native power, federal officials adjusted their colonial objectives. Congress began categorizing Native groups as either hostile or pacified, and debated whether the policy of honoring treaties and maintaining financial obligations had run its course. To many observers, only the military—which had grown exponentially and would never contract in terms of size or budget to prewar levels—could overcome the obstacle of Native power. Fiscal arguments for treaties began to lose traction. A consensus emerged within the Indian affairs administration to reject a return to the antebellum status quo. In 1871, Congress abolished the system of treaty making that had grounded federal trusteeship for nearly a century. Unfettered by diplomacy, officials dismissed principles of protection and reciprocity core to Indigenous understandings of trusteeship. In their place emerged a prerogative to act as uncontested guardians over Native nations newly categorized as wards.

When the war came, federal officials were accustomed to making up fiduciary practice as they went along. But the sundering of the very government that acted as trustee to Native nations held no precedent. When the South seceded, it withdrew abruptly from the United States' fiscal state. South Carolina led the pack, abandoning interest payments to the Office of Indian Affairs in January 1861. Louisiana and North Carolina stopped in April, with Florida, Georgia, Tennessee, and Virginia (the largest debtor to the trust funds) joining them that July. A divided Missouri also stopped payments in July, although it would resume them in

1863. Arkansas would not have paid interest either way, having repudiated its debts in 1841. Indiana, which had not formally repudiated, had nonetheless failed to resume interest payments after its defaults twenty years earlier, adding a Union state to the list of Civil War delinquents. Union Commissioner of Indian Affairs William P. Dole made halfhearted attempts to collect interest on nonpaying bonds. By December 1861, however, he had given up.[4]

Secession was so destructive because trust portfolios had been assembled by administrators with the discretion to channel wealth to the states of their choice. Many trust investments dated to the late 1830s, when Jacksonian appointees had strongly favored Southern states. But a significant portion were of a more recent vintage. In 1851, under the direction of Commissioner of Indian Affairs Luke Lea, the Office of Indian Affairs resumed investment of trust funds in state bonds under the guise that the prohibition on state investments, in place since the defaults of the early 1840s, did not apply to money released from matured bonds. Lea's chief clerk, Charles Mix, lavished funds from a variety of trusts on Virginia, investing $793,800 in the state in one year alone. Among the various public works now financed by Indian trust fund money was the James River and Kanawha Canal Company, a state-financed firm that owned 170 slaves.[5]

A second, smaller borrowing boom among states that had avoided defaults in the 1840s began in 1853, creating demand for credit and further tempting officials to invest trust funds in their preferred states. After a financial panic in 1857, bond yields lifted, and the Treasury recommended buying up discounted securities to cheapen the cost of annuities in the long term. Congress repealed the 1841 ban, and soon after, Interior Secretary Jacob Thompson and Commissioner of Indian Affairs James W. Denver—from North Carolina and Virginia, respectively—poured money into the heavily discounted bonds of slaveholding states.[6] As a result, at the Civil War's outbreak, 78 percent of the nearly $4.8 million held in trust had been invested in southern state bonds—and 63 percent in states that eventually seceded from the Union.[7] The consequence of a portfolio so skewed toward now seceded states was a deficiency of interest payments that would grow to $99,808 by January 1862, with no prospect for resumption on the horizon. Were the war to last more than a year, officials realized, they would quickly owe hundreds of thousands of dollars to Native nations.[8]

As the severity of the financial disarray dawned on federal officials in Washington, the war loomed over Indian Territory. Secession would rouse

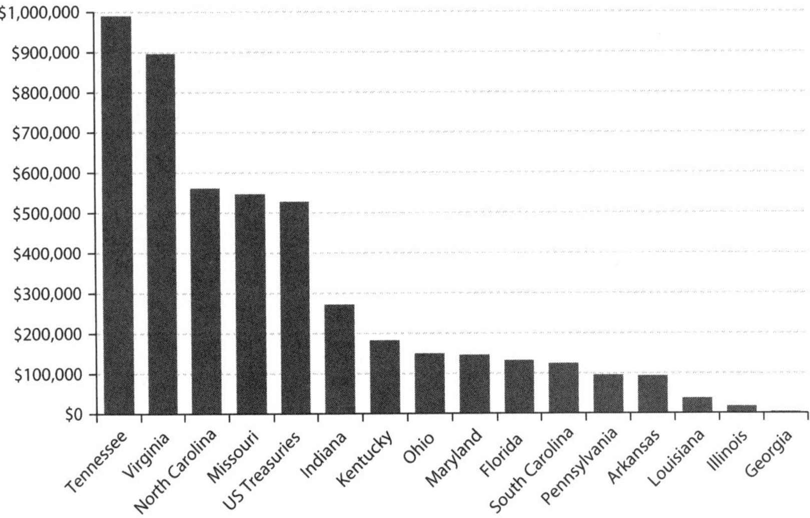

Indian trust fund investments in state and federal bonds, 1860. *Sources: ARCIA* 1860, 242; S. Ex Doc. No. 36-3, at 313 (1860).

bitter conflicts within nations over slavery, but it also arrived at a moment of mounting fiscal confidence that informed how leaders responded to the war. Across the previous decade, with growing assertiveness, Native treasurers and other statesmen liaising with the Office of Indian Affairs had insisted on intact national payments to fund public institutions and infrastructure, demanded adequate and accurate reporting on their trust funds, and even requested specific investments. After negotiating a $200,000 perpetual fund assigned for the purpose of education in 1856, Creek leaders expressed dissatisfaction with the 5 percent rate of return promised by the treaty and requested Louisiana state bonds, which they calculated would yield an additional $3,400 per year. "Their leading men well understand that money is worth more than five per cent per annum," an Indian agent commented.[9] Choctaw delegates similarly complained in 1858 that the Office of Indian Affairs had shifted their funds from Alabama bonds to lower-yielding Virginia bonds and demanded a restoration of their prior 6 percent rate of return. Observing the Chickasaw Nation, one agent marveled that "little remains for an agent to do" since the nation "have taken on themselves the entire management of their own fiscal affairs."[10]

An unfortunate event in Washington, however, interrupted nations' progress and prefigured the destruction to come. In late 1860, newspapers reported that a well-known military contractor, William Hepburn Russell, had, along with a clerk, stolen $870,000 in state bonds assigned to three separate Indian trust funds from an iron chest kept in the Office of Indian Affairs. Russell had stolen the securities to keep afloat his distressed business ventures (which included the iconic transcontinental mail line, the Pony Express). He had used the bonds to provide additional collateral to creditors for millions of dollars in debts he had promised to repay with future income from the War Department generated through his businesses' freighting contracts. The scandal tarnished President James Buchanan's administration, already notorious for corruption. But the theft also indicated how a revolving door between the Office of Indian Affairs and the Indian claims business encouraged fraud. Russell had met his accomplice, clerk Godard Bailey, through former Commissioner of Indian Affairs Luke Lea, who had transitioned to work as a claims agent after retiring from public office. Although Lea denied any involvement in the theft, one of his companies had issued a series of suspiciously timed and unexplained payments to Bailey in the weeks he abetted Russell.[11]

A few months after news of the bond theft broke, Choctaw delegate Peter Pitchlynn arrived at the Office of Indian Affairs. Citing the robbery, Pitchlynn demanded a tally of any losses his nation might have suffered, a full inventory of bonds held on their behalf, and, as a safeguard against future thefts, for each bond to be stamped prominently with the word "Choctaw." Commissioner of Indian Affairs Dole dutifully promised to deliver a full inventory and assured Pitchlynn that the Choctaw bonds remained intact and in his possession.[12]

Unbeknownst to the commissioner, however, the Choctaws' concern about the theft had been little more than a pretext to learn precisely how much of their funds were invested in Southern states and thereby to gauge the potential financial impact of secession. "Should the Government of the United States go to pieces," Choctaw Senator Peter Folsom had warned Pitchlynn, "there will be no Trustees to hold those bonds . . . and it will be absolutely necessary to obtain possession of them for the nation."[13] Soon after receiving the statement, which documented their $471,000 investment in bonds issued by Virginia and Missouri, the Choctaws requested that the federal government turn over the securities immediately. "We can use the bonds without serious loss now," the delegates explained, "& prefer to dispose of them at once rather than run the risk of further depreciation."[14] When the federal government refused, the Choctaws missed their opportunity to liquidate their investments before they became effectively worthless. Were it not followed by the Civil War, Russell and Bailey's theft would have been no more than a passing scandal. Instead, it was a dress rehearsal for a much larger betrayal to come.

{⊱⋆⋆⊰◯⊱⋆⋆⊰}

As the secession crisis unfolded in early 1861, most Native leaders hesitated to engage in order to protect their financial stake in the Union. Pitchlynn, who continued to lobby Congress for the Choctaws' net proceeds claim, warned against making an enemy of the same government that owed his nation hundreds of thousands of dollars (of which he stood to collect a substantial fee). Speaking in council, he reminded his audience that "the Choctaws are completely tied up, by Treaties, with the government of the United States" and that "all our invested funds are now in the hands of President Lincoln." Only treaties were guarantees "for our country & our monies."[15]

The commencement of all-out war in late April made neutrality far more difficult to sustain. Indian agents stationed in southern Indian Territory uniformly defected to the Confederacy. Nine days after the fall of Fort Sumter, secessionist volunteers from neighboring Arkansas and northern Texas forced a retreat of Union forces at Fort Smith in Arkansas and Fort Arbuckle, Fort Cobb, and Fort Washita in Indian Territory. Their evacuation marked the total withdrawal of the federal government from the region. Native polities were suddenly exposed to an array of secessionist recruitment tactics, ranging from suasion to threats on their lives. Creek *miko* Oktarharsars Harjo, also known as Sands, learned that he had a $5,000 bounty on his head because he refused to denounce the Union. One missionary who had fled to Kansas related how Confederate vigilantes charging through Indian Territory had declared that if any nations were to withhold an alliance, twenty thousand Texans would "wipe them from the face of the earth."[16]

Just as secession had broken apart trust investments, the formation of battle lines threw up barriers to the delivery of annuities to Indian Territory. Even before the war's outbreak, Indian agents had spent thousands on armed guards to ward off thieves and keep round-the-clock watch over the boxes of coined gold. Once confederates from neighboring Arkansas and Texas swept through the region, annuities became a serious liability. William Coffin, appointed southern superintendent of Indian affairs after his predecessor defected to the Confederacy, transmitted the funds he had on hand to New York City as a matter of precaution. Even still, Coffin feared capture and torture by Confederate operatives who might not believe he no longer had any gold to give up. In light of these dangers and the expenses of overcoming them, Commissioner of Indian Affairs William P. Dole decided

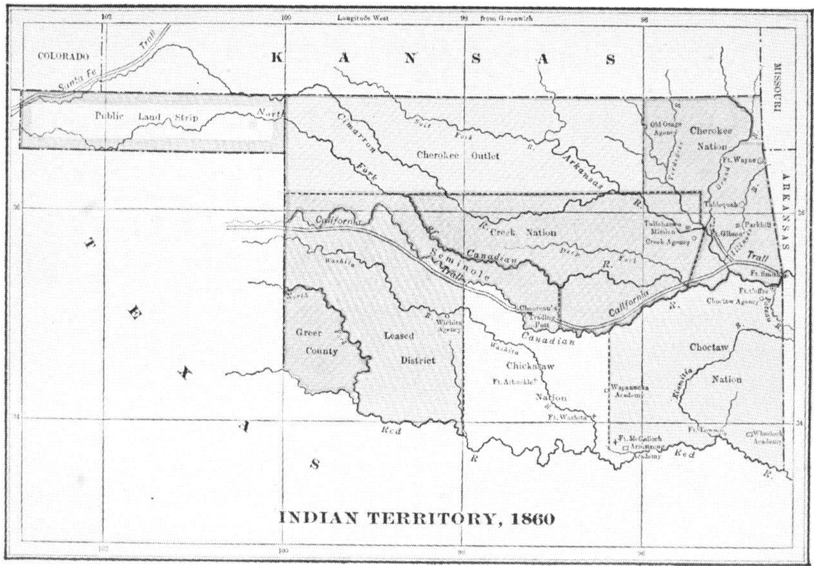


Indian Territory, 1860. *Source:* Charles Henry Roberts, *The Essential Facts of Oklahoma History and Civics* (B. H. Sanborn, 1914).

that fall to withhold annuities from Indian Territory to prevent the funds from falling "into the hands of the rebels as booty."[17]

Little noticed in the Union's Eastern command centers, the desertion of Indian Territory forts and suspension of annuities appeared from the Indigenous vantage point as a monumental event. Writing as an exile in his own nation, increasingly overrun by Confederates and their sympathizers, Creek *miko* Opothle Yohola reached out to President Abraham Lincoln for assistance. Addressing him as "our Great Father," Opothle Yohola reminded him of his treaty obligations to defend the Creeks "from all interference from any people." But now "the wolf has come" and their "Great Father" was nowhere to be found.[18] A resolution in the Chickasaw Legislature calling for the nation to support the Confederacy excoriated the Union for "withdrawing" and for "withholding, unjustly and unlawfully, our money placed in the hands of the Government of the United States as trustee, to be applied for our benefit." Without funds or protection, the resolution continued, the Chickasaws could not "escape the storm which is about to burst upon the South."[19]

{~~~W~~~}

The Confederate States wanted to assume trusteeship over their Native neighbors for the same reasons that had motived the United States since the late eighteenth century. Annuities could stave off costly military retribution from nations incentivized to loyalty, and treaties of protection could establish preemptive claim on lands desired for a slaveholder empire. In April 1861, Confederate President Jefferson Davis appointed Albert Pike as an emissary to Indian Territory. Pike's ongoing—and sizable—interest in the Choctaws' net proceeds claim meant that he held a personal stake in crafting a Confederate Indian affairs policy that assumed financial obligations to Native allies. As Pike explained to the Confederate Secretary of State Robert Toombs, Native polities had no reason to join the Confederacy were it not to assure them payment of annuities and protection of funds held in trust. "Why should they," Pike asked, "if we will not bind ourselves to give them what they hazard in giving us?"[20]

Once in Indian Territory, Pike traveled from nation to nation, reassuring each council convened for his visit that the Confederacy would fully assume the obligations of trusteeship: Its own commissioner of Indian Affairs would collect interest on Southern bonds, and its Congress would supplement interest payments on Northern state and federal securities, replace any uninvested funds held on behalf of nations by the federal government, and generally maintain any payments promised in treaties signed with the United States. In exchange, nations would need only join the Confederacy's war.

Pike's proposition elicited a range of reactions. Majorities within the largely proslavery Chickasaw and Choctaw Nations anticipated that their interests would align more closely with the Confederacy. But Pike found less unanimity among the Creeks and Seminoles, where slavery was less hegemonic, and in the Cherokee Nation, where a secretive abolitionist society aspired to usurp planters' political control. The Comanches agreed because they welcomed the opportunity to forge an alliance with an old enemy, Texas, yet did so at the expense of friendship with the Kiowas, who swore never to join the South. Nearly every nation counted slaveholders willing to entertain an alliance with the Confederacy, however, and even the more reluctant statesmen harbored legitimate fears of Union designs for the West, since free-soil advocates had as wantonly as their proslavery opponents flooded onto unceded reservations during the catastrophe of Bleeding Kansas.[21]

By early October 1861, Pike had signed treaties with every nation in Indian Territory. His compacts with the Cherokees, Chickasaws, Choctaws, Creeks, and Seminoles were his most significant. These nations not only enjoyed the largest trust funds but also possessed sufficient numbers and capacity to raise regiments for the Confederate military. A call to arms reached Indian Territory just over two weeks later.[22]

The Confederacy consolidated its fiduciary policy during a provisional Congress held in Montgomery, Alabama, in early 1861. Delegates vested fiduciary custody over all "money, bonds, and securities" belonging to Indigenous polities in the Confederate Treasury and authorized the secretary of war to draw the amounts necessary to disburse interest payments in specie, a striking ambition for a nascent state engulfed by war.[23] Interest owed on Southern bonds held by the Union would be withheld and rerouted to the Native trust beneficiaries that had signed agreements with Pike. Trusteeship would solidify military alliances, bolster the Confederacy's legitimacy, and, its leaders hoped, allow the extension of its empire toward the Pacific, not least by protecting its proclaimed territory of Arizona. Yet maintaining annuities owed to nations in the Southwest would prove far more difficult than satisfying obligations in Indian Territory. In November 1861, the Confederate Congress appropriated $25,000 to purchase presents for the Comanches—but the costs of shipment across the desert prevented the goods from being delivered.[24] Confederate Commissioner of Indian Affairs S. S. Scott urged additional appropriations, acknowledging that, while expensive, "the remuneration received by the Confederate Government, for this outlay of money, is peace on the frontier."[25]

Going into the war, the Union held a considerable economic edge over the Confederacy. The North boasted double the railroad milage, four times the banking capital, and ten times the annual manufacturing output of the South. These endowments would eventually prove decisive in its triumph, but the Union's war began inauspiciously. Lincoln had inherited a $76.4 million debt from President Buchanan, who had spent liberally on military campaigns in the West despite a financial panic in the first year of his term. A war unlike any the country had experienced would demand unprecedented means. Lincoln's opening plea to Congress requested $400 million, a sum large enough to finance the recent war against Mexico five times over. It barely lasted the Union to the summer.[26]

In July 1861, the Battle of Bull Run brought the Confederate Army a mere thirty miles southwest of Washington, bringing into focus the conflict's severity and the inadequacy of the Union's present means. After a month of unpleasant negotiations, Treasury Secretary Salmon P. Chase secured from a consortium of New York City bankers a $150 million loan. Bank credit helped, but only cash in hand could purchase war supplies at scale, and abroad—so Chase stunned bankers by demanding an immediate installment of $50 million in specie, draining nearly the entirety of the nation's $63 million in reserves and forcing banks to suspend the convertibility of their banknotes by December.[27]

Meanwhile, the customary sources of wartime financing—overseas capital—sat out of reach. A select few British financiers invested on their personal accounts, but no major houses were willing to lend to the Union. Many cited the uncertainty of the conflict, but their memories of American states' defaults and repudiations in the early 1840s were still fresh. In November 1861, two Confederate emissaries boarded a British steamer headed from Havana to London, where they planned to secure diplomatic recognition for the South. Union officers intercepted the vessel and arrested both men, prompting an outcry from Prime Minister Lord Palmerston, who threatened an Anglo-American war. Federal war bonds sank, dragging the Union's finances to a nadir. By this point, the Union Army and Navy were spending between $1.5 and $2 million per day, with customs duties—the stalwart source of revenue for the federal government— amounting to a mere $160,000 per day. Chase's initial loan evaporated, specie disappeared from circulation, and by February 1862 the government owed around $45 million to military suppliers.[28]

A full-blown military-fiscal crisis was underway, and to overcome it the federal government would exercise new powers of economic intervention that ultimately transformed the nature and scale of its imperial project. Over the outcries of New York City bankers, Congress created a national legal tender to cover outstanding war expenditures. Greenbacks, named for the color of their ink, held value that rested solely on the "faith of the government" (as the law that enacted them stated) rather than their convertibility specie. Originally convertible into Treasury bonds, greenbacks became in March 1863 a true fiat currency. At the same time, the Union constructed a robust system of internal taxation, overseen by the newly created Internal Revenue Service. To bolster its currency financing, Congress also authorized $500 million in Union war bonds, which carried 6 percent interest and bore flexible maturations of between five and twenty years—earning them the shorthand title "five-twenties." A subsequent issuance of $830 million in small-denomination bonds found a broad investor base in a public eager to contribute to the war effort, bringing the total raised to $1.3 billion—or nearly seventy-nine times what the government had borrowed for its war against Mexico.[29]

Native wealth flowed into the Union's swelling military-fiscal state. From January 1862 onward, any new Indian trust fund investments were in federal bonds alone. The decision to invest trust funds in war bonds pegged Native wealth to the vicissitudes of the conflict and to the Union's prospects for victory. In June 1863 the commissioner of Indian affairs commissioned a broker to sell off investments belonging to the Peoria Nation, which needed cash to pay debts and purchase agricultural implements. After a Confederate victory in Virginia's contested Shenandoah Valley, the broker warned of a "*very heavy* depression in U.S. or Gov't Stocks" since "the continued progress of the Rebels into our Territory has caused holders of US Stocks to throw them on to the market causing a heavy decline." If the Union Army gained an advantage within ten days, he reckoned, he could liquidate the bonds without so much sacrifice.[30] Sure enough, the market rallied when news of a Union victory at Gettysburg reached New York City. The broker sold off the bonds as planned, writing that the "news we have is so glorious & our successes so great & positive . . . we need have no fear in the future."[31]

As the Union developed the fiscal state it needed to match the enormity of the war, Congress declined to deploy this expanded capacity toward upholding its duties as a trustee. Two overlapping categories of Native trust beneficiaries now suffered from financial losses: victims of the bond theft, and victims of the total depreciation caused by secession. The government stalled on reimbursing either, while withholding redemption altogether for nations considered unworthy. Once a major scandal, the theft of the Indian trust funds bonds receded from the headlines once the Civil War began. Despite grand jury indictments for Russell, Bailey, and Secretary of War John Floyd, all escaped prosecution. By July 1863 the government owed $83,995 in interest to nations affected by the theft. With $514,000 of state bonds stolen from their account, the Lenapes suffered the greatest loss. Two other Kansas nations, a confederated band of Kaskaskias, Peorias, Piankashaws, and Weas, and the Iowa Nation, each had $157,000 and $77,000 stolen from their trust funds, respectively. All suffered from famines and railroad crews' timber theft during the war and pled for their direly needed overdue annuities. After ignoring their supplications for a year and a half, Congress finally issued a reimbursement in July 1862.[32]

Congress also equivocated on its responsibility to replace principal and interest owed by rebelling states to the Indian trust funds. Upon

**Table 7.1.** Indian Trust Fund Bonds, Stolen and Nonpaying

| Nation | Nominal value of bonds stolen in 1860 | Nominal value of nonpaying Confederate bonds | Total |
|---|---|---|---|
| Lenapes | $514,000 | $187,000 | $701,000 |
| Cherokees | $83,000 | $572,500 | $655,500 |
| Choctaws | — | $471,000 | $471,000 |
| Kaskaskias, Peorias, Piankashaws, and Weas | $197,000 | $98,000 | $295,000 |
| Creeks | — | $149,800 | $149,800 |
| Iowas | $76,000 | $55,000 | $131,000 |
| United Nations of Odawa, Ojibwe, and Potawatomi | — | $73,000 | $73,000 |
| Menominees | — | $28,000 | $28,000 |
| Kansas | — | $20,000 | $20,000 |
| Odawas and Ojibwes | — | $14,000 | $14,000 |
| Senecas and Shawnees | — | $10,000 | $10,000 |
| Odawas of Blanchard's Fork | — | $8,000 | $8,000 |
| Osages | — | $7,000 | $7,000 |
| Chickasaws | — | $5,000 | $5,000 |
| Odawas | — | $5,000 | $5,000 |
| Odawas of Roche de Boeuf | — | $1,000 | $1,000 |
| Total | $870,000 | $1,704,300 | $2,574,300 |

*Source:* "Statement of the description of the Abstracted Bonds [. . .]," Unregistered Letters Received Relating to Trust Funds, 1828–1869, Box 1, Records Relating to Indian Trust Funds, Records of the Indian Division, Records of the Department of the Interior, NARA II; *ARCIA* 1863, 485.
*Note:* One $1,000 bond removed for reasons unrelated to the bond theft excluded from calculations.

Commissioner Dole's urging, the House had included a controversial provision in the annual Indian appropriation bill that provided $350,220 in overdue interest on the more than $1.7 million in nonpaying securities. Without any precedent to consider, few legislators agreed on whether the government was obligated to cover the debts of states that no longer formed a part of the Union. Senator and Committee of Indian Affairs Chair James Doolittle denounced the House measure, comparing secession to a "flood, or fire, or an earthquake" for which trustees bore no responsibility.[33] But as Iowa senator (and future secretary of the interior) James Harlan pointed out, the federal government had exhibited questionable diligence in holding on to stocks that "were falling in the market, until they became worthless." Even if investments in Southern state bonds had been made in good faith, Harlan suggested that an ensuing "want of reasonable care" would not pass muster "in the eye of a court of equity."[34]

Once again, disruptions to the returns on trust investments provoked a set of unanswered questions about the federal government's fiduciary purview: What *were* trust funds? Were they risk-bearing investments like any other, subject to the losses caused by unpredictable events? Or were they nation-to-nation obligations, to be upheld regardless of the United States' economic misadventures? These same questions had arisen fifty years earlier, when the demise of the First Bank of the United States led federal officials to shift the Senecas' trust investments into lower-yielding federal securities. By insisting on the treaty-bound nature of trust obligations, the Senecas had persuaded federal officials to supplement the reduced interest payments to maintain the $6,000 payment promised by the 1797 Treaty of Big Tree. Decades later, when the state defaults of the early 1840s left tens of thousands of dollars owed to the Indian trust funds, Congress heeded the Office of Indian Affairs' insistence on covering overdue annuities to avert a multinational "Indian war" against the United States. Now Southern states' debts to the Indian trust funds spurred a different response, with Congress refusing to backstop seceded states. In a petition protesting the Senate's refusal "to recognize the liability of the United States," John Ross and other Cherokee delegates situated this repudiation within the federal government's larger failure as a trustee—a trustee that had, in treaty after treaty, promised the Cherokee Nation protection. "It is well known to every body how this guarantee was kept in the Spring of 1861, and from that time to this," the petition noted, in a pointed understatement.[35]

❦

The Cherokees' predicament indicated a larger shift underway in federal policy. In July 1862, with Union military capacity expanding and rumors of a Confederate-Native conspiracy spreading, Congress nullified treaties with "any Indian tribe . . . in actual hostility to the United States."[36] Directed primarily at the apparently Confederate-allied Cherokees, Chickasaws, Choctaws, Creeks, and Seminoles, the law failed to specify how any Native nation could safely be labeled hostile given that many were as internally fractured as the United States. The law inspired the federal government to assert a broader disavowal of its obligations to Native people under the cover of retribution to their aggressions.

First levied against alleged Confederates, charges of hostility spread to the multitude of Native peoples determined to protect their homelands from an invasion that long predated the war. Antebellum settlers had come to view the erstwhile "permanent Indian frontier," the line of posts dotting the western borders of Arkansas and Missouri, as a starting line for a westward sprint. With routes to California, New Mexico, and Oregon departing from eastern Kansas, Indian Territory—conceived as a space to permanently isolate removed peoples—had become a way station. Unauthorized settler highways laced across regions once considered beyond defensible lines. These routes ran through territories nominally acquired from Britain and Mexico in the 1840s but that belonged, in fact, to a multitude of Indigenous nations, including formidable equestrian powers like the Arapahoes, Cheyennes, Comanches, and Lakotas. With their decentralized political formations and nimble military units, domination of competitive trades in horses, guns, and captives, and expertise in raiding, Plains nations daunted the Union military, forcing it to abandon its conventional reliance on artillery in favor of mounted troops. Settler trespasses across the Great Plains only accelerated during the Civil War, incurring a response from Indigenous peoples that United States lawmakers divorced from its context and explained as an ingrained trait: hostility.[37]

Less than a month after Congress rendered treaty agreements conditional, a convulsion of violence in Minnesota branded the eastern Dakotas as quintessential hostiles. Despite rumors of a Confederate conspiracy, the 1862 Dakota war in fact stemmed from a twofold failure of federal trusteeship: first, to protect their homelands from settler incursions, and second, to maintain financial obligations. The Mdewankton and Wahpekute Dakotas had received $1.41 million for their remaining lands within Iowa and Minnesota Territory in a treaty that most Dakotas had rejected as fraud. The bulk of this sum was to be kept in trust in the Treasury at a 5 percent rate of return, with the interest disbursed annually as aid for agriculture and schooling. But few if any annuities were ever delivered, and those that were the Indian agent made conditional on the performance of agricultural or manual labor. In the summer of 1862, amid a famine and after months of delays, Dakotas learned that their long-awaited annuities would be paid in an unacceptable form: greenbacks, which circulated at a 25 percent discount relative to the price of gold. For many Dakotas forced by federal neglect to rely on traders charging exorbitant rates for food, depreciated paper notes would only worsen hunger. In Mdewakanton leader Wambditanka's recollection, it was only once the Dakotas were told that "the government was in a great war, and gold was scarce, and paper money had taken its place" that "the war talk started up."[38]

That August, Mdewakanton war leader Little Crow led attacks on the Lower Sioux Indian agency and adjacent trader stores, where his forces seized direly needed provisions. Several hundred settlers and many more Dakotas perished in the clashes that followed, with General John Pope overseeing a vengeful campaign. By the fall, Pope had taken around fifteen hundred Dakotas as prisoners, thirty-eight of whom were hanged in what remains the largest mass execution in the country's history.[39]

The Dakotas were not the only nation pushed to take up arms in response to unkept commitments to supply annuities and subsistence. Throughout the Civil War, and for years after its conclusion, annuities were withheld, delayed, or forfeited to settlers as compensation for depredations. When promised annuities did arrive, they seemed intended to mock their recipients. One annuity delivered to the Arapahoes and Cheyennes consisted of rotting coffee, recycled hospital uniforms, and tattered blankets. Like other famished and indebted peoples, the Arapahoes and Cheyennes responded to these failures of trusteeship by raiding on caravans and into settlements, acts the military treated as treaty violations meriting unbridled retribution.[40]

The Dakotas were not the only nation enraged by the substitution of fiat currency for the specie that they were owed. Ojibwe bands who had received annuities in precious metal since the 1840s protested paper money payments in the spring of 1863 as a violation of their treaty. The next fall, Ojibwe leader Hole in the Day warned that "paper money" would be "the same to us as receiving no annuities, for the amount of goods we will receive from our traders for our annuities will be as nothing to our great wants."[41] Hole in the Day's criticisms only grew more valid as greenbacks continued to depreciate, trading at a 60 percent discount by July 1864. Nations that did successfully insist on specie began to hoard it as a hedge against inflation. By 1865, an Indian agent reported that Potawatomis in Kansas—a group that included the United Nations of Odawa, Ojibwe, and Potawatomi—had "treasured up" around $4,000 in gold, which he estimated to be worth $5,600 on the money market.[42]

Mineral strikes, settler trespassing, and unmet financial obligations kept the flame of war alive on the Plains. While some in Congress recognized the role of failed trusteeship in the pattern, for others such rampant conflict reinforced the idea that certain Indigenous peoples were unrepentantly hostile and thus beyond the reach of any civilian engagement. Only the use of force could succeed, according to this thinking, and this option no longer seemed so expensive amid a parallel war of staggering scale. Suppressing the South had entailed a massive military-fiscal mobilization that now dwarfed civilian spending, making it newly possible to argue for using military force rather than annuities and treaties to pacify hostile nations. In 1861, Congress spent roughly $2.9 million on civilian Indian affairs and $35.4 million on military spending. By 1864, the country was spending less on civilian Indian affairs—only $2.6 million—while military spending had billowed to roughly $776.5 million, about three hundred times more than civilian spending on Indian affairs.[43] At the peak of its wartime capacity, it seemed the Union could afford to reconsider its obligations to Native peoples.

Slavery had inspired the South's rebellion, and it would hasten its collapse. From its founding, the Confederacy had relied almost entirely on issuances of securities and Treasury notes to finance its insurgency. Lacking the diversified economy and immigration-boosted population of the North, the Confederacy held fewer options for war mobilization than its rival. It chose to double down on cotton cultivation rather than sacrifice slave labor to the war effort. Cotton bales became the foundation of the Confederate fiscal state, serving as collateral for a secret loan from a French banking house. Since the Confederate Treasury accepted cotton as a means of payment for bond subscriptions, cotton even circulated as a kind of legal tender.[44]

This brittle fiscal structure rested on the Confederacy's commodity exports, which in turn relied on its commercial networks. The Union's blockade of occupied ports and destruction of the railroads that fed them failed to stop ships laden with bales of southern cotton from sailing east. But it still caused a ninefold increase in transport costs and undermined the collateral offered to British financiers, who eventually pivoted toward less vexing sources of cotton. As Confederate bonds slid in value, so too did Confederate currency. Slaveholding states had, before the war, declined to create robust systems of taxation that might have undermined the political power of the planter class, and the Confederacy's own reluctance to tax left it especially vulnerable to inflation. A flurry of increasingly worthless paper financed the final years of the rebellion.[45]

Hamstrung financially, the Confederacy limped forward as a trustee to Native allies. Confederate plans to sweep the trans-Mississippi West had ended abruptly in March 1862 with a loss at the Battle of Pea Ridge on the Arkansas-Missouri border. Union control of the Ozark Plateau severed

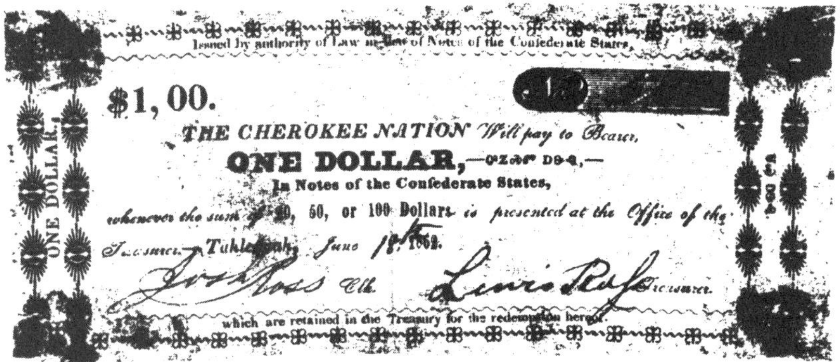

A Cherokee Nation treasury bill, backed by Confederate currency and printed in June 1862. Signed by Principal Chief John Ross and Treasurer Lewis Ross. *Source:* Oklahoma Historical Society.

Confederate communications between Richmond, Virginia, and Indian Territory, exacerbating the logistical challenges of supplying annuities and goods to its ostensible Native allies. Fearing "disastrous consequences" if doubts about the Confederacy's competency as a trustee were to fester, Confederate Indian Commissioner Scott headed for Indian Territory, his journey slow and halting given the disjointed operation of trains across the western theater. Arriving in mid-October, Scott disbursed more than $210,000 in annuities, meeting with Cherokee, Chickasaw, Choctaw, Creek, and Seminole leaders in a bid to restore goodwill.[46]

Yet the Confederacy's financial hardships had only begun. Food riots erupted across the home front, the Confederacy's specie scarcity worsened, and inflation soared, with prices rising almost thirtyfold. In May 1862, the Confederacy began offering annuities in cotton and, eventually, in heavily depreciated currency, making it difficult if not impossible for Native nations to import manufactured goods. As recently elected Choctaw Principal Chief Peter Pitchlynn pointed out, the delivery of annuities in discounted notes amounted to "a tax of thirty three and one third cents on the dollar" that "in spirit and in fact" violated their treaty with the Confederacy, which had exempted them from taxation.[47] In a desperate attempt to make up for annuities they could no longer deliver, Confederate officials arranged to ship whatever cotton could be raised from slaveholder plantations across Indian Territory nations to Mexico so that Native nations could "obtain necessaries."[48] At this point the Confederacy had grown desperate enough to contemplate freeing slaves who served in its military. But too many had already risen up and fled, mounting a general strike that would deal the Confederacy its fatal blow.[49] On April 9, 1865, Confederate General Robert E. Lee surrendered to the Union at Appomattox.

Before its bitter end, the Civil War brought unprecedented misery to Indian Territory. After refusing to sign a treaty with the Confederacy, Opothle Yohola had led roughly eleven thousand Creeks and self-emancipating slaves, many women and children, on a brutal exodus to Union camps in Kansas. Evacuees endured the war on the cusp of famine, lacking proper shelter, clothing, blankets, or even axes to cut firewood. In their first winter hundreds died of exposure, and hundreds more underwent amputations. Roughly two thousand ponies lay dead of starvation along the Verdigris River; in the spring of 1862, the stench emanating from their carcasses forced Indian agents to abandon the camp. Successive waves of refugees, mostly women and children, arrived as the war wore on, driven from their homes first by Cherokee Confederate General Stand Watie's scorched-earth campaign, then by starvation, and then by an aborted Union expedition that had once again left Indian Territory unprotected. When refugees were finally repatriated in 1864, they arrived too late in the season to plant crops on land scarred beyond recognition. Cattle theft by both Confederate and Union armies had decimated Natives' once-prosperous ranches: One 1865 estimate counted three hundred thousand cattle stolen from Indian country by Union forces alone. At an average value of $15 per head, losses amounted to roughly $4,500,000. As one Union officer remarked on surveying the destruction visited on the Cherokees, who suffered most from thefts and military impressment, "the 'protection' we are now giving would ruin any country on earth."[50]

The end of the war brought hope for an end to the destruction, but it also presented an immediate threat to Native nations that stood accused of hostility to United States. Whether or not the federal government would reconcile with putatively hostile nations was uncertain, but in the end boiled down, as before, to questions of military and fiscal capacity. At the war's end, twenty thousand troops were stationed on hundreds of posts along the frontier, separated by thousands of miles, from Dakota Territory to Kansas to California. While the US military would never contract to its prewar levels, postwar demobilization nonetheless diminished the allure of relying on armed force alone to contain Native nations.[51] Ultimately, the federal government resumed its financial obligations to onetime hostiles, albeit in a form that dispensed with any vestiges of reciprocity. The repercussions of this altered trusteeship would ripple outward, affecting even those who had remained on the margins of the conflict.

That the government did not want another all-out war was plain to leaders across Indian Territory. At one international council, Chickasaw Governor Winchester Colbert reminded his counterparts that treaties had always appealed to the United States for fiscal reasons. It remained "cheaper for the Federal Government to make good Treaties than to fight a number of Indian Tribes," he reasoned.[52] Federal officials did, in fact, desire a cheaper option than renewed combat, and they considered a reconciliation with allegedly Confederate-aligned nations a priority. Pacification of alleged rebels would free up resources for the military to invade the West.

Federal officials spent the spring and summer of 1866 preparing to contain Indian Territory by negotiating treaties with delegates who streamed into Washington. Each treaty exacted punitive land cessions, features that portended the government's bellicose plans for the West after the Civil War. In a display of arbitrariness, the Creek and Seminole Nations—who had opposed the Confederacy in the greatest number and fled en masse to Union refugee camps in Kansas—were compelled to give up the most land. The Creeks ceded more than three million acres, while the Seminole ceded their entire domain—more than two million acres—and agreed to relocate onto two hundred thousand acres on the western edge of Creek territory. Branded as traitors to the Union despite their divisions, the Cherokees were compelled to open a strip of Western land called the Cherokee Outlet for settlement by other Indigenous peoples forced to relocate to Indian Territory. By employing an attorney, John Latrobe, who also held a stake in the net proceeds claim (and thus in the restoration of antebellum treaties), the Chickasaws and Choctaws received the most lenient terms, despite their more unified support for the Confederacy. The nations surrendered a district already leased to the federal government for the price of $300,000—three-fourths assigned to the Choctaws and one-fourth to the Chickasaws.[53]

Dispossession was only one purpose of the 1866 treaties, however. They also intended to free slaves within nations that had not agreed to do so of their own accord, pitting emancipation against Native sovereignty. In the case of the Chickasaws and Choctaws, trusteeship became a cudgel to impose abolition: their compensation would be held in trust until both nations enfranchised former slaves. If the nations failed to do so, according to the treaty, the government would instead distribute the sum to their former slaves. Both Chickasaw and Choctaw governments were loath to obey this edict, calling instead for freedpeople's expulsion.

In November 1866 the Chickasaw legislature voted unanimously to forfeit their share of compensation held in trust. Choctaws granted citizenship to freedpeople in 1883, but the Chickasaws would never recognize as members of their nation the people they had enslaved.[54]

Even as they issued dictates to Native signatories, the treaties of 1866 promised to restore former treaty obligations, including annuities. It was clear to all involved, however, that this promise would take some effort to keep. Soon after signing, Native leaders began requesting financial statements from their federal trustee. "Our people are anxious to understand fully the condition of their funds in the hand of the Government," a Chickasaw delegation composed of Colbert Carter, Holmes Colbert, Winchester Colbert, and Edmund Pickens wrote. "What stocks have matured & been redeemed and the proceeds re-invested?" they asked. "What sold or exchanged for other securities"?[55] Chickasaw delegates inquired about specific investments, including Ohio bonds that had matured in 1856. Suspecting some of their annuities had been spent on provisioning refugees in Kansas, the Choctaws requested a statement documenting misappropriations and demanded "all their available funds at as early a day as possible."[56]

The prospects for a prompt restoration of trust assets and annuities were not good. Supervision of the Indian trust funds had devolved during the chaotic antebellum period—when the bond theft occurred—and only worsened during the war itself. Amid the upheaval, the Office of Indian Affairs had lost track not only of interest owed by states but of the investments it held in the first place. An 1867 inventory revealed that the Office of Indian Affairs held over $4,291,800 in federal and state securities, with more than half of this amount representing state bonds that no longer paid any interest. Nations that had nominally joined the Confederacy were the worst hit. Even before adding in overdue interest, the Creeks were owed $149,800 in nonpaying bonds, the Choctaws $471,000, and the Cherokees a whopping $572,500 (on top of the $83,000 still owed the Cherokees from the 1860 theft). Yet many ostensibly "loyal" nations like the Lenapes, Senecas, and Shawnees had also been affected. The Odawa, Ojibwe, and Potawatomis saw roughly 40 percent of their education fund wiped out by secession.[57]

Once again the federal government would find itself covering for delinquent states. In 1865, President Andrew Johnson encouraged Southern states to repudiate any war bonds issued to finance the rebellion. By 1868 every former Confederate state had done so, and for good measure, the Fourteenth Amendment to the Constitution prohibited federal assumption of Confederate debts. But these repudiations did not apply to antebellum debts (those held by the Indian trust funds)—of which Southern states still owed $105 million. These bonds held dismal value, if any: Georgia's 6 percent bonds had lost around one-fourth of their face value, South Carolina's circulated at a bit more than one-third of their face value, and certain issuances from Florida, Virginia, and Louisiana were entirely worthless.[58] To keep annuities flowing, Congress began supplementing nonexistent interest, much as it had after the defaults of the early 1840s. Not for the first time, the federal government faced the quandary of how to compel states to honor debts to Native nations.

Indigenous leaders worried that federal laxity toward Southern states would compromise their finances. In 1870, Holmes Colbert of the Chickasaws, Lewis Downing of the Cherokees, and Peter Pitchlynn of the Choctaws, among others, wrote to the Office of Indian Affairs to stipulate that distressed states must repay trusts in full and that, most important, "gold should be demanded" for both "principal and interest."[59] On this latter point the letter cited *Hepburn v. Griswold*, a case decided the year before by the US Supreme Court, in which the justices rejected the status of paper money as legal tender for debts incurred prior to the issuance of greenbacks in 1862. Astute legal reasoning alone could not preserve their nations' nearly century-old specie annuity standard against a consolidating monetary union, however. *Hepburn* would be reversed a year later, states continued to pay interest to their creditors in greenbacks, and the Office of Indian Affairs passed them on to dissatisfied nations as annuities.[60]

Collecting on debts owed to the trust funds would take years, and more than one method. States that had remained within the Union were relatively easy to hold accountable. In 1868 the Office of Indian Affairs arranged for the Treasury to garnish sums owed by the federal government to Indiana, Missouri, and West Virginia (which had inherited some of Virginia's antebellum debts) as reimbursement for sums spent financing their own procurement in the war's chaotic early months. Extracting funds from the former confederate states posed a steeper challenge. After the war, with Southern states desperately insolvent, Congress spent around $94,000 per year substituting its own funds for the interest owed by Arkansas, Florida, Louisiana, North Carolina, South Carolina, Tennessee, and Virginia. Congress neglected to appropriate funds for the Chickasaw Nation, since their trust fund remained under the Treasury's control rather than that of the Office of Indian Affairs. Only in 1878, after a forceful petition from Chickasaw Governor B. F. Overton that cited jurists

Hugo Grotius, Emmerich Vattel, and Chancellor James Kent on the duty to honor antebellum debts after the return of peace, did the Chickasaws receive the $220,290 owed them. Yet even these payments to the Chickasaws and others covered the overdue interest alone, leaving the principal outstanding. It would take until 1895, thirty years after the end of the Civil War, for the federal government to return to the Indian trust funds the more than $1,330,000 in principal still owed them by Southern states.[61]

While clerks in the Office of Indian Affairs sorted through fragmented trust fund ledgers and correspondence, both civilian and military officials stationed in the field launched a campaign to impose order on the West. They faced Indigenous military power that exceeded what the United States had confronted in recent memory but also potentials for extractive industry too alluring to ignore. The West's mineral resources caused an explosive pattern of settlement and demanded a novel colonial strategy focused on opening and policing routes of overland travel, especially transcontinental railroads.

Starting with an 1858 gold strike in Colorado, mining booms on Native land had punctuated the Civil War era in regular succession, erupting at sites spread from Colorado's Pikes Peak to Arizona to Montana. Prospectors disenchanted by diminishing returns on older mines flocked to the latest lodes, creating rushes of migration across unceded territories. Early arrivals might have secured tentative permission from Natives willing to work as guides or to trade with travelers, but by the mid-1860s corridors west had become war zones. Caravans streamed through land belonging to the Arapahoes, Lakotas, and Northern Cheyennes toward gold strikes in Montana and Washington Territories. Raiding and counterattacks along the Bozeman Trail would rage until 1868. Miners headed to Arizona trespassed on Apache land, incurring raids from Mescalero and Mimbres Apaches on the Rio Grande Valley and brutal military campaigns in response.[62]

Native raids on intruding settlers were sometimes opportunistic, seizing food, goods, or captives, and sometimes retaliatory, punishing violations according to Native laws and conventions. No matter the justification, the US military uniformly interpreted them as wanton aggression that merited violent response, including indiscriminate massacres. In the Sand Creek Massacre of 1864, Colonel John M. Chivington and his Colorado volunteers slaughtered 148 peaceful southern Arapahoes and

Cheyennes, mostly women and children. Many who fled Chivington's forces carried war pipes to neighboring Arapaho and Cheyenne bands and to their Lakota allies, who swept through the South Platte River Valley, tearing up telegraph wires, raiding wagon trains, and effectively isolating Denver from the east.[63]

More land was ceded by treaty during the Civil War than in any other comparable period, but treaties had never failed so resoundingly in their aim of disarming Native signatories. Before the Civil War, apart from the spectacular insurgency of the Seminoles in Florida—an exception that only reinforced federal officials' faith in the wisdom of avoiding war—treaties had largely succeeded in seizing Native land without provoking major armed conflicts. Now treaties no longer quieted violence but rather formed a part of its escalation, as military leaders on both sides considered truce-breaking cause for redoubled force. Reverberations of broken treaties across the West altered fiduciary colonial's fiscal logic. The costs of war and of keeping peace through annuities no longer counterbalanced one another, but instead soared simultaneously. Both nonmilitary spending on Indian affairs and military spending on Indian wars roughly doubled in 1865. Warfare was still five times as expensive, but peace no longer seemed so cheap.[64]

One notorious example of an emergent cycle of treaty making, treaty breaking, and avenging followed postwar negotiations with the Arapahoes, Cheyennes, and Lakotas. An 1866 treaty with the Brule and Oglala Lakotas committed $70,000 in annuities to secure safe passage for travelers on the Bozeman Trail, but Oglala Lakota military leader Red Cloud had not signed and refused to abide by its terms. Before the treaty could be ratified, in December 1866, Red Cloud's war party ambushed a military detachment protecting the Bozeman Trail under the command of Captain William Fetterman, killing all eighty-one soldiers. In response, General William Tecumseh Sherman, who now presided over an immense military theater spread from the Mississippi River to the Rocky Mountains, declared an all-out war on the Northern Plains. Writing to his brother, Sherman concluded that the Lakotas and their Northern Cheyenne allies "must be exterminated, for they cannot & will not settle down, and our people will force us to it."[65] Bursts of fighting that followed thwarted the progress of the Union Pacific Railroad as it crept along the Bozeman Trail. Red Cloud's War was only one example among the many escalations that erupted along travel corridors and in mineral enclaves. Between 1865 and 1898, according to the US Army's own count, it engaged Native militaries in combat more than 940 times.[66]

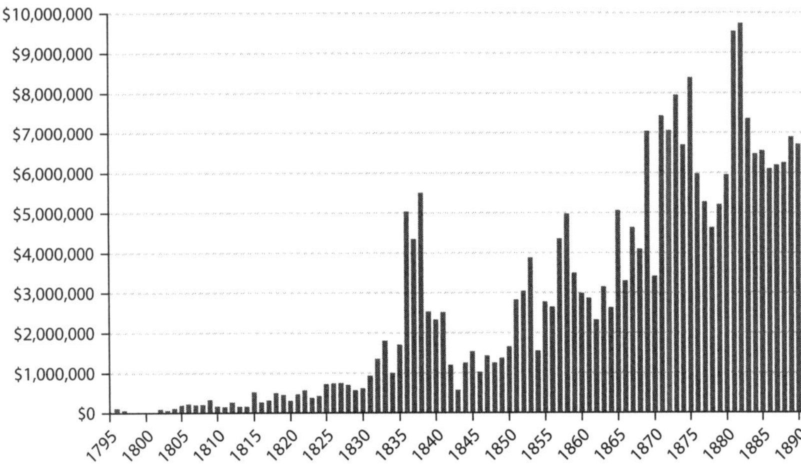

Federal civil expenditures on Indian affairs, 1795–1890. *Source:* US Department of the Interior, Census Office, *Report on Indians Taxed and Indians Not Taxed in the United States (Except Alaska)* (GPO, 1894).

What military commanders and lawmakers alike recognized was that winning the so-called Indian Wars would demand infrastructural investment on a scale that only the federal government could provide. Sectional competition over the best route west had prevented a major railroad bill until the 1862 Pacific Railway Act, which aimed to construct a logistics corridor that would keep the West, and especially California, for the Union. The path to transcontinental railroads would prove more convoluted than Congress hoped, but the act nonetheless aspired to a nationally coordinated transportation system unthinkable since President Andrew Jackson vetoed legislative efforts on constitutional grounds. In addition to expediting military logistics and cutting the costs of overland shipments by 250 percent, transcontinental lines acted as weapons in their own right, obstructing the movement of bison, horses, and people across the Plains, starving nations of their resources and weakening their strategic positions. In the words of Senator William Steward of Nevada, Native peoples "can only be permanently conquered by railroads. The locomotive is the sole solution to the Indian question."[67]

Railroads would hardly conquer the West on their own, but their spread nonetheless encapsulated an alignment of state and capital forces necessary to overcome Native power. Even as a leviathan the government still faced daunting logistical impediments in the West. Combining with corporations brought its colonial objectives within reach. State governments

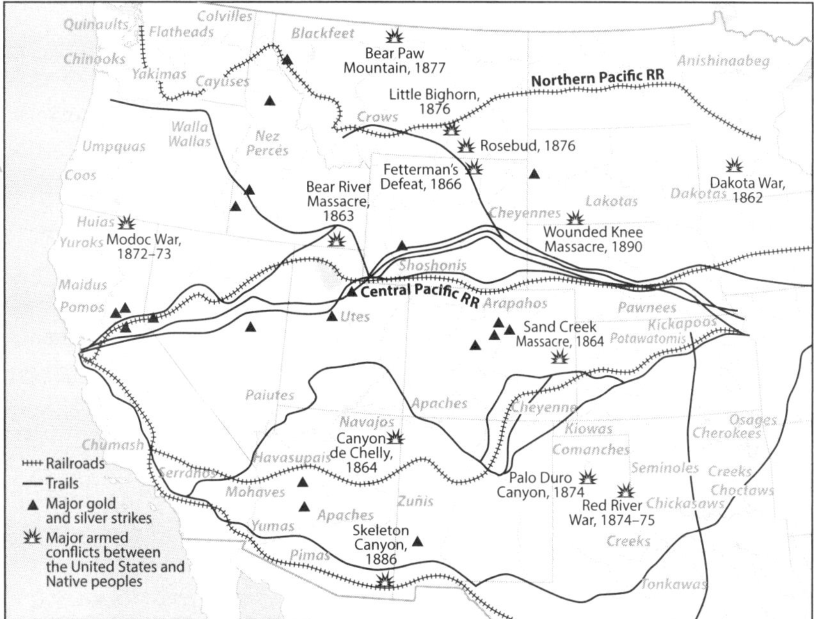


Transit routes, mineral strikes, and warfare in the West. Colonial violence erupted in the West along travel corridors and mining sites, where conflicts repeatedly escalated into massacres of Native civilians. *Source:* Map created by Shane Kelley.

had chartered a bumper crop of manufacturing and extractive enterprises during the war, and a postwar investment boom driven by war bonds and the National Banking Acts bred new corporations. Railroads were direct beneficiaries of the federal government's financial interventions. Congress authorized more than \$64.6 million in federal bonds to capitalize railroad companies under the 1862 and 1864 Pacific Railway Acts. Like states' borrowing a generation earlier, federal borrowing to build infrastructure constituted a form of seemingly taxless finance that in actuality shifted corporate risk onto citizens. This was especially true in the case of railroads. Because of the Railway Acts' sloppy construction, Congress wound up covering interest payments for railroad companies. Were the corporations to go bankrupt, Congress would recoup its investment only after private creditors were paid.[68]

Congress's charitable terms of credit incentivized a venture that involved nearly insurmountable challenges and otherwise made little economic sense. Transcontinental railroads would ultimately span thousands of miles and crosscut imposing mountain ranges—notably, the Sierra Nevada, which rises more than 14,500 feet above sea level. Aside from pockets of settler density in California and in mining towns nestled in rugged terrain, most of the lines would course through land inhabited only by Indigenous peoples—not exactly a customer base companies could rely on for revenue. Business was concentrated at terminal stops, which meant it would begin only once the line was complete. In short, railroad companies needed a major partner, and the Pacific Railroad Acts supplied an immense and up-front capitalization, as well as assurances to hedge the significant risks involved.[69]

Railroads drove forward the federal government's continued transformation into a colonial developmental state. Unlike state governments, Congress held unmediated authority over public lands and could make of them a financial resource for infrastructural development. By the end of President Ulysses S. Grant's term in office, railroad corporations had received more than 127.6 million acres in land grants. Much of this land remained in Indigenous possession, making the spadework of dispossession the government's most critical contribution. Only once the government seized Native land by treaty, negotiated rights of way through any unceded territories, and deployed military attachments to defend construction crews did railroads snake their way across the West. Unstinting assistance was in the government's own financial interest, since so much public money had been put on the line. "Now that the government has assumed the obligation to guarantee the bonds of the Pacific Railroad," then-General Grant wrote to Sherman in the winter of 1867, "it becomes a matter of great pecuniary interest to see it completed as soon as possible."[70]

Railroads represented a new interpenetration of imperial aims and imperatives to profit and came at a moment in which the fiscal logic of trusteeship was breaking down. The costs of war and of keeping peace through annuities no longer counterbalanced one another, but instead soared simultaneously as the government redoubled its efforts to conciliate through civil means. Shortly after his inauguration, President Grant announced a "peace policy" and appointed a Board of Indian Commissioners to advise Commissioner of Indian Affairs Ely S. Parker, a Tuscarora Seneca and Grant's former Civil War secretary. Composed of Northern merchants, industrialists, and Quaker missionaries, the board permitted capitalists to steer Indian policy for the first time, under the guise of philanthropy. Although the board was branded as in the interests of pacification, Congress expected it to rein in profligate spending on Indian affairs—especially annuities. Commissioners set about closely regulating payments, monitoring open bids for goods and rations, auditing Indian agents' vouchers, and rejecting any expenses they deemed excessive.[71]

Despite the board's efforts, civil spending on Indian affairs topped $7 million in 1869, a sum that exceeded the previous record by more than $1.5 million. While the costs of peacekeeping spiraled, the military's outsized presence in the West and its reputation as a rationalized and reliable bureaucracy made it a serious rival to the civilian Indian affairs administration. Conflicts of authority sharpened between territorial and military officials, who governed overlapping domains without clear priority of command. Proposals to transfer the Office of Indian Affairs to the military, an idea first popularized by General John Pope after the 1862 Dakota War, gained traction in Congress, with the House passing two transfer bills in 1867 and 1868.[72] Both failed in the Senate, but they represented another swell of arguments against treaties and the financial obligations they carried.

By 1871, these strains of criticism converged in a debate that consumed both houses of Congress. The parameters of acceptable debate over Native nations and their sovereignty warped and widened. Proponents of an entirely militarized approach pointed to treaties' inefficacy as truces, arguing that only war could bring peace with so-called hostile Indians. "Have we ever succeeded in securing peace with the Indians on the plains or on the frontier," asked James Cavanaugh, a Democratic territorial delegate from Montana, "until they had been soundly thrashed?"[73] An approach to all-out armed invasion that dispensed with treaties altogether had been tested in the antebellum years, in Oregon and more notoriously still in California, where a decades-long genocide launched in 1846 eliminated four-fifths of the Indigenous population. Republican Senator Thomas Fitch of Nevada advocated placing this option back on the table, praising "an exterminating war, carried on by volunteers from the Territory of Nevada and the State of California," and recommending more of the same.[74] With armed violence presumed intractable, the government's continued honoring of financial commitments—and its forging of new obligations in yet more treaties—struck many legislators as absurd. Even California Representative Aaron Sargent, a defender of a more pacific approach, opposed annuities as a means of persuading "Indians not to make war upon us, not to murder our citizens" when in fact "they are simply the wards of the Government, to whom we furnish means of existence."[75]

Over the course of these debates, annuities took on new guises. In the eyes of peace policy advocates they constituted philanthropy; to hawkish lawmakers they amounted to humiliating tribute. Both definitions indicated a growing consensus that annuities were nonbinding and discretionary, eclipsing their status as solemn obligations between sovereigns.

Much had changed over the course of the war to allow such a consensus to form. A crisis of secession had collapsed trust investments and caused federal officials to break financial promises. When Congress considered making amends and repaying what was owed to nations who had seen their wealth stolen or suddenly devalued, lawmakers began deploying a distinction between pacified and hostile Indians that encouraged the idea that treaties were conditional. New treaties were made and broken, and violence spread, seeming to discredit treaties' effectiveness. By the Civil War's end, what was most offensive to Congress about the current form of federal trusteeship was not the quantity of money being spent on seizing the West—although that was certainly the subject of many a congressional jeremiad—but the *quality* of this spending: the idea that the federal government could be bound to pay Native people anything at all.

So, too, had the politics of fiscal spending changed, widening the circle of stakeholders in federal Indian policy. Because the Union had created new, more visible forms of taxation to assist in funding the war—including an income tax—lawmakers could now frame the cost of treaties as a drain on citizens. When it came time to approve yet another soaring Indian appropriation bill in March 1871, Republican senator James Stewart of Nevada berated Congress for "taxing the white people, taxing the washerwomen, to feed Indian chiefs that live in idleness."[76] Unsurprisingly, treaty claims resurfaced as an object of criticism. The Civil War had interrupted but not abated the rush of petitions from Native peoples, their attorneys, and their traders demanding compensation for stolen lands and unpaid money. As calls to end treaties mounted, Congress once again moved to thwart claims by prohibiting Native nations from drawing contracts with outsiders.

The long-standing Choctaw net proceeds claim, for money raised on their homelands sold under an 1830 treaty, acquired infamy in this period. In 1859, in response to Peter Pitchlynn's tireless lobbying, the Senate had determined that just over $2,232,500 was owed to the nation, an astonishing sum (to compare, in that fiscal year the General Land Office only collected around $1,628,000 from sales in the public domain). Two years later, as shots broke out at Fort Sumter, Congress approved a first installment to the Choctaws of $500,000, to be paid half in cash and half in bonds. The eruption of a war in which the Choctaws became enemies of the Union delayed the delivery of the bonds indefinitely and significantly complicated the rest of the payment. Over half of the cash portion was successfully delivered to the Choctaw agent, who promptly absconded with it to the Confederacy. The remainder took the form of a draft on a

New York City bank that the Choctaws found nearly impossible to cash. When, against all odds, tens of thousands of dollars in gold did reach Doaksville, in Choctaw territory, it was quickly partitioned among the Choctaw delegates and their retinue of attorneys. Eager for more, the men revived the claim after the war, submitting an appeal for the remaining $250,000 in bonds to Congress, an impressive sum that nonetheless fell short by $1,833,000 of the amount Congress had admitted it owed— leaving the door open to demands for the rest in the future. Appalled, the House refused to authorize the bond payment until 1871. To lawmakers, the fact that a treaty negotiated by a prior administration more than three decades earlier could continue to impose such a staggering fiscal burden served as a warning against future negotiations.[77]

Treaties also attracted opposition from the public, although not primarily for their impact on tax bills. In the era after the 1862 Homestead Act, national sentiment turned against railroad treaties. In the years before the war, treaties signed in Kansas had allowed railroad companies to capture land directly, skirting public auctions and the hassle of eminent domain. Railroad treaties persisted despite the controversy, and settlers' opposition increased now that they considered Native lands across the continent theirs to rightfully inherit for little more than a filing fee. An 1868 treaty with the Osages granted prime territories to the Leavenworth, Lawrence, & Galveston Railroad, exasperated prospective homesteaders, brought congressional ire with treaties to a boil, and led the House to summarily refuse Indian affairs appropriations for that year.[78]

The Osage treaty would eventually squeak through Congress, but the outrage its ratification incited dealt a final blow to the form of fiduciary colonialism that had facilitated territorial expansion for nearly a century. On March 3, 1871, in a clause appended to that year's routine Indian appropriation bill, Congress abolished the practice of treaty making altogether. No longer would the federal government recognize Native peoples "as an independent nation, tribe, or power . . . with whom the United States may contract by treaty."[79]

<hr>

For nations with treaties in hand, 1871 was less a watershed year than a bellwether of what was yet to come. Treaties already ratified would remain in force, trusts already established would not dissolve, and annuities would—at least for the moment—continue to flow. But the rest of Indian Country suddenly faced a strain of fiduciary colonialism unencumbered by the principles of protection and reciprocity that treaties had, at least in theory, enshrined. Trusteeship now served an ascendant principle of plenary power, which held that Congress enjoyed unlimited and exclusive authority over Native nations, a doctrine that by the late nineteenth century would stretch to overseas jurisdictions in Guam, the Philippines, and Puerto Rico. Through executive orders, presidents and their subordinates confined Indigenous peoples to reservations that were created, altered, and revoked at will. Executive orders were applied most arbitrarily to Apache bands and other peoples in the territories of Arizona and New Mexico who remained, in the words of Acting Commissioner of Indian Affairs H. R. Clum, among the "Indians most difficult of management."[80] In the fall of 1871, for example, Indian commissioner Vincent Coyler affirmed a portion of Apache and Yavapai homelands in the Verde Valley as a reservation, where the government intended to consolidate all Apache bands. Another order annulled the reservation the very next year, and in 1875 the military pushed its inhabitants from the Verde Valley onto the San Carlos Reservation, another creature of executive fiat.[81]

Yet one vestige of treaties remained. Most agreements promised to set aside portions of the proceeds of ceded lands for the dispossessed nation. Whatever sum remained after deducting the costs of surveys, sale, removal, and subsistence would be held in trust by the Office of Indian Affairs, kept in the Treasury, and invested in federal bonds.[82] In this respect, post-1871 agreements bore a striking resemblance to the Chickasaw removal treaties of 1832 and 1834, which were crafted to make removal self-financing at a moment when President Andrew Jackson held fierce and competing desires to dispossess Native peoples and eliminate the national debt. Resurrected and generalized after 1871, this particular mode of compensation allowed once more for confiscations that spared the public purse while preserving federal control over Native wealth.

The endurance of compensated dispossession signaled that a trusteeship hollowed out of sovereign recognition and reciprocity served federal aims just fine. In fact, control became even more useful as these aims grew more ambitious. Once Indigenous peoples were no longer recognized "as an independent nation, tribe, or power," they could be diminished to the status of wards. On a rhetorical level, the term was not new: in his 1831 opinion in *Cherokee v. Georgia*, Supreme Court Justice John Marshall had remarked that the relationship between Native nations and the United States "resembles that of a ward to his guardian."[83] But there were important legal distinctions between trusteeship and guardianship as it operated within Anglo-American law. Whereas trusts could be created for beneficiaries of sound mind, guardianship was reserved solely for minors and incompetents—persons lacking the ability to reason or consent.[84]

Post-1871 wardship was, then, no rhetorical flourish or analogy but rather a formal policy resting on a steepening racial hierarchy. Federal institutions like the Smithsonian nurtured the nascent discipline of ethnology, which applied Darwinian theories to the study of Indigenous cultures, sharpening once hazy connotations of racial inferiority. Ethnology's notion of primitivism supplied a convenient justification for guardianship, a legal status that extended beyond the simple management of the ward's estate to the custody of their person, beyond a specific pool of assets to the entirety of a ward's wealth.[85]

So went federal trusteeship in this period. Per capita annuity distributions became an even broader and better-enforced standard than in the antebellum period in which they had emerged. In most cases annuities were now delivered in goods, even to nations that had once received specie or other forms of cash. Receiving goods instead of money evacuated any autonomy Native peoples once held over the allocation of their wealth within their nations. Where once Native leaders could insist on certain items, demand better-quality merchandise, or choose to spend funds on institutions or debts instead, agents alone now dictated whether funds would be spent on schools or on food, on blankets or on arms. To thwart nations from converting their goods into other commodities or cash, Indian agents prohibited the sale of any rations or goods, stamped metal items to ensure that they would not be traded, and, in the words of one executive order, provided "hostiles" with only enough to meet "absolute wants," a strategy of pacification that operated by keeping Native people at a level of bare subsistence.[86]

Cultivating scarcity gave Indian agents greater leverage. Expanding a policy first tested on the Dakotas during the Civil War—a policy that dovetailed neatly with a standard of per capita annuities—the Office of Indian Affairs made the receipt of annuities and rations conditional on the performance of labor. Only if "able-bodied men" worked would they receive a share of annuities, recast as wages granted rather than compensation already owed. At least one Indian agent in an arid location complained that he could not enforce such a rule if his wards possessed "nothing but their hands to work with." Yet, after early experiments, Congress made the policy mandatory in 1875. In agencies where the annuity wage system took root, the Office of Indian Affairs boasted of manifold benefits: Laboring men received government aid, grasped the virtues of hard work, and saved Congress thousands of dollars on contracts. Whether cutting firewood, splitting rails, moving hay, or even transporting their own

Unidentified Native boys in a metalworking shop at the Carlisle Indian
Industrial School in Pennsylvania, 1904. The school, the first of its kind, was
opened in 1879 by Richard Henry Pratt, who believed that regimented waged
labor would allow Native children to assimilate into the United States. *Source:*
Prints and Photographs Division, Library of Congress.

nations' annuities and rations, Native men received a fraction of what settlers would have demanded in wages. Not coincidentally, practices rolled
out across Indian agencies resembled those imposed on freedpeople in the
occupied South. As one Commissioner of Indian Affairs asserted, a resolution to "this whole Indian problem" demanded "a process similar to that
pursued with the negroes."[87]

Trusteeship had always been presented as an alternative to costlier
force. Wardship incorporated force, made it routine and intimate, applied
to the person rather than the people, at home rather than in the field
of war. Antebellum reservations, while terminals for trails of tears, had
nonetheless merited defense as a space of relative autonomy for nations.
Eastern Indian Territory nations had adapted to reservations and, even
after the end of treaties, managed to sustain degrees of self-governance
over institutions, like schools, which they long had nurtured. Reservations
created after the war operated differently. On lands ceded by the Cherokees, Chickasaws, Choctaws, Creeks, and Seminoles in 1866, the Interior

Department carved out diminutive reservations for nations driven from Kansas that settled in Indian Territory's northeastern corner, and, more problematically, for Plains nations, many considered hostile, that would be forced to surrender and then remain confined to tracts in the territory's western half. In a pattern repeated in reservations created across the West, Indian agents implemented a smothering form of social engineering that, by forcing newly confined peoples to farm without adequate resources or training, quite literally starved them, encouraging disease and death. Alternative forms of subsistence, like hunting or off-reservation waged labor, were accessible only with the permission of Indian agents, creating a state of virtual incarceration.[88]

Once the initiative of Native nation builders, education became mandatory and antithetical to nationhood, designed to interrupt the transmission of lifeways from one generation to another. In 1879, General Henry Pratt opened the Carlisle Indian Industrial School in Pennsylvania, applying his experience overseeing military discipline and penal confinement to the school. Pratt aimed to drive a wedge between generations, to prevent Indigenous children from inheriting knowledge and practices that, in his eyes, obstructed their complete integration into settler society. Funds that nations had earmarked for education flowed toward boarding schools that, by separating children from their kin, intended to cleanse them of their languages and divest them of their cultures, even confiscating the clothes they wore and cropping the hair on their heads on arrival. Parents who tried to hold their children back were deprived of rations and annuities. Cramped into close quarters, deprived of adequate nutrition, and subjected to abuse, a minimum of 831 Indigenous children died of infectious diseases at boarding schools in the fifty-five years after the Carlisle School's founding, with hundreds more Natives succumbing on reservations when sick students were sent home and illness spread.[89]

Under the guise of guardianship, fiduciary colonialism now reached beyond its original aim of land dispossession toward the very shattering of Native sovereignty. Congress contemplated converting Indian Territory into a territory like any other, governed by a federal appointee rather than by the nations themselves, dividing reservations into allotments held as private property, and, perhaps most disturbing, declaring Native persons United States citizens under the Fourteenth Amendment—a move that would effectively dissolve their nations and amount to "forced extinction," in the words of one Creek protest.[90] Calls for a total dissolution of Native nationhood gained traction. Leaders of a few Native nations were even willing to gamble on the allotment of their lands and assimilate to the

United States as citizens rather than remain under the government's yoke. For other Native leaders, however, trusteeship only became more deserving of defense as a last tether to an era in which their people had counted as treaty-worthy sovereigns.

Few avenues other than the issuance of legal claims remained open to contest plenary power in the dark decades to come. When Native leaders mounted these challenges, they kept alive in their statements a vision of trusteeship lost to those who acted in its name. "Your government has assumed the guardianship over the Indians," wrote Choctaw Principal Chief Isaac L. Garvin in one message to Congress. "You must remember that it is a sacred and responsible trust, and as a nation you must answer to the God of nations for your faithful or unfaithful administration."[91]

# Epilogue

THE PAST AND FUTURE OF TRUSTEESHIP

LAURA CORNELIUS KELLOGG sat facing eleven senators, each leafing through drafts of the Indian appropriations bill for the coming 1914 fiscal year. After nearly two months of hearings, some members of the Committee on Indian Affairs had grown impatient. But Chair William J. Stone insisted on allowing Kellogg to speak. "I shall proceed to dissect the Indian situation from the Indian's standpoint," Kellogg began, commanding the attention of the entire chamber. In her view, Native people were mired in an economic stagnancy of the government's making. After decades of colonial administration reservations were "an environment of deficits: there is no industrial system, no money in circulation, and what money does enter the reservation loses its elasticity at once; there grows up a discrimination against the Indian in business; he must pay higher interest and give more security in the local banks; these things all combine to make him a pauper."[1] Kellogg spoke at a moment of heightened concern over the depth of Native poverty, which struck Congress as stemming from a failure to adapt to modernity. To Kellogg, the failures were those of a federal trustee who impeded development on reservations and, more fundamentally, of a capitalist property regime ill-suited to realize Native societies' economic potentials.

An Oneida woman born on the reservation in Wisconsin, Kellogg had attended private school, taught at Sherman Industrial School, and studied law at several prestigious universities, including Barnard, Cornell, and Stanford. She had traveled abroad and spent several years immersed in intellectual circles across Europe. Two years before her testimony to the Senate, she had cofounded the Society of American Indians, the first

Native-led reform organization to address the so-called Indian Question. Despite her pioneering role, Kellogg's views diverged from many of her society peers, who approached the Pan-Indian organization as a vehicle to advance Native equality and eventually integrate Native people as citizens into the United States. To Kellogg, those aims fell far short of what Indigenous peoples could accomplish. Since her time at Sherman, Kellogg had been a strident opponent to boarding schools that, in her view, only conditioned "subservience." They also epitomized the fiduciary paradigm that had arisen after the pivotal abolition of treaties in 1871, in which money originating in treaty obligations had been reallocated to unilaterally administered assimilative programs.[2]

Kellogg instead had a plan that she named Lolomi—her approximation of a Hopi word meaning both "good" and "beautiful"—that would completely reorganize reservation economies. An advocate for reawakening the Haudenosaunee clan systems that had once structured kinship relations, and an admirer of enduring traditional enterprises like Navajo ranching, Kellogg believed that Native societies possessed unique capacities. The problem was how to convert their resources—especially the people and their land—into durable wealth. Lolomi would do so by creating a federally chartered corporation grounded in communist principles for each Native nation. Each citizen would donate a portion of allotted lands to communal property, granting them a share of the corporation— and a single vote in its governance—while working for a wage that would be equalized across all forms of labor. What Kellogg called a "communistic idea of capital" would allow Lolomi to distribute evenly the wealth of a reconstituted Native homeland.[3]

Kellogg's vision of common ownership stood in stark contrast to a growing movement of reformers who held that only the individuation and privatization of wealth could resolve the Indian Question. Sixteen years after Congress had abolished treaties, it passed the Dawes Act, marking a new phase in the history of dispossession through the compulsory dismemberment of communal land. The act dictated that tracts of 160 acres be assigned to each household, with smaller plots for individuals. Subsequent laws extended allotment to reservations initially exempted, including those in Indian Territory. Through this process, Kellog's home reservation, once sixty-five thousand acres, dwindled by 95 percent between 1892 and 1934, leaving her nation with only ninety acres over which it could exercise its sovereignty.[4]

Allotment's premise was that property ownership would act as a tutor, arousing industriousness and a salutary pursuit of self-interest. Yet officials believed immediate ownership would be premature, and so kept trusteeship in place as they weaned nations from collective ownership. Under to the Dawes Act and succeeding legislation, allotments would remain in trust for a period of twenty-five years, at which point title converted to fee simple. When that day arrived, conditions on allotments lifted abruptly, and thousands of newly minted proprietors were forced to weather market pressures on their own. Thousands of allotment holders lost land rapidly through tax foreclosure, investor manipulation, court order, and fraud. Within forty-five years, ninety-one million acres were transferred into settler possession, cutting Indian Country to one-third of its original size. Some allotment holders never gained clean title to their land, however, because they were deemed incompetent to own it. For them, the trust period extended indefinitely, with the somewhat ironic effect of preventing their dispossession. This uneven lifting of restrictions on sale produced a checkerboard pattern that persists today, in which tracts kept in trust and still subject to Native jurisdiction mix incoherently with private land in settler possession.[5]

A far more significant expansion of fiduciary control began after allotment surveys were complete. Any residual land, deemed surplus, was nominally "purchased" by the federal government (a strange transaction, given that nations were given no alternative—but, of course, perfectly consistent with the history of treaty making). These funds were not distributed to nations, but kept on the Treasury's books, where they accrued 3 percent interest. As acre after acre of supposedly surplus reservation land was transferred to the General Land Office, funds held in trust billowed, increasing by more than five and half times in less than a decade to reach nearly $234 million in 1920, a sum equivalent to $24 billion today.[6] Even more compelling for advocates of allotment was that the Dawes Act and its related legislation permitted the government to draw on these funds to finance increasingly expensive assimilation programs—boarding schools, in particular. Here was a far broader sense in which allotment sustained fiduciary colonialism, one that ledgers could not document: Allotment promoted the contrived idea that Congress knew better than nations how to organize their economies, and it appealed to its enactors as a form of conquest on the cheap.

It was only a matter of time before allotment's enthusiasts would pursue the individuation of money held in common. Starting in 1907, Congress began commuting national annuities into lump sums and allowed individuals to withdraw their personal shares. Allotments generated revenue from agricultural, mineral, timber, and grazing leases, which Indian superintendents deposited at local banks on behalf of individuals. Allottees considered competent could draw and spend that money freely; those considered incompetent could not, and their money collected in an individual trust fund. When Congress finally brought allotment to a halt in 1934, it extended indefinitely restrictions on the eleven million acres of allotments still held in trust and stipulated that any future lands restored to reservations would be held in trust as well. Revenue generated from leases on trust allotments, as well as any other restricted funds, trickled into what were by then called Individual Indian Money accounts.[7]

Apportioning money in this way struck Kellogg as preposterous. If an "individual Indian has $500 in assets," she pointed out in one essay, "this is no kind of a start to the ostracized, unskilled, uneducated man." But if hundreds of these sums were pooled together, she reasoned, "we have a capitalization big enough to promote an independent industry."[8] Kellogg's arguments were somewhat ironic in light of her own biography: She would later in life face credible accusations that she defrauded the Oneidas of funds raised to cover the legal costs of a land claim. Her apparent crime contradicted her stated principles, but it did not weaken the logic of her argument. Only by reconstituting a common stock of land—and, emphatically, a common stock of money—could nations recover from allotment's shattering impact. To ensure that the value of national funds benefited their shared owners, Kellogg proposed investment in a banking system and life insurance. These financial institutions had failed to take root on reservations, she argued, not because of Native ineptitude but because of federal policies that had denied Native people the right to govern their own money. When Elouise Cobell founded the Blackfeet National Bank in 1987, and grew it despite federal policies that withheld her own nation's deposits, she offered living proof of Kellogg's point.[9]

In the spring of 1973, Ada Deer sat facing Representatives Manuel Lujan Jr. and Lloyd Meeds, who had traveled to an unassuming visitors center in Keshena, Wisconsin, to preside over a remote hearing for the House Subcommittee on Indian Affairs. A Menominee woman, Deer was born on the reservation, raised in Milwaukee, and attended college at the University of Wisconsin, where she became the first Menominee to graduate with a bachelor's degree, and then Columbia University's School of Social Work, where she became the first Native person to earn a master's degree. After stints in the Bureau of Indian Affairs and as a social worker in Minneapolis, Deer moved back to Wisconsin, a few hours from her childhood home. By then, the Menominee Reservation where she grew up no longer existed.[10]

Years before, under the administration of President Harry Truman, Congress had initiated a policy called termination. In a series of laws, Congress dissolved targeted nations, revoked their federal trust protections, and unceremoniously proclaimed their members United States citizens. Indian agencies were shuttered, the services they had provided withdrawn. State jurisdiction spread across reservations that were now counties like any others. Most important, the trust relationship was severed and the government's fiduciary role abandoned. Assets held in trust were liquidated, transferred to private corporations, and divided into one-time per capita payments.[11]

The Menominees had been chosen as the first nation to be terminated because of their prosperity, built on stable political institutions and a thriving forestry enterprise. The policy came into effect in 1961 and within a matter of years, their once-robust economy crumbled. The nation was forced into expensive contracts with neighboring counties for basic infrastructure, and were suddenly responsible for steep state taxes, which compelled the nation to sell its utility companies and lay off workers at its lumber mill. Menominee county became the poorest in Wisconsin. A tuberculosis outbreak spread with devastating outcomes because the county lacked a hospital, or even a full-time physician. Worse, a corporation in which settlers held a majority of voting shares now controlled Menominee assets, including their forests and lumber mill, and had begun selling off lakeside properties to outsiders. Deer and other Menominees were appalled by the corporation's decisions and began organizing to reclaim governance of their homelands. By 1973 they had made headway. A bill to restore the Menominees' trust relationship to the federal government came before Congress, and it was to urge that bill's passage that Deer attended the hearing held at the Keshena visitors' center that day.[12]

Termination was supposed to put an end to the long history of federal trusteeship and the financial obligations it entailed. Among the most vexing of these obligations were Native claims. In 1881, the Choctaws had succeeded in bringing their fifty-year-old net proceeds claim before the Court of Claims after securing special legislation from Congress. Dozens of other nations acted on the precedent, submitting claims that the government owed them for land, resources, and annuities. Between 1881 and 1946, the court heard 142 Native claims, thirty-five of which were successful—to an extent. Judges recognized claims totaling $49.4 million. Yet because the court allowed awards to be offset by "gratuities," the claimants only received $20 million.[13]

Gratuities were defined by the court as funds spent on the claimant nation in excess of the compensation promised them by treaty in the years since that treaty was signed. Anything from salaries for Indian agents, police, judges, and interpreters, to the maintenance and repair of agency buildings, to the costs of teachers and tuition—all were tallied by the General Accounting Office in exhaustive audits and subject to categorization as a gratuity. It was an impressive contortion of history, in which the very costs of Indian affairs administration, including the costs of dispossession, forced relocation, containment to reservations, and compulsory assimilationist education were all retroactively defined as surplus compensation and deducted from what the government admitted that it owed. Among the judgments dramatically offset by gratuities was one awarded to the Blackfeet Nation in 1935. The court found that the government owed the Blackfeet nearly $6,131,000 in compensation for lands effectively stolen by executive order in 1874. Yet it allowed over $5,500,000 in gratuities, leaving the Blackfeet with only $622,466. After lawyers took around one-third of that amount as their fee, the government distributed a per capita payment of eighty-five dollars to the nation's members and placed the rest in trust in the hands of the defendant—that is, in the US Treasury.[14]

Even as the General Accounting Office scythed away at the court's judgments, lawmakers considered claims to be tethers keeping the government bound to trusteeship. To create a clean slate and end trust obligations once and for all, Congress created the Indian Claims Commission in 1947. Lawmakers, Indian affairs officials, and even judges explicitly framed the resolution of claims for monetary restitution as a final step toward termination. Some nations with successful claims were even awarded judgments made contingent on termination. It was only after they were told that their per capita share of an $8.5 million claim award hung in the balance that a majority of Menominees voted in favor of the policy. Another election—held after the implications of termination were fully explained—overturned the vote, but officials ignored it.[15]

The truth was that the Menominees had never wanted termination, Deer told the congressmen. "Termination represented a gigantic and revolutionary forced change," she stated, one that had brought only immiseration and, most painfully, the undermining of self-governance. Termination needed to end, yet Deer emphasized that restoring the trust relationship should not revert the Menominee to a status quo of fiduciary control. "We want Federal protection," Deer emphasized, "not Federal domination."[16] Congress passed the Menominee Restoration Act that December, inspiring dozens of other nations to successfully challenge their own termination.

Termination's architects had altogether ignored allotment's cautionary tale. Abandoning trusteeship in favor of wholesale privatization did not liberate Native wealth but rather revoked exactly the elements of trusteeship Indigenous peoples had demanded since the dawn of fiduciary colonialism: protection from the United States' own citizens and recognition of their sovereignty over their internal affairs. By swiftly dismantling trusteeship, termination destroyed nations' ability to decide through their own political process how their wealth would be collected, invested, and to what ends it should be spent. Laura Cornelius Kellogg, a fierce advocate of self-government, had witnessed termination's foreshadowing in the devastation of allotment. For this reason, she had reminded Congress that every Native nation was entitled to "the highest protection in the land, the protection of the United States Government."[17]

In August 1992, Elouise Cobell sat across from three senators to discuss Individual Indian Money accounts. In addition to working as her nation's comptroller and running the Blackfeet National Bank, Cobell had for years assisted Blackfeet citizens who could not make heads or tails of their accounts. One man named James Mad Dog Kennerly had inherited allotment land that hosted up to five working oil wells at a time, yet his royalties averaged a mere thirty dollars per month. An elderly woman, Bernice Skunk Cap, had tried to withdraw money from her trust fund after suffering a fire that destroyed her home. Officials told her she was not "competent" enough to withdraw the $2,400 that had accrued in her account, sending her home with only $1,000. When she returned a week later to collect the rest, they told her the money was gone. As these stories accumulated and Cobell's own frustrations deepened, she joined forces with other Native leaders, forming the Intertribal Monitoring Association on Trust Funds (ITMA) in 1991.[18]

Cobell testified that day in her capacity as chairperson of ITMA. She began by recounting one of her earliest encounters with the bureaucracy of the Individual Indian Money accounts. One summer she had worked at the Blackfeet Indian Agency, "a very dismal office," she recalled, with a "small window about this big that looked out into a hallway of rows of very, very hard benches." Every morning Cobell watched as elders filed into the agency, sat in discomfort, and waited to request their own money from the superintendent. One day, Cobell "could no longer tolerate the hurt and humiliation that my people were suffering." She stormed into

Elouise Cobell listens as Deputy Secretary of the Interior David Hayes, foreground, testifies at a 2009 Senate Indian Affairs Committee hearing in Washington, DC. *Source:* AP Photo / Evan Vucci.

the agent's office to insist that he give those waiting outside a moment of his time, only to find him sound asleep. The story encapsulated the willful negligence and incompetence of federal trusteeship and conveyed how trust funds had come to degrade their beneficiaries. "For too long we have been cut off from our trust funds," Cobell stated. "We sit with $2 billion in a bank, and not any of it working in Indian communities for us."[19]

In the century after the Dawes Act, Individual Indian Money accounts had devolved into absurdity. With each inheritance, the allotments that underpinned individual trusts were partitioned among descendants, splintering interests in leases and royalties into fractions of an ancestral whole. A 1994 Interior Department report estimated roughly 550,000 fractionated interests of less than 2 percent. One General Accounting Office survey found that on a sample of twelve reservations, more than 20 percent of allotments had been divided into fifty fractions or more. As a result, heirs received sums so small that only after several years could sufficient income accrue for the account holder to receive a single cent.[20]

An insult to beneficiaries, these sums also suggested how complex trust accounting had become for a federal trustee shortsighted enough to allow fractionization to run rampant. By the time Cobell testified before the Senate, the Bureau of Indian Affairs employed five separate accounting

systems for the Indian trust funds, none of which could be reconciled with one another. A special trustee appointed in 1994 to assess the system found that there were 32,319 unreconciled transactions, totaling $2.4 billion; twelve different nonintegrated databases, and numerous cases of routine record destructions; 15,599 unexplained duplicate accounts; 54,192 accounts without an address, amounting to $42.1 million (one such account contained more than $1.2 million); 15,912 accounts amounting to more than $24 million, belonging to beneficiaries who had reached the age threshold to withdraw but were never granted access; and more than $36 million in 21,002 accounts belonging to deceased individuals.[21]

By then, Cobell's patience with Congress had run thin. Lawmakers had responded to the enormity of trust fund mismanagement by proposing an abrupt privatization, a plan ITMA advocates warned would augur a second era of termination. ITMA instead demanded participation in federal trust fund oversight. But as it worked toward reform legislation, Congress summarily rejected ITMA's involvement. In a development that at once embodied the progress made since termination and the limits of representation within an intractable bureaucracy, President Bill Clinton appointed Ada Deer to head the Bureau of Indian Affairs. Deer, who had fought to restore the federal trust relationship with her nation, now struggled to honor that trust within a derelict administration. "I feel like I'm carrying 500 years of history on my shoulders," she told reporters.[22]

In 1996, after the failure of a major trust fund reform bill in Congress, Elouise Cobell filed a federal lawsuit against the Department of the Interior for its mismanagement of the Individual Indian Money accounts. Represented by the Native American Rights Fund, Cobell was the suit's lead plaintiff along with four other individuals—Mildred Kleghorn, James Louis LaRose, Thomas Maulson, and Earl Old Person—who sued on behalf of a class of an estimated five hundred thousand Individual Indian Money account beneficiaries. *Cobell v. Babbitt*—later *Cobell v. Salazar*, after a reappointment of the interior secretary—was the largest class-action lawsuit ever certified against the US federal government. The case would wind its way through the courts for nearly fourteen years, generating over thirty-five hundred court filings, more than eighty published opinions, and 250 days of hearings.[23]

The most vexing aspect of the litigation was the federal government's inability to undertake even a partial reconciliation of the Individual Indian Money accounts given the state of the Interior Department's records and bookkeeping systems. The government even failed to produce records for the five named plaintiffs, despite a court mandate. The fruitless search cost nearly $20 million. By 2003, Congress estimated that complying with the court's injunction to provide a historical accounting that dated back merely to 1994 would cost upwards of $6 billion.[24]

In December 2009, Cobell and the other plaintiffs reached a settlement with the federal government for a total of $3.4 billion, the largest class-action settlement ever paid by the United States. Unlike most suits of that kind, the settlement did not represent compensation or damages but simply a restitution of funds that already belonged to the plaintiff class. Class members would receive direct payments from a pool of $1.5 billion. Nearly two billion dollars was devoted to reversing allotment's division of collective lands, with the federal government purchasing fractionated parcels from owners and restoring them to Native nations. Echoing Kellogg, counsel for the plaintiffs explained that the fund's purpose was "to make this more productive land by having it consolidated and then under tribal control."[25] In another provision, the settlement financed scholarships for Native students pursuing postsecondary education. Like so many Indigenous leaders before her, Cobell saw trust funds' best use as an endowment for education. In her own words, the scholarship fund would "establish a great legacy for Indian children and grandchildren, providing them the education necessary to break the cycle of poverty that has held too many Indians in its grip for generations."[26]

The federal district court finalized the *Cobell* settlement in 2011. The following year, forty-one Native nations that had filed separate lawsuits concerning trust fund mismanagement reached a $1 billion settlement, to be divided among the plaintiffs. Indian Country received news of the settlements with mixed emotion. Many were dismayed that the *Cobell* settlement precluded further litigation. Others expressed disappointment in the sum awarded, citing a 2005 estimate of federal liability from Attorney General Alberto Gonzales that topped $200 billion. One editorial by a class member entitled to a $500 payment considered the amount too trivial to make any "real difference in the lives of most account holders," a result that "can hardly be considered justice in any real sense of the word." Instead it was "a way to put an ugly chapter in American history to rest for the perpetrators."[27] For Cobell, however, reaching a settlement meant bringing restitution to claimants before they were laid to rest. "Time takes a toll, especially on elders living in abject poverty," Cobell explained to the *Los Angeles Times* in 2009. "Many of them died as we continued to struggle to settle this suit. Many more would not survive long to see a financial gain, if we had not settled now."[28] Less than a year after seeing the settlement signed into law, and before receiving her own share of compensation, Elouise Cobell died of cancer at the age of sixty-five.[29]

⟨━━━⟩⊙⟨━━━⟩

Fiduciary colonialism has a history nearly as long as that of the United States. Cobell and the countless Native leaders who came before her endured a colonial regime invented to build an empire with relatively meager resources. Trusteeship had been a promise broken from the start, a vow to protect Native people hollowed by self-interest. It remained in force because it granted a growing empire efficient and mutable control. Sheltered by impunity, trusteeship only decayed further as the years passed by. Yet from their first encounters with trusteeship, Indigenous peoples had found within its confines a path toward self-determination that rested not on unconditional independence but on a solemn and reciprocal commitment to the federal government. What they understood was that trusteeship was an alliance—an asymmetrical one, but an alliance between sovereigns and their peoples nevertheless. And it still is today. That means that trusteeship belongs not only to Native nations, but to all of us who live on their land and under a government that signed treaties in our name.

*ARCIA*  *Annual Report of the Commissioner of Indian Affairs*
(Government Printing Office, various years).

ASP  American State Papers

BIA  Records of the Bureau of Indian Affairs, Record Group 75,
National Archives and Records Administration, Washington, DC.

GPO  Government Printing Office, Washington, DC

LROIA  Letters Received by the Office of Indian Affairs 1824–1880
(National Archives Microfilm Publication M234), General Records of the Bureau of Indian Affairs, Records of the Bureau of
Indian Affairs, Record Group 75, National Archives and
Records Administration, Washington, DC. Accessed online
at https://catalog.archives.gov/id/159715232. Cited by reel
number, with digital image number(s) in brackets.

LSCR  Letters Sent Concerning Chickasaw Removal, 1832–1861, Records Relating to Indian Removal, Records of the Bureau
of Indian Affairs, Record Group 75, National Archives
and Records Administration, Washington, DC.

LSITF  Letters Sent Concerning Indian Trust Funds, Records
Concerning Trust Funds, Records of the Finance Division,
Records of the Office of Indian Affairs, Records of the Bureau
of Indian Affairs, Record Group 75, National Archives
and Records Administration, Washington, DC.

LSOIA  Letters Sent by the Office of Indian Affairs 1828–1880 (National
Archives Microfilm Publication M21), General Records of the
Bureau of Indian Affairs, Records of the Bureau of Indian
Affairs, Record Group 75, National Archives and Records
Administration, Washington, DC. Accessed online at https://
catalog.archives.gov/id/2105779. Cited by reel and page number.

NARA  National Archives and Records Administration, Washington, DC.

NARA II  National Archives and Records Administration, College
Park, MD.

PPPH  Peter Pitchlynn Papers, Helmerich Center for American Research, Gilcrease Museum, Tulsa, OK.

SWLR  Letters Sent/Received by the Secretary of War Relating to Indian Affairs, 1800–1824, Records of the Office of the Secretary of War Relating to Indian Affairs, 1794–1824, Records of the Bureau of Indian Affairs, Record Group 75, National Archives and Records Administration, Washington, DC.

SWLS  Letters Sent/Received by the Secretary of War Relating to Indian Affairs, 1800–1824, Records of the Office of the Secretary of War Relating to Indian Affairs, Records of the Bureau of Indian Affairs, Record Group 75, National Archives and Records Administration, Washington, DC.

TTFC  MS Correspondence of the Secretary of the Treasury Relating to the Administration of Trust Funds for the Chickasaw and Other Indian Tribes ("S" Series), 1834–1872, General Records of the Department of the Treasury, 1775–2005, Records of the Bureau of Indian Affairs, Record Group 75, National Archives and Records Administration, Washington, DC.

**NOTES**

## *Introduction*

1. Brenda Norrell, "Blackfeet National Bank: Crisis Yielded First Fruit in Indian Country," *Indian Country Today*, April 5, 2000; Ryan Hall, *Beneath the Backbone of the World: Blackfoot People and the North American Borderlands, 1720–1877* (University of North Carolina Press, 2021); Pekka Hämäläinen, "The Rise and Fall of Plains Indian Horse Cultures," *Journal of American History* 90, no. 3 (2003): 847; Andrew C. Isenberg, *The Destruction of the Bison: An Environmental History, 1750–1920* (Cambridge University Press, 2000), 130–31; Donna Feir, Rob Gillezeau, and Maggie Jones, "The Slaughter of the North American Bison and Reversal of Fortunes on the Great Plains," Center for Indian Country Development Working Paper Series 1-2019 (Federal Reserve Bank of Minneapolis, 2019); Clark Wissler and Alice Beck Kehoe, *Amskapi Pikuni: The Blackfeet People* (State University of New York Press, 2012), 45–46; John C. Ewers, *The Blackfeet: Raiders on the Northwestern Plains* (University of Oklahoma Press, 1958), 277–96; Julia Whitty, "Elouise Cobell's Accounting Coup," *Mother Jones*, September–October, 2005, https://www.motherjones.com/politics/2005/09/accounting-coup-0/; Bethany Berger, "Elouise Cobell: Bringing the United States to Account," in *"Our Cause Will Ultimately Triumph": Profiles in American Indian Sovereignty*, ed. Tim Alan Garrison (Carolina Academic Press, 2014), 183–95.

2. Nancy Traver, "Activist's Suit Tackles Goliath; Native American Succeeds Against U.S. Government," *Chicago Tribune*, October 9, 2002; Michael J. Kennedy, "Truth and Consequences on the Reservation," *Los Angeles Times*, July 7, 2002; Berger, "Elouise Cobell," 184–85.

3. "Treaty with the Blackfeet, 1855," in *Indian Affairs: Laws and Treaties*, vol. 2, *Treaties*, ed. Charles J. Kappler (Government Printing Office [GPO], 1904), 736–40; Wissler and Kehoe, *Amskapi Pikuni*, 36–37; Hall, *Beneath the Backbone of the World*, 130–43; S. Doc. No. 118-54 (1896); Sheila McManus, *The Line Which Separates: Race, Gender, and the Making of the Alberta-Montana Borderlands* (University of Nebraska Press, 2005), 57–82; Benjamin Hoy, *A Line of Blood and Dirt: Creating the Canada-United States Border Across Indigenous Land* (Oxford University Press, 2021).

4. 43 Stat. 21 (1924). Blackfeet et al. Nations v. United States, 81 Ct. Cl. Docket E-427 (1935).

5. Traver, "Activist's Suit Tackles Goliath"; Elouise Cobell, "Can Indian Trust Fund Debacle Ever Be Resolved?," *Denver Post*, March 3, 2002.

6. Elouise Cobell, "Elouise Cobell—Keynote Address," Dartmouth College Native American Leadership and Economic Development Conference, October 15, 2010, YouTube, https://www.youtube.com/watch?v=JuzqjhhW23g; Norrell, "Blackfeet National Bank"; Kathleen M. Beans, "Financing Indian Country," *RMA Journal* 88, no. 6 (2006): 8–10; *Review of the Bureau of Indian Affairs' Management of the $1.7 Billion Indian Trust Fund: Hearing Before the Natural Resources Subcommittee of*

*the House Committee on Government Operations*, 101th Cong., 92–94 (1989); *BIA Management of Indian Trust Funds: Hearing Before the Subcommittee on Native American Affairs of the House Committee on Natural Resources, on H.R. 1846, Native American Trust Fund Accounting and Management Reform Act of 1993 and H.R. 4833, American Indian Trust Fund Management Reform Act of 1994*, 103rd Cong. 23 (1994); *BIA Management of Indian Trust Funds: Oversight Hearing Before the Subcommittee on Native American Affairs of the House Committee on Natural Resources*, 103rd Cong. 100 (1993). The Blackfeet National Bank was purchased by the Native American Bank in 2001.

7. *Indian Trust Fund Management: Oversight Hearing on the Management of Indian Trust Funds by the U.S. Government, Before Senate Select Committee on Indian Affairs*, 102nd Cong. 4–5 (1992); *Indian Trust Fund Oversight: Hearing Before the Select Committee on Indian Affairs, United States Senate*, 99th Cong. 27–28 (1986); *Review of the Bureau of Indian Affairs' Management of the $1.7 Billion Indian Trust Fund: Hearing Before the Natural Resources Subcommittee of the House Committee on Government Operations*, 101th Cong. 74–84 (1989); *The Interior Department's Failure to Correct Serious Problems in the Management of the Indian Trust Funds: Hearing Before the Environment, Energy, and Natural Resources Subcommittee on of the House Committee on Government Operations*, 103rd Cong. 70 (1994).

8. Paul Stuart, *Nations Within a Nation: Historical Statistics of American Indians* (Greenwood, 1987), 9, 15. 1871 figure excludes allotted lands. For accounts of Anglo-American property and its predication on ideas of improvement and civilization in colonial contexts, see Andrew Fitzmaurice, *Sovereignty, Property, and Empire, 1500–2000* (Cambridge University Press, 2014); Christopher Tomlins, *Freedom Bound: Law, Labor, and Civic Identity in Colonizing English America, 1580–1865* (Cambridge University Press, 2010), 93–132; Craig Yirush, *Settlers, Liberty, and Empire: The Roots of Early American Political Theory* (Cambridge University Press, 2011); Brenna Bhandar, *Colonial Lives of Property: Law, Land, and Racial Regimes of Ownership* (Duke University Press, 2018), 33–76; and Robert Nichols, *Theft Is Property: Dispossession and Critical Theory* (Duke University Press, 2020). On the use of criminal jurisdiction to "perfect" settler claims across territory, see Lisa Ford, *Settler Sovereignty: Jurisdiction and Indigenous People in America and Australia, 1788–1836* (Harvard University Press, 2010).

9. For more on annuities, see Emilie Connolly, "Fiduciary Colonialism: Annuities and Native Dispossession in the Early United States," *American Historical Review* 127, no. 1 (2022): 223–53. For annuities in the Canadian context, see George Colpitts, "Treaty 6 Cree Annuity Spending in the Territorial Economy of Western Canada, 1873–1905," *Ethnohistory* 67, no. 1 (2020): 29–48; and Brian Gettler, *Colonialism's Currency: Money, State, and First Nations in Canada, 1820–1950* (McGill-Queen's University Press, 2020).

10. Gerald T. White, *A History of the Massachusetts Hospital Life Insurance Company* (Harvard University Press, 1955), 28–32; Richard Price, *Observations on Reversionary Payments, on Schemes for Providing Annuities for Widows, and for Persons of Old Age* [. . .], vol. 1 (T. Cadell, 1783), 64–180; Sharon Ann Murphy, *Investing in Life: Insurance in Antebellum America* (Johns Hopkins University Press, 2010); Timothy L. Alborn, *Regulated Lives: Life Insurance and British Society, 1800–1914* (University of Toronto Press, 2009), 210–13. On gift diplomacy, see Neal Salisbury, *Manitou*

*and Providence: Indians, Europeans, and the Making of New England, 1500–1643* (Oxford University Press, 1982), 48–49; Gregory Evans Dowd, *War Under Heaven: Pontiac, the Indian Nations, and the British Empire* (Johns Hopkins University Press, 2002), 27, 73–74; Stephen R. Potter, *Commoners, Tribute, and Chiefs: The Development of Algonquian Culture in the Potomac Valley* (University of Virginia Press, 1993), 17–18; Jenny Hale, *Pulsipher, Subjects unto the Same King: Indians, English, and the Contest for Authority in Colonial New England* (Philadelphia: University of Pennsylvania Press, 2005), 8–37; and Wilbur R. Jacobs, *Diplomacy and Indian Gifts: Anglo-French Rivalry Along the Ohio and Northwest Frontiers, 1748–1763* (Stanford University Press, 1950). Landmark histories of Indigenous dispossession include Jean O'Brien, *Dispossession by Degrees: Indian Land and Identity in Natick, Massachusetts, 1650–1790* (Cambridge University Press, 1997); Stuart Banner, *How the Indians Lost Their Land: Law and Power on the Frontier* (Harvard University Press, 2007); Allan Greer, *Property and Dispossession: Natives, Empires, and Land in Early Modern North America* (Cambridge University Press, 2008); and Paula Mitchell Marks, *In a Barren Land: American Indian Dispossession and Survival* (William Morrow, 1998). On treaties, see Colin G. Calloway, *Pen and Ink Witchcraft: Treaties and Treaty Making in American Indian History* (Oxford University Press, 2013); Dorothy V. Jones, *License for Empire: Colonialism by Treaty in Early America* (University of Chicago Press, 1982), 157–86; and Francis Paul Prucha, *American Indian Treaties: The History of a Political Anomaly* (University of California Press, 1994). Historian Robert Lee has found that Indian title to lands encompassed by the Louisiana Purchase was extinguished for roughly a quarter of the minimum price that the federal government would accept once offered for sale in the public domain. See Robert Lee, "Accounting for Conquest: The Price of the Louisiana Purchase of Indian Country," *Journal of American History* 103, no. 4 (2017): 938.

11. Colin Calloway, ed, "Treaties by Right of Conquest," in *Early American Indian Documents: Treaties and Laws, 1607–1789*, vol. 18, ed. Alden Vaughan (University Publications of America, 1994), 278–81; Colin Calloway, *The Victory with No Name: The Native American Defeat of the First American Army* (Oxford University Press, 2014). On genocide, see Karl Jacoby, "'The Broad Platform of Extermination': Nature and Violence in the Nineteenth Century American Borderlands," *Journal of Genocide Research* 10, no. 2 (2008): 249–67; Benjamin Madley, "Reexamining the American Genocide Debate: Meaning, Historiography, and New Methods," *American Historical Review* 120, no. 1 (2015): 98–139; Jeffrey Ostler, "'To Extirpate the Indians': An Indigenous Consciousness of Genocide in the Ohio Valley and Lower Great Lakes, 1750s–1810," *William and Mary Quarterly* 72, no. 4 (2015): 587–622; Brendan C. Lindsay, *Murder State: California's Native American Genocide, 1846–1873* (University of Nebraska Press, 2015); Benjamin Madley, *An American Genocide: The United States and the California Indian Catastrophe, 1846–1873* (Yale University Press, 2016); Robert Aquinas McNally, *The Modoc War: A Story of Genocide at the Dawn of America's Gilded Age* (Bison Books, 2017); and Jeffrey Ostler, *Surviving Genocide: Native Nations and the United States from the American Revolution to Bleeding Kansas* (Yale University Press, 2019). For an argument against the use of genocide and for the term ethnic cleansing, see Gary Clayton Anderson, "The Native Peoples of the American West: Genocide or Ethnic Cleansing?" *Western Historical Quarterly* 47, no. 4 (2016): 407–34; Gary Clayton Anderson, *Ethnic Cleansing and the Indian: The*

*Crime That Should Haunt America* (University of Oklahoma Press, 2014). Historians continue to debate the utility of settler colonialism, given its rigid insistence on elimination at the expense of recognizing enduring Indigenous power, among other critiques. See Patrick Wolfe, *Settler Colonialism and the Transformation of Anthropology: The Politics and Poetics of an Ethnographic Event* (Cassell, 1999); Patrick Wolfe, "Land, Labor, Difference: Elementary Structures of Race," *American Historical Review* 106, no. 3 (2001): 866–905; Patrick Wolfe, "Settler Colonialism and the Elimination of the Native," *Journal of Genocide Research* 8, no. 4 (2006): 387–409; Lorenzo Veracini, *Settler Colonialism: A Theoretical Overview* (Palgrave Macmillan, 2010); Anna Johnston and Alan Lawson, "Settler Colonies," in *A Companion to Postcolonial Studies*, ed. Henry Schwarz and Sangeeta Ray (Blackwell, 2005), 360–76; and Mahmood Mamdani, "Settler Colonialism: Then and Now," *Critical Inquiry* 41, no. 3 (2015): 596–614. For critical discussions of Patrick Wolfe's theory and settler colonial studies more generally, see Jeffrey Ostler and Nancy Shoemaker, eds., "Forum: Settler Colonialism in Early American History," *William and Mary Quarterly* 76, no. 3 (2019): 361–450; John Mack Faragher, "Commentary: Settler Colonial Studies and the North American Frontier," *Settler Colonial Studies* 4, no. 2 (2014): 181–91; Nancy Shoemaker, "A Typology of Colonialism," *Perspectives on History* 53, no. 7 (2015): 29–30; Patricia Limerick, "Comments on Settler Colonialism and the West," *Journal of the West* 56, no. 4 (2017): 90–96; Tim Rowse, "Indigenous Heterogeneity," *Arena Journal* 37, no. 8 (2012): 297–310; and Shannon Speed, "Structures of Settler Capitalism in Abya Yala," *American Quarterly* 69, no. 4 (2017): 783–90.

12. On the United States' continental empire, see Michael A. Blaakman, Emily Conroy Krutz, and Noelani Arista, eds., *The Early Imperial Republic: From the American Revolution to the U.S.-Mexican War* (University of Pennsylvania Press, 2023); Brian Delay, "Indian Polities, Empire, and the History of American Foreign Relations," *Diplomatic History* 39, no. 5 (2015): 927–42; Bethel Saler, *The Settler's Empire: Colonialism and State Formation in America's Old Northwest* (University of Pennsylvania Press, 2015); Walter L. Hixson, *American Settler Colonialism: A History* (Palgrave Macmillan, 2013); Walter T. K. Nugent, *Habits of Empire: A History of American Expansion* (Alfred A. Knopf, 2008). For overviews of the United States' fiscal-military state, see Max M. Edling, *A Hercules in the Cradle: War, Money, and the American State, 1783–1867* (University of Chicago Press, 2014); and Paul A. C. Koistinen, *Beating Plowshares into Swords: The Political Economy of American Warfare, 1606–1865* (University Press of Kansas, 1996). Two often-cited references for the debate over state capacity and centralization are William Novak, "The Myth of the 'Weak' American State," *American Historical Review* 113, no. 3 (2008): 754–57; and the contrasting Stephen Skowronek, *Building a New American State: The Expansion of National Administrative Capacities* (Cambridge University Press, 1982), 29. A more recent clarification can be found in Stephen Skowronek, "Present at the Creation: The State in Early American Political History," *Journal of the Early Republic* 38, no. 1 (2018): 95–103. Overviews of the state strength debate include Gautham Rao, "The New Historiography of the Early Federal Government: Institutions, Contexts, and the Imperial State," *William and Mary Quarterly* 77, no. 1 (2020): 97–128; Ariel Ron and Gautham Rao, "Introduction: Taking Stock of

the State in Nineteenth-Century America," *Journal of the Early Republic* 38, no. 1 (2018): 61–66; and Brian Balogh, "The State of the State Among Historians," *Social Science History* 27, no. 3 (2003): 455–63. Two influential formulations that argue, along Novak's lines, for substantial yet diffuse, concealed, and delegated power are Brian Balogh, *A Government out of Sight: The Mystery of National Authority in Nineteenth-Century America* (Cambridge University Press, 2009); and Elisabeth S. Clemens, "Lineages of the Rube Goldberg State: Building and Blurring Public Programs, 1900–1940," in *The Art of the State: Rethinking Political Institutions*, ed. Ian Shapiro, Stephen Skowronek, and Daniel Galvin (New York University Press, 2006), 187–215. For works that helpfully disaggregate federal, state, and local governments, see Max M. Edling, *Perfecting the Union: National and State Authority in the US Constitution* (Oxford University Press, 2021); Nicolas Barreyre and Claire Lemercier, "The Unexceptional State: Rethinking the State in the Nineteenth Century (France, United States)," *American Historical Review* 126, no. 2 (2021): 481–503; and Naomi R. Lamoreaux and John Joseph Wallis, "Economic Crisis, General Laws, and the Mid-Nineteenth-Century Transformation of American Political Economy," *Journal of the Early Republic* 41, no. 3 (2021): 403–34. Historians of the American West have long recognized the immense importance of the federal government's colonial activities in developing the region, and, conversely, the immense importance of the West for the institutional development of the federal government. See, for example, William Bergmann, *The American National State and the Early West* (Cambridge University Press, 2012); Richard White, *"It's Your Misfortune and None of My Own": A New History of the American West* (University of Oklahoma Press, 1991); and Patricia Limerick, *The Legacy of Conquest: The Unbroken Past of the American West* (W. W. Norton, 1987). Yet, as Rachel St. John, "State Power in the West in the Early American Republic," *Journal of the Early Republic* 38, no.1 (2018): 87–94, argues, the West was also the region in which the limits of state power were most apparent. Trust funds were invested in federal 6 percent bonds used to finance the War of 1812, in Treasury notes used to finance the Mexican-American War, and in Union war bonds. For each issuance, see Rafael A. Bayley, *The National Loans of the United States, from July 4, 1776, to June 30, 1880* (GPO, 1882), 48–60, 70–73, 78–89. See also Edling, *A Hercules in the Cradle*, 108–44, 145–77, 178–221; and David K. Thompson, *Bonds of War: How Civil War Financial Agents Sold the World on the Union* (University of North Carolina Press, 2022). For the United States' use of wars as a pretext for invasions of Indigenous territories, see Deborah Rosen, *Border Law: The First Seminole War and American Nationhood* (Harvard University Press, 2015); Jennifer Denetdale, *The Long Walk: The Forced Navajo Exile* (Chelsea House, 2007); Gary Clayton Anderson and Alan R. Woolworth, eds., *Through Dakota Eyes: Narrative Accounts of the Minnesota Indian War of 1862* (Minnesota Historical Society, 1988); and Robert Wooster, *American Military Frontiers: The United States Army in the West, 1783–1900* (University of New Mexico Press, 2009), 48–54, 135–55. On the regularity and often undeclared status of so-called Indian wars, see Samuel Watson, "Military Learning and Adaptation Shaped by Social Context: The U.S. Army and Its 'Indian Wars,' 1790–1890," *Journal of Military History* 82, no. 2 (2018): 373–438; and Bruce Vandervoort, *Indian Wars of Mexico, Canada, and the United States, 1812–1900* (Routledge, 2006). On "small wars" across global empires, see Lauren Benton, *They Called It Peace: Worlds of Imperial Violence* (Princeton University Press, 2024).

13. Measured as a share of gross domestic product per capita. "Purchasing Power Today of a US Dollar Transaction in the Past," MeasuringWorth, 2025, https://www .measuringworth.com/ppowerus.

14. On infrastructural power, see Michael Mann, "The Autonomous Power of the State: Its Origins, Mechanisms and Results," *European Journal of Sociology* 25, no. 2 (1984): 185–213. On colonialism through settler infrastructures, see Nick Estes, *Our History Is the Future: Standing Rock Versus the Dakota Access Pipeline, and the Long Tradition of Indigenous Resistance* (Verso Books, 2019); and Winona LaDuke and Deborah Cowen, "Beyond Wiindigo Infrastructure," *South Atlantic Quarterly* 119, no. 2 (2020): 243–68. H.R. Rep. No. 25-892 (1838); Sen. Ex. Doc. 36-3, at 313 (1860); *ARCIA* 1860, 236.

15. There is a growing literature on Native history and the history of capitalism, with many important projects in the pipeline. See, for example, Noah Ramage, "Phoenix on Fire: The Cherokee Nation from Reconstruction to Denationalization" (PhD diss., University of California–Berkeley, 2024); Gustave Lester, "Land, Fur, and Copper: The Union of Settler Colonialism and Industrial Capitalism in the Great Lakes Region, 1815–1842," *Early American Studies* 21, no. 1, (2023) 122–65; Claudio Saunt, *Unworthy Republic: The Dispossession of Native Americans and the Road to Indian Territory* (W. W. Norton, 2020), 173–227; Calvin Schermerhorn, "'The Time Is Now Just Arriving When Many Capitalists Will Make Fortunes': Indian Removal, Finance, and Slavery in the Making of the American Cotton South," in *Linking the Histories of Slavery: North America and Its Borderlands*, ed. Bonnie Martin and James F. Brooks (School for Advanced Research Press, 2015), 151–70; Andrew Needham, *Power Lines: Phoenix and the Making of the Modern Southwest* (Princeton University Press, 2014); Colleen O'Neill, *Working the Navajo Way: Labor and Culture in the Twentieth Century* (University Press of Kansas, 2005); Brian C. Hosmer and Colleen M. O'Neill, *Native Pathways: American Indian Culture and Economic Development in the Twentieth Century* (University Press of Colorado, 2004); and Brian Hosmer, *American Indians in the Marketplace: Persistence and Innovation Among the Menominees and Metlakatlans* (University Press of Kansas, 1999). For a survey of earlier works, see Alexandra Harmon, Colleen O'Neill, and Paul C. Rosier, "Interwoven Economic Histories: American Indians in a Capitalist America," *Journal of American History* 98, no. 3 (2011): 698–722. For model works on Native history from economic historians, see Ann M. Carlos and Frank D. Lewis, *Commerce by a Frozen Sea: Native Americans and the European Fur Trade* (University of Pennsylvania Press, 2010); Ann M. Carlos, Donna L. Feir, and Angela Redish, "Indigenous Nations and the Development of the U.S. Economy: Land, Resources, and Dispossession," *Journal of Economic History* 82, no. 2 (2022): 516–55; Linda Barrington, *The Other Side of the Frontier: Economic Explorations into Native American History* (Westview, 1999). See also forthcoming dissertations from Zada Ballew (University of Madison, WI) and Sam Schirvar (University of Pennsylvania). For histories of capitalism as reliant on state violence and imperial warfare, see Lindsay Schakenbach Regele, "A Brief History of the History of Capitalism, and a New American Variety," *Enterprise and Society* 25,

no. 1 (2024): 2–26; and Sven Beckert, *Empire of Cotton: A Global History* (Alfred A. Knopf, 2014). For surveys of the nineteenth-century historiography on the new history of American capitalism, see Seth Rockman, "What Makes the History of Capitalism Newsworthy?," *Journal of the Early Republic* 34, no. 3 (2014): 439–66; Sven Beckert and Seth Rockman, "Introduction: Slavery's Capitalism," in *Slavery's Capitalism: A New History of American Economic Development*, ed. Sven Beckert and Seth Rockman (University of Pennsylvania Press, 2016), 1–28; Dael A. Norwood, "What Counts? Political Economy, or Ways to Make Early America Add Up," *Journal of the Early Republic* 36, no. 4 (2016): 753–82; Sven Beckert and Christine Desan, "Introduction," in *American Capitalism: New Histories*, ed. Sven Beckert and Christine Desan (Columbia University Press, 2018), 1–34; and Hannah Farber, "Practical Americans," *William and Mary Quarterly* 78, no. 2 (2021): 339–57. As Justin Leroy, Destin Jenkins, and Peter James Hudson, "Introduction: The Old History of Capitalism," in *Histories of Racial Capitalism*, ed. Justin Leroy and Destin Jenkins (Columbia University Press, 2021), 1–26, point out, the "new" history of capitalism should be traced more accurately to foundational works of the 1930s and 1940s by W. E. B. Du Bois, C. L. R. James, Eric Williams, and Claudia Jones. See also Peter James Hudson, "The Racist Dawn of Capitalism: Unearthing the Economy of Bondage," *Boston Review*, March 14, 2016, https://www.bostonreview .net/articles/peter-james-hudson-slavery-capitalism. Drawing on Cedric Robinson's seminal *Black Marxism: The Making of the Black Radical Tradition* (University of North Carolina Press, 2021), scholars of racial capitalism refuse class-reductionist theories of capitalism, which is to say, analyses that treat class conflict as if it were ontologically prior to inequalities of race or gender. While indebted to scholarship on racial capitalism, this book addresses mechanisms of dispossession and subordination that targeted Native sovereignty first and foremost; racism developed alongside and through trusteeship but was not its motive. On the importance of recognizing Native sovereignty and racialization as conceptually distinct, and on the contemporary conflation of Native peoples' legal and ethnic status in order to undermine Indigenous sovereignty, see Joanne Barker, "Introduction," in *Sovereignty Matters: Locations of Contestation and Possibility in Indigenous Struggles for Self-Determination* (University of Nebraska Press, 2006), 23–24; Matthew L. M. Fletcher, "The Original Understanding of the Political Status of Indian Tribes," *St. John's Law Review* 82, no. 1 (2008): 153–82; and Mary K. Nagle, "Nothing to Trust: The Unconstitutional Origins of the Post–Dawes Act Trust Doctrine," *Tulsa Law Review* 48 (2012–13): 63–92.

16. H.R. Rep. No. 27-296, at 120–21 (1843); *ARCIA* 1841, 278–79; Namsuk Kim and John Joseph Wallis, "The Market for American State Government Bonds in Britain and the United States, 1830–43," *Economic History Review* 58, no. 4 (2005): 736–64; Reginald McGrane, *Foreign Bondholders and American State Debts* (Macmillan, 1935), 9. Economist Wesley C. Mitchell, *Business Cycles*, vol. 1 (National Bureau of Economic Research, 1927), 387, counted at least eleven financial panics or crises in the nineteenth century alone. For an overview of financial crises in the United States, see Scott Reynolds Nelson, *A Nation of Deadbeats: An Uncommon History of America's Financial Disasters* (Alfred A. Knopf, 2012). For an analysis of settler colonialism attentive to the regularity of crisis, see James Belich, *Replenishing the Earth:*

*The Settler Revolution and the Rise of the Anglo-World, 1783–1939* (Oxford University Press, 2009).

17. H.R. Rep. No. 27-296, at 99, 120–21 (1843); *ARCIA* 1841, 278–79; Charles Macalester to Levi Woodbury, February 2, 1836, Vol. 1, TTFC, 13–14.

18. Emily S. Rosenberg, *Financial Missionaries to the World: The Politics and Culture of Dollar Diplomacy, 1900–1930* (Duke University Press, 1999); Cyrus Veeser, *A World Safe for Capitalism: Dollar Diplomacy and America's Rise to Global Power* (Columbia University Press, 2002); Ellen D. Tillman, *Dollar Diplomacy by Force: Nation-Building and Resistance in the Dominican Republic* (University of North Carolina Press, 2016); Allan E. S. Lumba, *Monetary Authorities: Capitalism and Decolonization in the American Colonial Philippines* (Duke University Press, 2022); James Hudson, *Bankers and Empire: How Wall Street Colonized the Caribbean* (University of Chicago Press, 2017); Carlos Marichal, *A Century of Debt Crisis in Latin America: From Independence to the Great Depression, 1820–1930* (Princeton University Press, 1989). On the legal theories of sovereignty and reputation that justify the compulsory repayment of sovereign debts, see Odette Lienau, *Rethinking Sovereign Debt: Politics, Reputation, and Legitimacy in Modern Finance* (Harvard University Press, 2014). For histories of finance and colonialism, see K-Sue Park, "Money, Mortgages, and the Conquest of America," *Law and Social Inquiry* 41, no. 4 (2016): 1006–35; and Catherine Comyn, "Te Peeke o Aotearoa: Colonial and Decolonial Finance in Aotearoa New Zealand, 1860s–1890s," in *The Entangled Legacies of Empire: Race, Finance and Inequality*, ed. Paul Robert Gilbert, Clea Bourne, Max Haiven, and Johnna Montgomerie (Manchester University Press, 2023). For contemporary forms of financialized colonialism, see Alyosha Goldstein, "Finance and Foreclosure in the Colonial Present," *Radical History Review* 118 (2014): 42–63; and Rocío Zambrana, *Colonial Debts: The Case of Puerto Rico* (Duke University Press, 2021).

19. K-Sue Park, "Self-Deportation Nation," *Harvard Law Review* 132, no. 7 (2019): 1878–1941. See also Donna L. Akers, "Decolonizing the Master Narrative: Treaties and Other American Myths," *Wicazo Sa Review* 29, no. 1 (2014): 58–76; and Vine Deloria, *Behind the Trail of Broken Treaties: An Indian Declaration of Independence* (Delacorte, 1974).

20. On Indigenous understandings of treaty making, see Robert A. Williams, *Linking Arms Together: American Indian Treaty Visions of Law and Peace, 1600–1800* (Oxford University Press, 1997), 98–123; and Heidi Kiiwetinepinesiik Stark, "Marked by Fire: Anishinaabe Articulations of Nationhood in Treaty Making with the United States and Canada," *American Indian Quarterly* 36, no. 2 (2012): 119–49.

21. Frederick Pollock and Frederic William Maitland, *The History of English Before the Time of Edward I*, 2nd ed., vol. 2 (Cambridge University Press, 1923), 228–31; Austin Wakeman Scott, *The Law of Trusts*, 4 vols. (Little, Brown, 1939); Lawrence M. Friedman, *Dead Hands: A Social History of Wills, Trusts, and Inheritance Law* (Stanford University Press, 2009), 111–24; Carole Shammas, Marylynn Salmon, and Michel Dahlin, *Inheritance in America: From Colonial Times to the Present* (Rutgers University Press, 1987), 3–5, 57–64; Elizabeth Blackmar, "Inheriting Property and Debt: From Family Security to Corporate Accumulation," in Zakim and Kornblith, *Capitalism Takes Command*, 98–102; Peter Dobkin Hall, *The Organization of American Culture, 1700–1900: Private Institutions, Elites, and the Origins of*

*American Nationality* (New York University Press, 1982), 68–72, 97–123; Gregory S. Alexander, *Commodity and Propriety: Competing Visions of Property in American Legal Thought, 1776–1970* (University of Chicago Press, 1997), 122–24; John Morley, "The Common Law Corporation: The Power of the Trust in Anglo-American Business History," *Columbia Law Review* 116, no. 8 (2016): 2145–97; John H. Langbein, "The Contractarian Basis of the Law of Trusts," *Yale Law Journal* 105 (1995): 632–41; Peter Dobkin Hall, "What the Merchants Did with Their Money: Charitable and Testamentary Trusts in Massachusetts, 1780–1880," in *Entrepreneurs: The Boston Business Community, 1700–1850,* ed. Conrad Edick Wright and Katherine Viens (Massachusetts Historical Society, 1997), 365–417; Tamara Plakins Thornton, *Nathaniel Bowditch and the Power of Numbers: How a Nineteenth-Century Man of Business, Science, and the Sea Changed American Life* (University of North Carolina Press, 2016), 135–60; Jeffrey Sklansky, *Sovereign of the Market: The Money Question in Early America* (University of Chicago Press, 2017), 215–25; Naomi R. Lamoreaux, *The Great Merger Movement in American Business, 1895–1904* (Cambridge University Press, 1985); Richard Franklin Bensel, *The Political Economy of American Industrialization, 1877–1900* (Cambridge University Press, 2000, 314–21; William G. Roy, *Socializing Capital: The Rise of the Large Industrial Corporation in America* (Princeton University Press, 1997), 148–54; Richard White, "From Antimonopoly to Antitrust," in *Antimonopoly and American Democracy,* ed. Daniel A. Crane and William J. Novak (Oxford University Press, 2023), 83–118; Katharina Pistor, *The Code of Capital: How the Law Creates Wealth and Inequality* (Princeton University Press, 2019), 42–43, 81–82. James Kent, *Commentaries on American Law,* 2nd ed., vol. 4 (O. Halstead, 1832), 289–310, dates trusts' history to Roman law. William Blackstone, *Commentaries on the Laws of England,* vol. 2 (Sweet, Maxwell, Stevens and Sons, 1836), 174, notes that the rule against perpetuities limits trusts' duration to "a life or lives in being, and one and twenty years afterwards."

22. On imperial legalities, see Christopher Tomlins and Bruce H. Mann, eds., *The Many Legalities of Early America* (University of North Carolina Press, 2001); Lauren Benton, *A Search for Sovereignty: Law and Geography in European Empires, 1400–1900* (Cambridge University Press, 2010); Ken MacMillan, *Sovereignty and Possession in the English New World: The Legal Foundations of Empire, 1576–1640* (Cambridge University Press, 2006); Lauren Benton and Richard J. Ross, eds., *Legal Pluralism and Empires, 1500–1850* (New York University Press, 2013); Saliha Belmessous, ed., *Native Claims: Indigenous Law against Empire, 1500–1920* (Oxford University Press, 2011); and Kathryn Hermes, "The Law of Native Americans, to 1815," in *The Cambridge History of Law in America,* ed. Michael Grossberg and Christopher Tomlins (Cambridge University Press; 2008): 32–62.

23. For works that date the trust responsibility to a trilogy of cases decided by Chief Justice John Marshall (*Johnson v. McIntosh, Cherokee Nation v. Georgia,* and *Worcester v. Georgia*), see Reid Peyton Chambers, "Judicial Enforcement of the Federal Trust Responsibility to Indians," *Stanford Law Review* 27, no. 5 (1975): 1213–48; Vine Deloria and Clifford M. Lytle, *American Indians, American Justice* (University of Texas Press, 1983), 30; Petra M. Shattuck and Jill Norgren, *Partial Justice: Federal Indian Law in a Liberal Constitutional System* (Berg, 1991), 115–21; and David Wilkins, *Hollow Justice,* 142–83. For works that date the trust responsibility

to twentieth-century jurisprudence, see Milner S. Ball, "Constitution, Court, Indian Tribes," *American Bar Foundation Research Journal* 12, no. 1 (1987): 1–140; and Francis Paul Prucha, *The Indians in American Society: From the Revolutionary War to the Present* (University of California Press, 1985), 80–104. See also Gilbert L. Hall, *Duty of Protection: The Federal Indian Trust Relationship*, 2d ed. (Institute for the Development of Indian Law, 1981).

24. On trusteeship as a legitimation for New World empires, see Robert A. Williams Jr., *The American Indian in Western Legal Thought: The Discourses of Conquest* (Oxford University Press, 1990), 104–5; Anthony Pagden, *Lords of all the World: Ideologies of Empire in Spain, Britain, and France c. 1500–1800* (Yale University Press, 1995), 86–89; Anthony Anghie, *Imperialism, Sovereignty, and the Making of International Law* (Cambridge University Press, 2004), 13–31; and Seth Davis, "Empire and the Political Economy of Fiduciary Law," in *Transnational Fiduciary Law*, ed. Seth Davis, Thilo Kuntz, and Gregory Shaffer (Cambridge University Press, 2024), 237–60. As Patricia Seed, *American Pentimento: The Invention of Indians and the Pursuit of Riches* (University of Minnesota Press, 2001), 62–63, notes, the root of Spanish empire's term for its forced labor system, *encomienda*, is *encomendar*, "to entrust." For accounts tracing British imperial trusteeship to late eighteenth-century reformers, see William Bain, *Between Anarchy and Society: Trusteeship and the Obligations of Power* (Oxford University Press, 2003), 27–52; and Andrew Porter, "Trusteeship, Anti-Slavery and Humanism," in *The Oxford History of the British Empire*, vol. 3, ed. Andrew Porter (Oxford University Press, 1999): 198–220. Trusteeship structured modern empires through the 1884–85 Berlin Conference and the League of Nations' Mandate System. William Bain, "'Repaying the National Debt to Africa': Trusteeship, Property and Empire," *Theoria: A Journal of Social and Political Theory* 59, no. 133 (2012): 1–20; Ronald Hyam, "Bureaucracy and 'Trusteeship' in the Colonial Empire," in *The Oxford History of the British Empire*, vol. 4, ed. Andrew Porter (Oxford University Press, 1999), 255–79. On Roman law, see Lauren Benton and Benjamin Straumann, "Acquiring Empire by Law: From Roman Doctrine to Early Modern European Practice," *Law and History Review* 28, no. 1 (2010): 1–38. See also R. H. Helmholz, "Roman Law of Guardianship in England, 1300–1600," *Tulane Law Review* 52, no. 2 (1977–78): 223–57. New England colonies employed a guardianship system that persisted after the Revolution, and which prefigured federal trusteeship in several respects, including in the management of Native land and money. See Daniel Mandell, *Behind the Frontier: Indians in Eighteenth-Century Eastern Massachusetts* (University of Nebraska Press, 1996), 25, 113–14, 143–56; Wendy St. Jean, "Inventing Guardianship: The Mohegan Indians and Their 'Protectors,'" *New England Quarterly* 72, no. 3 (1999): 362–87; Jean O'Brien, *Firsting and Lasting: Writing Indians out of Existence in New England* (University of Minnesota Press, 2010), 145–99; Deborah A. Rosen, *American Indians and State Law: Sovereignty, Race, and Citizenship, 1790–1880* (University of Nebraska Press, 2007), 9–10, 162–66; and William Apess, *Indian Nullification of the Unconstitutional Laws of Massachusetts* (Jonathan Howe, 1835).

25. On protection, empire, and international law, see Lauren Benton, "Shadows of Sovereignty: Legal Encounters and the Politics of Protection in the Atlantic World," in *Encounters Old and New in World History: Essays Inspired by Jerry H. Bentley*, ed. Alan Karras and Laura J. Mitchell (University of Hawai'i Press, 2017), 136–50; Lauren A. Benton, Adam Clulow, and Bain Attwood, eds., *Protection and Empire:*

*A Global History* (Cambridge University Press, 2018); N. Bruce Duthu, *Shadow Nations: Tribal Sovereignty and the Limits of Legal Pluralism* (Oxford University Press, 2013), 13, 74–128; Gregory Ablavsky, "Species of Sovereignty, Native Nationhood, the United States, and International Law, 1783–1795," *Journal of American History* 106, no. 3 (2019): 591–613; MacMillan, *Sovereignty and Possession*; and Benton and Straumann, "Acquiring Empire by Law."

26. Robert N. Clinton, "The Proclamation of 1763: Colonial Prelude to Two Centuries of Federal-State Conflict over the Management of Indian Affairs," *Boston University Law Review* 69, no. 2 (1989): 329–85; Robert Lee, "The Indian Boundary Line and the Imperialization of U.S.-Indian Affairs," in Blaakman et al., *The Early Imperial Republic*, 27–44; Colin Calloway, *The Scratch of a Pen: 1763 and the Transformation of North America* (Oxford University Press, 2006); Lauren Benton and Lisa Ford, *Rage for Order: The British Empire, and the Origins of International Law, 1800–1850* (Harvard University Press, 2016), 85. On preemption within the United States, see Michael A. Blaakman, "'Haughty Republicans,' Native Land, and the Promise of Preemption," *William and Mary Quarterly*, 78 no. 2 (2021): 243–50.

27. Emer de Vattel, *The Law of Nations* (T. and J. W. Johnson, 1853), 2; Tim Alan Garrison, *The Legal Ideology of Removal: The Southern Judiciary and the Sovereignty of Native American Nations* (University of Georgia Press, 2002), 125–50; Jill Norgren, *The Cherokee Cases: The Confrontation of Law and Politics* (University of Oklahoma Press, 1996). On Indigenous peoples' engagement with the law of nations, see Ablavsky, "Species of Sovereignty"; Melissa A. Stock, "Sovereign or Suzerain: Alexander McGillivray's Argument for Creek Independence after the Treaty of Paris of 1783," *Georgia Historical Quarterly* 92, no. 2 (2008): 149–76; and Craig Bryan Yirush, "Claiming the New World: Empire, Law, and Indigenous Rights in the Mohegan Case, 1704–1743," *Law and History Review* 29, no. 2 (2011): 333–73. Taiaiake Alfred, *Peace, Power, Righteousness: An Indigenous Manifesto* (Oxford University Press, 1999), 55–72, argues that the category of sovereignty is a European fiction anathema to Indigenous forms of power and governance, yet European empires exercised far more flexible and shared forms of sovereignty than the absolutist and coercive definition Alfred employs. On sovereignty within empires, see Ann Laura Stoler, "On Degrees of Imperial Sovereignty," *Public Culture* 18, no. 1 (2006): 125–46. On divided sovereignty, see Edward Keene, *Beyond the Anarchical Society: Grotius, Colonialism and Order in World Politics* (Cambridge University Press, 2002); Duthu, *Shadow Nations*, 15, 111; K. Tsianina Lomawaima, "Federalism: Native, Federal, and State Sovereignty," in *Why You Can't Teach United States History Without American Indians*, ed. Susan Sleeper-Smith, Jean M. O'Brien, Nancy Shoemaker, and Scott Manning Stevens (University of North Carolina Press, 2015), 273–86; and Gregory Evans Dowd, "Indigenous Peoples Without the Republic," *Journal of American History* 104, no. 1 (2017): 19–41. On Native sovereignty as liminal to the bounded nation-state, see Kevin Bruyneel, *The Third Space of Sovereignty: The Postcolonial Politics of U.S.-Indigenous Relations* (University of Minnesota Press, 2007).

28. David E. Wilkins and K. Tsianina Lomawaima, *Uneven Ground: American Indian Sovereignty and Federal Law* (University of Oklahoma Press, 2001), 64–97; Williams, *Linking Arms Together*; Nancy Shoemaker, *A Strange Likeness: Becoming Red and White in Eighteenth-Century North America* (Oxford University Press, 2004), 117–18; Richard White, *The Middle Ground: Indians, Empires, and Republics in the*

*Great Lakes Region, 1650–1815* (Cambridge University Press, 1991), 269–314; Patricia Galloway, "'The Chief Who Is Your Father': Choctaw and French Views of the Diplomatic Relation," in *Powhatan's Mantle: Indians in the Colonial Southeast*, ed. Gregory A. Waselkov, Peter H. Wood, and Tom Hatley (University of Nebraska Press, 2006), 345–70; Cynthia Cumfer, *Separate Peoples, One Land: The Minds of Cherokees, Blacks, and Whites on the Tennessee Frontier* (University of North Carolina Press, 2007), 78–85; Michael J. Witgen, *An Infinity of Nations: How the Native New World Shaped Early North America* (University of Pennsylvania Press, 2012), 50–54; Peter Cook, "Onontio Gives Birth: How the French in Canada Became Fathers to Their Indigenous Allies, 1645–73," *Canadian Historical Review* 96, no. 2 (2015): 165–93; Elspeth Martini, "Visiting Indians, Nursing Fathers, and Anglo-American Empire in the Post–War of 1812 Western Great Lakes," *William and Mary Quarterly* 73, no. 3 (2021): 459–90; Daniel Rey-Bear and Matthew Fletcher, "We Need Protection from Our Protectors: The Nature, Issues, and Future of the Federal Trust Responsibility to Indians," *Michigan Journal of Environmental and Administrative Law* 6, no. 2 (2017): 397–461; Jean Dennison, *Colonial Entanglement: Constituting a Twenty-First-Century Osage Nation* (University of North Carolina Press, 2012); Scott Richard Lyons, *X-Marks: Native Signatures of Assent* (University of Minnesota Press, 2010).

29. Given the euphemistic veneer of *removal*, some scholars have begun to use the term *deportation* instead. Yet deportation refers to the expulsion of individuals from territories belonging to the deporting nation-state, not the expulsion of nations *as nations* from their own territories. Contemporaries used Indian removal to describe the latter, making it a better term, albeit not ideal. For works invoking deportation, see Saunt, *Unworthy Republic*; and Park, "Self-Deportation Nation," 1878–941. Once restricted to Jackson's era and focused on the Southeast, histories of Indian removal now encompass the North and often reach back to the nation's founding. Landmark works include Tim Alan Garrison, *The Legal Ideology of Removal: The Southern Judiciary and the Sovereignty of Native American Nations* (University of Georgia Press, 2002); Michael D. Green, *The Politics of Indian Removal: Creek Government and Society in Crisis* (University of Nebraska Press, 1982); Amanda L. Paige, Fuller L. Bumpers, and Daniel F. Littlefield Jr., *Chickasaw Removal* (Chickasaw Press, 2010); Theda Perdue and Michael D. Green, *The Cherokee Nation and the Trail of Tears* (Penguin, 2007); John P. Bowes, *Land Too Good for Indians: Northern Indian Removal* (University of Oklahoma Press, 2016); and Samantha Seeley, *Race, Removal, and the Right to Remain: Migration and the Making of the United States* (Omohundro Institute and University of North Carolina Press, 2021).

30. Felix S. Cohen, *Handbook of Federal Indian Law* (GPO, 1942), 195–202; Laurence Schmeckebier, *The Office of Indian Affairs: Its History, Activities and Organization* (Johns Hopkins Press, 1927), 191–96.

31. Mechekeeleta [La Gros] to Secretary of War, January 1826, LROIA 416 [23–25].

32. *BIA Management of Indian Trust Funds: Hearing Before the Subcommittee on Native American Affairs of the Committee on Natural Resources, House of Representatives*, 103rd Cong., 2nd Sess. 153 (1994).

## *Chapter One: Strategies of Succession*

1. Address of Seneca Sachems, Enclosed in Erastus Granger to Department of War, December 9, 1811, Vol. 1811–1812, SWLR.

2. Address of Seneca Sachems.

3. Michael A. Blaakman, *Speculation Nation: Land Mania in the Revolutionary American Republic* (University of Pennsylvania Press, 2023); Allan Greer, *Property and Dispossession: Natives, Empires, and Land in Early Modern North America* (Cambridge University Press, 2008), 389–436.

4. Address of Seneca Sachems.

5. Carl Benn, *The Iroquois in the War of 1812* (University of Toronto Press, 1998), 63–65.

6. E. James Ferguson, *The Power of the Purse: A History of American Public Finance, 1776–1790* (University of North Carolina Press, 1961), 3–24; Edwin Perkins, *American Public Finance and Financial Services, 1700–1815* (Ohio University Press, 1994), 96; Max M. Edling, *A Hercules in the Cradle: War, Money, and the American State, 1783–1867* (University of Chicago Press, 2014), 24–25; Richard Sylla, "Experimental Federalism: The Economics of American Government, 1789–1914," in *The Cambridge Economic History of the United States*, vol. 2, *The Long Nineteenth Century*, ed. Stanley L. Engerman and Robert E. Gallman (Cambridge University Press, 2000), 498; Farley Grubb, *The Continental Dollar: How the American Revolution Was Financed with Paper Money* (University of Chicago Press, 2023).

7. Max M. Edling, *Perfecting the Union: National and State Authority in the US Constitution* (Oxford University Press, 2021), 5, 12; Alexander Hamilton, "Report on Public Credit," January 14, 1790, in *ASP: Finance*, vol. 1, ed. Walter Lowrie and Matthew St. Clair Clarke (Gales and Seaton, 1832), 15–16, 26–27; Eliga H. Gould, *Among the Powers of the Earth: The American Revolution and the Making of a New World Empire* (Harvard University Press, 2012), 127–29; Colin G. Calloway, *The American Revolution in Indian Country: Crisis and Diversity in Native American Communities* (Cambridge University Press, 1995); Alan Taylor, *The Divided Ground: Indians, Settlers, and the Northern Borderland of the American Revolution* (Alfred A. Knopf, 2006), 114–15.

8. Alexander Hamilton, "National Bank," December 14, 1790, in *ASP: Finance*, 1:68.

9. Alexander Hamilton, "Plan for Disposing of the Public Lands," July 20, 1790, in *ASP: Public Lands*, vol. 1, ed. Walter Lowrie (Gales and Seaton, 1834), 8–9; Thomas Jefferson, "Opinion on the Constitutionality of the Bill for Establishing a National Bank," February 15, 1791, in *The Papers of Thomas Jefferson*, vol. 19, *January 1791–March 1791*, ed. Julian P. Boyd (Princeton University Press, 1974), 275–82.

10. Farley Grubb, "U.S. Land Policy: Founding Choices and Outcomes, 1781–1802," in *Founding Choices: American Economic Policy in the 1790s*, ed. Douglas A. Irwin and Richard Sylla (University of Chicago Press, 2011), 264; Perkins, *American Public Finance*, 219–20.

11. Susan Sleeper-Smith, *Indigenous Prosperity and American Conquest: Indian Women of the Ohio River Valley, 1690–1792* (Omohundro Institute / University of North Carolina Press, 2018), 13–66, 170; Patrick Griffin, *American Leviathan: Empire, Nation, and Revolutionary Frontier* (Hill and Wang, 2007), 97–122; Eric Hinderaker,

*Elusive Empires: Constructing Colonialism in the Ohio Valley, 1673–1800* (Cambridge University Press, 1997), 189–224; "Treaties by Right of Conquest," in *Early American Indian Documents: Treaties and Laws, 1607–1789*, vol. 18, *Revolution and Confederation*, ed. Colin G. Calloway (University Publications of America, 1994), 278–81; David Nichols, *Red Gentlemen, White Savages: Indians, Federalists, and the Search for Order on the American Frontier* (University of Virginia Press, 2008), 31–34; Colin Calloway, *The Victory with No Name: The Native American Defeat of the First American Army* (Oxford University Press, 2014), 27; Michael Witgen, "A Nation of Settlers: The Early American Republic and the Colonization of the Northwest Territory," *William and Mary Quarterly* 76, no. 3 (2019): 391–98; Bethel Saler, *The Settler's Empire: Colonialism and State Formation in America's Old Northwest* (University of Pennsylvania Press, 2015); Greg Ablavsky, *Federal Ground: Governing Property and Violence in the First U.S. Territories* (Oxford University Press, 2021), 51–78; Timothy J. Shannon, "The Ohio Company and the Meaning of Opportunity in the American West, 1786–1795," *New England Quarterly* 64, no. 3 (1991): 393–413.

12. Calloway, *The Victory with No Name*, 45; John Sugden, *Blue Jacket: Warrior of the Shawnees* (University of Nebraska Press, 2003), 77.

13. Wiley Sword, *President Washington's Indian War: The Struggle for the Old Northwest* (University of Oklahoma Press, 1985), 137–39, 155–91; Calloway, *The Victory with No Name*, 64–92; Rob Harper, *Unsettling the West: Violence and State Building in the Ohio Valley* (University of Pennsylvania Press, 2018), 119–72.

14. Alexander Hamilton to George Washington, April 10, 1791, in *The Papers of Alexander Hamilton*, vol. 8, *Feb. 1791–July 1791*, ed. Harold C. Syrett (Columbia University Press, 1965), 269; Alexander Hamilton to Rufus King, July 8, 1791, in *Papers of Alexander Hamilton*, 8:531–32.

15. Pub. L. Ch. 28-1, 3 Stat. 222 (1791); Pub. L. Ch. 27-2, 1 Stat. 241 (1792); Calloway, *The Victory with No Name*, 142; Robert Wooster, *American Military Frontiers: The United States Army in the West, 1783–1900* (University of New Mexico Press, 2009), 7–14; Ablavsky, *Federal Ground*, 76; Alexander Hamilton, "Message on Public Debt," December 3, 1792, in *The Works of Alexander Hamilton*, ed. Henry Cabot Lodge, vol. 3 (G. P. Putnam's Sons, 1903), 46; George Washington to Alexander Hamilton, May 7, 1792, Series 2, Letterbooks 1754–1799, George Washington Papers, Library of Congress.

16. Alan Taylor, *American Colonies* (Viking, 2001), 443; U.S. Bureau of the Census, *Historical Statistics of the United States, Colonial Times to 1970* (GPO, 1975), vol. 1, 8; Nicole Eustace, *1812: War and the Passions of Patriotism* (University of Pennsylvania Press, 2012), 6–8; Blaakman, *Speculation Nation*, 106–14; Mark Barrow Jr., *Nature's Ghosts: Confronting Extinction from the Age of Jefferson to the Age of Ecology* (University of Chicago Press, 2009), 15–46; Brian W. Dippie, *The Vanishing American: White Attitudes and U.S. Indian Policy* (Wesleyan University Press, 1982); Jean O'Brien, *Firsting and Lasting: Writing Indians Out of Existence in New England* (University of Minnesota Press, 2010); Robert F. Berkhofer, *The White Man's Indian: Images of the American Indian from Columbus to the Present* (Alfred A. Knopf, 1978), 29–30; Henry Knox to George Washington, July 7, 1789, in *The Papers of George Washington*, vol. 3, *Presidential Series, June–September 1789*, ed. W. W. Abbot (University of Virginia Press, 1989), 134–41.

17. Daniel K. Richter, *The Ordeal of the Longhouse: The Peoples of the Iroquois League in the Era of European Colonization* (Omohundro Institute / University of North Carolina Press, 1992), 252–70; Richter, *Trade, Land, Power: The Struggle for Eastern North America* (University of Pennsylvania Press, 2013), 69–96; "Deed Determining the Boundary Line Between the Whites and Indians," November 5, 1768, in *Documents Relative to the Colonial History of the State of New-York*, vol. 8, ed. E. B. O'Callaghan (Weed, Parsons, 1857), 135–37; Colin G. Calloway, *Pen and Ink Witchcraft: Treaties and Treaty Making in American Indian History* (Oxford University Press, 2013), 49–95; William J. Campbell, *Speculators in Empire: Iroquoia and the 1768 Treaty of Fort Stanwix* (University of Oklahoma Press, 2012).

18. Calloway, *The American Revolution in Indian Country*, 33–45, 51–53, 129–57; Barbara Graymont, *The Iroquois in the American Revolution* (Syracuse University Press, 1972), 10, 192–222; Karim Tiro, "A 'Civil' War? Rethinking Iroquois Participation in the American Revolution," *Explorations in Early American Culture* 4 (2000): 148–65; Alyssa Mt. Pleasant, "After the Whirlwind: Maintaining a Haudenosaunee Place at Buffalo Creek, 1780–1825" (PhD diss., Cornell University, 2007), 23–64, 74.

19. Blaakman, *Speculation Nation*, 215–50; Blake A. Watson, *Buying America from the Indians: "Johnson v. McIntosh" and the History of Native Land Rights* (University of Oklahoma Press, 2012), 165–70; Greer, *Property and Dispossession*, 408–9.

20. Taylor, *The Divided Ground*, 143–203; Karim M. Tiro, *The People of the Standing Stone: The Oneida Nation from Revolution Through the Era of Removal* (University of Massachusetts Press, 2011), 65–95; Laurence M. Hauptman, *Conspiracy of Interests: Iroquois Dispossession and the Rise of New York State* (Syracuse University Press, 1999), 27–97; Blake McKelvey, "Historic Aspects of the Phelps and Gorham Treaty of July 4–8, 1788," *Rochester History* 1, no. 1 (1939): 1–24.

21. Clarence L. Ver Steeg, *Robert Morris, Revolutionary Financier: With an Analysis of His Earlier Career* (Octagon Books, 1976), 4–5; Charles Rappleye, *Robert Morris: Financier of the American Revolution* (Simon and Schuster, 2010), 105; Perkins, *American Public Finance*, 106–36; Barbara Ann Chernow, *Robert Morris, Land Speculator, 1790–1801* (Arno, 1978), 40–67; Paul D. Evans, *The Holland Land Company* (Buffalo Historical Society Publications, 1924), 3–35, 177–93.

22. Henry Knox to George Washington, June 15, 1789, in *ASP: Indian Affairs*, vol. 1, ed. Walter Lowrie and Matthew St. Clair Clarke (Gales and Seaton, 1832), 13–14; Henry Knox to George Washington, July 7, 1789, in *ASP: Indian Affairs*, 1:53; January 4, 1790 Report of Henry Knox, in *ASP: Indian Affairs*, 1:59–64; Hannah Farber, *Underwriters of the United States: How Insurance Shaped the American Founding* (Omohundro Institute / University of North Carolina Press, 2021), 156.

23. George Washington to Senate, March 26, 1792, in *ASP: Indian Affairs*, 1:225. Henry Knox to George Washington, June 15, 1789, in *ASP: Indian Affairs*, 1:13–14; Reginald Horsman, *Expansion and American Indian Policy, 1783–1812* (Michigan State University Press, 1967), 55–64; Nichols, *Red Gentlemen, White Savages*, 125.

24. George Washington, "Speech of the President of the United States to the Chiefs and Representatives of the Five Nations of Indians, in Philadelphia," March 23, 1792, in *ASP: Indian Affairs*, 1:229; Colin G. Calloway, *The Indian World of George Washington: The First President, the First Americans, and the Birth of the Nation* (Oxford University Press, 2018), 407; Jon W. Parmenter, "The Iroquois and the Native

American Struggle for the Ohio Valley, 1754–1794," in *Sixty Years' War for the Great Lakes, 1754–1814*, ed. Larry L. Nelson and David Curtis Skaggs (Michigan State University Press, 2012), 105–20; Lisa Brooks, *The Common Pot: The Recovery of Native Space in the Northeast* (University of Minnesota Press, 2008), 106–62; Isabel T. Kelsay, *Joseph Brant, 1743–1807: Man of Two Worlds* (Syracuse University Press, 1984), 345–46; Graymont, *The Iroquois in American Revolution*, 14; Alyssa Mt. Pleasant, "Independence for Whom? Expansion and Conflict in the Northeast and Northwest," in *The World of the Revolutionary American Republic: Land, Labor, and the Conflict for a Continent*, ed. Andrew Shankman (Routledge, 2014), 116–33.

25. Thomas S. Abler, ed. *Chainbreaker: The Revolutionary War Memoirs of Governor Blacksnake as Told to Benjamin Williams* (University of Nebraska Press, 1989), 197.

26. Abler, *Chainbreaker*, 199; Anthony F. C. Wallace, *The Death and Rebirth of the Seneca* (Vintage, 1972), 164–65.

27. Sugden, *Blue Jacket*, 136; Taylor, *The Divided Ground*, 277–78; "Journal of a Treaty Held in 1793, with the Indian Tribes North-West of the Ohio, by Commissioners of the United States," in *ASP: Indian Affairs*, 1:356.

28. Francis Paul Prucha, *The Sword of the Republic: The United States Army on the Frontier, 1783–1846* (Macmillan, 1969), 37; Calloway, *The Victory with No Name*, 150; Sword, *President Washington's Indian War*; Timothy Pickering to Anthony Wayne, April 8 1795, in *Anthony Wayne, A Name in Arms: Soldier, Diplomat, Defender of Expansion Westward of a Nation*, ed. Richard C. Knopf (University of Pittsburgh Press, 1960), 393–403; Cong. Globe, 26th Cong., 1st Sess., Appendix, 201 (1840); "Treaty with the Wyandot, Etc.," in *Indian Affairs: Laws and Treaties*, vol. 2, *Treaties*, ed. Charles Kappler (GPO, 1904), 39–45; Andrew Cayton, "'Noble Actors' upon 'the Theatre of Honour': Power and Civility in the Treaty of Greenville," in *Contact Points: American Frontiers from the Mohawk Valley to the Mississippi*, ed. Andrew Cayton and Fredrika J. Teute (Omohundro Institute / University of North Carolina Press, 1998), 235–69.

29. Timothy Pickering to Anthony Wayne, April 8, 1795, in *Campaign into the Wilderness: The Wayne-Knox-Pickering-McHenry Correspondence*, vol. 4, ed. Richard C. Knopf (Ohio State Museum, 1955), 402.

30. "Treaty with the Wyandot," 39–45; Samantha Seeley, *Race, Removal, and the Right to Remain: Migration and the Making of the United States* (Omohundro Institute / University of North Carolina Press, 2021).

31. "Treaty with the Wyandot," 39–45.

32. Michael A. Blaakman, "The Marketplace of American Federalism: Land Speculation Across State Lines in the Early Republic," *Journal of American History* 107, no. 3 (2020): 585–86, 603.

33. Gould, *Among the Powers of the Earth*, 137–43; Peter Kastor, *The Nation's Crucible: The Louisiana Purchase and the Creation of America* (Yale University Press, 2004), 38; Robert Morris to Anthony Wayne, March 27, 1795, Box 4, Robert Morris Papers, Huntington Library, San Marino, CA.

34. Gregory Ablavsky, "Beyond the Indian Commerce Clause," *Yale Law Journal* 124, no. 4 (2015): 1012–52; Ablavsky, *Federal Ground*, 79–108.

35. Francis Paul Prucha, *American Indian Policy in the Formative Years: The Indian Trade and Intercourse Acts, 1790–1834* (Harvard University Press, 1962).

36. Blaakman, *Speculation Nation*, 272–76, 283–84; Barbara Ann Chernow, "Robert Morris: Genesee Land Speculator," *New York History* 58, no. 2 (1977): 197–220. For a discussion of how Morris's imprisonment fit into the development of a general bankruptcy law, see Bruce H. Mann, *A Republic of Debtors: Bankruptcy in the Age of American Independence* (Harvard University Press, 2002), 212, 253–61.

37. James Bruff, Speech to Seneca and Responses, September 23, 1796, Vol. 15, Henry O'Reilly Collection, New York Historical (hereafter cited as O'Reilly Collection).

38. Robert Morris to Thomas Morris, March 6, 1797, Microfilm Edition, Reel 9, Frame 279, Papers of Robert Morris, Manuscript Division, Library of Congress (hereafter cited as Papers of Robert Morris); Norman B. Wilkinson, "Robert Morris and the Treaty of Big Tree," *Mississippi Valley Historical Review* 40, no. 2 (1953): 262; Thomas S. Abler, *Cornplanter: Chief Warrior of the Allegany Senecas* (Syracuse University Press, 2007), 121. Morris had originally intended to also bring Farmer's Brother and Red Jacket, but he appears to have run out of funds before he could host them. Robert Morris to Thomas Morris, March 26, 1796, Reel 9, Frames 763–65, Papers of Robert Morris.

39. Abler, *Cornplanter*, 1–3, 87–88; Michael Leroy Oberg, *Peacemakers: The Iroquois, the United States, and the Treaty of Canandaigua, 1794* (Oxford University Press, 2016), 47; Taylor, *The Divided Ground*, 246–47; Christopher Densmore, *Red Jacket: Iroquois Diplomat and Orator* (Syracuse University Press, 1999), 40–42.

40. Cornplanter Address, February 28, 1797, Vol. 12, O'Reilly Collection.

41. Cornplanter, "Indian Speech Made at Treaty Negotiations in September 1797," Papers of the War Department, 1784–1800, Roy Rosenzweig Center for History and New Media, George Mason University, https://wardepartmentpapers.org/s/home/item/59281; Robert Morris to Thomas Morris, March 6, 1797, Frame 279, Reel 10, Papers of Robert Morris.

42. "Rough Memoranda of Treaty of Geneseo in Aug. and Sept. 1797," Vol. 15, O'Reilly Collection, 31.

43. "Rough Memoranda"; Densmore, *Red Jacket*, xiv; Taylor, *The Divided Ground*, 164–65.

44. Nancy Shoemaker, "The Rise or Fall of Iroquois Women," *Journal of Women's History* 2, no. 3 (1991): 39–57; Elizabeth Tooker, "Women in Iroquois Society," in *Extending the Rafters: Interdisciplinary Approaches to Iroquoian Studies*, ed. Michael K. Foster, Jack Campisi, and Mariann Mithun (State University of New York Press, 1984), 115–17; Oberg, *Peacemakers*, 102.

45. "Rough Memoranda."

46. "Rough Memoranda."

47. "Rough Memoranda."

48. Joseph Ellicott to Theophile Cazenove, September 25, 1797, in *Reports of Joseph Ellicott*, vol. 1 (Buffalo Historical Society, 1937).

49. Indenture of April 30, 1798 between Thomas Morris, Le Roy, Bayard, Evers, Vol. 13, O'Reilly Collection; Wilkinson, "Morris and the Treaty of Big Tree," 275; Thomas L. Ogden, Draft of Chancery Answer, Case of Herman Le Roy, William Bayard, and James McEvers, vs. Thomas Morris, Folder Anthony Wayne etc., Box 11, Ogden Family Papers, Clements Library, University of Michigan, Ann Arbor (hereafter cited as Ogden Papers).

50. Alexander Hamilton, "Public Credit," January 16 and 21, 1795, in *ASP: Finance*, 1:322. Public land distribution would not resume until 1796, after the end of warfare in the Ohio Country; see Malcolm Rohrbough, *The Land Office Business: The Settlement and Administration of American Public Lands, 1789–1837* (Oxford University Press, 1968), 20–22; and Ablavsky, *Federal Ground*, 76–78.

51. Julius Goebel Jr. and Joseph H. Smith, eds., *The Law Practice of Alexander Hamilton: Documents and Commentary*, vol. 3 (Columbia University Press, 1980), 611, 614–16, 633; Evans, *The Holland Land Company*, 206–7.

52. Gould, *Among the Powers of the Earth*, 14–47; David M. Golove and Daniel J. Hulsebosch, "A Civilized Nation: The Early American Constitution, the Law of Nations, and the Pursuit of International Recognition," *New York University Law Review* 85, no. 4 (2010): 932–1066; Francis Paul Prucha, *American Indian Treaties: The History of a Political Anomaly* (University of California Press, 1994), 70–74; Julius Goebel Jr. and Joseph H. Smith, eds., *The Law Practice of Alexander Hamilton: Documents and Commentary*, vol. 5 (Columbia University Press, 1980), 545; Alexander Hamilton to Theophile Cazenove in *The Papers of Alexander Hamilton*, vol. 26, *1802–1804*, ed. Harold C. Syrett (Columbia University Press, 1979), 759. Syrett's summary cites the Holland Land Company collection at Stadsarchief Amsterdam, yet archivists were unable to locate the original. See also Amalia D. Kessler, *Inventing American Exceptionalism: The Origins of American Adversarial Legal Culture, 1800–1877* (Yale University Press, 2017), 4, 21–51; Lawrence M. Friedman, *A History of American Law*, 3rd ed. (Simon and Schuster, 2005), xviii; and Stanley N. Katz, "The Politics of Law in Colonial America: Controversies over Chancery Courts and Equity Law in the Eighteenth Century," in *Perspectives in American History: Law in American History*, vol. 5, ed. Donald Fleming and Bernard Bailyn (Little, Brown, 1971), 257–84.

53. "Treaty: Ratified Indian Treaty 27: Agreement with Seneca—Genesee, New York, September 15, 1797," DigiTreaties, https://digitreaties.org/treaties/treaty/84565084/.

54. Claire Priest, *Credit Nation: Property Laws and Institutions in Early America* (Princeton University Press, 2021), 74–90; Claire Priest, "Creating an American Property Law: Alienability and Its Limits in American History," *Harvard Law Review* 120, no. 2 (2006): 385–459; K-Sue Park, "Money, Mortgages, and the Conquest of America," *Law and Social Inquiry* 41, no. 4 (2016): 1006–35; Elizabeth Blackmar, "Inheriting Property and Debt: From Family Security to Corporate Accumulation," in *Capitalism Takes Command: The Social Transformation of Nineteenth-Century America*, ed. Michael Zakim and Gary J. Kornblith (University of Chicago Press, 2012), 102; Peter Dobkin Hall, *The Organization of American Culture, 1700–1900: Private Institutions, Elites, and the Origins of American Nationality* (New York University Press, 1982), 68–72; Carole Shammas, Marylynn Salmon, and Michel Dahlin, *Inheritance in America: From Colonial Times to the Present* (Rutgers University Press, 1987), 5; John H. Langbein, "The Contractarian Basis of the Law of Trusts," *Yale Law Journal* 105, no. 3 (1995): 627–75; Lawrence M. Friedman, *Dead Hands: A Social History of Wills, Trusts, and Inheritance Law* (Stanford University Press, 2009), 111–17; Peter Dobkin Hall and George E. Marcus, "Why Should Men Leave Great Fortunes to Their Children? Class, Dynasty, and Inheritance in America," in *Inheritance and Wealth in America*, ed. Robert K. Miller Jr. and Stephen J. McNamee (Springer, 1998), 143–55.

55. Robert Morris to Theophile Cazenove, November 8, 1797, Reel 10, Frame 61, Papers of Robert Morris.

56. For more on this legal battle, see Emilie Connolly, "Strategies of Succession and the 1797 Treaty of Big Tree," *William and Mary Quarterly* 80, no. 1 (2023): 125–54.

57. Robert Morris to Theophile Cazenove, August 12, 1797, Reel 10, Frame 491, Papers of Robert Morris; Robert Morris to Jeremiah Wadsworth, August 15, 1797, Reel 10, Frames 505–6, Papers of Robert Morris.

58. Robert Morris to Theophile Cazenove, November 1, 1797, Reel 10, Frame 50, Papers of Robert Morris.

59. Robert Morris to Theophile Cazenove, Messrs. Leroy, Bayard, & McEvers, December 5, 1797, Reel 10, Frame 125, Papers of Robert Morris; John J. Vanderkemp to Thomas L. Ogden, March 21, 1828, Folder John J. Vanderkemp 4, Box 6, Ogden Papers; John J. Vanderkemp to Thomas L. Ogden, August 23, 1832, Folder John J. Vanderkemp 11, Box 7, Ogden Family Papers; Copy of Bank Stock Conferral from Thomas Willing to John Adams, n.d., Folder John J. Vanderkemp 4, Box 6, Ogden Papers.

60. "Halliday Jackson's Journal to the Seneca Indians, 1798–1800," *Pennsylvania History: A Journal of Mid-Atlantic Studies* 19, no. 2 (1952): 128–29.

61. Evans, *The Holland Land Company*, 198–99; Joseph Ellicott to Theophile Cazenove, August 29 1798, in *Reports of Joseph Ellicott*, vol. 1, ed. Robert Warwick Bingham (Buffalo Historical Society, 1937), 39.

62. Israel Chapin to James McHenry, September 9, 1798, Vol. 13, O'Reilly Collection; James McHenry to Israel Chapin, October 11, 1798, Vol. 13, O'Reilly Collection.

63. Lockwood R. Doty, *History of Livingston County, New York, From Its Earliest Traditions to the Present Together with Early Town Sketches* (W. J. Van Deusen, 1905), 259–60.

64. Israel Chapin to James McHenry, November 10 1798, Vol. 13, O'Reilly Collection.

65. James McHenry to John Adams, "Stipends, Dividends & Gift Sums to Indian Nations," January 27, 1799, Papers of the War Department, 1784–1800, Roy Rosenzweig Center for History and New Media, George Mason University, https://wardepartmentpapers.org/s/home/item/66236.

66. Israel Chapin to James McHenry, May 26, 1799, Vol. 13, O'Reilly Collection; Laurence Hauptman, *Conspiracy of Interests: Iroquois Dispossession and the Rise of New York State* (Syracuse University Press, 1999), 106–7; Orlando Allen, "Personal Recollections of Captains Jones and Parrish, and of the Payment of Indian Annuities in Buffalo," in *Publications of the Buffalo Historical Society*, vol. 6, ed. Frank H. Severance (Buffalo Historical Society, 1903), 541–46; James McHenry to Israel Chapin, October 11, 1798, Vol. 13, O'Reilly Collection. The Senecas also received a smaller annuity originating from New York State's purchase of islands in the Niagara River; see Allen, "Personal Recollections," 539–40; Israel Chapin to James McHenry, September 9, 1798, Vol. 13, Henry O'Reilly Collection; Theophile Cazenove to Israel Chapin, November 3, 1798, Vol. 13, O'Reilly Collection; and Le Roy, Bayard, and Evers to Chapin, November 11, 1798, Vol. 13, O'Reilly Collection.

67. Allen, "Personal Recollections," 542; Israel Chapin to James McHenry, January 10, 1798, Vol. 13, O'Reilly Collection; Address of Seneca sachems, enclosed by Erastus Granger to Department of War, December 9, 1811, Vol. 1811–1812, SWLR.

68. "Indian Speeches at Geneseo," November 12, 1801, Vol. 14, O'Reilly Collection.

69. Thomas Jefferson and Henry Dearborn to Seneca, Onondaga, Cayuga, Munsee Indians, February 24, 1802, in *The Papers of Thomas Jefferson*, vol. 36, *December 1801 to March 1802*, ed. Barbara B. Oberg (Princeton University Press, 2010), 632.

70. My thanks to Jamie Jacobs for the translation. See also Wallace Chafe, comp., *Seneca Words* (Onöndowa'ga:' Gawë:nö' [Seneca Language] Department, Seneca Nation, n.d.), accessed March 26, 2025, https://senecalanguage.com/wp-content/uploads/Seneca-Words-Chafe.pdf; and Allen, "Personal Recollections," 350.

71. Perkins, *American Public Finance*, 235–36; H. Wayne Morgan, "The Origins and Establishment of the First Bank of the United States," *Business History Review* 30, no. 4 (1956): 472–79; James O. Wettereau, "New Light on the First Bank of the United States," *Pennsylvania Magazine of History and Biography* 61, no. 3 (1937): 273–74.

72. Peter L. Rousseau and Richard Sylla, "Emerging Financial Markets and Early US Growth," *Explorations in Economic History* 42, no. 1 (2005): 4–9; Richard Sylla, "Financial Foundations: Public Credit, the National Bank, and Securities Markets," in *Founding Choices: American Economic Policy in the 1790s*, ed. Douglas A. Irwin and Richard Sylla (University of Chicago Press, 2019), 59–88.

73. Kastor, *The Nation's Crucible*, 37–38; Susan Gaunt Stearns, *Empire of Commerce: The Closing of the Mississippi and the Opening of Atlantic Trade* (University of Virginia Press, 2024).

74. Laurent Dubois, "The Haitian Revolution and the Sale of Louisiana: Or, Thomas Jefferson's (Unpaid) Debt to Jean Jacques Dessalines," in *Empires of the Imagination: Transatlantic Histories of the Louisiana Purchase*, ed. Peter J. Kastor and François Weil (University of Virginia Press, 2009), 93–116; Kastor, *The Nation's Crucible*, 39–41; J. E. Winston, "How the Louisiana Purchase Was Financed," *Louisiana Historical Quarterly* 12, no. 2 (1929): 191; Edling, *A Hercules in the Cradle*, 107.

75. Michael John Witgen, *Seeing Red: Indigenous Land, American Expansion, and the Political Economy of Plunder in North America* (Omohundro Institute / University of North Carolina Press, 2022), 35–90; Ora Brooks Peake, *A History of the United States Indian Factory System, 1795–1822* (Sage Books, 1954); David A. Nichols, *Engines of Diplomacy: Indian Trading Factories and the Negotiation of American Empire* (University of North Carolina Press, 2016); Lewis Cass to William H. Crawford, May 14, 1816, Folder September 1815–May 1816, Box 2, Lewis Cass Papers, Detroit Public Library; Stephen J. Rockwell, *Indian Affairs and the Administrative State in the Nineteenth Century* (Cambridge University Press, 2010), 81; Statement of Annuities, 1811, Vol. 1811, SWLR.

76. William Eustis to Erastus Granger, April 26, 1811, Vol. C, SWLS, 78; John T. Holdsworth, *The First Bank of the United States* (GPO, 1910), 107–8; Edling, *A Hercules in the Cradle*, 119–22; Callender Irvine to William Eustis, November 2, 1812, Vol. 1812–1813, SWLR.

77. Alan Taylor, *The Civil War of 1812: American Citizens, British Subjects, Irish Rebels, & Indian Allies* (Alfred A. Knopf, 2010), 228–29; John Armstrong to Six Nations, April 18, 1813, Vol. C, SWLS.

78. Benn, *The Iroquois in the War of 1812*, 127–51.

79. In 1813 another $6,200 was invested on behalf of the Senecas, likely due to the liquidation of an additional fifteen shares of stock purchased in 1804, 1806, and 1807,

as well as the biannual dividend on this stock. Callender Irvine to John Armstrong, June 6, 1813, Vol. 1813, SWLR. The War Department failed after 1811 to keep a careful accounting of revenues and expenditures relating to the Seneca fund. Charles Nourse Report, March 18, 1829, LROIA 808 [213]; Benn, *The Iroquois in the War of 1812*, 147–48.

80. James Monroe to Brothers of the Six Nations, March 11, 1815, Vol. C, SWLS, 202–4.

81. In March 1817, for example, Jasper Parrish took out $952 on the War Department's account in order to bring the Seneca dividend of $5,048 to an even $6,000; George Graham to Erastus Granger, March 19, 1817, Vol. D, SWLS, 16.

## *Chapter Two: Inheriting the Earth*

1. David Folsom to Cyrus Kingsbury, July 9, 1819, Box 1, Folder 2, Series I, J. L. Hargett Papers, Beinecke Library, Yale University (hereafter cited as Hargett Papers). Captains governed *iksas* (clans); see Richard White, *The Roots of Dependency: Subsistence, Environment, and Social Change Among the Choctaws, Pawnees, and Navajos* (University of Nebraska Press, 1983), 40.

2. Donna L. Akers, *Living in the Land of Death: The Choctaw Nation, 1830–1860* (Michigan State University Press, 2004), 114; H. B. Cushman, *History of the Choctaw, Chickasaw, and Natchez Indians* (Headlight, 1899), 72–73, 76–77; Folsom to Kingsbury, July 9, 1819.

3. On civilization policy as a strategy of dispossession through a forced transition to sedentary production and the appropriation of Indigenous labor, see Lori J. Daggar, *Cultivating Empire: Capitalism, Philanthropy, and the Negotiation of American Imperialism in Indian Country* (University of Pennsylvania Press, 2023); Bernard Sheehan, *Seeds of Extinction: Jeffersonian Philanthropy and the American Indian* (Omohundro Institute / University of North Carolina Press, 1973), 119–47; Christian B. Keller, "Philanthropy Betrayed: Thomas Jefferson, the Louisiana Purchase, and the Origins of Federal Indian Removal Policy," *Proceedings of the American Philosophical Society* 144, no. 1 (2000): 39–66; and Anthony F. C. Wallace, *Jefferson and the Indians: The Tragic Fate of the First Americans* (Harvard University Press, 1999), 161–74. See also Francis Paul Prucha, *The Great Father: The United States Government and the American Indians* (University of Nebraska Press, 1984), 142–54. On "flexible" state capacity, see Ira Katznelson, "Flexible Capacity: The Military and Early American Statebuilding," in *Shaped by War and Trade: International Influences on American Political Development*, ed. Ira Katznelson and Martin Shefter (Princeton University Press, 2002), 84–104.

4. James W. Covington, *The Seminoles of Florida* (University of Florida Press, 1993), 28–49; Robert V. Remini, *Andrew Jackson and His Indian Wars* (Viking, 2002), 94–108, 143–62; Nathaniel Millet, "The Radicalism of the First Seminole War and Its Consequences," in *Warring for America: Cultural Contests in the Era of 1812*, ed. Nicole Eustace and Fredrika J. Teute (Omohundro Institute / University of North Carolina Press, 2017), 164–201; Nancy Shoemaker, *A Strange Likeness: Becoming Red and White in Eighteenth Century North America* (Oxford University Press, 2004), 74–75; Colin G. Calloway, *Pen and Ink Witchcraft: Treaties and Treaty Making in*

*American Indian History* (Oxford University Press, 2013), 35; Robert A. Williams, *Linking Arms Together: American Indian Treaty Visions of Law and Peace, 1600–1800* (Oxford University Press, 1997), 47–61, 76–79; David Folsom to Elias Cornelius, October 1, 1818, Box 1, Folder 2, Hargett Papers.

5. Carla Gardina Pestana, *Protestant Empire: Religion and the Making of the British Atlantic World* (University of Pennsylvania Press, 2009); Jorge Cañizares-Esguerra, *Puritan Conquistadors: Iberianizing the Atlantic, 1550–1700* (Stanford University Press, 2006); Andrew Porter, *Religion Versus Empire? British Protestant Missionaries and Overseas Expansion 1700–1914* (Manchester University Press, 2004).

6. Drew McCoy, *The Elusive Republic: Political Economy in Jeffersonian America* (University of North Carolina Press, 1980), 17–37; Sheehan, *Seeds of Extinction*, 24–25, 148–94; Robert F. Berkhofer Jr., *Salvation and the Savage: An Analysis of Protestant Missions and American Indian Response, 1787–1862* (University Press of Kentucky, 1965); Emily Conroy-Krutz, *Christian Imperialism: Converting the World in the Early American Republic* (Cornell University Press, 2015), 14–15; "Speech of the President of the United States to the Chiefs and Representatives of the Five Nations of Indians, in Philadelphia," March 23, 1792, in *ASP: Indian Affairs*, vol. 1, ed. Walter Lowrie and Matthew St. Clair Clarke (Gales and Seaton, 1832), 229; Colin G. Calloway, *The Indian World of George Washington: The First President, the First Americans, and the Birth of the Nation* (Oxford University Press, 2018), 407; Claudio Saunt, *A New Order of Things: Property, Power, and the Transformation of the Creek Indians, 1733–1816* (Cambridge University Press, 2004), 139, 155–56, 164–76.

7. Theda Perdue, *"Mixed Blood Indians": Racial Construction in the Early South* (University of Georgia Press, 2003), 33–69. See also Claudio Saunt, Barbara Krauthamer, Tiya Miles, Celia E. Naylor, and Circe Sturm, "Rethinking Race and Culture in the Early South," *Ethnohistory* 53, no. 2 (2006): 399–405; R. David Edmunds, *The Shawnee Prophet* (University of Nebraska Press, 1983), 16–20, 33–39, 80–81; Gregory Evans Dowd, *A Spirited Resistance: The North American Indian Struggle for Unity, 1745–1815* (Johns Hopkins University Press, 1992), 124–39; Susan Sleeper-Smith, *Indigenous Prosperity and American Conquest: Indian Women of the Ohio River Valley, 1690–1792* (Omohundro Institute / University of North Carolina Press, 2018), 316–17.

8. Angie Debo, *The Rise and Fall of the Choctaw Republic* (University of Oklahoma Press, 1961), 40–41; Joel W. Martin, *Sacred Revolt: The Muskogees' Struggle for a New World* (Beacon, 1991), 116–17; J. Leitch Wright Jr., *Creeks and Seminoles: The Destruction and Regeneration of the Muscogulge People* (University of Nebraska Press, 1990), 155–84; Frank Lawrence Owsley, *Struggle for the Gulf Borderlands: The Creek War and the Battle of New Orleans, 1812–1815* (Library Press, 2017); Michael Green, *The Politics of Indian Removal: Creek Government and Society in Crisis* (University of Nebraska Press, 1982), 40–42; Saunt, *A New Order of Things*, 271–72; Jeffrey Ostler, *Surviving Genocide: Native Nations and the United States from the American Revolution to Bleeding Kansas* (Yale University Press, 2019), 173.

9. Green, *The Politics of Indian Removal*, 43; Saunt, *A New Order of Things*, 271–72. The United States upheld this fraudulent cession despite Creek protests that it violated international law under the 1814 Treaty of Ghent, which stipulated that Native lands taken during the war were to be restored to their original possessors.

Deborah Rosen, *Border Law: The First Seminole War and American Nationhood* (Harvard University Press, 2015), 105–6.

10. Lewis Cecil Gray, *History of Agriculture in the Southern United States to 1860*, vol. 2 (Carnegie Institution of Washington, 1933), 682–83; Adam Rothman, *Slave Country: American Expansion and the Origins of the Deep South* (Harvard University Press, 2005), 57; Daniel S. Dupre, *Alabama's Frontiers and the Rise of the Old South* (Indiana University Press, 2018), 249–52; John Hebron Moore, *The Emergence of the Cotton Kingdom in the Old Southwest: Mississippi, 1770–1860* (Louisiana State University Press, 1988), 4–6.

11. Gilbert C. Fite, "Development of the Cotton Industry by the Five Civilized Tribes in Indian Territory," *Journal of Southern History* 15, no. 3 (1949): 342–53; James Taylor Carson, "Dollars Never Fail to Melt Their Hearts: Native Women and the Market Revolution," in *Neither Lady nor Slave: Working Women of the Old South*, ed. Susanna Delfino and Michele Gillespie (University of North Carolina Press, 2002), 15–33; Jeffrey Washburn, "Directing Their Own Change: Chickasaw Economic Transformation and the Civilization Plan, 1750s–1830s," *Native South* 13 (2020): 94–119; Daniel H. Usner Jr., "American Indians on the Cotton Frontier: Changing Economic Relations with Citizens and Slaves in the Mississippi Territory," *Journal of American History* 72, no. 2 (1985): 297–317; Gavin Wright, *Slavery and American Economic Development* (Louisiana State University Press, 2006), 50–54; Gavin Wright, "Slavery and the Rise of the Nineteenth-Century American Economy," *Journal of Economic Perspectives* 36, no. 2 (2022): 132.

12. See Charles J. Kappler, ed., *Indian Affairs: Laws and Treaties*, vol. 2, *Treaties* (GPO, 1904), 124–26, 133–37, 140–44, 155, 174–81. One exceptionally large cession preceded this period, when the Choctaws were in 1805 compelled to sell lands in order to repay trade debts to the British trading firm Panton and Leslie. White, *The Roots of Dependency*, 96; Rothman, *Slave Country*, 41; William G. McLoughlin, *Cherokee Renascence in the New Republic* (Princeton University Press, 1986), 245; Robert V. Remini, *Andrew Jackson and His Indian Wars* (Viking, 2001), 101, 128.

13. "Quantity of Land Sold at the Land Offices Since their Institution [. . .]," in *ASP: Public Lands*, vol. 3 (Gales and Seaton, 1834), 371; Steven Deyle, *Carry Me Back: The Domestic Slave Trade in American Life* (Oxford University Press, 2005), 43.

14. Nathan O. Hatch, *The Democratization of American Christianity* (Yale University Press, 1989), 18–45; Martin E. Marty, *Righteous Empire: The Protestant Experience in America* (Dial, 1970); Kathleen D. McCarthy, *American Creed: Philanthropy and the Rise of Civil Society, 1700–1865* (University of Chicago Press, 2003), 7, 50–51; Kevin Butterfield, *The Making of Tocqueville's America: Law and Association in the Early United States* (University of Chicago Press, 2015), 24–25; Daniel Walker Howe, *What Hath God Wrought: The Transformation of America, 1815–1848* (Oxford University Press, 2007), 166–86; Conroy-Krutz, *Christian Imperialism*.

15. *The Society for Propagating the Gospel Among the Indians and Others in North America, 1787–1887* (Printed for the Society, University Press, 1887), 5–12; Howe, *What Hath God Wrought*, 165; McCarthy, *American Creed*, 32, 52; Johann N. Neem, "The Elusive Common Good: Religion and Civil Society in Massachusetts, 1780–1833," *Journal of the Early Republic* 24, no. 3 (2004): 388. See also William G.

McLoughlin, *New England Dissent: 1630–1833: The Baptists and the Separation of Church and State*, 2 vols. (Harvard University Press, 1971).

16. Elizabeth Blackmar, "Inheriting Property and Debt: From Family Security to Corporate Accumulation," in *Capitalism Takes Command: The Social Transformation of Nineteenth-Century America*, ed. Michael Zakim and Gary J. Kornblith (University of Chicago Press, 2012), 92–117; Carole Shammas, Marylynn Salmon, and Michel Dahlin, *Inheritance in America: From Colonial Times to the Present* (Rutgers University Press, 1987), 5; Peter Dobkin Hall, *The Organization of American Culture, 1700–1900: Private Institutions, Elites, and the Origins of American Nationality* (New York University Press, 1982), 70–72, 97, 110; Peter Dobkin Hall, "What the Merchants Did with Their Money: Charitable and Testamentary Trusts in Massachusetts, 1780–1880," in *Entrepreneurs: The Boston Business Community, 1700–1850*, ed. Conrad Edick Wright and Katherine Viens (Massachusetts Historical Society, 1997), 398–402; Robert F. Dalzell Jr., *Enterprising Elite: The Boston Associates and the World They Made* (Harvard University Press, 1987), 12; Peter Dobkin Hall and George E. Marcus, "Why Should Men Leave Great Fortunes to Their Children? Class, Dynasty, and Inheritance in America," in *Inheritance and Wealth in America*, ed. Robert K. Miller Jr. and Stephen J. McNamee (Springer, 1998), 143–45; William J. Curran, "The Struggle for Equity Jurisdiction in Massachusetts," *Boston University Law Review* 31, no. 3 (1951): 274–75; Tamara Platkins Thornton, *Nathaniel Bowditch and the Power of Numbers: How a Nineteenth-Century Man of Business, Science, and the Sea Changed American Life* (University of North Carolina Press, 2016), 142; David Grayson Allen, *Investment Management in Boston* (University of Massachusetts Press, 2015), 61–80; Donald Holbrook, *The Boston Trustee* (Marshall Jones, 1937).

17. John F. Schermerhorn, *Report to the Society for Propagating the Gospel Among the Indians*, vol. 2 (Society for Propagating the Gospel Among the Indians, 1814), 20, 14.

18. Conroy-Krutz, *Christian Imperialism*, 24–36; William G. McLoughlin, *Cherokees and Missionaries, 1789–1839* (Yale University Press, 1984), 103–14. In 1816 the American Board of Commissions for Foreign Missions held almost $4,140 in unspecified bank stock, and another $2,490 in stock of the Second Bank of the United States. *Report of the American Board of Commissions for Foreign Missions, Compiled from Documents Laid Before the Board at the Seventh Annual Meeting* (Samuel T. Armstrong, 1816). On the popularity of bank stock among benevolent associations, see McCarthy, *American Creed*, 45.

19. Robert Sparks Walker, *Torchlights to the Cherokees: The Brainerd Mission* (Macmillan, 1931), 16; McLoughlin, *Cherokees and Missionaries*, 108–9; McLoughlin, *Cherokee Renascence*, 198–99, 208–9; American Board of Commissioners for Foreign Missions, *First Ten Annual Reports of the American Board of Commissioners for Foreign Missions, with Other Documents of the Board* (Crocker and Brewster, 1834), 134–35; Gary E. Moulton, *John Ross: Cherokee Chief* (University of Georgia Press, 1978), 2–4, 6; Tiya Miles, *Ties That Bind: The Story of an Afro-Cherokee Family in Slavery and Freedom* (University of California Press, 2006), 104. On slavery in the Cherokee Nation in this period, see Theda Perdue, *Slavery and the Evolution of Cherokee Society, 1540–1866* (University of Tennessee Press, 1979), 50–67; and Fay A. Yarbrough, *Race and the Cherokee Nation: Sovereignty in the Nineteenth Century* (University of Pennsylvania Press, 2008), 25–56.

20. McLoughlin, *Cherokees and Missionaries*, 110; "American Aborigines," in American Board of Commissioners, *First Ten Annual Reports*, 154.

21. Circular of John C. Calhoun, September 3, 1819, in *ASP: Indian Affairs*, vol. 2, ed. Walter Lowrie and Walter S. Franklin (Gale and Seaton, 1834), 201; Martha Letitia Edwards, "Government Patronage of Indian Missions, 1789–1832" (PhD diss., University of Wisconsin–Madison, 1916), 79–80, 82–85. When Presbyterian missionaries arrived among the Chickasaw during this period, William Colbert granted them land in a similar arrangement. Otis W. Pickett, "T. C. Stuart and the Monroe Mission Among the Chickasaws in Mississippi, 1819–1834," *Native South* 8 (2015): 68. Edwards, "Government Patronage," 84–85; Joyce B. Phillips and Paul Gary Phillips, *The Brainerd Journal: A Mission to the Cherokees, 1817–1823* (University of Nebraska Press, 1998), 29, 32, 37

22. Clara Sue Kidwell, *Choctaws and Missionaries in Mississippi, 1818–1918* (University of Oklahoma Press, 1995), 54; Julie Reed, "Centering the Native South: A Roundtable on Native Pasts and Futures," paper presented at the annual meeting of the Society for Early Americanists, virtual meeting, March 5, 2021; Cherokee Deputation, February 5, 1818, Vol. 1818, SWLR. For a similar request from the Chickasaws, see Chinabee King et al, Chickasaw Memorial, February 10, 1817, Vol. 1817, SWLR.

23. Daggar, *Cultivating Empire*, 98–122; Krauthamer, *Black Slaves, Indian Masters: Slavery, Emancipation, and Citizenship in the Native American South* (University of North Carolina Press, 2013), 63–64; Miles, *Ties That Bind*, 39–41, 93–97; Cherokee Delegation to John C. Calhoun, March 8, 1819, Vol. 1819, SWLR; Theda Perdue, *Cherokee Women: Gender and Culture Change, 1700–1835* (University of Nebraska Press, 1998), 17–18, 116, 126–30; Fite, "Development of the Cotton Industry"; Path Killer to John Ross, January 10, 1816, in *The Papers of Chief John Ross*, vol. 1, ed. Gary E. Moulton (University of Oklahoma Press, 1985), 29; Cherokee Memorial Letter to George Graham, October 28, 1817, Vol. 1817, SWLR; and Cherokee Memorial Letter to James Monroe, November 22, 1817, Vol. 1817, SWLR; McLoughlin, *Cherokee Renascence*, 297–98.

24. Czarina C. Conlan, "David Folsom," *Chronicles of Oklahoma* 4, no. 4 (1926): 340–55; Cushman, *History of the Choctaw, Chickasaw, and Natchez Indians*, 328.

25. "Tenth Annual Meeting, American Board of Commissioners for Foreign Missions," in American Board of Commissioners, *First Ten Annual Reports*, 241–42, 244; Kidwell, *Choctaws and Missionaries*, 29–49; David Folsom to Elias Cornelius, September 3, 1819, Box 1, Folder 2, Series I, Hargett Papers; Cyrus Byington, *A Dictionary of the Choctaw Language*, ed. John R. Swanton and Henry S. Halbert (GPO, 1915), 101–2.

26. Cherokee Delegation, Washington City, February 5, 1818, Vol. 1818, SWLR.

27. Mikhelle Lynn Ross-Mulkey, "The Cherokee Phoenix: Resistance and Accommodation," *Native South* 5 (2012): 123–48. On the enduring significance of Sequoyah's syllabary for Cherokee nationhood, see Daniel Heath Justice, *Our Fire Survives the Storm: A Cherokee Literary History* (University of Minnesota Press, 2006).

28. Cherokee Delegation, February 5, 1818; McLoughlin, *Cherokee Renascence*, 252–54; Ard Hoyt to Samuel Worcester, January 11, 1819, Cherokee Mission, Vol. 2, Reel 737, Frame 349, American Board of Commissioners for Foreign Missions Archives, 1810–1961 (ABC 1–91), Houghton Library, Harvard University (hereafter cited as ABCFM Archives).

29. Ard Hoyt, Daniel S. Butrick, and William Chamberlin to Samuel Worcester, December 21, 1818, Cherokee Mission, Vol. 2, Reel 737, Frame 347, ABCFM Archives; Cherokee Delegation to Secretary of War, February 12, 1819, Vol. 1819, SWLR; Ard Hoyt, Daniel Butrick, Mood Hall, and William Chamberlin to Samuel Worcester, April 10, 1819, Cherokee Mission, Vol. 2, Reel 737, Frame 356, ABCFM Archives; "Treaty with the Cherokee, 1819," in Kappler, *Indian Affairs*, 2:177–79.

30. The Land Ordinance of 1785 set aside the proceeds of the sixteenth section of every township to finance common schools. See Paul Wallace Gates, *History of Public Land Law Development* (GPO, 1968), 65; Peter Onuf, *Statehood and Union: A History of the Northwest Ordinance* (Indiana University Press, 1987), 38–39.

31. Christina Snyder, *Slavery in Indian Country: The Changing Face of Captivity in Early America* (Harvard University Press, 2010), 5–6, 63, 100–102, 149–51; Perdue, *Cherokee Women*, 54–55; Cynthia Cumfer, *Separate Peoples, One Land: The Minds of Cherokees, Blacks, and Whites on the Tennessee Frontier* (University of North Carolina Press, 2007), 112–20; Miles, *Ties That Bind*, 69–72. Possessions were often buried alongside the deceased instead of inherited; see William L. Anderson, Jane L. Brown, and Anne F. Rogers, eds., *The Payne-Butrick Papers*, vol. 2 (University of Nebraska Press, 2010), 91; John Philip Reid, *A Law of Blood: The Primitive Law of the Cherokee Nation* (DeKalb: Northern Illinois University Press, 2006), 143–45; Rowena McClinton, "Possessions and Value: Cherokee Inheritance in the early Nineteenth Century," unpublished manuscript, 1992; Rennard Strickland, *Fire and the Spirits: Cherokee Law from Clan to Court* (University of Oklahoma Press, 1975), 55, 93–94; and "Cherokee Women, *Petition*, June 30, 1818," in *The Cherokee Removal: A Brief History with Documents*, ed. Theda Perdue and Michael D. Green (Bedford / St. Martin's, 2005), 132–34.

32. "September 11, 1808, Laws of Cherokee Nation," in *Documents of Native American Political Development: 1500s to 1933*, ed. David E. Wilkins (Oxford University Press, 1989), 111.

33. Strickland, *Fire and the Spirits*, 79–81; Theda Perdue, "Clan and Court: Another Look at the Early Cherokee Republic," *American Indian Quarterly* 24, no. 4 (2000): 562–69; Julie Reed, *Serving the Nation: Cherokee Sovereignty and Social Welfare, 1800–1907* (University of Oklahoma Press, 2016), 3; Nakia D. Parker, "'Regarded as an Appendage of His Family': Slavery, Family, and the Law in Indian Territory," *Journal of African American History* 106, no. 1 (2021): 27–51.

34. Cherokee Memorial Letter to James Monroe, November 22, 1817, Vol. 1817, SWLR.

35. "Address to Cherokee Delegation from Samuel Worcester, August 1819," in American Board of Commissioners, *First Ten Annual Reports*, 239.

36. "Treaties with Several Tribes," in *ASP: Indian Affairs*, 2:230, 240, 244. On the Treaty of Doaks Stand, see Cushman, *History of the Choctaw, Chickasaw, and Natchez Indians*, 60–68; White, *The Roots of Dependency*, 114–16; and Kidwell, *Choctaws and Missionaries*, 45–47.

37. "Treaties with Several Tribes," in *ASP: Indian Affairs*, 2:229–44; Cong. Globe, 26th Cong., 1st sess., 201 (Appendix); "Treaty with the Choctaw, 1820," in Kappler, *Indian Affairs*, 2:191–95; John C. Calhoun to Lewis Cass, March 27, 1819, Vol. D, SWLS, 277; "Treaty with the Osage, 1825," in Kappler, *Indian Affairs*, 2:217–21;

"Treaty with the Kansa, 1825," in Kappler, *Indian Affairs*, 2:222–25; "Treaty with the Chippewa, 1826," in Kappler, *Indian Affairs*, 2:268–71; "Treaty with the Potawatomi, 1826," in Kappler, *Indian Affairs*, 2:274.

38. On Cherokee understandings of federal protection and trusteeship, see David E. Wilkins and K. Tsianina Lomawaima, *Uneven Ground: American Indian Sovereignty and Federal Law* (University of Oklahoma Press, 2001), 81; and Cumfer, *Separate Peoples*, 87–89.

39. Return J. Meigs to John C. Calhoun, February 22, 1819, Correspondence and Miscellaneous Records, 1819–20, Microform 208: Records of the Cherokee Indian Agency in Tennessee, Reel 8, Image 42, RG 64, NARA.

40. John C. Calhoun to Henry Clay, "Progress of Civilizing Indians," January 15, 1820, in *ASP: Indian Affairs*, 2:201.

41. Andrew H. Browning, *The Panic of 1819: The First Great Depression* (University of Missouri Press, 2019), 216, 235; Malcolm Rohrbough, *The Land Office Business: The Settlement and Administration of American Public Lands, 1789–1837* (Oxford University Press, 1968), 140–98; Elbert Herring to John Ross et al., February 14, 1834, LSOIA 10, 48–49; Elbert Herring to John Ross et al., February 18, 1834, LSOIA 12, 123.

42. James Monroe, "Second Inaugural Address," in *A Compilation of the Messages and Papers of the Presidents*, vol. 2, ed. James D. Richardson (Bureau of National Literature, 1917), 661.

43. Charles Cutts, Resolution, April 19, 1820, Vol. 1820, SWLR; Ann Sanford, *Reluctant Reformer: Nathan Sanford in the Era of the Early Republic* (State University of New York Press, 2018), 48, 65; "Statement of All Annuities Payable by the United States [. . .]," in *ASP: Indian Affairs*, 2:218–20; Thomas McKenney to Thomas C. Stuart, October 31, 1826, M21 R3, LSOIA 3, 204–5.

44. "Funds," in American Board of Commissioners, *First Ten Annual Reports*, 250; American Board of Commissioners for Foreign Missions, *Eleventh Annual Report of the American Board of Commissioners for Foreign Missions* (Samuel T. Armstrong, 1820), 309; American Board of Commissioners for Foreign Missions, *Report of the American Board of Commissioners for Foreign Missions, Compiled from Documents Laid Before the Board* (Crocker and Brewster, 1821), 102–3; Jeremiah Evarts to Cyrus Kingsbury, March 8, 1821, in E. C. Tracy, *Memoir of the Life of Jeremiah Evarts, Esq.* (Crocker and Brewster, 1845), 137, 139; John Andrew, *From Revivals to Removal: Jeremiah Evarts, the Cherokee Nation, and the Search for the Soul of America* (University of Georgia Press, 1992), 115; Jeremiah Evarts to Samuel Worcester, April 2, 1821, in Tracy, *Memoir of the Life of Jeremiah Evarts*, 141.

45. American Board of Commissioners for Foreign Missions, *Twelfth Annual Report of the American Board of Commissioners for Foreign Missions* (Crocker and Brewster, 1821), 57–67; Kidwell, *Choctaws and Missionaries*, 51–61; David Folsom to Elias Cornelius, June 20, 1821, Box 1, Folder 2, Series I, Hargett Papers; David Folsom to Cyrus Byington, July 23, 1821, Box 1, Folder 1, Series I, Hargett Papers.

46. Delegation to John C. Calhoun, November 12, 1824, in *ASP: Indian Affairs*, 2:550.

47. Dawn Peterson, *Indians in the Family: Adoption and the Politics of Antebellum Expansion* (Harvard University Press, 2017), 10, 107–8, 173; Christina Snyder,

*Great Crossings: Indians, Settlers, and Slaves in the Age of Jackson* (Oxford University Press, 2017), 32–40; Frederick Hoxie, *This Indian Country: American Indian Activists and the Place They Made* (New York: Penguin, 2012), 49; Herman J. Viola, *Thomas L. McKenney: Architect of America's Early Indian Policy, 1816–1830* (Sage Books, 1974), 40–41, 45–46; William S. Belko, "John C. Calhoun and the Creation of the Bureau of the Indian Affairs: An Essay on Political Rivalry, Ideology, and Policy-making in the Early Republic," *South Carolina Historical Magazine* 105, no. 3 (2004): 170–97.

48. Peterson, *Indians in the Family*, 225; Snyder, *Great Crossings*, 25–28.

49. David Folsom and James L. McDonald, November 20, 1824, in *ASP: Indian Affairs*, 2:551 (emphasis in the original).

50. Statement from the General Land Office Forwarded by James McDonald, LROIA 169 [309]; Choctaw Delegation to Calhoun, November 22, 1824, *ASP: Indian Affairs*, 2:551–52.

51. David Folsom to Cyrus Kingsbury, January 14, 1825, Box 1, Folder 3, Series I, Hargett Papers.

52. Thomas McKenney to James McDonald, November 27, 1824, LSOIA 1, 242.

53. "Treaty with the Choctaw, 1825," in Kappler, *Indian Affairs*, 2:211–16.

54. David Folsom to Cyrus Byington, October 15, 1824, Box 1, Folder 1, Series I, Hargett Papers; David Folsom to Cyrus Kingsbury January 14, 1825, Box 1, Folder 3, Series I, Hargett Papers; Debo, *The Rise and Fall of the Choctaw Republic*, 50; Peterson, *Indians in the Family*, 234; Snyder, *Great Crossings*, 39, 43–45, 57; Kidwell, *Choctaws and Missionaries*, 92–99; Ella Wells Drake, "Choctaw Academy: Richard M. Johnson and the Business of Indian Education," *Register of the Kentucky Historical Society* 91, no. 3 (1993): 265; Evelyn Crady Adams, "Kentucky's Choctaw Academy, 1819–1842: A Commercial Enterprise," *Filson Club History Quarterly* 26 (1952): 28–36.

55. Snyder, *Great Crossings*, 28–29; Peterson, *Indians in the Family*, 234, 240–42; Kidwell, *Choctaws and Missionaries*, 100–102; Richard M. Johnson to War Department, September 27, 1825, and Richard M. Johnson to Indian Office, October 28, 1825, H.R. Doc. No. 26-109, at 10, 18–19 (1841); Adams, "Kentucky's Choctaw Academy," 29.

56. Peterson, *Indians in the Family*, 235, 244–51; Cyrus Kingsbury to Thomas McKenney, September 28, 1825, H.R. Doc. No. 26-109, at 12–13 (1841) (emphasis in the original).

57. Richard M. Johnson to Thomas Henderson, December 8, 1825, Henderson Papers, Filson Historical Society, Louisville, KY (hereafter cited as Henderson Papers); Richard M. Johnson to War Department, September 27, 1825, H.R. Doc. No. 26-109, at 10 (1841); Richard M. Johnson to Thomas Henderson, December 31, 1825, Henderson Papers.

58. Power of Attorney Draft, Richard M. Johnson for Thomas Henderson, December 1825, Henderson Papers; Drake, "Choctaw Academy," 283; Richard M. Johnson to Thomas Henderson, December 31, 1825, Henderson Papers (emphasis in the original).

59. James McDonald to Thomas McKenney, April 27, 1826, LROIA 169 [320–25].

60. Rev. Jedidiah Morse, *A Report to the Secretary of War of the United States on Indian Affairs, Comprising a Narrative of a Tour* [. . .] (S. Converse, 1822), 12; John C. Calhoun to Jedidiah Morse, February 7, 1820, Vol. D, SWLS, 362; Nicholas Guyatt, *Bind Us Apart: How Enlightened Americans Invented Racial Segregation* (Basic Books, 2016), 283–84; Tim Rowse, "Population Knowledge and the Practice of Guardianship," *American Nineteenth Century History* 15, no. 1 (2014): 15–42; Ostler, *Surviving Genocide*, 184.

## *Chapter Three: Banking on Removal*

1. Levi Colbert et al. to Andrew Jackson, November 22, 1832, LROIA 136 [278–93] (emphasis in the original).

2. Colbert et al. to Jackson, November 22, 1832. Emphasis added.

3. Or, as Jonathan Levy, *Ages of American Capitalism: A History of the United States* (Random House, 2021), xxiii, notes, the Chickasaw balanced "precautionary liquidity," the choice of security over profit, with "transactional liquidity," the ability to rapidly convert assets into cash.

4. Robbie Ethridge, *From Chicaza to Chickasaw: The European Invasion and the Transformation of the Mississippian World, 1540–1715* (University of North Carolina Press, 2010), 26–37, 251–52; James Atkinson, *Splendid Land, Splendid People: The Chickasaw Indians to Removal* (University of Alabama Press, 2004), 6–7; C. Margaret Scarry and John F. Scarry, "Native American 'Garden Agriculture' in Southeastern North America," *World Archaeology* 37, no. 2 (2005): 259–74.

5. On Chickasaw removal, see Amanda L. Paige, Fuller L. Bumpers, and Daniel F. Littlefield Jr., *Chickasaw Removal* (Chickasaw Press, 2010); Arrell M. Gibson, *The Chickasaws* (University of Oklahoma Press, 1971), 142–62; and Atkinson, *Splendid Land, Splendid People*, 180–236.

6. For a survey of the recurring settler attitude that Indigenous people are underserving of their money, see Alexandra Harmon, *Rich Indians: Native People and the Problem of Wealth in American History* (University of North Carolina Press, 2010). A growing literature addresses how money and banking sustain colonialism.

7. Christine Desan, *Making Money: Coin, Currency, and the Coming of Capitalism* (Oxford University Press, 2014), 37–38; Richard Sylla, "The Transition to a Monetary Union in the United States, 1787–1795," *Financial History Review* 13, no. 1 (2006): 73–95; Ronald Michener and Robert E. Wright, "Development of the US Monetary Union," *Financial History Review* 13, no. 1 (2006): 19–41. For general studies of banking in this period, see Sharon Ann Murphy, *Other People's Money: How Banking Worked in the Early American Republic* (Johns Hopkins University Press, 2017); Bray Hammond, *Banks and Politics in America, from the Revolution to the Civil War* (Princeton University Press, 1957); and Howard Bodenhorn, *State Banking in Early America: A New Economic History* (Oxford University Press, 2002). For a view of banks as infrastructure rather than intermediaries, see Morgan Ricks, "Money as Infrastructure," *Columbia Business Law Review* 757 (2018): 758–72. On the political debates that shaped the governance of money in the nineteenth-century United States, see Jeffrey Sklansky, *Sovereign of the Market: The Money Question in Early America* (University of Chicago Press, 2017).

8. Allan Gallay, *The Indian Slave Trade: The Rise of the English Empire in the South, 1670–1716* (Yale University Press, 2002), 127–54; Christina Snyder, *Slavery in Indian Country: The Changing Face of Captivity in Early America* (Harvard University Press, 2010), 63; Daniel H. Usner Jr., *Indians, Settlers, and Slaves in a Frontier Exchange Economy: The Lower Mississippi* (University of North Carolina Press, 1992), 16–17; David Nichols, "The Enterprise of War: The Military Economy of the Chickasaw Indians 1715–1815," in *The Native South: New Histories and Enduring Legacies*, ed. Tim Alan Garrison and Greg O'Brien (University of Nebraska Press, 2017), 33–46; Ethridge, *From Chicaza to Chickasaw*, 65–76.

9. H. B. Cushman, *History of the Choctaw, Chickasaw, and Natchez Indians* (Headlight, 1899), 392; Atkinson, *Splendid Land, Splendid People*, 100, 143, 183; Jesse D. Jennings, ed., "Rush Nutt's Trip to the Chickasaw Country," *Journal of Mississippi History* 9, no. 1 (1947): 34–61; Gibson, *The Chickasaws*, 131; Chickasaw Memorial Letter, February 10, 1817, Vol. 1817, SWLR; James Carson, "'Dollars Never Fail to Melt Their Hearts': Native Women and the Market Revolution," in *Neither Lady nor Slave: Working Women of the Old South*, ed. Michele Gillespie and Susanna Delfino (University of North Carolina Press, 2002), 15–33; Jeffrey Washburn, "Directing Their Own Change: Chickasaw Economic Transformation and the Civilization Plan, 1750s–1830s," *Native South* 13 (2020): 94–119; Report of Thomas McKenney to Secretary of War, October 10, 1827, LROIA 135 [308–11].

10. Guy B. Braden, "The Colberts and the Chickasaw Nation," *Tennessee Historical Quarterly* 17, no. 3 (1958): 222–49; Guy B. Braden, "The Colberts and the Chickasaw Nation (Continued)," *Tennessee Historical Quarterly* 17, no. 4 (1958): 318–35; Atkinson, *Splendid Land, Splendid People*, 130–31, 198–206; Gibson, *The Chickasaws*, 134; George S. Gaines, *The Reminiscences of George Strother Gaines: Pioneer and Statesman of Early Alabama and Mississippi, 1805–1843*, ed. James P. Pate (University of Alabama Press, 1998), 78; Cushman, *History of the Choctaw, Chickasaw, and Natchez Indians*, 390.

11. Most specie originated from beyond US borders until 1849, when a succession of mineral strikes triggered invasion after invasion of Native lands across the West. A foreshadowing came in 1828, when prospectors discovered gold on Cherokee land and began mining for commodity money's raw material. Georgia escalated its assault on the nation's sovereignty, carried out an extralegal lottery that sold off unceded Cherokee lands, and then enforced squatters' claims with paramilitary units assembled specifically for the mission. See Manuel Alejandro Bautista González, "A Little Known, Long-Lasting, and Borderless Monetary Affair: The History of the Mexican Silver Peso in Antebellum America, 1792–1860," paper presented at the Fourteenth International Meeting of Historians of Mexico, Chicago, September 21, 2014; Alejandra Irigoin, "The End of a Silver Era: The Consequences of the Breakdown of the Spanish Peso Standard in China and the United States, 1780s–1850s," *Journal of World History* 20, no. 2 (2009): 207–43; Angela Redish, *Bimetallism: An Economic and Historical Analysis* (Cambridge University Press, 2000), 27–34, 231; David A. Martin, "Bimetallism in the United States Before 1850," *Journal of Political Economy* 76, no. 3 (1968): 428–42; Christine Desan, "Coin Reconsidered: The Political Alchemy of Commodity Money," *Theoretical Inquiries in Law* 11, no. 1 (2010): 361–410; and David Williams, *The Georgia Gold Rush: Twenty-Niners, Cherokees, and Gold Fever* (University

of South Carolina Press, 1993). On coinage at the U.S. Mint, see Ann Marsh Daly, "Every Dollar Brought from the Earth: Money, Slavery, and Southern Gold Mining," *Journal of the Early Republic* 41, no. 4 (2021): 553–86.

12. Perry Mehrling, "The Inherent Hierarchy of Money," in *Social Fairness and Economics: Economic Essays in the Spirit of Duncan Foley*, ed. Lance Taylor (Routledge, 2012), 394–404; Christine Desan, "Money's Design Elements: Debt, Liquidity, and the Pledge of Value from Medieval Coin to Modern 'Repo,'" *Banking and Finance Law Review* 38 (2022): 331–53; Marcia Haag, "Legal Terms from the Choctaw Council Meetings of 1826–1828," *American Indian Culture and Research Journal* 42, no. 4 (2018): 78; Joshua R. Greenberg, *Bank Notes and Shinplasters: The Rage for Paper Money in the Early Republic* (University of Pennsylvania Press, 2020), 6–8; Murphy, *Other People's Money*, 38–70; Steven Mihm, *A Nation of Counterfeiters: Capitalists, Con Men, and the Making of the United States* (Harvard University Press, 2007).

13. H.R. Doc. No. 25-18 (1837); Jane Ellen Knodell, *The Second Bank of the United States: "Central" Banker in an Era of Nation-Building, 1816–1836* (Routledge, 2017), 15, 34; Washburn, "Directing Their Own Change," 100–101; Daniel H. Usner Jr., "American Indians on the Cotton Frontier: Changing Economic Relations with Citizens and Slaves in the Mississippi Territory," *Journal of American History* 72, no. 2 (1985): 299; Atkinson, *Splendid Land, Splendid Peoples*, 166–69, 199–200.

14. J. Neilly to William Eustis, December 13, 1811, Vol. 1811, SWLR.

15. George and Levi Colbert, quoted in James R. Atkinson, *History of the Chickasaw Indian Agency East of the Mississippi River* (n.p., 1998), 27.

16. Henry Sherburne to John C. Calhoun, November 28, 1818, Vol. 1818, SWLR.

17. Rowena McClinton, ed. *The Moravian Springplace Mission to the Cherokees* (University of Nebraska Press, 2010), 22.

18. John C. Calhoun to Henry Sherburn, April 1, 1819, SWLS, Vol. D, 280; L. Edwards to Henry Sherburn, April 9, 1819, Vol. D, SWLS, 283; Atkinson, *History of the Chickasaw Indian Agency*, 30. On the Panic of 1819, see Andrew H. Browning, *The Panic of 1819: The First Great Depression* (University of Missouri Press, 2019) and the essays collected in "Forum: The Panic of 1819," *Journal of the Early Republic* 40, no. 4 (2020): 665–740.

19. Atkinson, *Splendid Land, Splendid People*, 199–200, 209, 215; Atkinson, *History of the Chickasaw Indian Agency*, 30.

20. Lewis Cass and Duncan McArthur to George Graham, September 30, 1817, in *ASP: Indian Affairs*, vol. 2, ed. Walter Lowrie and Walter S. Franklin (Gale and Seaton, 1834), 139; Leonard U. Hill, *John Johnston and the Indians: In the Land of the Three Miamis* (Stoneman, 1957), 178–79; Sami Lakomaki, *Gathering Together: The Shawnee People Through Diaspora and Nationhood, 1600–1870* (Yale University Press, 2014), 154. For subsequent treaties with explicit commitments to payment of annuities in specie, see "Treaty with the Wyandot, etc., 1818," in *Indian Affairs: Laws and Treaties*, vol. 2, *Treaties*, ed. Charles J. Kappler (GPO, 1904), 62–63; "Treaty with the Potawatomi, 1818," in Kappler, *Indian Affairs*, 2:168–69; "Treaty with the Wea, 1818," in Kappler, *Indian Affairs*, 2:169–70; "Treaty with the Delaware, 1818," in Kappler, *Indian Affairs*, 2:170–71; "Treaty with the Miami, 1818," in Kappler, *Indian*

*Affairs*, 2:171–72; "Treaty with the Kickapoo, 1819," in Kappler, *Indian Affairs*, 2:182–83; "Treaty with the Chippewa, 1819," in Kappler, *Indian Affairs*, 2:185–87; "Treaty with the Chippewa, etc., 1821," in Kappler, *Indian Affairs*, 2:198–201; "Treaty with the Quapaw, 1824," in Kappler, *Indian Affairs*, 2:210–11; "Treaty with the Potawatomi, 1826," in Kappler, *Indian Affairs*, 2:273–76; and J. A. Eaton Circular, February 16, 1830, LROIA 433 [528].

21. These figures are compiled from Kappler, *Indian Affairs*, vol. 2, and H.R. Doc. No. 22-242 (1832). Figures are calculated using relative share of gross domestic product per capita; "Purchasing Power Today of a US Dollar Transaction in the Past," MeasuringWorth, 2024, https://www.measuringworth.com/ppowerus; H.R. Doc. No. 25-18 (1837). When the option to receive in goods or money was listed, I treated this sum as deliverable in goods. Salaries to Native peoples were treated as money, and services treated as goods; compiled from H.R. Doc. No. 23-474 (1834) with reference to Kappler, *Indian Affairs*, vol. 2.

22. Lewis E. Atherton, *The Frontier Merchant in Mid-America* (University of Missouri Press, 1971), 140–42.

23. George A. Schultz, *An Indian Canaan: Isaac McCoy and the Vision of an Indian State* (University of Oklahoma Press, 1972), 5, 11–15, 61–74; Isaac McCoy, *History of Baptist Indian Missions* (P. Force, 1840), 45, 319, 535–36. For evidence of Potawatomi annuities distributed directly as repayment to traders, see "Metra and Toisa to Thomas Robb: Certificate of Indebtedness," November 5, 1823, in *The John Tipton Papers*, vol. 1, *1809–1827*, ed. Nellie Armstrong Robertson and Dorothy Riker (Indiana Historical Bureau, 1942), 325–27; and Isaac McCoy, *Remarks on the Practicability of Indian Reform, Embracing their Colonization* (Lincoln and Edmands, 1827), 20.

24. [Lewis Cass], "Documents and Proceedings Relating to the Formation and Progress of a Board [. . .]," *North American Review* 66 (1830), 73. On a parallel discourse of Indigenous improvidence in Canada, see Gettler, *Colonialism's Currency*, 25, 76–79.

25. Pub. L. 21-148, 4 Stat. 411 (1830); Nicholas Guyatt, *Bind Us Apart: How Enlightened Americans Invented Racial Segregation* (Basic Books, 2016), 288–325; Willard Carl Klunder, *Lewis Cass and the Politics of Moderation* (Kent State University Press, 1996), 50–51; Ronald N. Satz, *American Indian Policy in the Jacksonian Era* (University of Nebraska Press, 1975), 31; Herman J. Viola, *Thomas L. McKenney: Architect of America's Early Indian Policy, 1816–1830* (Sage Books, 1974), 200–222; Alfred A. Cave, "Abuse of Power: Andrew Jackson and the Indian Removal Act of 1830," *Historian* 65, no. 6 (2003): 1330–53.

26. Total expenditures on Indian affairs under Jackson more than doubled from 1830 to 1832; Choctaw removal would ultimately cost more than $5 million. See H.R. Rep. No. 474-23, at 50 (1834); Ethan Davis, "An Administrative Trail of Tears: Indian Removal," *American Journal of Legal History* 50, no. 1 (2008–10): 73–75, 97; and Muriel Wright, "The Removal of the Choctaws to the Indian Territory, 1830–1833," *Chronicles of Oklahoma* 6, no. 2 (1928): 124.

27. "Treaty with the Seneca," in Kappler, *Indian Affairs*, 2:325–27; "Treaty with the Seneca, etc.," in Kappler, *Indian Affairs*, 2:327–31; "Treaty with the Shawnee, 1831," in Kappler, *Indian Affairs*, 2:331–34; "Treaty with the Ottawa, 1831," in Kappler, *Indian Affairs*, 2:335–39; Mary Stockwell, *The Other Trail of Tears: The*

*Removal of the Ohio Indians* (Westholme, 2014), 202–3; Lakomaki, *Gathering Together*, 162–63.

28. Andrew Jackson, "First Inaugural Address, March 4, 1829," in *A Compilation of the Messages and Papers of the Presidents, 1789–1897*, vol. 2, ed. James D. Richardson (Bureau of Natural Literature, 1908), 451; Robert V. Remini, *Andrew Jackson and the Bank War: A Study in the Growth of Presidential Power* (W. W. Norton, 1967), 58–59, 82–83, 120–21; Larry Schweikart, "Jacksonian Ideology, Currency Control and Central Banking: A Reappraisal," *Historian* 51, no. 1 (1988): 80–81; Andrew Jackson to John Coffee, October 23, 1831, in *The Papers of Andrew Jackson*, vol. 9, *1831*, ed. Daniel Feller, Laura-Eve Moss, Thomas Coens, and Erik B. Alexander (University of Tennessee Press, 2013), 639; Andrew Jackson to John Eaton, October 23, 1831, in Feller et al., *The Papers of Andrew Jackson*, 9:638.

29. John Eaton to Lewis Cass, January 21, 1833, LROIA 136 [381–82].

30. Chickasaw Treaty Journal [1832], Box 22B-C4, 23rd Cong., Records of Early Select Committees, Records of the United States Senate, RG 46, NARA (hereafter cited as Records of Early Select Committees). John Eaton was also appointed by Jackson as a treaty commissioner, but he did not arrive in time for negotiations—although he confirmed that Jackson had conveyed his wishes for the treaty directly to him and Coffee. John Eaton to Elbert Herring, December 30, 1832, LROIA 136 [268–69].

31. Chickasaw Treaty Journal; Paige et al., *Chickasaw Removal*, 39; See also Mary E. Young, *Redskins, Ruffleshirts, and Rednecks: Indian Allotments in Alabama and Mississippi 1830–1860* (University of Oklahoma Press, 1961), 27–41.

32. Chickasaw Delegates to John C. Calhoun, December 15, 1824, LROIA 135 [15–18]; Calhoun to Chickasaw Delegation, December 9, 1824, LSOIA 1, 258–59.

33. Thomas McKenney to Richard Smith, December 28, 1824, LSOIA 1, 274; Richard Smith to Thomas McKenney, December 28, 1824, LROIA 135 [107]; Thomas McKenney to Clement Smith, January 3, 1825, LSOIA 1, 278; Thomas McKenney to Thomas Stuart, October 31, 1826, LSOIA 3, 204–5.

34. Cushman, *History of the Choctaw, Chickasaw, and Natchez Indians*, 429; Chickasaw Treaty Journal.

35. Levi Colbert to Andrew Jackson, November 22, 1832, LROIA 136 [279–93].

36. Representatives of the Chickasaw Nation to Gen. John Coffee, Box 1, John Coffee Papers Relating to Negotiations with Cherokee, Creek, Choctaw and Chickasaw Nations, Beinecke Library, Yale University.

37. Colbert to Jackson, November 22, 1832.

38. Colbert to Jackson, November 22, 1832.

39. H.R. Rep. No. 87-21 (1829); Atkinson, *Splendid Land, Splendid People*, 224–27. The 1830 treaty stated that $15,000 in annuities promised the Chickasaws would "cease if the Chickasaw nation at any time become enemies of the United States"; United States Commissary General of Subsistence, *Correspondence on the Subject of the Emigration of Indians* [. . .], vol 5 (Duff Green, 1835), 250; "Unratified Treaty with the Chickasaw, 1830," in Kappler, *Indian Affairs*, 2:1035–42. The Treaty of Pontotoc Creek would also include a clause stipulating that the Chickasaw pledged never to make war on any other people "unless they are so Authorized by the United States." "Treaty with the Chickasaw, October 20, 1832," in *Kappler, Indian Affairs*, 2:418. See also Brian DeLay, *War of a Thousand Deserts: Indian Raids and the U.S.-Mexican War* (Yale University Press, 2008), 61–85; Pekka Hämäläinen, *The Comanche Empire*

(Yale University Press, 2009), 181–238; David La Vere, *Contrary Neighbors: Southern Plains and Removed Indians in Indian Territory* (University of Oklahoma Press, 2000), 67–68; and Muriel Wright, "Notes on Events Leading to the Chickasaw Treaties of Franklin and Pontotoc, 1830 and 1832," *Chronicles of Oklahoma* 34, no. 4 (1956): 477. Cherokees attempted a similar strategy in 1835. See John Ross, R. Taylor, Daniel McCoy, Samuel Gunter, and William Rogers to Lewis Cass, February 14, 1835, in *The Papers of Chief John Ross*, vol. 1, ed. Gary E. Moulton (University of Oklahoma Press, 1985), 321–23; John Ross to Friedrich Ludwig von Roenne, March 5, 1835 in *The Papers of Chief John Ross*, 1:330; and John Ross to Joaquin Maria del Castillo y Lanzas, March 22, 1835, in *The Papers of Chief John Ross*, 1:335.

40. Lewis Cass to C. C. Clay, March 6, 1834, Vol. 1, LSCR, 23; Chickasaw delegation to Andrew Jackson, March 7, 1834, Box SEN23B1-3, Records of Early Select Committees.

41. George Colbert, Pitman Colbert, and Ishtomotutka to Thomas Hart Benton and Theodore Frelinghuysen, Box 22B-C1, Records of Early Select Committees.

42. Andrew Jackson to John Coffee, November 6, 1832, in *The Papers of Andrew Jackson*, vol. 10, *1832*, ed. Daniel Feller, Thomas Coens, and Laura-Eve Moss (University of Tennessee Press, 2016), 554.

43. McCoy, *History of Baptist Missions*, 459.

44. Amos Kendall to Andrew Jackson, July 19, 1834, in *The Papers of Andrew Jackson*, vol. 12, *1834*, ed. Daniel Feller, Thomas Coens, Laura-Eve Moss, and Aaron Crawford (University of Tennessee Press, 2023), 368–69.

45. Statement of Bonds Received by Treasurer for Various Tribes, December 26, 1836, Vol. 1, TTFC, 140–41.

46. William Medill to G. W. Clinton, February 6, 1846, Vol. 1, LSITF, 143–44; Message of Governor Stevens T. Mason, February 1, 1836, in *Messages of the Governors of Michigan*, vol. 1, ed. George N. Fuller (Michigan Historical Commission, 1925), 171.

47. J. D. Beers to Levi Woodbury, July 14, 1836, Vol. 1, TTFC, 78; Levi Woodbury to J. D. Beers, July 21, 1836, Vol. 1, TTFC, 79; Statement of Bonds, December 26, 1836; Levi Woodbury to William Edmonston, September 7, 1835, Vol. 1, TTFC, 7–8; Levi Woodbury to J. M. Bass, April 20, 1836, Vol. 1, TTFC, 42–43; Johnathan M. Bass to Levi Woodbury, May 26, 1836, Vol. 1, TTFC, 56–57; Levi Woodbury to Johnathan M. Bass, June 6, 1836, Vol. 1, TTFC, 57; Levi Woodbury to Carey A. Harris, August 3, 1836, Vol. 1, TTFC, 85–86; *An Act to Charter the Union Bank of the State of Tennessee, Passed October 18, 1832* (Hunt, Tardiff, 1832), 6; H.R. Rep. 27-296, at 80, 98 (1841); Stanley John Folmsbee, *Sectionalism and Internal Improvements in Tennessee, 1796–1845* (East Tennessee Historical Society, 1939), 112–22, 141; "Treaty with the Cherokee, 1785," in Kappler, *Indian Affairs*, 2:8–11; Colin G. Calloway, *The American Revolution in Indian Country: Crisis and Diversity in Native American Communities* (Cambridge University Press, 1995), 182–212; Statement of Bonds, December 26, 1836.

48. Malcolm Rohrbough, *The Land Office Business: The Settlement and Administration of American Public Lands, 1789–1837* (Oxford University Press, 1968), 23, 137–41; William Brantley, *Banking in Alabama, 1816–1860*, vol. 1 (privately printed, 1961), 13; Daniel Dupre, "Ambivalent Capitalists on the Cotton Frontier: Settlement and Development in the Tennessee Valley of Alabama," *Journal of Southern History* 56, no. 2 (1990): 221; Daniel Dupre, *Alabama's Frontiers and the Rise of the Old*

*South* (Indiana University Press, 2018), 249–69; Browning, *The Panic of 1819*, 94–95, 104–13; Franklin Sammons, "The Fruit of the Yazoo Compromise," *Journal of the Early Republic* 40, no. 4 (2020): 671–76; Sharon Ann Murphy, *Banking on Slavery: Financing Southern Expansion in the Antebellum United States* (University of Chicago Press, 2023), 45–78; Larry Schweikart, *Banking in the American South from the Age of Jackson to Reconstruction* (Louisiana State University Press, 1987), 49–68.

49. Rohrbough, *The Land Office Business*, 137–40; Payson Jackson Treat, *The National Land System, 1785–1820* (E. B. Treat, 1910), 157; J. Mills Thornton, *Politics and Power in a Slave Society: Alabama, 1800–1860* (Louisiana State University Press, 2014), 15. The bulk of the Huntsville bank's capital came from its service as a depository for the Land Office. Brantley, *Banking in Alabama*, 1:13; Alabama General Assembly, *Acts Passed at the Fifth Annual Session of the General Assembly of Alabama* (William B. Allen, 1823), 3; Alabama House of Representatives, *Journal of the House of Representatives of the States of Alabama* [. . .] *Fifth Session* (William B. Allen, 1824), 9.

50. Richard Sylla, John B. Legler, and John J. Wallis, "Banks and State Public Finance in the New Republic: The United States, 1790–1860," *Journal of Economic History* 47, no. 2 (1987): 391–403; Brantley, *Banking in Alabama*, 1:319–20; Robin Einhorn, *American Taxation, American Slavery* (University of Chicago Press, 2006), 220–25; John Majewski, "Why Did Northerners Oppose the Expansion of Slavery? Economic Development and Education in the Limestone South," in *Slavery's Capitalism: A New History of American Economic Development*, ed. Sven Beckert and Seth Rockman (University of Pennsylvania Press, 2016), 277–98.

51. Knodell, *The Second Bank of the United States*, 16, 84, 107–30; Ralph Catterall, *The Second Bank of the United States* (University of Chicago Press, 1902), 164–85; Hammond, *Banks and Politics in America*, 251–85; Brantley, *Banking in Alabama*, 1:207–13. Jackson cast this policy as a populist takedown of an aristocratic institution, but the end result centralized control within his cabinet. With the "pet bank" system, Jackson's secretary of the Treasury personally directed the flow of federal funds, including specie, across a network of depositaries. Remini, *Andrew Jackson and the Bank War*, 168–69; Schweikart, *Banking in the American South*, 17–23; Larry Schweikart, "Jacksonian Ideology, Currency Control, and Central Banking: A Reappraisal," *Historian* 51, no. 1 (1988): 78–102. On the Second Bank in the cotton South, see Richard H. Kilbourne Jr., *Slave Agriculture and Financial Markets in Antebellum America* (Pickering and Chatto, 2006).

52. In the newer states of the South, the number of chartered banks grew from fourteen in 1832 to fifty in 1837. In Western states, the number of banks grew from twenty-three to sixty-seven over the same period. See Joseph Van Fenstermaker, "The Development of American Commercial Banking, 1782–1837" (PhD diss., University of Illinois, 1963), 100, 134, 139; Bodenhorn, *State Banking in Early America*, 234–45; and Jane Knodell, "Rethinking the Jacksonian Economy: The Impact of the 1832 Bank Veto on Commercial Banking," *Journal of Economic History* 66, no. 3 (2006): 546–47.

53. Schweikart, *Banking in the American South*, 50; Brantley, *Banking in Alabama*, 1:230; H.R. Rep. 296-27, at 70 (1842); J. H. Fitts, "History of Banking in Alabama," *Banking Law Journal* 12 (1895): 348–49.

54. Gaines, *The Reminiscences of George Strother Gaines*, 111–12.

55. Levi Woodbury to Charles Macalester, January 28, 1836, Vol. 1, TTFC, 11–12; Charles Macalester to Levi Woodbury, February 2, 1836, Vol 1, TTFC, 13–14; Brantley, *Banking in Alabama*, 1:313.

56. J. W. Garth to Levi Woodbury, March 25, 1836, Vol. 1, TTFC, 27; J. W. Garth to Levi Woodbury, March 25, 1836, Vol. 1, TTFC, 27; W. R. King to Levi Woodbury, March 28, 1836, Vol. 1, TTFC, 28–29; Levi Woodbury to William Edmondson, March 31, 1836, Vol. 1, TTFC, 34; Charles Macalester to Levi Woodbury, April 14, 1836, Vol. 1, TTFC, 39–40.

57. Levi Woodbury to J. D. Beers, March 30, 1836, Vol. 1, TTFC, 24. Woodbury realized that he lacked congressional authorization to invest the Chickasaw funds before the purchase from Beers was finalized, but he nonetheless authorized Beers to draw on his account before Senate approval, which came a few weeks later. Levi Woodbury to J. D. Beers, April 2, 1836, Vol. 1, TTFC, 25; 5 Stat. 10 (1836); H.R. Rep. 25-892, at 2–3 (1838); H.R. Rep. 27-296, at 70–71 (1842); "Exhibit of the State and Condition of the Banks of the State of Alabama, on 1st June 1837," in William Brantley, *Banking in Alabama, 1816-1860*, vol. 2 (privately printed, 1961), 294.

58. John G. Aikin, ed., *A Digest of the Laws of the State of Alabama*, 2nd ed. (D. Woodruff, 1836), 55–76; Resolution Adopted January 11, 1837, Folder 5: Resolutions of the Board of the State Bank, 1837, Box SG3296, Bank of the State of Alabama at Huntsville, Miscellaneous, Records and Resolutions, 1820–1848, Alabama Department of Archives and History; Calvin Schermerhorn, "'The Time Is Now Just Arriving When Many Capitalists Will Make Fortunes': Indian Removal, Finance, and Slavery in the Making of the American Cotton South," in *Linking the Histories of Slavery in North America and Its Borderlands*, ed. James F. Brooks and Bonnie Martin (School for Advanced Research Press, 2015), 158.

59. Knodell, "Rethinking the Jacksonian Economy," 552–53, 563; Bodenhorn, *State Banking in Early America*, 57–63; Murphy, *Banking on Slavery*, 28–29, 82; John Hebron Moore, *The Emergence of the Cotton Kingdom in the Old Southwest, Mississippi, 1770-1860* (Louisiana State University Press, 1988), 16.

60. Thomas M. Barker to Lewis Cass, July 17, 1834, LROIA 136 [485–86]; Articles of Association for the New York and Mississippi Land Company, Box 39, Folder 1059, Lewis Perry Curtis Family Papers, Sterling Library, Yale University (hereafter cited as Curtis Family Papers); David Hubbard to J. D. Beers, November 17, 1834, Box 39, Folder 1050, Curtis Family Papers; Dennis East, "Land Speculation in the Chickasaw Cession: A Study of the New York and Mississippi Land Company, 1835–1889" (master's thesis, University of Wisconsin–Madison, 1964), 6–10; Young, *Redskins, Ruffleshirts, and Rednecks*, 123–25; Claudio Saunt, *Unworthy Republic: The Dispossession of Native Americans and the Road to Indian Territory* (W. W. Norton, 2020), 188–91.

61. "The Tennessee Valley Railroad," *American Railroad Journal* 8, no. 31 (1852): 490; Tuscumbia, Cortland, and Decatur Railroad Stock, Box 41, Folder 1104, Curtis Family Papers; Brantley, *Banking in Alabama*, 2:23; East, "Land Speculation," 13–14; Saunt, *Unworthy Republic*, 188–91; James W. Silver, "Land Speculation Profits in the Chickasaw Cession," *Journal of Southern History* 10, no. 1 (1944): 86.

62. S. Doc. 24-15 (1836); Peter Rousseau, "Jacksonian Monetary Policy, Specie Flows, and the Panic of 1837," *Journal of Economic History* 62, no. 2 (2002): 460, 463;

Schweikart, *Banking in the American South*, 76; Richard H. Timberlake Jr., "The Specie Circular and Sales of Public Lands: A Comment," *Journal of Economic History* 25, no. 3 (1965): 414–16.

63. H.R. Rep. 26-172 (1840); Saunt, "Financing Dispossession"; James Durno to Levi Woodbury, July 28, 1836, Vol. 1, TTFC, 87–88; Levi Woodbury to James Durno, August 11, 1836, Vol. 1, TTFC, 89; H.R. Rep. 24-194 (1837). Stanley Lebergott, "The Demand for Land: The United States, 1820–1860," *Journal of Economic History* 45, no. 2 (1985): 205, points to the Treasury's purchase of $4.6 million in bonds issued by Alabama, Kentucky, and Maryland as a kind of monetary easing that prolonged land speculation, undermining the specie circular. See also Young, *Redskins, Ruffleshirts, and Rednecks*, 167.

64. "Regulations Prescribing the Mode of Executing Certain Duties Required by the Treaties with the Chickasaws [. . .]," Vol. 1, LSCR, 32–36; Gibson, *The Chickasaws*, 208; Duane Champagne, *Social Order and Political Change: Constitutional Governments Among the Cherokee, the Choctaw, the Chickasaw, and the Creek* (Stanford University Press, 1992), 162; Felix S. Cohen, *Handbook of Federal Indian Law* (GPO, 1942), 167–69; William Armstrong to C. A. Harris, September 28, 1838, LROIA 137 [242–44]; H.R. Rep. 27-741, at 67 (1842). See also Katherine Ellinghaus, "'A Little Home for Myself and Child': The Women of the Quapaw Agency and the Policy of Competency," *Pacific Historical Review* 84, no. 3 (2015): 307–32.

65. R. D. Barker to Jonathan Bell, June 25, 1841, LROIA 147 [205–11]. See also "A friend of the Indian" to "My Excellent Sir," October 1835, LROIA 136 [569–70].

66. James Robinson to Andrew Jackson, June 23, 1836, LROIA 145 [141–43] (emphasis in the original).

67. Gaston L. Litton, ed., "The Negotiations Leading to the Chickasaw-Choctaw Agreement, January 17, 1837," *Chronicles of Oklahoma* 17, no. 4 (1939): 417–27; Angie Debo, *The Rise and Fall of the Choctaw Republic* (University of Oklahoma Press, 1961), 71–72; Chickasaw chiefs to John Eaton and John Coffee, January 15, 1832, Folder 1832, Correspondence and Other Records, Records of the Cherokee Agency West, Record Group 75, NARA; Gibson, *The Chickasaws*, 163; "Treaty with the Choctaw and Chickasaw, 1837," in Kappler, *Indian Affairs*, 2:486; David La Vere, *Contrary Neighbors: Southern Plains and Removed Indians in Indian Territory* (University of Oklahoma Press, 2000), 66–82.

68. Schermerhorn, "'The Time is Now Just Arriving,'" 158; Memorial Letter to President Andrew Jackson signed by Ishtehotopa, Tishomingo, William McGilvery, Pistalatubby, Isaac Albertson, and Others, in Presence of J. M. Lish and Pitman Colbert, Pontotoc, February 17, 1837, LROIA 137 [148–50].

69. Journal of Emigrating Chickasaws, John Millard, LROIA 143 [111–19]; John Millard to [Commissioner of Indian Affairs], September 17, 1837, LROIA 143 [123–31]; Paige et al., *Chickasaw Removal*, 102; J. A. Phillips to C. A. Harris, July 4, 1837, LROIA 143 [149–51]; A. M. M. Upshaw to C. A. Harris, July 4, 1837, LROIA 143 [312–13]; C. A. Harris to R. D. C. Collins, July 6, 1837, Vol. 1, 177, LSCR; A. M. M. Upshaw to C. A. Harris, July 7, 1837, LROIA 143 [316]; C. A. Harris to J. A. Phillips, July 7, 1837, Vol. 1, 179, LSCR.

70. "AG" to Lewis Cass, received October 28, 1835, Folder Office, 11/3, 1837, Correspondence and Other Records, Records of the Cherokee Agency West, Record Group

75, NARA; Barbara Krauthamer, *Black Slaves, Indian Masters: Slavery, Emancipation, and Citizenship in the Native American South* (University of North Carolina Press, 2013), 42; Atkinson, *Splendid Land, Splendid People*, 234; William Armstrong to C. A. Harris, September 29, 1837, LROIA 137 [115].

71. Levi Woodbury to S. F. MacCracken, May 31, 1837, Vol. 1, TTFC, 239; C. A. Harris to S. Cooper, June 29, 1837, Vol. 1, LSCR, 175.

72. Jessica Lepler, *The Many Panics of 1837: People, Politics, and the Creation of a Transatlantic Financial Crisis* (University of Cambridge Press), 95–120; Peter Temin, *The Jacksonian Economy* (W. W. Norton, 1969), 120; Rousseau, "Jacksonian Monetary Policy, Specie Flows, and the Panic of 1837"; Alasdair Roberts, *America's First Great Depression: Economic Crisis and Political Disorder After the Panic of 1837* (Cornell University Press, 2012); Silver, "Land Speculation Profits in the Chickasaw Cession," 86.

73. J. A. Phillips to C. A. Harris, November 17, 1837, LROIA 143 [189–90]; J. D. Searight to C. A. Harris, April 15, 1837, LROIA 143 [211–12]; D. Vanderslice to C. A. Harris, May 12, 1837, LROIA 143 [354–55]; Paige et al., *Chickasaw Removal*, 76; Satz, *American Indian Policy*, 77–78; George B. Porter to Elbert Herring, April 15, 1833, LROIA 421 [343–45]; C. A. Harris to John Tipton, June 22, 1837, in *The John Tipton Papers*, vol. 3, *1834–1839*, ed. Nellie Armstrong Robertson and Dorothy Riker (Indiana Historical Bureau, 1942), 410; John Tipton to C. A. Harris, June 25, 1837, in Robertson and Riker, *The John Tipton Papers*, 3:410; John Garland to C. A. Harris, June 15, 1837, LROIA 422 [465–67]; John Garland to C. A. Harris, June 26, 1837, LROIA 422 [472–73]; John Garland to C. A. Harris, July 24, 1837, LROIA 422 [490–91]. For the use of land offices as banks, see C. A. Harris to James Adams, November 7, 1837, LSOIA 22, 512–13; and *ARCIA* 1839, 123–24.

74. Harris to Cooper, June 29, 1837, 175; C. A. Harris to J. R. Poinsett, September 1, 1837, Vol. 1, LSCR, 202–3; Levi Woodbury to Martin Van Buren, July 5, 1837, Vol. 1, TTFC, 244–45; Statement, Vol. 1, TTFC, 284–85. For the Panic of 1837's impact on cotton and slave markets, see Walter Johnson, *River of Dark Dreams: Slavery and Empire in the Cotton Kingdom* (Harvard University Press, 2013), 281–83; Joshua D. Rothman, *Flush Times and Fever Dreams: A Story of Capitalism and Slavery in the Age of Jackson* (University of Georgia Press, 2012), 157–208, 293–98.

75. Chickasaw Chiefs to the President, September 9, 1838, Sen 25B-C10, Papers of the Senate, RG 46, NARA.

76. William Armstrong to C. A. Harris, June 29, 1838, LROIA 137 [232–34].

77. Petition from Chickasaws to A. M. M. Upshaw, April 1, 1840, LROIA 138 [11–12].


## *Chapter Four: Money Flows*

1. *Daily Union*, October 10, 1845; *Ohio Statesman*, October 22, 1845; Richard Smith Elliott, *Notes Taken in Sixty Years* (Cupples, Upham, 1884), 200–201; Solomon W. Roberts, "Reminisces of the First Railroad over the Alleghany Mountain," *Pennsylvania Magazine of History and Biography* 2, no. 4 (1878): 374.

2. Tamara Platkins Thornton, "Capitalist Aesthetics: Americans Look at the London and Liverpool Docks," in *Capitalism Takes Command: The Social Transformation of Nineteenth-Century America*, ed. Michael Zakim and Gary J. Kornblith

(University of Chicago Press, 2012), 169–98; Will B. Mackintosh, "Mechanical Aesthetics: Picturesque Tourism and the Transportation Revolution in Pennsylvania," *Pennsylvania History: A Journal of Mid-Atlantic Studies* 81, no. 1 (2014): 88–105; Trust Fund Journals, Vol. 1, Journals and Ledgers for Indian Trust Funds, Records Concerning Indian Trust Funds, BIA, NARA, 48, 57; *ARCIA* 1842, 387–88.

3. C. A. Harris to Benjamin F. Butler, December 14, 1836, LSOIA 20, 285; "Report on Funds," January 2, 1840, LROIA 854 [180–82]; *Sun* (Baltimore), October 24, 1845; "Indian Delegation," *Daily Union* (Washington, DC), October 24, 1845; "Indian Affairs—The Pottawatomies—Their Visit to the President," *Daily Union* (Washington, DC), October 31, 1845; "Interesting Scene at the White House—Presentation of the Pottawatomi Indians to the President," *New York Herald*, November 1, 1845; William Medill to Thomas P. Andrews, T. H. Harvey, and Gideon Matlock, May 2, 1846, LSOIA 38, 223–25; "The Pottawatomies—Another Conference with the President," *New York Herald*, November 23, 1845.

4. Michael John Witgen, *Seeing Red: Indigenous Land, American Expansion, and the Political Economy of Plunder in North America* (Omohundro Institute / University of North Carolina Press, 2022), 274.

5. Helen Hornbeck Tanner, *Atlas of Great Lakes Indian History* (University of Oklahoma Press, 1987), 2–9.

6. Michael McDonnell, *Masters of Empire: Great Lakes Indians and the Making of America* (Hill and Wang, 2015), 22, 75–76, 88–89, 245–46; Patty Loew, *Indian Nations of Wisconsin: Histories of Endurance and Renewal* (Wisconsin Historical Society Press, 2013), 99; Heidi Kiiwetinepinesiik Stark, "Marked by Fire: Anishinaabe Articulations of Nationhood in Treaty Making with the United States and Canada," *American Indian Quarterly* 36, no. 2 (2012): 119–49; Heidi Bohaker, *Doodem and Council Fire: Anishinaabe Governance Through Alliance* (University of Toronto Press, 2020), 11, 19.

7. Susan Sleeper-Smith, *Indigenous Prosperity and American Conquest: Indian Women of the Ohio River Valley, 1690–1792* (Omohundro Institute / University of North Carolina Press, 2018), 28–42; Cary Miller, *Ogimaag: Anishinaabeg Leadership, 1760–1845* (University of Nebraska Press, 2010), 47–58.

8. McDonnell, *Masters of Empire*, 100–118; Heidi Bohaker, "*Nindoodemag*: The Significance of Algonquian Kinship Networks in the Eastern Great Lakes Region, 1600–1701," *William and Mary Quarterly* 63, no. 1 (2006): 23–52; Alfred H. Meyer, "Circulation and Settlement Patterns of the Calumet Region of Northwest Indiana and Northeast Illinois," *Annals of the Association of American Geographers* 44, no. 3 (1954): 245–74; Carolyn Podruchny, Frederic W. Gleach, and Roger Roulette, "Putting Up Poles: Power, Navigation, and Cultural Mixing in the Fur Trade," in *Gathering Places: Aboriginal and Fur Trade Histories*, ed. Carolyn Podruchny and Laura Peers (University of British Columbia Press, 2010), 25–47.

9. Tanner, *Atlas of Great Lakes Indian History*, 105–7; Alec R. Gilpin, *The War of 1812 in the Old Northwest* (Michigan State University Press, 1958), 139; Ann Durkin Keating, *Rising Up from Indian Country: The Battle of Fort Dearborn and the Birth of Chicago* (University of Chicago Press, 2012), 141; John William Nelson, *Muddy Ground: Native Peoples, Chicago's Portage, and the Transformation of a Continent* (University of North Carolina Press, 2023), 144–49; John C. Calhoun, quoted in John Lauritz Larson, *Internal Improvement: National Public Works and the Promise of*

*Popular Government in the Early United States* (University of North Carolina Press, 2001), 65.

10. Nelson, *Muddy Ground*, 152–83; William Cronon, *Nature's Metropolis: Chicago and the Great West* (W. W. Norton, 1991), 60; James W. Putnam, *The Illinois and Michigan Canal: A Study in Economic History* (University of Chicago Press, 1918), 1–29.

11. John G. Clark, *The Grain Trade in the Old Northwest* (University of Illinois Press, 1966), 23–30; George Rogers Taylor, *The Transportation Revolution 1815–1860* (Routledge, 1951), 158–59; Susan Gaunt Stearns, *Empire of Commerce: The Closing of the Mississippi and the Opening of Atlantic Trade* (University of Virginia Press, 2024), 148; Paul W. Gates, *The Farmer's Age: Agriculture, 1815–1860* (M. E. Sharpe, 1960), 159–62; Paul Fatout, *Indiana Canals* (Purdue University Press, 1972), 10–11, 22–38; Louis C. Hunter, *Steamboats on the Western Rivers: An Economic and Technological History* (Harvard University Press, 1949), 1–26.

12. Carter Goodrich, *Government Promotion of American Canals and Railroads, 1800–1890* (New York: Columbia University Press, 1960), 52–53; Nathan Miller, *The Enterprise of a Free People: Aspects of Economic Development in New York State During the Canal Period, 1792–1838* (Cornell University Press, 1962), 77–111, 115; *Preliminary Report of Inland Waterways Commission*, 60th Cong., 1st sess., 1980, S. Doc. No. 325, 215; Taylor, *The Transportation Revolution*, 137; Brian Murphy, *Building the Empire State: Political Economy in the Early Republic* (University of Pennsylvania Press, 2015), 164–88; Laurence M. Hauptman, *Conspiracy of Interests: Iroquois Dispossession and the Rise of New York State* (Syracuse University Press, 1999), 124, 144–61; Mary Conable, "A Steady Enemy: The Ogden Land Company and the Seneca Indians" (PhD diss., University of Rochester, 1994), 57–58; Robert Greenhalgh Albion and Jennie Barnes Pope, *The Rise of New York Port, 1815–1860* (Charles Scribner's Sons, 1939).

13. George B. Porter to Elbert Herring, March 16, 1833, LROIA 132 [325–28]; Patrick J. Jung, *The Black Hawk War of 1832* (University of Oklahoma Press, 2007), 69–92; John Hall, *Uncommon Defense: Indian Allies in the Black Hawk War* (Harvard University Press, 2009), 120–44, 153, 217; John Bowes, *Land Too Good for Indians: Northern Indian Removal* (University of Oklahoma Press, 2016), 5, 151–53.

14. Lewis Cass to Thomas Owen, George Porter, and William Weatherford, April 8, 1833, LSOIA 10, 210–14; Charles J. Latrobe, *The Rambler in North America, 1832–1833* (Harper and Brothers, 1835), 203–4; R. David Edmunds, *The Potawatomis: Keepers of the Fire* (University of Oklahoma Press, 1987), 248–49; Bowes, *Land Too Good for Indians*, 149–81; James Clifton, *The Prairie People: Continuity and Change in Potawatomi Indian Culture, 1665–1965* (University of Iowa Press, 1998), 238–41; Anselm J. Gerwing, "The Chicago Indian Treaty of 1833," *Journal of the Illinois State Historical Society* 57, no. 2 (1964): 117–42.

15. "Journal of the Treaty Concluded at Chicago on the 26th and 27th Sep. 1833," Ratified treaty no. 189, Documents Relating to the Negotiation of the Treaty of September 26, 1833, with the United Chippewa, Ottawa, and Potawatomi Indians, Roll 3, Frame 68, Ratified Treaty no. 189, Documents Relating to the Negotiation of Ratified and Unratified Treaties with Various Tribes of Indians, National Archives Microfilm Publication T494, BIA, NARA; Latrobe, *The Rambler in North America*, 204.

16. Michael Witgen, *An Infinity of Nations: How the Native New World Shaped Early North America* (University of Pennsylvania Press, 2012), 77–78; Miller, *Ogimaag*, 42–43, 65–82, 103–10; Clifton, *The Prairie People*, 119, 161–64, 289; Edmunds, *The Potawatomis*, 216; John William Nelson, "Sigenauk's War of Independence: Anishinaabe Resurgence and the Making of Indigenous Authority in the Borderlands of Revolution," *William and Mary Quarterly* 78, no. 4 (2021): 656–57; James A. Clifton, "Merchant, Solider, Broker, Chief: A Corrected Obituary of Captain Billy Caldwell," *Journal of the Illinois State Historical Society* 71, no. 3 (1978): 186–87; "Journal of the Treaty Concluded at Chicago," 25–26.

17. Clifton, *The Prairie People*, 239–40; James W. Van Hoeven, "Salvation and Indian Removal: The Career Biography of the Rev. John Freeman Schermerhorn, Indian Commissioner" (PhD diss., Vanderbilt University, 1971), 150–51, 160–67, 171–228. Shortly after the 1833 Chicago treaty, while still serving as removal commissioner, Schermerhorn attempted to purchase Potawatomi reservations located on the Wabash River through local merchants, but they dismissed him, calling his price a "a shameful offer" that the Potawatomi would have refused. Schermerhorn to Allen Hamilton and Cyrus Taber, January 10, 1834, Folder 7, Box 2, Hamilton Family Papers, Manuscripts Section, Indiana State Library, Indianapolis; "Journal of the Treaty Concluded at Chicago," 30.

18. "Treaty with the Chippewa, Etc., 1833," in *Indian Affairs: Laws and Treaties*, vol. 2, *Treaties*, ed. Charles J. Kappler (GPO, 1904), 402–15.

19. "Treaty with the Ottawa, Etc., 1821," in Kappler, *Indian Affairs*, 2:200; Isaac McCoy to William Staughton, September 6, 1821, Isaac McCoy Papers, Kansas Collection, RH MF 100, Kenneth Spencer Research Library, University of Kansas.

20. *ARCIA* 1841, 238; Henry Van Der Bogart to William Van Der Bogart, September 15, 1833, Henry Van Der Bogart Papers, Chicago Historical Society (hereafter cited as Van Der Bogart Papers); Henry Van Der Bogart to David Demarest, October 7, 1833, Van Der Bogart Papers; Henry Van Der Bogart to Walter Monteith, October 14, 1833, Van Der Bogart Papers; US Civil Service Commission, *Official Register of the United States* (GPO, 1833).

21. George Porter to Elbert Herring, September 28, 1833, Ratified Treaty no. 189, Documents Relating to the Negotiation of Ratified and Unratified Treaties with Various Tribes of Indians, NARA.

22. "Treaty with the Wyandot, Etc.," in Kappler, *Indian Affairs*, 2:39; Cameron M. Shriver, "Indians, Empires, and the Contest for Information in Colonial Miami and Illinois Countries" (PhD diss., Ohio State University, 2016), 33–34; Bert Anson, *The Miami Indians* (University of Oklahoma Press, 1970), 139–76; George Porter and William Marshall to Lewis Cass, November 16, 1833, LROIA 416 [111].

23. Shriver, "Indians, Empires, and the Contest for Information," 35, 309–13; Susan Sleeper-Smith, *Indigenous Prosperity and American Conquest: Indian Women of the Ohio River Valley, 1690–1792* (University of North Carolina Press, 2018), 150–56; Stuart Rafert, *The Miami Indians of Indiana: A Persistent People, 1654–1994* (Indiana Historical Society, 1996), 27; Bradley J. Birzer, "Entangling Empires, Fracturing Frontiers: Jean Baptiste Richardville and the Quest for Miami Autonomy, 1760–1841" (PhD diss., Indiana University, 1998), 93–94; Karen Marrero, "'She Is Capable of Doing a Good Deal of Mischief': A Miami Woman's Threat to Empire in

the Eighteenth-Century Ohio Valley," *Journal of Colonialism and Colonial History* 6, no. 3 (2005), https://doi.org/10.1353/cch.2006.0015.

24. S. Doc. No. 19-47, at 2–3 (1826); Fatout, *Indiana Canals*, 37–39; John Bell Rae, "Federal Land Grants in the Aid of Canals," *Journal of Economic History* 4, no. 2 (1944): 167–77; Rafert, *The Miami Indians of Indiana*, 91–94.

25. Daniel Feller, *The Public Lands in Jacksonian Politics* (University of Wisconsin Press, 1984), 141–42, 234n72; Larson, *Internal Improvement*, 181–93, 204–5; Daniel Walker Howe, *What Hath God Wrought: The Transformation of America, 1815-1848* (Oxford University Press, 2007), 358–60; Carlton Jackson, "The Internal Improvement Vetoes of Andrew Jackson," *Tennessee Historical Quarterly* 25, no. 3 (1966): 261–79; B. U. Ratchford, *American State Debts* (Duke University Press, 1941), 88; John Joseph Wallis, Richard E. Sylla, and Arthur Grinath III, "Sovereign Debt and Repudiation: The Emerging-Market Debt Crisis in the U.S. States, 1839–1843," Working Paper No. 19753 (National Bureau of Economic Research, September 2004), 9–10; Fatout, *Indiana Canals*, 50.

26. William Crawford Linton to Nicholas McCarty, January 1, 1834, Canal Fund Commissioners Letter Book, 1832–1834, Records of the Auditor of the State, Internal Improvement Papers, Indiana State Archives, 23–24; Nicholas McCarty to John Tipton, June 5, 1834, in *The John Tipton Papers*, Vol. 3, *1834–1839*, ed. Nellie Armstrong Robertson and Dorothy Riker (Indiana Historical Bureau, 1942), 58; Fatout, *Indiana Canals*, 56; Reginald McGrane, *Foreign Bondholders and American State Debts* (Macmillan, 1935), 11; William Crawford Linton, Jeremiah Sullivan, Nicholas McCarty to S. V. Wilden, June 6, 1834, Canal Fund Commissioners Letter Book, 1832–1834, Indiana State Archives, 58–59.

27. William Crawford Linton to Nicholas McCarty, Indianapolis, February 17, 1834, Canal Fund Commissioners Letter Book 1832–1834, Indiana State Archives, 39; Nicholas McCarty and Samuel Hanna to Elbert Herring, March 11, 1835, LROIA 133 [136–37]; Elbert Herring to Samuel Ward, March 16, 1835, LSOIA 15, 163–64; John Ward & Co. to D. Kurtz, March 26, 1835, LROIA 133 [322–24]; Elbert Herring to Samuel Ward, March 26, 1835, LROIA 133 [324–26]; Elbert Herring to Samuel Ward, March 21, LSOIA 15, 187; Meeting of May 26, 1835, Canal Fund Commissioner Record Book, Book 1, Indiana State Archives, 27. Ward received a $174.56 brokerage fee for his services; "Abstract from Trust Fund Day Book No. 1," June 1, 1837, Folder Special File 21, Box 6, Special Files Relating to Indian Trust Funds 1833–1898, Records of the Department of the Interior, Indian Division, Records of the Office of the Secretary of the Interior, RG 48, NARA II. Only three months later, New York firm Prime, Ward, & King would purchase $40,000 dollars of Wabash and Erie Canal bonds for only a five percent premium; Meeting of August 28, 1835, Canal Fund Commissioner Record Book, Indiana State Archives, 32; Bessie Keeraan Roberts Document, Comparet Family Collection, Folder S1122, Manuscripts Division, Indiana State Library; Elbert Jay Benton, *The Wabash Trade Route in the Development of the Old Northwest* (Johns Hopkins University Press, 1903), 49.

28. C. A. Harris to Levi Woodbury, December 22, 1836, Vol. 1, TTFC 171; Levi Woodbury to C. A. Harris, December 27, 1836, Vol. 1, TTFC, 177; Bond Statement for 1838, Vol. 2, Miscellaneous Records Concerning Finances, ca. 1797–1881, BIA, NARA, 388–89.

29. C. A. Harris to Joel Poinsett, March 15, 1838, LROIA 438 [24–25]; "Treaty with the Sauk and Foxes, 1837," in Kappler, *Indian Affairs*, 2:495–97; "Treaty with the Winnebago, 1837," in Kappler, *Indian Affairs*, 2:497–99; C. A. Harris to Benjamin F. Butler, November 4, 1836, LSOIA 20, 93; Mary E. Young, *Redskins, Ruffleshirts, and Rednecks: Indian Allotments in Alabama and Mississippi 1830–1860* (University of Oklahoma Press, 1961), 91–93; Ronald N. Satz, *American Indian Policy in the Jacksonian Era* (University of Nebraska Press, 1975), 157–59; H.R. Rep. No. 25-892, at 2–3 (1838).

30. Namsuk Kim and John Joseph Wallis, "The Market for American State Government Bonds in Britain and the United States, 1830–1843," *Economic History Review* 58, no. 4 (2005): 736–64; Wallis et al., "Sovereign Debt and Repudiation," 1–6.

31. See, for example, J. D. Beers to Elbert Herring, February 17, 1836, LROIA 853 [8]; Thomas D. Lewis to J. D. Beers, February 17, 1836, LROIA 853 [10–12]; J. D. Beers to Elbert Herring, March 4, 1836, LROIA 853 [21–22]; John Smith to Charles A. Harris, March 28, 1837, LROIA 853 [417–34]; Jonathan Tilford to C. A. Harris, February 3, 1837, LROIA 853 [494–529]; W. H. Evans to C. A. Harris, May 17, 1837, LROIA 853 [663–67]; Amos Kendall to T. Hartley Crawford, December 10, 1838, LROIA R853 [683]; Joshua Pilcher to T. Hartley Crawford, June 26, 1839, LROIA 853 [973–75]; and Miscellaneous Records Concerning Finances, Vol. 4, Records of the Finance Division, BIA, NARA, 188–89.

32. Stephen Aron, *American Confluence: The Missouri Frontier from Borderland to Border State* (Indiana University Press, 2006), 231; John Smith to C. A. Harris, March 28, 1837, LROIA 853 [415]; John Smith to C. A. Harris, March 29, 1837, LROIA 853 [436]; *Journal of the Senate of the State of Missouri at the First Session, Tenth General Assembly* (Calvin Gunn, 1839), 19; "Missouri Bonds," *Cleveland Daily Herald*, November 27, 1837; "Multiple News Items," *Arkansas State Gazette*, December 5, 1837; John Ray Cable, *The Bank of the State of Missouri* (PhD diss., Columbia University, 1923), 166, 174–76; [John Smith] to Charles A. Harris, March 28, 1837, LROIA 853, [778–80]; C. A. Harris to John Smith, March 29, 1837, LROIA 853 [798–99]; C. A. Harris to S. Cooper, April 27, 1838, LROIA 853 [781–82]; C. A. Harris to John Smith, June 28, 1837, LROIA 853 [790–91]; John Smith to C. A. Harris, July 13, 1837, LROIA 853 [788–89]; C. A. Harris to John Smith, August 9, 1837, LROIA 853 [786–88]; John Smith to C. A. Harris, October 9, 1837, LROIA 853 [795]; C. A. Harris to Theodore McGill, September 9, 1837, LSOIA 22, 306–7; H.R. Rep. No. 25-892 (1838); C. A. Harris to John Smith, November 1, 1837, LSOIA 22, 504; Levi Woodbury to Thomas H. Benton, September 13, 1837, Treasury Correspondence Concerning Chickasaw Trust Fund, Vol. 1, TTFC, 265; C. A. Harris to Thomas H. Benton, December 2, 1837, LROIA 853 [796–97]; "Sales at the Stock Exchange, January 2," *New York Spectator*, January 4, 1838; Cable, *The Bank of State of Missouri*, 174.

33. R. M. Johnson to C. A. Harris, March 7, 1837, LROIA 853 [295]; "State Bonds," *Daily Commercial Bulletin*, January 2, 1837; *Journal of the House of the General Assembly of the Commonwealth of Kentucky* (A. G. Hodges, 1837), 22.

34. Andrew Jackson to Levi Woodbury, May 17, 1837, LROIA 853 [308].

35. Levi Woodbury to Andrew Jackson, May 29, 1837, Vol. 1, TTFC, 238; C. A. Harris to Andrew Jackson, June 14, 1837, LSOIA 21, 481; Jackson, "The Internal Improvement Vetoes"; Howe, *What Hath God Wrought*, 358–60; John Reynolds to

Carey A. Harris, April 20, 1837, LROIA 853 [415]; C. A. Harris to John Reynolds, May 4, 1837, LSOIA 21, 362.

36. Isaac Bronson to John J. Stuart, March 5, 1840, LROIA 854 [94–96].

37. C. A. Harris to Jacob Brown, May 4, 1837, LROIA 853 [106–07]; Jacob Brown to C. A. Harris, June 11, 1837, LROIA 853 [109]; Cody Lynn Berry, "Territorial Capitalism: Early Arkansas Banking and Indian Removal, 1819–1860" (MA thesis, University of Arkansas–Little Rock, 2016), 42–43; W. B. Worthen, *Early Banking in Arkansas* (Democrat Printing, 1906), 26; "Money Market," *New York Herald*, May 4, 1837.

38. Poinsett Notation on T. H. Crawford to Joel Poinsett, October 23, 1838, Box 1, Unregistered Letters Received Relating to Trust Funds, 1828–1869, Records Relating to Indian Trust Funds, Records of the Indian Division, Records of the Department of the Interior, RG 48, NARA II; William Clarence Evans, "The Public Debt of Arkansas: Its History from 1836 to 1885" (master's thesis, University of Arkansas, 1928), 14, 17; William Field to T. Hartley Crawford, September 6, 1838, LROIA 853 [670–71]; William Field to J. R. Palmer, September 16, 1840, LROIA 854 [44–45]; T. Hartley Crawford to William S. Fulton, November 13, 1838, LSOIA 25, 355; Berry, "Territorial Capitalism," 52–54; Arkansas v. Carey A. Harris, 3 Pike, 570 (AK 1842); James S. Conway and Others, *Ex Parte*, 4 Pike 302 (AK 1843).

39. H.R. Rep. No. 25-892, at 2–3 (1838).

40. Wallis et al., "Sovereign Debt and Repudiation," 7–8, 16–22; "Inaugural Address to the General Assembly, December 3, 1834," in *Messages and Papers Relating to the Administration of Noah Noble, Governor of Indiana, 1831–1837*, ed. Dorothy Riker and Gayle Thornbrough (Indiana Historical Bureau 1958), 340–41; H.R. Rep. 27-296, at 47 (1842); John Joseph Wallis, "The Property Tax as a Coordinating Device: Financing Indiana's Mammoth Internal Improvement System, 1835–1842," *Explorations in Economic History* 40, no. 3 (2003): 225.

41. Report of the State Board of Internal Improvements, 1839, in *Documents of the Senate of Indiana, Twenty-Fourth Session* (Douglass & Noel, 1840), 27; Wallis et al., "Sovereign Debt and Repudiation," 9–10.

42. Wallis, "The Property Tax as a Coordinating Device," 229.

43. S. Doc. No. 25-106 (1838); Ronald N. Satz, *American Indian Policy in the Jacksonian Era* (University of Nebraska Press, 1974), 110; Anson, *The Miami Indians*, 200–204; Bert Anson, "The Fur Traders in Northern Indiana, 1796–1850" (PhD diss., Indiana University, 1953), 195–251.

44. "Treaty with the Miami, 1838," in Kappler, *Indian Affairs*, 2:519–22; Paul Wallace Gates, "Introduction," in *The John Tipton Papers*, vol. 1, *1809–1827*, ed. Nellie Armstrong Robertson and Dorothy Riker (Indiana Historical Bureau, 1942), 17–22; H.R. Doc. No. 24-2 (1837); H.R. Doc. No. 25-185 (1838); S. Doc. No. 26-190 (1841); Melissa Rinehart, "Miami Resistance and Resilience During the Removal Era," in *Contested Territories: Native Americans and Non-Natives in the Lower Great Lakes, 1700–1850*, ed. Charles Beatty-Medina and Melissa Rinehart (Michigan State University Press, 2012), 142–43.

45. Clifton, *The Prairie People*, 283–86, 299; John P. Bowes, *Exiles and Pioneers: Eastern Indians in the Trans-Mississippi West* (Cambridge University Press, 2007), 77–81; Edmunds, *The Potawatomis*, 267–68; Henry Schoolcraft to [Commissioner of Indian Affairs], July 10, 1837, LROIA 133 [513–14].

46. R. David Edmunds, "Potawatomis in the Platte Country: An Indian Removal Incomplete," *Missouri Historical Review* 68, no. 4 (1974): 375–92; Aron, *American Confluence*, 230; S. Doc. No. 23-4 (1834).

47. Lewis Cass to Thomas Owens, June 26, 1834, LSOIA 13, 69–72; Billy Caldwell et al., enclosed in Thomas Owen to Lewis Cass, August 22, 1834, LROIA 132 [430–32] (emphasis in the original).

48. Billy Caldwell et al. to Thomas Owen, October 1, 1834, enclosed in Thomas Owen to Lewis Cass, October 3, 1834, LROIA 132 [448–51]; Edmunds, "Potawatomis in the Platte Country," 378; Toponebee et al. to Senate, February 11, 1835, Folder B-C6, Records of Early Select Committees, 23rd Cong., 1789–1921, Records of the United States Senate, RG 46, NARA; Clifton, *The Prairie People*, 290; Thomas Owen to Lewis Cass, November 17, 1834, LROIA 132 [466–67]; Shingbequay et al. to Secretary of War, November 1834, LROIA 132 [492–93].

49. C. A. Harris to Lewis Sands, October 3, 1837, LSOIA 22, 369. John Tipton and Isaac McCoy promoted the plan to consolidate both groups on Osage River land. Isaac McCoy to John Tipton, May 29, 1837, in *The John Tipton Papers*, vol. 3, *1834–1839*, ed. Nellie Armstrong Robertson and Dorothy Riker (Indiana Historical Bureau, 1942), 405–6; Clifton, *The Prairie People*, 291; Henry Atkinson to C. A. Harris, August 8, 1837, LROIA 134 [97–98]; Billy Caldwell to John Gantt, September 24, 1839, LROIA 215 [471–72]; Billy Caldwell, Matawa, Wabonsa, et al. to Stephen W. Kearney, September 13, 1837, LROIA 215 [141–42]; Stark, "Marked by Fire"; Bohaker, *Doodem and Council Fire*, 105, 118–19.

50. Gholson Kercheval to Carey A. Harris, September 20, 1836, LROIA 133 [401]; Elbert Herring to J. B. F. Russell, May 31, 1836, LSOIA 18, 470–71; Christina Snyder, *Great Crossings: Indians, Settlers, and Slaves in the Age of Jackson* (Oxford University Press, 2017), 170–84; Thomas McKenney to Joseph M. Street, April 13, 1830, LSOIA 6, 384–86; Elbert Herring to R. M. Johnson, July 24, 1834, LSOIA 13, 258–60; R. M. Johnson to Thomas Henderson, February 18, 1834, Folder 9, Henderson Papers, Filson Historical Society, Louisville, KY (hereafter cited as Henderson Papers); R. M. Johnson to Thomas Henderson, January 10, 1835, Folder 10, Henderson Papers; Elbert Herring to R. M. Johnson, August 1, 1834, LSOIA 13, 295–96; T. Hartley Crawford to Joshua Pilcher, May 22, 1840, LSOIA 28, 405–6.

51. Gholson Kercheval to Carey A. Harris, February 10, 1836, LROIA 134 [263]. For the next decade, the United Nations would continue to oppose sending children to the Choctaw Academy and insist on a school "in their own country" at Council Bluffs—in vain. See, for example, Samuel Cooper to Joshua Pilcher, May 14, 1840, LROIA 215 [544–45]; and T. Hartley Crawford to Thomas Harvey, October 10, 1844, LSOIA 35, 497.

52. C. A. Harris to Thomas Henderson, January 5, 1838, LSOIA 23, 146–47; Elbert Herring to Thomas Henderson, March 7, 1835, LSOIA 15, 140; R. M. Johnson to Thomas Henderson, December 10, 1837, Folder 12, Henderson Papers; H.R. Doc. No. 26-109, at 121, 135–36, 140–41 (1841); Snyder, *Great Crossings*, 111–17, 219–35, 259; T. Hartley Crawford to Samuel Milroy, January 13, 1840, LSOIA 28, 25; Carey A. Harris to Benjamin Reynolds, March 13, 1837, Vol. 1, LSCR, 134; T. Hartley Crawford to Joshua Pilcher, January 22, 1840, LSOIA 28, 46–47; T. Hartley Crawford to J. J. Douglass, March 2, 1840, LSOIA 28, 154–55.

53. Edwin James to George McGuire, September 28, 1837, LROIA 215 [139–40]; Stephen Cooper Annual Report, December 31, 1839, LROIA 215 [300–305]; Ethan Allen Hitchcock to C. A. Harris, November 4, 1837, Folder 1, Box 1, Ethan Allen Hitchcock Collection on Indian Removal, Beinecke Rare Book and Manuscript Library, Yale University; C. A. Harris to E. A. Hitchcock, October 17, 1838, LSOIA 25, 289; C. A. Harris to Joel Poinsett, June 22, 1838, LSOIA 24, 387–88.

54. C. A. Harris to Benjamin F. Butler, December 14, 1836, LSOIA 20, 285; Samuel Hanna, "A Financial History of Maryland, 1789–1848" (PhD diss., Johns Hopkins University, 1906), 102–56, 229–35; Larson, *Internal Improvement*, 88–91; Josiah F. Polk to C. A. Harris, August 31, 1837, LROIA 853 [79]; C. A. Harris to William Lewis, August 25, 1837, LSOIA 22, 260.

55. Birzer, "Entangling Empires, Fracturing Frontiers," 178; Rafert, *The Miami Indians of Indiana*, 97–98; Anson, *The Miami Indians*, 206–7.

56. Rinehart, "Miami Resistance and Resilience," 150–52; Elizabeth Lindsey Palmer Oral History, Indian-Pioneer History S-149, Western History Collection, University of Oklahoma Digital Collections.

57. George Strack, George Ironstrack, Daryl Baldwin, Kristina Fox, Julie Olds, Robbyn Abbitt, and Melissa Rinehart, *myaamiaki aancihsaaciki: A Cultural Exploration of the Miami Removal Route* (Miami Tribe of Oklahoma, 2011); Anson, *The Miami Indians*, 224–25, 229. The Wabash and Erie Canal would not reach the Ohio River (at Evansville) until 1853; Benton, *The Wabash Trade Route*, 76. See also William Medill to Thomas Harvey, November 3, 1846, LSOIA 39, 5; "The Miami Indians—Emigration—Indian Debts," *Indiana State Sentinel*, October 8, 1846; "Emigration of the Miami Indians," *Indiana State Sentinel*, October 29, 1846; "Indian Emigration," *Logansport (IN) Telegraph*, November 14, 1846.

58. Wallis, "The Property Tax as a Coordinating Device," 240; Glen E. Holt, "The Birth of Chicago: An Examination of Economic Parentage," *Journal of the Illinois State Historical Society* 76, no. 2 (1983): 87–90; Clark, *The Grain Trade*, 87; Cronon, *Nature's Metropolis*, 60–66; Roger L. Ransom, "Canals and Development: A Discussion of the Issues," *American Economic Review* 54, no. 3 (1964): 374–76; Ronald Shaw, "The Canal Era in the Old Northwest," in *Transportation and the Early Nation: Papers Presented at an American Revolution Bicentennial Symposium* (Indiana Historical Society, 1982), 93–95.

## Chapter Five: American Insecurities

1. James Clifton, *The Prairie People: Continuity and Change in Potawatomi Indian Culture, 1665–1965* (University of Iowa Press, 1998), 329; William H. Goode, *Outposts of Zion: With Limnings of Mission Life* (Poe and Hitchcock, 1864), 67; Grant Foreman, *Advancing the Frontier, 1830–1860* (University of Oklahoma Press, 1933), 205, 212.

2. Ethan Allen Hitchcock, *A Traveler in Indian Territory: The Journal of Ethan Allen Hitchcock, Late Major-General in the United States Army*, ed. Grant Foreman (University of Oklahoma Press, 1996), 36–37; Goode, *Outposts of Zion*, 69–70; Tim Alan Garrison, "Pan-Nationalism as a Crisis Management Strategy: John Ross and the Tahlequah Conference of 1843," in *Between Settler and Indigenous Governance*,

ed. Timothy Rouse and Lisa Ford (Routledge, 2012), 53–54; Foreman, *Advancing the Frontier*, 211–12; Cherokee Nation, *The Constitution and Laws of the Cherokee Nation: Passed at Tahlequa in the Cherokee Nation, 1839–51* (Cherokee Nation, 1852), 6. On the council's legacy, see Lewis Downing to Abraham Lincoln, December 20, 1864, LROIA 836 [86–91].

3. Goode, *Outposts of Zion*, 67, 72–73; P. M. Butler to T. Hartley Crawford, June 30, 1843, LROIA 442 [781–83]; *ARCIA* 1843, 422–23; Susan A. Miller, *Cooacoochee's Bones: A Seminole Saga* (University Press of Kansas, 2003), 49–50; James W. Covington, *The Seminoles of Florida* (Library Press, 2017), 108–9; Kathleen DuVal, *The Native Ground: Indians and Colonists in the Heart of the Continent* (University of Pennsylvania Press, 2006), 196–248; "Treaty with the Great and Little Osage, 1825," in *Indian Affairs: Laws and Treaties*, vol. 2, *Treaties*, ed. Charles J. Kappler (GPO, 1904), 246–48; Louis F. Burns, *A History of the Osage People* (University of Alabama Press, 2004), 147–71.

4. Goode, *Outposts of Zion*, 74; P. M. Butler to T. Hartley Crawford, June 30, 1843, LROIA 442 [781–83].

5. B. U. Ratchford, *American State Debts* (Duke University Press, 1941), 80–82; John Joseph Wallis, Richard E. Sylla, and Arthur Grinath III, "Sovereign Debt and Repudiation: The Emerging-Market Debt Crisis in the U.S. States, 1839–1843," Working Paper No. 19753 (National Bureau of Economic Research, September 2004): 12–22; John Joseph Wallis, "The Depression of 1839 to 1843: States, Debts, and Banks," unpublished manuscript, National Bureau of Economic Research / University of Maryland, 2005; Namsuk Kim and John Joseph Wallis, "The Market for American State Government Bonds in Britain and the United States, 1830–43," *Economic History Review* 58, no. 4 (2005): 736–64.

6. Robert N. Clinton, "The Dormant Indian Commerce Clause," *Connecticut Law Review* 27 (1995): 1055–247; Gregory Ablavsky, "Beyond the Indian Commerce Clause," *Yale Law Journal* 124, no. 4 (2015): 1012–52; H.R. Rep. No. 25-892 (1838).

7. Ronald Satz, *American Indian Policy in the Jacksonian Era* (University of Nebraska Press, 1975), 97. On pre-1830s removals and the right to remain, see Samantha Seeley, *Race, Removal and the Right to Remain: Migration and the Making of the United States* (Omohundro Institute / University of North Carolina Press, 2021).

8. "Treaty with the Florida Tribes of Indians, 1823," in Kappler, *Indian Affairs*, 2:203; John K. Mahon, *History of the Second Seminole War, 1835–1842* (University of Florida Press, 1985), 43; James W. Covington, *The Seminoles of Florida*, 63.

9. Mahon, *History of the Second Seminole War*, 101–6; Covington, *The Seminoles of Florida*, 74–88; John T. Ellisor, *The Second Creek War: Interethnic Conflict and Collusion on a Collapsing Frontier* (University of Nebraska Press, 2010), 192–93; George H. Walton, *Fearless and Free: The Seminole Indian War, 1835–1842* (Bobbs-Merrill, 1977), 88–102; Robert Wooster, *American Military Frontiers: The United States Army in the West, 1783–1900* (University of New Mexico Press, 2009), 89; Jeffrey Ostler, *Surviving Genocide: Native Nations and the United States from the American Revolution to Bleeding Kansas* (Yale University Press, 2019), 286.

10. D. W. Meinig, *The Shaping of America: A Geographical Perspective on 500 Years of History*, vol. 2, *Continental America, 1800–1867* (Yale University Press, 1995), 92.

11. Isaac McCoy, *History of Baptist Indian Missions* (P. Force, 1840), 333–49; George A. Schultz, *An Indian Canaan: Isaac McCoy and the Vision of an Indian State* (University of Oklahoma Press, 1972), 101–22; Claudio Saunt, *Unworthy Republic: The Dispossession of Native Americans and the Road to Indian Territory* (W. W. Norton, 2020), 104–7.

12. William E. Unrau, *The Rise and Fall of Indian Country, 1825–1855* (University Press of Kansas, 2007), 17–37; Meinig, *The Shaping of America*, 92–94.

13. Unrau, *The Rise and Fall of Indian Country*, 37–58; Stephen Aron, *American Confluence: The Missouri Frontier from Borderland to Border State* (Indiana University Press, 2006), 109–10.

14. Gregory Smithers, *The Cherokee Diaspora: An Indigenous History of Migration, Resettlement, and Identity* (Yale University Press, 2005), 48–50; Williard H. Rollings, *The Osage: An Ethnohistorical Study of Hegemony on the Prairie-Plains* (University of Missouri Press, 1992), 220–22, 237–46, 251–54; Kathleen DuVal, *The Native Ground: Indians and Colonists in the Heart of the Continent* (University of Pennsylvania Press, 2007), 196–226, 233; Frankie Bauer, "Civilized Settlement & Nomadic Dominion: Inter-Tribal Treaties and Grand Councils Between the Cherokee and Osage Indians, 1817–1828" (MA, Western Carolina University, 2018); James Barbour to William Clark, July 14, 1826, LSOIA R3, 146–47; William E. Unrau, *Indians of Kansas: The Euro-American Invasion and Conquest of Kansas Indians* (Kansas State Historical Society, 1991), 51–55.

15. David La Vere, *The Texas Indians* (Texas A&M University Press, 2003), 154, 160, 168; Sami Lakomaki, *Gathering Together: The Shawnee People Through Diaspora and Nationhood, 1600–1870* (Yale University Press, 2014), 184–87; Gary Clayton Anderson, *The Conquest of Texas: Ethnic Cleansing in the Promised Land, 1820–1875* (University of Oklahoma Press, 2005), 26, 105–19, 127–38, 157–58.

16. H.R. Doc. 25-59 (1838); Lindsay Schakenbach Regele, *Flowers, Guns, and Money: Joel Roberts Poinsett and the Paradoxes of American Patriotism* (University of Chicago Press, 2023), 140–41. Between 1837 and 1842, US Army personnel averaged 10,838. See *Historical Statistics of the United States, Millennial Edition Online*, "Table Ed26-47: Military Personnel on Active Duty, by Branch of Service and Sex: 1789–1995," accessed Sept. 7, 2020; Wooster, *American Military Frontiers*, 90–92.

17. Wooster, *American Military Frontiers*, 90.

18. Christina Snyder, *Great Crossings: Indians, Settlers, and Slaves in the Age of Jackson* (Oxford University Press, 2017), 157–59; Donna L. Akers, *Living in the Land of Death: The Choctaw Nation, 1830–1860* (Michigan State University Press, 2004), 114, 117–19; Theda Perdue, "Clan and Court: Another Look at the Early Cherokee Republic," *American Indian Quarterly* 24, no. 4 (2000): 562–69; Julie Reed, *Serving the Nation: Cherokee Sovereignty and Social Welfare, 1800–1907* (University of Oklahoma Press, 2016), 5, 35; Henry C. Benson, *Life Among the Choctaw Indians, and Sketches of the South-West* (Swormstedt and A. Poe, 1860), 174.

19. Benson, *Life Among the Choctaw Indians*, 251–54; William G. McLoughlin, *After the Trail of Tears: The Cherokees' Struggle for Sovereignty, 1839–1880* (University of North Carolina Press, 1993), 34–58; [S. C. Stambaugh and Amos Kendall,] *A Faithful History of the Cherokee Tribe of Indians, from the Period of our First Intercourse with Them, Down to the Present Time* (Jesse E. Dow, 1846); S. Rep. Com. No. 31-176

(1850); Amos Kendall, *A Letter to the Hon. George E. Badger in Relation to the Claim of A. & J. E. Kendall Against the United States, for Certain Wrongs Done Them* (Buell and Blanchard, 1852).

20. Ostler, *Surviving Genocide*, 361; Angie Debo, *The Road to Disappearance: A History of the Creek Indians* (University of Oklahoma Press, 1941), 108; Russell Thornton, *American Indian Holocaust and Survival: A Population History Since 1492* (University of Oklahoma Press, 1987), 94–101; Anne Hyde, *Empires, Nations, and Families: A History of the North American West, 1800–1860* (University of Nebraska Press, 2011), 336–37; Snyder, *Great Crossings*, 157.

21. Hitchcock, *A Traveler in Indian Territory*, 249–50; Petition from Stone Love, James Wolfe, et al., January 26, 1839, LROIA 144 [12–13]; Thomas E. Wilson to Jonathan Bell, July 27, 1841, LROIA 923 [450–51]; Snyder, *Great Crossings*, 168; Ostler, *Surviving Genocide*, 352.

22. 1834 Draft of Choctaw Constitution, Folder 145, PPPH; Choctaw Nation, *The Constitution and Laws of the Choctaw Nation, Together with the Treaties of 1855, 1865 and 1866*, comp. Joseph P. Folsom (William P. Lyon and Son, 1869), 22; Cherokee Nation, *The Constitution and Laws of the Cherokee Nation*, 5–15, 34, 131; Benson, *Life Among the Choctaw Indians*, 28–32; William Armstrong, Report of September 30, 1841, LROIA 923 [343–60]; Isaac Albertson, Slone Love, et al. to John C. Spencer, May 6, 1843, LROIA 138 [1072–74]; Joseph Bryan to T. Hartley Crawford, October 29, 1844, LROIA 139 [28–29]; William Armstrong to William Medill, January 11, 1846, LROIA 139 [234–36]; Nicholas Parillo, *Against the Profit Motive: The Salary Revolution in American Government, 1780–1940* (Yale University Press, 2013).

23. Thomas H. Crawford to L. M. Butler, August 8, 1843, LSOIA 34, 169. On Cherokee values regarding social welfare, see Reed, *Serving the Nation*, 5–6; Debo, *The Road to Disappearance*, 114–15; and Foreman, *Advancing the Frontier*, 97. On Indigenous protocols governing asylum and expulsion, see Elizabeth N. Ellis, *The Great Power of Small Nations: Indigenous Diplomacy in the Gulf South* (University of Pennsylvania Press, 2023).

24. Clara Sue Kidwell, *Choctaws and Missionaries in Mississippi, 1818–1918* (University of Oklahoma Press, 1995), 159–75; Roland Hinds, "Early Creek Missions," *Chronicles of Oklahoma* 17, no. 1 (1939): 53; R. M. Loughridge to James Logan, October 22, 1847, LROIA 783 [1054–57]. The 1830 Treaty with the Choctaw reserved $60,000 for varied educational expenses, and the 1835 Treaty with the Choctaw reserved $214,000; see "Treaty with the Choctaw, 1830," in Kappler, *Indian Affairs*, 2:315; and "Treaty with the Cherokee, 1835," Kappler, *Indian Affairs*, 2:444.

25. Thomas H. Crawford to Thomas Henderson, March 13, 1841, LSOIA 30, 168.

26. Benson, *Life Among the Choctaw Indians*, 61–63; Goode, *Outposts of Zion*, 38–39; Snyder, *Great Crossings*, 262.

27. *ARCIA* 1841, 271–73; Armstrong Report of September 30, 1841; Hitchcock, *A Traveler in Indian Territory*, 36; Goode, *Outposts of Zion*, 67, 176, 187; William P. Ross, *The Life and Times of Hon. William P. Ross* (Weldon and Williams, 1893), n.p. [6]; Muriel H. Wright, "Organization of Counties in the Choctaw and Chickasaw Nations," *Chronicles of Oklahoma* 8, no. 3 (1930): 318; "Progress of Cherokee Civilization," *New York Herald*, November 18, 1844.

28. Hitchcock, *A Traveler in Indian Territory*, 41, 45. Benson, *Life Among the Choctaw Indians*, 42–43; Armstrong Report of September 30, 1841.

29. Hitchcock, *A Traveler in Indian Territory*, 93, 172, 186.

30. William Clark to Edwin James, November 30, 1837, LROIA 134 [463]; Billy Caldwell et al. to William Alley, February 18, 1838, LROIA 215 [204–5]; Billy Caldwell to John Dougherty, November 10, 1838, LROIA 215 [362]. Harris only allowed $1,000 to hire a farmer, who was eventually dismissed after the department refused to supply him with agricultural implements; see C. A. Harris to William Clark, April 10, 1838, LSOIA 24 [39]. See also Richard Elliot, *Notes Taken in Sixty Years* (R. P. Studley, 1883), 184; and Chabenee, Chenagewee, Akbetakeshee, et al. to John Dougherty, May 8, 1838, LROIA 215 [242–43].

31. C. A. Harris to E. A. Hitchcock, October 17, 1838, LSOIA 25, 289; E. A. Hitchcock to C. A. Harris, March 20, 1838, LROIA 215 [288–89]; C. A. Harris to William Clark, April 5, 1838, LSOIA 24, 17–18; C. A. Harris to E. A. Hitchcock, August 8, 1838, LSOIA 25, 51. A few villages of Odawa, Ojibwe, and Potawatomis that relocated to the Osage River did receive agricultural provisions; see T. Hartley Crawford to St. Joseph and Prairie Potts, December 25, 1841, LSOIA 31, 321; T. Hartley Crawford to D. D. Mitchell, May 17, 1843, LSOIA 34, 3; and T. Hartley Crawford to Thomas Harvey, June 18, 1844, LSOIA 35, 289.

32. Petition of Shabonay, Padagoshuck, Joseph La Framboise et al., February 21, 1842, LROIA 215 [754]; James Deaderick to D. D. Mitchell, February 23, 1842, LROIA 215 [749–51]; James Deaderick to T. Hartley Crawford, April 3, 1842, LROIA 215 [778–79]; T. Hartley Crawford to D. D. Mitchell, May 18, 1842, LSOIA 32, 178–80; John B. Luce to D. D. Mitchell, March 28, 1843, LROIA 215 [1015–16]; T. Hartley Crawford to D. D. Mitchell, August 22, 1843, LSOIA 34, 201.

33. William Medill to T. H. Benton, January 5, 1846, LSOIA 37, 317–19; William Medill to Henry Dodge, January 10, 1846, LSOIA 37, 334; William Medill to Henry Dodge, January 30, 1846, LSOIA 37, 369; William Medill to Henry Dodge, January 10, 1846, LSOIA 37, 334.

34. Brian C. Hosmer, *American Indians in the Marketplace: Persistence and Innovation Among the Menominees and Metlakatlans, 1870–1920* (University Press of Kansas, 1999); David L. Mausel, Anthony Waupochick Jr., and Marshall Pecore, "Menominee Forestry: Past, Present, Future," *Journal of Forestry* 115, no. 5 (2017): 366–69.

35. John Ross to National Council, January 6, 1845, in Gary E. Moulton, ed., *The Papers of Chief John Ross*, vol. 2 (University of Oklahoma Press, 1985), 192–93; "An Act Authorizing the Making of a Loan from the General and Orphan School Fund," passed January 17, 1845, in Cherokee Nation, *Constitution and Laws of the Cherokee Nation*, 124; John Ross to William L. Marcy, August 9, 1845, in *The Papers of Chief John Ross*, vol. 2, ed. Gary E. Moulton (University of Oklahoma Press, 1985), 269–70; T. Hartley Crawford to John Ross et al., August 1, 1845, LSOIA 37, 38; William L. Marcy to John Ross et al., August 14, 1846, LSOIA 37, 486.

36. John Joseph Wallis, "What Caused the Crisis of 1839?" Historical Working Paper No. 133 (National Bureau of Economic Research, April 2001); H.R. Rep. No. 27-296, at 122 (1843); Reginald McGrane, *Foreign Bondholders and American State Debts* (Macmillan, 1935), 8–9; Ratchford, *American State Debts*, 9, 93; Jay

Sexton, *Debtor Diplomacy: Finance and American Foreign Relations in the Civil War Era 1837–1873* (Clarendon Press, 2014), 23; Leland Jenks, *The Migration of British Capital to 1875* (Thomas Nelson and Sons, 1927), 73–84; Namsuk Kim and John Joseph Wallis, "The Market for American State Government Bonds in Britain and the United States, 1830–43," *Economic History Review* 58, no. 4 (2005): 737; Richard Sylla, Review of Peter Temin, *The Jacksonian Economy*, *EH.net*, n.d., accessed March 31, 2025, https://eh.net/book_reviews/the-jacksonian-economy/; "Money Market," *Morning Herald* (New York), May 13, 1839; "Money Market and City News," *Morning Post* (London), June 17, 1839.

37. Ralph Hidy, *The House of Baring in American Trade and Finance: English Merchant Bankers at Work, 1763–1861* (Harvard University Press, 1949), 254–59; Kathryn Boodry, "August Belmont and the World the Slaves Made," in *Slavery's Capitalism: A New History of American Economic Development*, ed. Sven Beckert and Seth Rockman (University of Pennsylvania Press, 2016), 163–78; Circular, House of Baring, quoted in Hidy, *The House of Baring*, 283; McGrane, *Foreign Bondholders*, 24–26.

38. Daniel Webster, *Webster on the Currency: Speech of Hon. Daniel Webster, at the Merchants' Meeting, in Wall Street, New York, on Monday, September 28, 1840*, ed. Arthur J. Stansbury (E. French, 1840), 15–16.

39. S. Doc. No. 26-153 (1840); H.R. Rep. No. 27-296 (1842); McGrane, *Foreign Bondholders*, 28; John Larson, *Internal Improvement: National Public Works and the Promise of Popular Government* (University of North Carolina Press, 2001), 6, 192–93.

40. Colin Read, *The Rising in Western Upper Canada, 1837–8: The Duncombe Revolt and After* (University of Toronto Press, 1982), 115–16; H. Doc. No. 25-73 (1838); Howard Jones, *To the Webster-Ashburton Treaty: A Study in Anglo-American Relations, 1783–1843* (University of North Carolina Press, 1977), 20–27, 36–41, 48–49; J. Doty to J. R. Poinsett, February 20, 1840, LROIA 440 [140–41]; Extract of "Citizen" to J. Doty, February 3, 1840, LROIA 440 [146–47].

41. Duff Green to John Calhoun, January 1842, in *Correspondence of John Calhoun*, ed. J. Franklin Jameson (GPO, 1899), 841–43.

42. Jenks, *The Migration of British Capital*, 106; Roberts, *America's First Great Depression*, 67; Hidy, *The House of Baring*, 290–92; Sexton, *Debtor Diplomacy*, 39.

43. Brian DeLay, *War of a Thousand Deserts: Indian Raids and the U.S.-Mexican War* (Yale University Press, 2008), 76–78; La Vere, *The Texas Indians*, 172–75; Nathaniel Amory to Daniel Webster, May 19, 1841, LROIA 923 [431–33]; John Forsyth to Joel Poinsett, July 17, 1839, LROIA 439 [548–51]; John Forsyth to Joel Poinsett, March 4, 1840, LROIA 440 [463–65].

44. La Vere, *The Texas Indians*, 172–75; Lakomaki, *Gathering Together*, 191; Smithers, *The Cherokee Diaspora*, 103–4; Wooster, *American Military Frontiers*, 108–9.

45. William J. Sloan to H. L. Heiskell, March 4, 1841, LROIA 923 [426–27]; A. M. M. Upshaw to Matthew Arbuckle, February 5, 1841, LROIA 923 [289–90].

46. Nakia D. Parker, "A Slave State in Embryo: Indian Territory, Native Sovereignty, and the Expansion of Slavery's Empire," in *The Early Imperial Republic: From the American Revolution to the U.S.-Mexican War*, ed. Noelani Arista, Emily Conroy-Krutz, and Michael A. Blaakman (University of Pennsylvania Press, 2023), 118–36; William Armstrong to T. Hartley Crawford, April 9, 1842, LROIA 923 [514–16].

47. Thomas E. Wilson to Jonathan Bell, July 27, 1841, LROIA 923, [450–51]; Ethan Allen Hitchcock to John C. Spencer, March 20, 1842, in Hitchcock, *A Traveler in Indian Territory*, 255–57; S. Doc. No. 27-1, at 177–78 (1842); Wooster, *American Military Frontiers*, 97.

48. Waubonsee, Shabbne, Patecoshuck, Half Day, Puckwon, Wabonme, Shatee, Meawmese to John Tyler, March 29, 1844, LROIA R216 [107–8]; Clifton, *Prairie People*, 326–27.

49. Pekka Hamalainen, *The Comanche Empire* (Yale University Press, 2009), 148–51, 153–54, 165, 171–75, 223–32; Delay, *War of a Thousand Deserts*, 80–83, 95; David J. Silverman, *Thundersticks: Firearms and the Violent Transformation of Native America* (Harvard University Press, 2016), 239–41; Louis F. Burns, *A History of the Osage People* (University of Alabama Press, 2004), 152–53.

50. Silverman, *Thundersticks*, 241; Hitchcock, *A Traveler in Indian Country*, 28, 182, 257; *ARCIA* 1842, 452–54; A. M. M. Upshaw to T. Hartley Crawford, September 2, 1843, LROIA 138 [1240–42].

51. Grant Foreman, *Pioneer Days in the Early Southwest* (Arthur H. Clark, 1926), 275–79; Foreman, *Advancing the Frontier*, 199.

52. William Armstrong to Thomas H. Crawford, April 12, 1842, LROIA 923 [508]; *ARCIA* 1842, 446.

53. T. Hartley Crawford, quoted in Satz, *American Indian Policy*, 228.

54. Covington, *The Seminoles of Florida*, 106–9; "Statement of Balances Due Tribes on Trust Fund interest," Box 1, Unregistered Letters Received Relating to Trust Funds, 1828–1869, Records Relating to Indian Trust Funds, Records of the Indian Division, Records of the Department of the Interior, RG 48, NARA II; Exhibit B, Vol. 1, TTFC, 416.

55. S. Doc. No. 250106, at 5 (1838); C. A. Harris to Capt. E. A. Hitchcock, July 3, 1837, LSOIA 22 [58–59]; S. Doc. No. 25-198, at 198 (1838); Gregory Evans Dowd, "Michigan Murder Mysteries: Death and Rumor in the Age of Indian Removal," in *Enduring Nations: Native Americans in the Midwest*, ed. R. David Edmunds (University of Illinois Press), 129; C. A. Harris to E. P. Gaines, July 28, 1837, LSOIA 22 [169–70].

56. S. Doc. No. 25-106 (1838).

57. William H. Brantley, *Banking in Alabama, 1816–1860*, vol. 1 (privately printed, 1961), 320; Wallis et al., "Sovereign Debt and Repudiation," 16; William Armstrong to T. Hartley Crawford, February 28, 1842, LROIA 171 [157]; William Armstrong to T. Hartley Crawford, June 22, 1842, LROIA 171 [165–66]; William Armstrong to T. Hartley Crawford, November 1, 1842, LROIA 923 [580–81].

58. Memorial Letter from Chickasaw to John C. Spencer, October 26, 1842, LROIA 138 [1047–48].

59. William Armstrong to T. Hartley Crawford, June 22, 1842, LROIA 171 [165–66]; T. Hartley Crawford to Robert Stuart, August 13, 1842, LSOIA 32, 379; D. D. Mitchell to T. Hartley Crawford, September 1, 1842, LROIA 753 [127].

60. Crawford to J. L. Dawson et al., May 21, 1842, LSOIA 32, 192; *ARCIA* 1843, 386–87; Rich W. Cummins to D. D. Mitchell, July 2, 1842, Vol. 8, Collection 741, US Office of Indian Affairs, Central Superintendency, St. Louis, Missouri, William Clark Papers, Kansas Historical Society (hereafter cited as Clark Papers), 61; Robert A.

Callaway to D. D. Mitchell, October 24, 1843, Vol. 7, Collection 741, U.S. Office of Indian Affairs, Central Superintendency, St. Louis, Missouri, Clark Papers; Daniel Miller to D. D. Mitchell, June 24, 1842, LROIA 215 [876–77]; George Evans to T. H. Crawford, July 2, 1842, LROIA 854 [417–18].

61. John C. Spencer to Walter Forward, July 19, 1842, LSOIA 32, 336–37.

62. The act stipulated that the sums expended would "be reimbursed out of the interest when collected"; Pub. L. 27-275, 2 Stat. 576 (1842).

63. Ethan Allen Hitchcock to John C. Spencer, April 29, 1842, LROIA 138 [858–59]; Bond totals compiled from S. Rep. No. 27-116 (1841); Robert J. Walker to John W. Davis, February 4, 1846, Vol. 1, 578–80, MS Correspondence of the Secretary of the Treasury Relating to the Administration of Trust Funds for the Chickasaw and Other Indian Tribes, General Records of the Department of the Treasury; S. Rep. No. 28-49 (1845).

64. Ethan Allen Hitchcock to John C. Spencer, April 29, 1842, LROIA 138 [861–64]; Memorial Letter from Chickasaw to John C. Spencer, October 26, 1842, LROIA 138 [1047–49]; William Armstrong to T. Hartley Crawford, August 18, 1843, LROIA 138 [1082–83]; Amanda L. Paige, Fuller L. Bumpers, and Daniel F. Littlefield Jr., *Chickasaw Removal* (Chickasaw Press, 2010), 59; Arrell M. Gibson, *The Chickasaws* (University of Oklahoma Press, 1971), 184–205; Hitchcock, *A Traveler in Indian Territory*, 164–65, 168–69, 197–98; Joseph Dukes to [Commissioner of Indian Affairs], September 4, 1841, LROIA 138 [255–58]; S. Rep. No. 28-160, at 36 (1845); T. Hartley Crawford to Daniel Saffarans, October 1, 1842, Vol. 2, LSCR, 232–33; T. Hartley Crawford to J. M. Porter, June 26, 1843, Vol. 2, LSCR, 305–6; Daniel Saffarans to John C. Spencer, October 20, 1841, LROIA 854 [306–8]; T. Hartley Crawford to William Wilkins, December 7, 1844, Vol. 1, LSITF, 85.

65. Foreman, *Advancing the Frontier*, 99–104; Hitchcock to Spencer, April 29, 1842, LROIA 138 [861–64]; Chickasaw Memorial to T. Hartley Crawford, February 21, 1843, LROIA 138 [1100–1101].

66. Cong. Globe, 27th Cong., 1st Sess. 419–22 (1841); Davis Rich Dewey, *Financial History of the United States* (Longmans, Green, 1912), 235; Cong. Globe, 27th Cong., 1st Sess. 422 (1841). Linn's state, Missouri, had received $63,000 in investments from the Indian trust funds; H.R. Rep. No. 25-892, at 2–3 (1838).

67. Pub. L. 27-25, 1 Stat. 465 (1841).

68. L. Ray Gunn, *The Decline of Authority: Public Economic Policy and Political Development in New York, 1800–1860* (Cornell University Press, 1988), 146–47, 164, 184–85; John J. Wallis, "Constitutions, Corporations, and Corruption: American States and Constitutional Change, 1842 to 1852," *Journal of Economic History* 65, no. 1 (2005): 212–14; Naomi R. Lamoreaux and John Joseph Wallis, "Economic Crisis, General Laws, and the Mid-Nineteenth-Century Transformation of American Political Economy," *Journal of the Early Republic* 41, no. 3 (2021): 403–34.

69. Paul Fatout, *Indiana Canals* (Purdue University Press, 1972), 123–24; Jenks, *The Migration of British Capital*, 107.

70. *ARCIA* 1850, 139–40; Jonathan Sperber, *The European Revolutions, 1848–1851* (Cambridge University Press, 1994), 105–47; Niall Ferguson, "Political Risk and the International Bond Market Between the 1848 Revolution and the Outbreak of the First World War," *Economic History Review* 59, no. 1 (2006): 70–112; Sexton, *Debtor*

*Diplomacy*, 53–57; Max M. Edling, *A Hercules in the Cradle: War, Money, and the American State, 1783–1867* (University of Chicago Press, 2014), 166–74.

71. Aims McGuinness, *Path of Empire: Panama and the California Gold Rush* (Cornell University Press, 2008), 54–83; Leonard L. Richards, *The California Gold Rush and the Coming of the Civil War* (Alfred A. Knopf, 2007), 144–67; David M. Potter, *The Impending Crisis, 1848–1861* (Harper and Row, 1976), 63–89; Kevin Waite, *West of Slavery: The Southern Dream of a Transcontinental Empire* (University of North Carolina Press, 2021).

72. P. M. Butler to William Armstrong, May 18, 1845, LROIA 923 [787]; Notes on Grand Council in Creek Nation, May 12, 1845, LROIA 923 [793].

73. Foreman, *Advancing the Frontier*, 235; John M. Richardson to Samuel M. Rutherford, September 1, 1848, in *ARCIA* 1848, 161–62; Vere, *Contrary Neighbors*, 118.

74. Silverman, *Thundersticks*, 244–45.

## Chapter Six: Unsettled Claims

1. S. Doc. No. 28-49 (1845).

2. Daniel Carpenter, *Democracy by Petition: Popular Politics in Transformation, 1790–1870* (Harvard University Press, 2021), 121–22.

3. James Clifton, *The Prairie People: Continuity and Change in Potawatomi Indian Culture, 1665–1965* (University of Iowa Press, 1998), 329–40; G. W. Ewing Memorandum to Thomas Andrews, November 21, 1845, Thomas Patrick Andrews Papers, 1845–1850, Western Americana Collection, Beinecke Rare Book and Manuscript Library, Yale University (hereafter cited as Andrews Papers); G. W. Ewing to Thomas Andrews, November 30, 1845, Andrews Papers; G. W. Ewing to Thomas Andrews, December 8, 1845, Andrews Papers; George W. Ewing, "Confidential Suggestions as to How the Treaty with the Potawatomies May Be Made," March 16, 1846, Box Ayer MS 3067, Newberry Library, Chicago (emphasis in the original).

4. "Treaty with the Potawatomi Nation, 1846," in *Indian Affairs: Laws and Treaties*, vol. 2, *Treaties*, ed. Charles J. Kappler (GPO, 1904), 557–60.

5. H.R. Rep. Com. No. 31-489, at 74 (1850). In 1851 the Ewings and their business partner Alexis Coquillard secured a contract to carry out the removal of a group of Odawa, Ojibwe, and Potawatomis at fifty-five dollars per head, which eventually yielded them a 50 percent profit rate on the more than $35,000 paid them by the government. Robert A. Trennert, "The Business of Indian Removal," *Wisconsin Magazine* 63, no. 1 (1979): 36–50. See also "Treaty with the Potawatomi Nation, 1846," in Kappler, *Indian Affairs*, 2:557–59; and W. G. & G. W. Ewing, Traders, Claims Against the Potawatomi Indians, Treaty of June 1846, Special File No. 101, Special Files of the Office of Indian Affairs, 1807–1904, Microform Publication M574, Roll 15, BIA, NARA.

6. James L. Clayton, "The Growth and Economic Significance of the American Fur Trade, 1790–1890," in *Aspects of the Fur Trade: Selected Papers of the 1965 North American Fur Trade Conference*, ed. Dale L. Morgan (Minnesota Historical Society, 1967), 68; Jay Gitlin, "Private Diplomacy to Private Property: States, Tribes, and Nations in the Early National Period," *Diplomatic History* 22, no. 1 (1998): 85–99; H.R. Rep. No. 27-741, at 68 (1842).

7. Sources produced by Indigenous claimants reveal their legal strategies and interpretation even though they are almost always filtered through the mediation of non-Native actors like attorneys, bureaucrats, politicians, or judges. See Saliha Belmessous, ed., *Native Claims: Indigenous Law Against Empire, 1500–1920* (Oxford University Press, 2012), 3–15. On attorneys' contingency fees in this period, see Peter Karsten, "Enabling the Poor to Have Their Day in Court: The Sanctioning of Contingency Fee Contracts, a History to 1940," *DePaul Law Review* 47 (1998): 231–60.

8. "Thomas Forsyth to Lewis Cass, St. Louis, October 24, 1831: Draper Mss. 6T152r164," *Ethnohistory* 4, no. 2 (1957): 198–210; Susan Sleeper-Smith, *Indigenous Prosperity and American Conquest: Indian Women of the Ohio River Valley, 1690–1792* (Omohundro Institute / University of North Carolina Press, 2018), 162–209; James Axtell, *Beyond 1492: Encounters in Colonial North America* (Oxford University Press, 1992), 134; David J. Wishart, *Fur Trade in the American West, 1807–1840: A Geographical Synthesis* (University of Nebraska Press, 1979), 64, 92; Bert Anson, "The Fur Traders in Northern Indiana, 1796–1850" (PhD diss., Indiana University, 1953), 86, 95, 152–53; Michael John Witgen, *Seeing Red: Indigenous Land, American Expansion, and the Political Economy of Plunder in North America* (Omohundro Institute / University of North Carolina Press, 2022), 145–46; Bethel Saler, *The Settler's Empire: Colonialism and State Formation in America's Old Northwest* (University of Pennsylvania Press, 2015), 112, 141; Jay Gitlin, *The Bourgeois Frontier: French Towns, French Traders, and American Expansion* (Yale University Press, 2010), 87; David Lavender, *The Fist in the Wilderness* (Doubleday, 1964), xiii.

9. H.R. Doc. No. 25-229, at 36 (1839); James L. Clayton, "The Impact of Traders' Claims on the American Fur Trade," in *The Frontier in American Development: Essays in Honor of Paul Wallace Gates*, ed. David M. Ellis (Cornell University Press, 1969), 307, 311–12; Sen. Doc. No. 25-198 (1838); "Thomas Forsyth to Lewis Cass," 201; Anson, "The Fur Traders in Northern Indiana," 122.

10. For discussions of Indian agent corruption in later periods, see Ryan Hall, "Patterns of Plunder: Corruption and the Failure of the Indian Reservation System, 1851–1887," *Western Historical Quarterly* 55, no. 1 (2024): 21–37; William Unrau, "The Civilian as Indian Agent: Villain or Victim?," *Western Historical Quarterly* 3, no. 4 (1972): 405–20; Jerome O. Steffen, *William Clark: Jeffersonian Man on the Frontier* (University of Oklahoma Press, 1977), 73; John E. Sunder, *Joshua Pilcher: Fur Trader and Indian Agent* (University of Oklahoma Press, 1968); Robert A. Trennert Jr., "The Fur Trader as Indian Administrator: Conflict of Interest or Wise Policy?," *South Dakota History* 5, no. 1 (1974): 1–19; Gitlin, *The Bourgeois Frontier*, 70; John D. Haeger, "The American Fur Company and the Chicago of 1812–1835," *Journal of the Illinois State Historical Society* 61, no. 2 (1968): 117–39; Witgen, *Seeing Red*, 149, 253; Susan Sleeper-Smith, *Indian Women and French Men: Rethinking Cultural Encounter in the Western Great Lakes* (University of Massachusetts Press, 2001); Lucy Eldersveld Murphy, *Great Lakes Creoles: A French-Indian Community on the Northern Borderlands, Prairie du Chien, 1750–1860* (Cambridge University Press, 2014); Tanis Thorne, *The Many Hands of My Relations: French and Indians on the Lower Missouri* (University of Missouri Press, 1996).

11. *ARCIA* 1838, 465; W. M. Bateman to Elbert Herring, April 4, 1835, LROIA 76 [413–14].

12. *ARCIA* 1837, 614; *ARCIA* 1841, 239; Anthony F. C. Wallace, *Jefferson and the Indians: The Tragic Fate of the First Americans* (Belknap Press of Harvard University Press, 1999), 19–20; Christian B. Keller, "Philanthropy Betrayed: Thomas Jefferson, the Louisiana Purchase, and the Origins of Federal Indian Removal Policy," *Proceedings of the American Philosophical Society* 144, no. 1 (2000): 39–66; Ronald N. Satz, *American Indian Policy in the Jacksonian Era* (University of Nebraska Press, 1974), 110.

13. Isaac McCoy, *History of Baptist Indian Missions: Embracing Remarks on the Former and Present Condition of the Aboriginal Tribes and Their Settlement Within the Indian Territory, and Their Future Prospects* (H. and S. Raynor, 1840), 495; Witgen, *Seeing Red*, 207.

14. Pub. L. 24-62, 5 Stat. 29 (1836); and Gitlin, "Private Diplomacy to Private Property." Only a handful of treaties signed in the 1800s and 1810s had addressed trade debts.

15. H.R. Rep. No. 23-474, at 80–81 (1834); H.R. Rep. No. 27-741, at 35 (1842); *ARCIA* 1837, 659; Gitlin, *The Bourgeois Frontier*, 74. In addition to the dozens submitted to the Office of Indian Affairs, at least twenty trader claims were heard in Congress between 1842 and 1847. See Maggie Blackhawk, Daniel Carpenter, Tobias Resch, and Benjamin Schneer, "Replication Data for: Congressional Representation by Petition: Assessing the Voices of the Voteless in a Comprehensive New Database, 1789–1949," V1, 2020, https://doi.org/10.7910/DVN/JMOXQI.

16. R. David Edmunds, "'Designing Men, Seeking a Fortune': Indian Traders and the Potawatomi Claims Payment of 1836," *Indiana Magazine of History* 77, no. 2 (1981): 114.

17. Robert A. Trennert, *Indian Traders on the Middle Border: The House of Ewing, 1827–54* (University of Nebraska Press, 1981), 35–36; Anson, "The Fur Traders in Northern Indiana," 205–54; George W. Ewing to William G. Ewing, November 14, 1839, Box 4, Folder Oct.–Dec. 1839, Ewing Family Papers, Indiana State Library.

18. Annuities also kept the American Fur Company afloat during the economic downturn of 1837–43. See Clayton, "The Impact of Traders' Claims on the American Fur Trade," 316–17.

19. H.R. Rep. No. 27-741, at 14, 26, 58–59, 79 (1842); Thomas H. Crawford to William Lewis, December 2, 1841, LSCR, 158; Thomas H. Crawford to John Tyler, February 4, 1842, LSCR, 194–95.

20. Dennis East, "Land Speculation in the Chickasaw Cession: A Study of the New York and Mississippi Land Company, 1835–1889" (MA thesis, University of Wisconsin–Madison, 1964), 6–10; Amanda L. Paige, Fuller L. Bumpers, and Daniel F. Littlefield Jr., *Chickasaw Removal* (Chickasaw Press, 2010), 59; Mary Elizabeth Young, *Redskins, Ruffleshirts, and Rednecks: Indian Allotments in Alabama and Mississippi, 1830–1860* (University of Oklahoma Press, 1961), 120–21.

21. P. G. Randolph to Benjamin Reynolds, October 7, 1830, LSOIA 7, 54; Young, *Redskins, Ruffleshirts, and Rednecks*, 66; S. Doc. No. 28-168 (1844); Claudio Saunt, *Unworthy Republic: The Dispossession of Native Americans and the Road to Indian Territory* (W. W. Norton, 2020), 204–5.

22. Thomas M. Barker to Lewis Cass, July 17, 1834, LROIA 136 [485–86]; "A friend of the Indian" to "My Excellent Sir," October 1835, LROIA 136 [569–70]; James W. Silver, "Land Speculation Profits in the Chickasaw Cession," *Journal of Southern History* 10, no. 1 (1944): 84–92; East, "Land Speculation in the Chickasaw Cession," 17; Saunt, *Unworthy Republic*, 209; Abstract of Chickasaw Testimony, Box 4, Special Files Relating to Indian Trust Funds, 1833–1898, Records of the Indian Division, Records of the Secretary of the Interior, RG 48, NARA II.

23. H.R. Rep. No. 24-663 (1836); Sen. Doc. No. 25-25 (1837); H.R. Rep. No. 27-271 (1843); S. Rep. No. 28-160 (1845); S. Doc. No. 28-168 (1844); Satz, *American Indian Policy*, 86–87; Young, *Redskins, Ruffleshirts, and Rednecks*, 193.

24. See for example, "Treaty with the Seneca, 1831," in Kappler, *Indian Affairs*, 2:326; "Treaty with the Seneca, etc., 1831," in Kappler, *Indian Affairs*, 2:329; "Treaty with the Shawnee, 1831," in Kappler, *Indian Affairs*, 2:332; "Treaty with the Ottawa, 1831," in Kappler, *Indian Affairs*, 2:336; "Treaty with the Wyandot, 1832," in Kappler, *Indian Affairs*, 2:339; "Treaty with the Creeks, 1832," in Kappler, *Indian Affairs*, 2:342; "Treaty with the Seminoles, 1832," in Kappler, *Indian Affairs*, 2:344; "Treaty with the Chickasaws, 1832," in Kappler, *Indian Affairs*, 2:357; "Treaty with the Kickapoos, 1832," in Kappler, *Indian Affairs*, 2:366; "Treaties with the Shawnee, etc., 1832," in Kappler, *Indian Affairs*, 2:371; "Treaties with the Kaskaskia, etc., 1832," in Kappler, *Indian Affairs*, 2:376; and "Treaty with the Menominee, 1832," in Kappler, *Indian Affairs*, 2:378.

25. Sen. Doc. No. 29-135 (1846); William G. McLoughlin, *After the Trail of Tears: The Cherokees' Struggle for Sovereignty, 1839-1880* (University of North Carolina Press, 1993), 41.

26. H.R. Doc. No. 27-219, at 15–16, 91, 105 (1843).

27. 1831 Choctaw Poem, Folder 110A, PPPH.

28. S. Rep. No. 27-116 (1841); Memorial Letter of Chickasaw Commissioners to William Armstrong, March 8, 1839, LROIA 137 [484–86]; Petition from Chickasaws to A. M. M. Upshaw, April 1 1840, LROIA 138 [11–12]; William Armstrong to T. Hartley Crawford, February 28, 1842, LROIA 138 [334]; E. A. Hitchcock to J. C. Spencer, April 29, 1842, LROIA 138 [858–59]; Chickasaw Memorial Letter to John C. Spencer, October 26, 1842, LROIA 138 [1047–49]; T. Hartley Crawford to A. M. M. Upshaw, December 20, 1842, Vol. 2, LSCR, 270; Isaac Alberson et al. to J. C. Spencer, May 6, 1843, LROIA 138 [1072–74]; Trust Fund Journals, Vol. 1, Records of the Finance Division, BIA, NARA, 72, 80, 83, 92, 107, 131; Ishtehotopa, Tishomingo, William McGilvery, Pistalatubby, Isaac Albertson, et al. to Andrew Jackson, February 17, 1837, LROIA 137 [148–50].

29. Lately Thomas, *Between Two Empires: The Life Story of California's First Senator, William McKendree Gwin* (Houghton Mifflin, 1969), 19; Rachel St. John, "The Unpredictable America of William Gwin: Expansion, Secession, and the Unstable Borders of Nineteenth-Century North America," *Journal of the Civil War Era* 6, no. 1 (2016): 56–84; Hallie Mae McPherson, "William McKendree Gwin, Expansionist" (PhD diss., University of California–Berkeley, 1931), 6, 8–9, 49–56; James P. Shenton, *Robert John Walker, a Politician from Jackson to Lincoln* (Columbia University Press, 1961), 13–14; S. Doc. 23-151 (1835); Young, *Redskins, Ruffleshirts, and Rednecks*, 53–54, 65–71; Gordon T. Chappell, "Some Patterns of Land Speculation

in the Old Southwest," *Journal of Southern History* 15, no. 4 (1949): 463–77; Saunt, *Unworthy Republic*, 202–8; J. F. Bivins, "The Life and Character of Jacob Thompson," in *Historical Papers, Legal and Biographical Studies, Historical Society of Trinity College* (A.M.S. Press, 1898): 85; Franklin L. Riley, "Choctaw Land Claims," in *Publications of the Mississippi Historical Society*, vol. 8 (Mississippi Historical Society, 1904), 353–54.

30. H.R. Rep. No. 42-98, at 475–76, 480 (1873); "Charles E. Mix," in *The Commissioners of Indian Affairs, 1824–1977*, ed. Robert M. Kvasnicka and Herman J. Viola (University of Nebraska Press, 1979), 77–79; William M. Wiecek, "The Origin of the United States Court of Claims," *Administrative Law Review* 20, no. 3 (1968): 395.

31. H.R. Rep. Com. No. 31-489, at 13–14, 238 (1850); William Armstrong to T. Hartley Crawford, June 10, 1845, LROIA 139 [144–46]; Duane Champagne, *Social Order and Political Change: Constitutional Governments Among the Cherokee, the Choctaw, the Chickasaw, and the Creek* (Stanford University Press, 1992), 162–63, 194–95; William Armstrong to T. Hartley Crawford, July 27, 1845, LROIA 139 [151–52]; C. A. Harris to R. D. C. Collins, April 3, 1837, Vol. 1, LSCR, 140–41; C. A. Harris to J. A. Philips, April 3, 1837, Vol. 1, LSCR, 142; A. M. M. Upshaw to C. A. Harris, July 7, 1837, LROIA 143 [319]; C. A. Harris to J. A. Phillips, July 7, 1837, Vol. 1, LSCR, 179; C. A. Harris to A. M. M. Upshaw, June 13, 1838, Vol. 1, LSCR, 263–65; H.R. Rep. No. 27-604 (1842); Paige et al., *Chickasaw Removal*, 102; Holmes Colbert, *Exceptions to the Account Stated, Under the Direction of the Secretary of the Interior* [. . .] (McGill, 1869); H.R. Rep. Com. No. 31-489, at 13–14 (1850); List of Attorneys Having Contracts for Services with Indians and Indian Tribes, Special File No. 18, Records of the Indian Division, Office of the Secretary of the Interior Special Files, 1848–1907, BIA, NARA II.

32. "Treaty with the Chickasaws, 1834," in Kappler, *Indian Affairs*, 2:422; Chickasaw Delegation to Andrew Jackson, March 7, 1834, Box B1-3, 23rd Cong., Records of Early Select Committees, 1789–1921, BIA, NARA; Order of Andrew Jackson, December 12, 1836, Vol. 1, TTFC, 136–37; S. Doc No. 28-49 (1845); Gregory C. Sisk, "A Primer on the Doctrine of Federal Sovereign Immunity," *Oklahoma Law Review* 51, no. 4 (2005): 443–46; Louis Jaffee, "Suits Against Governments and Officers: Sovereign Immunity," *Harvard Law Review* 77, no. 1 (1963): 1–39.

33. H.R. Rep. Com. No. 31-489, at 13 (1850); S. Rep. No. 28-49 (1845).

34. S. Rep. No. 28-49 (1845).

35. On the enduring centrality of reciprocity in post-Mississippian cultures, see Robbie Ethridge, *From Chicaza to Chickasaw: The European Invasion and the Transformation of the Mississippian World, 1540–1715* (University of North Carolina Press, 2010), 251–52. On reciprocity as a tenet of Indigenous law, see Katherine A. Hermes, "The Law of Native Americans, to 1815," in *The Cambridge History of Law in America*, vol. 1, *Early America (1580–1815)*, ed. Michael Grossberg and Christopher Tomlins (Cambridge University Press, 2008), 37–44; Lisa Ford, *Settler Sovereignty: Jurisdiction and Indigenous People in America and Australia* (Harvard University Press, 2010), 35.

36. H.R. Doc. No. 37-93, at 2–3 (1843).

37. Remarkably, the Senate Judiciary Committee initially granted the Chickasaw request, but Mississippi representative Jacob Thompson blocked the bill's passage in

the House, prompting Gwin to challenge him to a duel. See S. Rep. No. 28-49 (1845); Cong. Globe, 28th Cong., 2nd Sess., 394 (1845); Shenton, *Robert John Walker*, 67; and P. L. Rainwater, "Letters to and from Jacob Thompson," *Journal of Southern History* 6, no. 1 (1940): 103.

38. H.R. Rep. Com. No. 31-489, at 14 (1850); Young, *Redskins, Ruffleshirts, and Rednecks*, 67–68; Henry Cohen, *Business and Politics in America from the Age of Jackson to the Civil War: The Career Biography of W. W. Corcoran* (Greenwood, 1971), xv, 6–9, 118–19. The attorneys were Robert G. Corwin and Caleb B. Smith (a former representative from Indiana and future secretary of the interior under President Abraham Lincoln). Smith was also, at the time, serving on the Board of Mexican Commissioners, which reviewed claims stemming from the 1848 Treaty of Guadelupe Hidalgo. See H.R. Rep. Com. No. 31-489, at 14 (1850).

39. Reverdy Johnson to Thos. Ewing, January 3, 1850, in H.R. Rep. Com. No. 31-489, at 217–18 (1850); Cohen, *Business and Politics in America*, 121; Orestus Browning to Thomas Ewing, January 7, 1850, Vol. 3, LSCR, 87–88; Reverdy Johnson to Thomas Ewing, March 7, 1850, in H.R. Rep. Com. No. 31-489, at 218–19 (1850); "Remarks of Mr. Gwin," Cong. Globe, 31st Cong., 1st Sess., app., 387 (1851).

40. Johnson to Ewing, January 3, 1850; Reverdy Johnson to Thomas Ewing, March 7, 1850, in H.R. Doc. No. 31-55, at 2145–46 (1851); H.R. Rep. Com. No. 31-489, at 12 (1850). In 1888 the US Court of Claims recommended that this amount be repaid to the Chickasaws. Chickasaw Nation v. United States, 19 Ct. Cl. 133 (1884); H.R. Ex. Doc. No. 50-42 (1888).

41. Sen. Ex. Doc. No. 30-28 (1849); Sen. Ex. Doc. No. 32-32 (1852); Amos Kendall, *A Letter to the Hon. George E. Badger in Relation to the Claim of A. & J. E. Kendall Against the United States, for Certain Wrongs Done Them* (Buell and Blanchard, 1852); [S. C. Stambaugh and Amos Kendall,] *A Faithful History of the Cherokee Tribe of Indians, from the Period of our First Intercourse with Them, Down to the Present Time* (Jesse E. Dow, 1846); David R. M. Beck, *Siege and Survival: History of the Menominee Indians, 1634–1856* (University of Nebraska Press, 2002), 176–80; S. Ex. Doc. No. 34-72, at 6–7 (1856); Cohen, *Business and Politics in America*, 121; Charles Roll, *Colonel Dick Thompson: The Persistent Whig* (Indiana Historical Bureau, 1948), 116–22.

42. Pub. L. Ch. 29-66, 9 Stat. 203 (1847), 203.

43. William Medill to Thomas Harvey, August 30, 1847, LSOIA 40, 33; William Medill to Samuel Rutherford, September 1, 1847, LSOIA 40, 42.

44. Medill to Harvey, August 30, 1847.

45. *ARCIA* 1848, 19; H.R. Rep. Com. No. 31-489 (1850); Pub. L. Ch. 32-108, 10 Stat. 41 (1852), 41–56; *ARCIA* 1854, 230.

46. Pub. L. Ch. 29-34, 9 Stat. 20 (1846); H.R. Rep. No. 29-53 (1847); Pub. L. Ch. 29-66, 9 Stat. 203 (1847).

47. T. Hartley Crawford Circular, August 9, 1842, in *ARCIA* 1842, 386.

48. William Medill to James McKisick, October 25, 1847, LSOIA 40, 139; William Medill to James McKisick, November 19, 1847, LSOIA 40, 165–66.

49. "Treaty with the Potawatomi Nation," in Kappler, *Indian Affairs*, 2:558–59.

50. Ratified Treaty No. 249: Documents Relating to the Negotiation of the Treaty of October 13, 1846, with the Winnebago Indians, 59–60, Documents Relating to the

Negotiation of Ratified and Unratified Treaties with Various Tribes of Indians, 1801–1869, BIA, NARA; Tim Rowse, "Population Knowledge and the Practice of Guardianship," *American Nineteenth Century History* 15, no. 1 (2014): 15–42.

51. Daniel Kurtz to S. T. Jamison, November 4, 1834, LSOIA 14, 135; R. David Edmunds, "The Prairie Potawatomi Removal of 1833," *Indiana Magazine of History* 68, no. 3 (1972): 248. For earlier relationships between the Kickapoos and Western Potawatomis, see James Clifton, *Prairie People*, 236; and William Medill to Thomas Harvey, September 9, 1848, LSOIA 41, 228.

52. Orestus Browning to J. C. Mason, March 30, 1850, LSOIA 43, 110. Despite this ultimatum, the Potawatomi continued to live among the Kickapoo and request annuities without success. See, for example, W. H. Richardson to Luke Lea, August 18, 1851, LROIA 678 [134]. Northern bands of Kickapoos and the Potawatomis they hosted signed an articles of agreement in 1851 formalizing their relationship and the sharing of their resources. A. M. Gibson, *The Kickapoos: Lords of the Middle Border* (University of Oklahoma Press, 1963), 117–18.

53. *ARCIA* 1850, 48 (emphasis in the original).

54. Orestus Browning to D. D. Mitchell, April 13, 1850, LSOIA 43, 128–29.

55. William Medill to Thomas H. Harvey, February 20, 1849, LSOIA 41, 495.

56. Orestus Browning to A. M. Mitchell, March 2, 1850, LSOIA 43, 52–55.

57. S. Rep. Com. No. 32–181 (1852); Young, *Redskins, Ruffleshirts, and Rednecks*, 52–62; Clara Sue Kidwell, *The Choctaws in Oklahoma: From Tribe to Nation, 1855–1970* (University of Oklahoma Press, 2007), 19.

58. Thomson McKinney to Forbis Leflore, October 28, 1850, Box 1, Folder 36, J. L. Hargett Collection of Choctaw Nation Papers, Yale Collection of Western Americana, Beinecke Rare Book and Manuscript Library, Yale University (hereafter cited as Hargett Collection); Thomson McKinney to Forbis Leflore, November 18, 1850, Box 1, Folder 36, Hargett Collection; Kidwell, *The Choctaws in Oklahoma*, 19–20; *ARCIA* 1848, 23–24, 108–9; Choctaw Nation, *The Constitution and Laws of the Choctaw Nation, Together with the Treaties of 1855, 1865 and 1866*, comp. Joseph P. Folsom (William P. Lyon and Son, 1869), 121.

59. Carolyn Thomas Foreman, "New Hope Seminary, 1844–1897," *Chronicles of Oklahoma* 22, no. 3 (1944): 272–73; G. W. Hawkins to Thomson McKinney, September 30, 1855, Box 1, Folder 1855–56, Hargett Collection.

60. Thomson McKinney to Forbis LeFlore, January 25, 1851, Box 1, Folder 36, Hargett Collection; Thompson McKinney to Forbis Leflore, February 12, 1851, Box 1, Folder 37, Hargett Collection.

61. McKinney to Leflore, February 12, 1851; Elsie M. Lewis, "Robert Ward Johnson: Militant Spokesman of the Old South-West," *Arkansas Historical Quarterly* 13 (1954): 16–30. McKinney graduated from Choctaw Academy in 1836; see Certificate from the Choctaw Academy to Thompson McKinney, December 24, 1836, Choctaw Nation Papers, Western Historical Collection, Oklahoma University.

62. Thomson McKinney to Forbis LeFlore, February 4, 1851, Box 1, Folder 36, Hargett Collection.

63. McKinney to Leflore, February 12, 1851.

64. Like others in the Office of Indian Affairs, Luce had received extra pay from the Chickasaw fund at the rate of fifty dollars per month for his clerical work; see

John B. Luce to J. R. Poinsett, December 24, 1848. See also Robert Mills, *Guide to the National Executive Offices and the Capitol of the United States* (P. Force, 1841), 100; McKinney to Leflore, October 28, 1850; and McKinney to LeFlore, February 4, 1851.

65. McKinney to Leflore, February 12, 1851.

66. Pub. L. No. 32-66, 10 Stat. 15 (1852); *ARCIA* 1851, 268–69, 300–301; Choctaw Nation, *Constitution and Laws of the Choctaw Nation*, 121; Thomson McKinney to Forbis Leflore, August 10, 1851, Box 1, Folder 37, Hargett Collection; Thomson McKinney to Forbis Leflore, December 21, 1851, Box 1, Folder 37, Hargett Collection; Thomson McKinney to Forbis LeFlore, September 6, 1852, Box 1, Folder 37, Hargett Collection; Kidwell, *The Choctaws in Oklahoma*, 19–20; W. David Baird, *Peter Pitchlynn: Chief of the Choctaws* (University of Oklahoma, 1986), 95; Thomson McKinney to Forbis Leflore, August 24, 1853, Box 1, Folder 38, Hargett Collection.

67. Choctaw Nation, *Papers Relating to the Claims of the Choctaw Nation Against the United States, Arising Out of the Treaty of 1830* (A. O. P. Nicholson, 1855); Colin Calloway, *The Chiefs Now in This City: Indians and the Urban Frontier in Early America* (Oxford University Press, 2021), 42–70; *Daily Union* (Washington, DC), March 31, 1853.

68. Order in Council by Chiefs and Headmen of Wyandot Nation, 1842, Folder 6, John M. Armstrong Manuscript Collection, Helmerich Research Center, Gilcrease Museum, Tulsa, OK (hereafter cited as Armstrong Collection); Sen. Doc. No. 29-13 (1846); T. W. Bartley to John M. Armstrong, June 22, 1846, Folder 41, Armstrong Collection; Power of Attorney from Shawnee Band of Missouri, July 14, 1852, Folder 112, Armstrong Collection; Order in Council of Munsee Nation, Folder 80, Armstrong Collection.

69. Baird, *Peter Pitchlynn*, 67, 71–72.

70. Kidwell, *The Choctaws in Oklahoma*, 20–22; Baird, *Peter Pitchlynn*, 97–98; Peter Pitchlynn to Thomson McKinney, March 2, 1854, Box 1, Folder 45, Hargett Collection.

71. Choctaw Nation, *Papers Relating to the Claims of the Choctaw Nation*, 16.

72. Kidwell, *The Choctaws in Oklahoma*, 20–24; Baird, *Peter Pitchlynn*, 97–98, 117–19; Walter Lee Brown, *A Life of Albert Pike* (University of Arkansas Press, 1997), 303–4; Remarks on the "History" of the Claim of the Choctaw Indians [. . .], Folder 2301, PPPH; S. Rep. Com. No. 36-283 (1860).

73. Robert Wooster, *American Military Frontiers: The United States Army in the West, 1783–1900* (University of New Mexico Press, 2009), 117, 119; D. W. Meinig, *The Shaping of America: A Geographical Perspective on 500 Years of History*, vol. 2, *Continental America, 1800–1867* (Yale University Press, 1995), 159; Samuel Watson, "Military Learning and Adaptation Shaped by Social Context: The U.S. Army and Its 'Indian Wars,' 1790–1890," *Journal of Military History* 82, no. 2 (2018): 401–2; Durwood Ball, *Army Regulars on the Western Frontier, 1848–1861* (University of Oklahoma Press, 2001); Robert M. Utley, *Frontiersmen in Blue: The United States Army and the Indian, 1848–1865* (Macmillan, 1967); *ARCIA* 1851, 271–72; Robert A. Trennert Jr., *Alternative to Extinction: Federal Indian Policy and the Beginnings of the Reservation System, 1846–1851* (Temple University Press, 1975), 45–60; Francis P.

Prucha, *The Great Father: The United States Government and the American Indians*, vol. 1 (University of Nebraska Press, 1984), 328–32; Rachel St. John, "State Power in the West in the Early American Republic," *Journal of the Early Republic* 38, no. 1 (2018): 87–94.

74. Max Edling, *Hercules in the Cradle: War, Money, and the American State, 1783–1867* (University of Chicago Press, 2014), 147–53; Rafael A. Bayley, *The National Loans of the United States, from July 4, 1776, to June 30, 1880* (GPO, 1882), 70–73; Treaty of Peace, Friendship, Limits, and Settlement [. . .], in *Treaties and Conventions Concluded Between the United States and Other Powers Since July 4, 1776* (GPO, 1873), 562–73. For the history of these claims, which preceded the Mexican-American War, see Peter M. Jonas, "William Parrot, American Claims, and the Mexican War," *Journal of the Early Republic* 12, no. 2 (1992): 213–40. Richard Griswold del Castillo, *The Treaty of Guadelupe Hidalgo: A Legacy of Conflict* (University of Oklahoma Press, 1990), 58–59; U.S. Bureau of the Census, *Report on Indians Taxed and Not Taxed in the United States (Except Alaska) at the Eleventh Census* (GPO, 1894), 641.

75. See, for example, H.R. 617, 22nd Cong. (1832); S. 146, 29th Cong. (1847); S. 92, 28th Cong (1845); Larry C. Skogen, *Indian Depredation Claims, 1796–1920* (University of Oklahoma Press, 1996); Kristin A. Collins, "'Petitions Without Number': Widows' Petitions and the Early Nineteenth-Century Origins of Marriage-Based Entitlements," *Law and History Review* 31, no. 1 (2013): 1–60; Carpenter, *Democracy by Petition*, 66–67; Maggie McKinley, "Petitioning and the Making of the Administrative State," *Yale Law Journal* 127, no. 6 (2018): 1538–637.

76. Wiecek, "The Origin of the United States Court of Claims," 395–98; David Wilkins, *Hollow Justice: A History of Indigenous Claims in the United States* (Yale University Press, 2013), 8–9, 11; Floyd D. Shimomura, "The History of Claims Against the United States: The Evolution from a Legislative Toward a Judicial Model of Payment," *Louisiana Law Review* 45 (1985): 625–700. Both cases were dismissed, in 1876 and 1878. "Creek Nation v. The United States, Attorney Albert Pike, March 3, 1856," Vol. 1, Cases 1–1014, 5/23/1855–5/8/1857, General Court Dockets, 1855–1959, Records of the U.S. Court of Claims, RG 123, NARA, 130; "Muscogee and Creek Nation of Indians v The United States, Atty Albert Pike, March 13, 1856," Vol. 1, Cases 1–1014, 5/23/1855–5/8/1857, General Court Dockets, 1855–1959, Records of the U.S. Court of Claims, RG 123, NARA, 132.

77. *ARCIA* 1851, 289–90; *ARCIA* 1853, 362; *ARCIA* 1856, 622; Pekka Hämäläinen, *Lakota America: A New History of Indigenous Power* (Yale University Press, 2019), 220–35; Jeffrey Ostler, *The Plains Sioux and U.S. Colonialism from Lewis and Clark to Wounded Knee* (Cambridge University Press, 2004), 36–43; Stan Hoig, *White Man's Paper Trail: Grand Councils and Treaty-Making on the Central Plains* (University Press of Colorado, 2006); Paul Conrad, *The Apache Diaspora: Four Centuries and Displacement* (University of Pennsylvania Press, 2021), 185–86.

78. *ARCIA* 1851, 274.

79. See, for example, "Treaty with the Ottawa and Chippewa, 1855," in Kappler, *Indian Affairs*, 2:725–30; "Treaty with the Chippewa of Saginaw, 1855," in Kappler, *Indian Affairs*, 2:733–35; "Treaty with the Creeks, etc., 1856," in Kappler, *Indian*

*Affairs*, 2:756–763; and "Treaty with the Chippewa—Red Lake and Pembina Bands, 1863," in Kappler, *Indian Affairs*, 2:853–855.

## Chapter Seven: The Fall and Rise of Fiduciary Colonialism

1. *ARCIA* 1861, 810; George W. Riggs to Moses Kelly, February 21, 1861, Unregistered Letters Received Related to Trust Funds, Box 2, Records Relating to Indian Trust Funds, Records of the Indian Division, Records of the Office of the Secretary of the Interior, RG 48, NARA II.

2. On the Civil War's reverberations across Native territories and implications for federal-Native relations, see Elliott West, "Reconstructing Race," *Western Historical Quarterly* 34 (2003): 6–26; Elliott West, *The Last Indian War: The Nez Perce Story* (Oxford University Press, 2009), 97–104; Gregory P. Downs, *After Appomattox: Military Occupation and the Ends of War* (Harvard University Press, 2015), 100–103, 144–45; Pekka Hämäläinen, "Reconstructing the Great Plains: The Long Struggle for Sovereignty and Dominance in the Heart of the Continent," *Journal of the Civil War Era* 6, no. 4 (2016): 481–509; and Khal Schneider, "Distinctions That Must Be Preserved: On the Civil War, American Indians, and the West," *Civil War History* 62, no. 1 (2016): 36–54.

3. Sean Patrick Adams, "Wartime Political Economy," in *A Companion to the U.S. Civil War*, vol. 2, ed. Aaron Sheehan-Dean (Wiley Blackwell, 2014), 1073–86; Peter A. Coclanis, "The American Civil War in Economic Perspective: Basic Questions and Some Answers," *Southern Cultures* 2, no. 2 (1996): 163–75; Steven Hahn, *A Nation Without Borders: The United States and Its World in an Age of Civil Wars, 1830–1910* (Penguin, 2016); Richard Franklin Bensel, *Yankee Leviathan: The Origins of Central State Authority in America, 1859–1877* (Cambridge University Press, 1990); Heather Cox Richardson, *The Greatest Nation of the Earth: Republican Economic Policies During the Civil War* (Harvard University Press, 1997); Emma Teitelman, "The Properties of Capitalism: Industrial Enclosures in the South and the West after the American Civil War," *Journal of American History* 106, no. 4 (2020): 879–900.

4. "Statement of Nonpaying Stocks," March 15, 1862, Vol. 3, LSITF, 16–22; Trust Fund Journal, Vol. 2, Journals and Ledgers for Indian Trust Funds, Records Concerning Indian Trust Funds, BIA, NARA, 261; John J. Cisco to William Dole, January 27, 1863, Box 2, Unregistered Letters Received Relating to Trust Funds, NARA II. For Missouri's financial disarray as a result of secessionism, see Mark W. Geiger, *Financial Fraud and Guerrilla Violence in Missouri's Civil War, 1861–1865* (Yale University Press, 2010); and William Dole to Caleb Smith, December 23, 1861, Vol. 3, LSITF, 2.

5. *ARCIA* 1850, 138–41; Proposal from Selden Withers & Co., May 23, 1851, LROIA 855 [701–3]; Charles Mix to Alex H. H. Stuart, June 20, 1851, Box 2, Unregistered Letters Received Relating to Trust Funds, NARA II; Charles Mix to Selden, Withers, Co., July 8, 1851, Vol. 1, LSITF, 374; Charles Mix to Selden, Withers & Co, July 14, 1851, Vol. 1, LSITF, 380; Luke Lea to A. H. H. Stuart, February 5, 1852, LROIA 855 [780–81]; Aaron Hall, "Slaves of the State: Infrastructure and Governance through Slavery in the Antebellum South," *Journal of American History* 106, no. 1 (2019): 39.

6. B. U. Ratchford, *American State Debts* (Duke University Press, 1941), 122–23; H.R. Ex. Doc. No. 35-3, at 269 (1857); *ARCIA* 1856, 570.

7. S. Ex. Doc. No. 36-3, at 313 (1860); *ARCIA* 1860, 242.

8. The Office of Indian Affairs calculated a total projected shortage of $378,183 by July 1863, which included $131,400 in interest missing on the bonds stolen by Godard Bailey and William Russell, as well as $28,403 owed by a still-delinquent Indiana. "Statement of Nonpaying Stocks," March 15, 1862, Vol. 3, LSITF, 16–22.

9. *ARCIA* 1857, 491.

10. Choctaw Delegation to George Manypenny, April 7, 1858, Folder 1508, PPPH; Regulations Adopted by Chickasaw Tribe at Boiling Springs, Folder 487, PPPH; *ARCIA* 1853, 400.

11. William H. Russell to William Waddell, August 30, 1859, Box 2, Folder 175, Russell, Majors, & Waddell Papers, Huntington Library, San Marino, CA (hereafter cited as Russell, Majors, & Waddell Papers); William H. Russell to William Waddell, June 29, 1860, Box 3, Folder 190, Russell, Majors, & Waddell Papers; Thomas P. Akers to William Waddell, December 26, 1860, Box 4, Folder RW 1, Russell, Majors, & Waddell Papers; Will Bagley and David L. Bigler, *The Mormon Rebellion: America's First Civil War, 1857-1858* (University of Oklahoma Press, 2011), 201, 244; Raymond W. Settle and Mary Lund Settle, *War Drums and Wagon Wheels: The Story of Russell, Majors, and Waddell* (University of Nebraska Press, 1966); Raymond W. Settle and Mary Lund Settle, *Saddles and Spurs: The Pony Express Saga* (Bonanza Books, 1955); H.R. Ex. Doc. No. 36-17 (1860). An inventory after the theft revealed one bond had been withdrawn years before by Senator G. N. Fitch, who had removed one $1000 Tennessee bond belonging to the Potawatomi education fund, apparently to determine whether interest could be paid on it; see H.R. Rep. No. 36-78, at 34, 134–35, 141 (1861). "The Great National Robbery," *New-York Daily Tribune*, December 25, 1860; "The Great National Robbery," *New-York Daily Tribune*, December 26, 1860; and "Our Washington Letter: The Indian Trust Fund Robbery," *Chicago Tribune*, December 29, 1860. Ironically, Bailey had criticized Californian missions for their financial exploitation of Native labor while serving as interim Commissioner of Indian Affairs. *ARCIA* 1858, 649–57; Schneider, "Distinctions That Must Be Preserved."

12. Peter P. Pitchlynn, Israel Folsom, and Peter Folsom to William P. Dole, March 16, 1861, File 13: Papers Concerning the Affairs of the Choctaw and Chickasaw, Box 4, Folder 3, Special Files Relating to Indian Trust Funds, Records of the Indian Division, Records of the Department of the Interior, RG 48, NARA II; Statement of Choctaw Funds, March 18, 1861, File 13: Papers Concerning the Affairs of the Choctaw and Chickasaw, Box 4, Folder 3, Special Files Relating to Indian Trust Funds, Records of the Indian Division, Records of the Department of the Interior, RG 48, NARA II.

13. Folsom also suggested that the Choctaw obtain direct assurances of payment from the states in whose bonds their funds were invested. Peter Folsom to Peter P. Pitchlynn, January 19, 1861, Peter Pitchlynn Papers, Native American Manuscripts, Western Historical Collection, University of Oklahoma Libraries.

14. Choctaw Delegates to William Dole, March 15, 1861, Folder 1877, PPPH.

15. W. David Baird, *Peter Pitchlynn: Chief of the Choctaws* (University of Oklahoma Press, 1986), 113–21; Undated Address Given by Peter Pitchlynn, Folder 1899, PPPH.

16. Alvin M. Josephy, *The Civil War in the American West* (Vintage Books, 1991), 34–35; Mary Jane Warde, *When the Wolf Came: The Civil War and the Indian*

*Territory* (University of Arkansas Press, 2013), 47–51; Edmund J. Danziger, *Indians and Bureaucrats: Administering the Reservation Policy During the Civil War* (University of Illinois Press, 1974), 166–67; William H. Emory Report, May 19, 1861, in *Official Records of the Union and Confederate Navies in the War of the Rebellion*, ser. 1, vol. 1 (GPO, 1894), 648–49; E. H. Carruth to William Coffin, July 11, 1861, LROIA 834 [952–57]; Charles R. Keith to Col. H. B. Branch, August 24, 1861, LROIA 834 [900–901]. On Confederates' coercive methods of consolidating secessionism generally, see Stephanie McCurry, *Confederate Reckoning: Power and Politics in the Civil War South* (Harvard University Press, 2010), 38–84. See also Annie Heloise Abel, *The Slaveholding Indians*, vol. 3, *The American Indian Under Reconstruction* (Arthur H. Clark, 1915), 67n141; C. H. Carruth to Maj. Gen. Hunter, November 26, 1861, in *Report of the Commissioner of Indian Affairs, Accompanying the Annual Report of the Secretary of the Interior, for the Year 1861* (GPO, 1861), 46–47.

17. See, for example, *ARCIA* 1857, 492; William G. Coffin to William Dole, July 17, 1861, LROIA 834 [926–27]; and *ARCIA* 1861, 628.

18. Opotheleyohola and Ouktahnaserharjo [Ochtarsarsharjo] to Abraham Lincoln, August 15, 1861, quoted in Annie Heloise Abel, *The Slaveholding Indians, Volume 1: As Slaveholder and Secessionist* (Arthur H. Clark, 1919), 245–46n491.

19. "Resolutions of the Senate and House of Representatives of the Chickasaw Legislature Assembled, May 25, 1861," in *Official Records of the Union and Confederate Navies in the War of the Rebellion*, ser. 1, vol. 3 (GPO, 1881) 585–86.

20. Hahn, *A Nation Without Borders*, 202–4; Kevin Waite, *West of Slavery: The Southern Dream of a Transcontinental Empire* (University of North Carolina Press, 2021); Walter Johnson, *River of Dark Dreams: Slavery and Empire in the Cotton Kingdom* (Harvard University Press, 2013), 303–29; Matthew Karp, *This Vast Southern Empire: Slaveholders at the Helm of American Foreign Policy* (Harvard University Press, 2016); Albert Pike to Robert Toombs, May 20, 1861, in *Official Records of the Union and Confederate Navies*, ser. 1, vol. 3, 580–81; [Congress of the Confederate States of America], *Message of the President and Report of Albert Pike* (Enquirer Book and Job Press, 1861), 13–14; Troy Smith, "Nations Colliding: The Civil War Comes to Indian Territory," *Civil War History* 59, no. 3 (2013): 279–319; Brad Agnew, "Our Doom as a Nation Is Sealed: The Five Nations in the Civil War," in *The Civil War and Reconstruction in Indian Territory*, ed. Bradley Clampitt (University of Nebraska Press, 2015), 64–87; Walter Lee Brown, *A Life of Albert Pike* (University of Arkansas Press, 1997), 303–18.

21. David Hubbard to John Ross and Benjamin McCulloch, June 12, 1861, in *Official Records of the Union and Confederate Navies in the War of the Rebellion*, ser. 1, vol. 13 (GPO, 1885), 497–98; [Congress of the Confederate States of America], *Message of the President*, 4–5; "Civil War," Indian-Pioneer History Collection, ed. Grant Foreman, Vol. 69, University of Oklahoma Libraries Digital Collections; William G. Coffin to William Dole, June 3, 1861, LROIA 834 [914–15]; W. S. Robertson to William Dole, September 30, 1861, LROIA 834 [1071–72]; Evan Long to William Dole, October 31, 1861, LROIA 834 [1014–17]; Agnew, "Our Doom as a Nation is Sealed"; Barbara Krauthamer, *Black Slaves, Indian Masters: Slavery, Emancipation, and Citizenship in the Native American South* (University of North Carolina Press, 2013), 98–99; Fay A. Yarbrough, *Choctaw Confederates: The American Civil War in Indian*

*Country* (University of North Carolina Press, 2021), 90–91, 94–95; David A. Chang, *The Color of the Land: Race, Nation, and the Politics of Landownership in Oklahoma, 1832–1929* (University of North Carolina Press, 2010), 35–38; Warde, *When the Wolf Came*, 53–61; William G. McLoughlin, *After the Trail of Tears: The Cherokee's Struggle for Sovereignty, 1839–1880* (University of North Carolina Press, 1993), 176–200; Clarissa W. Confer, *The Cherokee Nation in the Civil War* (University of Oklahoma Press, 2007), 33–34, 49–59; H. Craig Miner Warde and William E. Unrau, *The End of Indian Kansas: A Study of Cultural Revolution, 1854–1871* (University Press of Kansas), 7–9, 14–24; Nicole Etcheson, *Bleeding Kansas: Contested Liberty in the Civil War Era* (University Press of Kansas, 2004), 29; Paul W. Gates, *Fifty Million Acres: Conflicts over Kansas Land Policy, 1854–1890* (University of Oklahoma Press, 1997), 23.

22. "Treaty with the Creek Nation, July 10, 1861," in *The Statutes at Large of the Provisional Government of the Confederate States of America*, ed. J. M. Matthews (R. M. Smith, 1864), 289–310; "Treaty with the Choctaws and Chickasaws, July 12, 1861," in Matthews, *The Statutes at Large*, 312–31; "Treaty with the Seminole Nation, Aug. 1, 1861," in Matthews, *The Statutes at Large*, 332–45; "Treaty with the Cherokees, Oct. 7, 1861," in Matthews, *The Statutes at Large*, 394–411; Warde, *When the Wolf Came*, 54, 60–61. Pike estimated that a force of between thirty-five hundred and five thousand Native men could be raised from Indian Territory; Albert Pike to R. W. Johnson, May 11, 1861, in *Official Records of the Union and Confederate Navies*, ser. 1, vol. 3, 572–74. By December 1861 the Confederacy had raised four regiments of Cherokee, Chickasaw, Choctaw, Creek, and Seminole soldiers, counting more than four thousand troops; see Abel, *The Slaveholding Indians*, vol, 1, *The American Indian as Slaveholder and Secessionist* (Arthur H. Clark, 1915), 252; and Douglas Cooper Proclamation to Cherokees, Creeks, Choctaws, Chickasaws, Seminoles, etc., October 23, 1861, Folder 1911, PPPH. See also Laurence M. Hauptman, *Between Two Fires: American Indians in the Civil War* (Free Press, 1995).

23. Act of January 10, 1862, in Matthews, *The Statutes at Large*, 239–40. See also "Act of April 8, 1862," in *Public Laws of the Confederate States of America, Passed at the First Session of the First Congress, 1862*, ed. James M. Matthews (R. M. Smith, 1862), 11–25.

24. Waite, *West of Slavery*, 141–78; Megan Kate Nelson, *The Three-Cornered War: The Union, the Confederacy, and Native Peoples in the Fight for the West* (Scribner, 2020) 5–14; Confederate States of America, Department of War, *Report of the Commissioner of Indian Affairs, March 13, 1862* (n.p., 1862), 5.

25. Confederate States of America, *Report of the Commissioner of Indian Affairs, March 13, 1862*, 9.

26. Thomas Weber, *The Northern Railroads in the Civil War, 1861–1865* (New York: Columbia University Press, 1952), 3–14; Bensel, *Yankee Leviathan*, 187; Jane Flaherty, *The Revenue Imperative: The Union's Financial Policies During the American Civil War* (Pickering and Chatto, 2009), 35–60; Max Edling, *Hercules in the Cradle: War, Money, and the American State, 1783–1867* (University of Chicago Press, 2014), 178.

27. James M. McPherson, *Battle Cry of Freedom: The Civil War Era* (Oxford University Press, 1988), 339–68; Flaherty, *The Revenue Imperative*, 74–75; Bray Hammond, *Sovereignty and an Empty Purse: Banks and Politics in the Civil War* (Princeton University Press, 1970), 71–106.

28. Jay Sexton, *Debtor Diplomacy: Finance and American Foreign Relations in the Civil War Era, 1837–1873* (Oxford University Press, 2005), 82–121; David K. Thomson, *Bonds of War: How Civil War Financial Agents Sold the World on the Union* (University of North Carolina Press, 2022), 93; Howard Jones, *Blue and Gray Diplomacy: A History of Union and Confederate Foreign Relations* (University of North Carolina Press, 2010), 83–112; Richardson, *The Greatest Nation of the Earth*, 41–46; Hammond, *Sovereignty and an Empty Purse*, 129–64; Flaherty, *The Revenue Imperative*, 85; Edling, *Hercules in the Cradle*, 188–90.

29. Joshua R. Greenberg, *Bank Notes and Shinplasters: The Rage for Paper Money in the Early Republic* (University of Pennsylvania Press, 2020), 159–90; Sharon Ann Murphy, *Other People's Money: How Banking Worked in the Early American Republic* (Johns Hopkins University Press, 2017), 133–62; Richardson, *The Greatest Nation of the Earth*, 47–48, 82–83, 107–36; Bensel, *Yankee Leviathan*, 169; Edling, *Hercules in the Cradle*, 192–96; W. E. Brownlee, *Federal Taxation in America: A History* (Cambridge University Press, 2016), 58–92; Ariel Ron and Sofia Valeonti, "The Money War: Democracy, Taxes and Inflation in the U.S. Civil War," *Cambridge Journal of Economics* 47, no. 2 (2023): 263–88; Christine Desan, "The Monetary Structure of Economic Activity: A Constitutional Analysis," *Law and Contemporary Problems* 86, no. 4 (2024): 77–110; Flaherty, *The Revenue Imperative*, 84–88; Thomson, *Bonds of War*, 55–84; Rafael A. Bayley, *The National Loans of the United States, from July 4, 1776, to June 30, 1880* (GPO, 1882), 70–71. For the wartime creation of the US Department of Agriculture, see Ariel Ron, *Grassroots Leviathan: Agricultural Reform and the Rural North in the Slaveholding Republic* (Johns Hopkins University Press, 2020).

30. Charles Mix to Caleb Smith, January 24, 1862, Vol. 3, LSITF, 10–11; *ARCIA* 1863, 156–57. For fluctuations in the London market value of Union bonds during the conflict, see Sexton, *Debtor Diplomacy*, figure 4, 97. See also Batiste Peoria, Yellow Beaver, and Taconah to Commissioner of Indian Affairs, May 1, 1863, LROIA 856 [1051–55]; Confederated Wea Indians Grant of Power of Attorney to Baptiste Peoria et al., LROIA 856 [1057–58]; William Dole to Baptiste Peoria et al., May 14, 1863, LROIA 856 [1060]; D. R. Martin to William Dole, June 31, 1863, LROIA 856 [992–93]; McPherson, *Battle Cry of Freedom*, 648.

31. D. R. Martin to William Dole, July 6, 1863, LROIA 856 [1021–22]; William Dole to D. R. Martin, July 14, 1863, Unregistered Letters Received Related to Trust Funds, Box 1, Records of the Indian Division, Records of the Office of the Secretary of the Interior, RG 48, NARA II.

32. Settle and Settle, *War Drums and Wagon Wheels*, 150–52; "Abstracted Bonds, Interest A/C," Ledgers for Indian Trust Funds, 1836–1865, Vol. 3, Records Concerning Indian Trust Funds, Records of the Finance Division, BIA, NARA, 3; *ARCIA* 1861, 200–201; John P. Bowes, *Exiles and Pioneers: Eastern Indians in the Trans-Mississippi West* (Cambridge University Press, 2007), 198–200; Brice Obermeyer and John P. Bowes, "'The Lands of My Nation': Delaware Indians in Kansas, 1829–1869," *Great Plains Quarterly* 36, no. 1 (2016): 1–30; Miner and Unrau, *The End of Indian Kansas*, 28–53; Charles Mix to H B. Branch, January 22 1862, LSOIA 67, 271; S. Mis. Doc. No. 37-100 (1862); H.R. Mis. Doc. No. 37-91, at 59 (1861).

33. Cong. Globe, 38th Cong. 1st Sess. 2870 (1864).

34. Cong. Globe, 38th Cong. 1st Sess. 2872 (1864).

35. "To the Senate and House of Representative, June 14, 1864," in *The Papers of Chief John Ross*, vol. 2, ed. Gary E. Moulton (University of Oklahoma Press, 1985), 590–91.

36. Pub. L. 37–135, 12 Stat. 512 (1862).

37. Nick Estes, *Our History Is the Future: Standing Rock Versus the Dakota Access Pipeline, and the Long Tradition of Indigenous Resistance* (Verso Books, 2019), 89–132; Elliott West, *Continental Reckoning: The American West in the Age of Expansion* (University of Nebraska Press, 2023), 75; John David Unruh, *The Plains Across: The Overland Emigrants and the Trans-Mississippi West, 1840–60* (University of Illinois Press, 1979), 156–200; Robert G. Athearn, *William Tecumseh Sherman and the Settlement of the West* (University of Oklahoma Press, 1956), 27; Samuel Watson, "Military Learning and Adaptation Shaped by Social Context: The U.S. Army and Its 'Indian Wars,' 1790–1890," *Journal of Military History* 82, no. 2 (2018): 402–6; Russell Frank Weigley, *History of the United States Army* (Indiana University Press, 1984), 267–68.

38. Gary Clayton Anderson, *Kinsmen of Another Kind: Dakota-White Relations in the Upper Mississippi Valley, 1650–1862* (St. Paul: Minnesota Historical Society Press, 1997), 184–87, 208–15, 247–49; Ari Kelman, "From Manassas to Mankato: How the Civil War Bled into the Indian Wars," in *Indian Cities: Histories of Indigenous Urbanization*, ed. Kent Blansett, Cathleen D. Cahill, and Andrew Needham (University of Oklahoma Press, 2022), 75–94; "Treaty with the Sioux—Mdewakanton and Wahpakoota Bands, 1851," in *Indian Affairs: Laws and Treaties*, vol. 2, *Treaties*, ed. Charles J. Kappler (GPO, 1904), 591–93; Wesley C. Mitchell, *History of the Greenbacks* (University of Chicago Press, 1903), 201; Gary Clayton Anderson and Alan R. Woolworth, eds., *Through Dakota Eyes: Narrative Accounts of the Minnesota Indian War of 1862* (Minnesota Historical Society, 1988), 27.

39. Lincoln pardoned the remaining prisoners. Nichols, *Lincoln and the Indians*, 94–117. See also Anderson, *Kinsmen of Another Kind*, 247–54; Michel Clodfelter, *The Dakota War: The United States Army Versus the Sioux, 1862–1865* (McFarland, 1998); Scott W. Berg, *38 Nooses: Lincoln, Little Crow, and the Beginning of the Frontier's End* (Vintage Books, 2012) 6–7, 26–27, 41–42, 75, 78–79, 111–12, 239–40, 277.

40. *ARCIA* 1868, 472; Stan Hoig, *White Man's Paper Trail: Grand Councils and Treaty-Making on the Central Plains* (University Press of Colorado, 2006), 131, 134–37; Jeffrey Ostler, *The Plains Sioux and U.S. Colonialism from Lewis and Clark to Wounded Knee* (Cambridge University Press, 2004), 130. For examples of delayed, inadequate, or missing annuities, see US Senate, *Condition of the Indian Tribes: Report of the Joint Special Committee, Appointed Under Joint Resolution of March 3, 1865* (GPO, 1867), 5, 7, 8, 10–12, 16, 365, 392, 400.

41. *ARCIA* 1863, 461–62; *ARCIA* 1864, 577.

42. Mitchell, *History of the Greenbacks*, 200–205; Irwin Unger, *The Greenback Era: A Social and Political History of American Finance, 1865–1879* (Princeton University Press, 1964), 15; *ARCIA* 1865, 560.

43. US Department of the Interior, Census Office, *Report on Indians Taxed and Indians Not Taxed in the United States* (GPO, 1894), 641; Mark Wilson, *The Business of Civil War: Military Mobilization and the State, 1861–1865* (Johns Hopkins University Press, 2006), 38, table. Pekka Hämäläinen, *Lakota America: A New History of Indigenous Power* (Yale University Press, 2019), 176.

44. Armstead L. Robinson, *Bitter Fruits of Bondage: The Demise of Slavery and the Collapse of the Confederacy, 1861–1865* (University of Virginia Press, 2005), 148–50; Stanley Lebergott, "Why the South Lost: Commercial Purpose in the Confederacy, 1861–1865," *Journal of American History* 70, no. 1 (1983): 58–74; John C. Schwab, *The Confederate States of America 1861–1865: A Financial and Industrial History of the South During the Civil War* (Charles Scribner's Sons, 1901), 6, 12–13, 30–31.

45. William G. Thomas III, *The Iron Way: Railroads, the Civil War, and the Making of Modern America* (Yale University Press, 2011), 134–38; Michael Brem Bonner and Peter McCord, *The Union Blockade in the American Civil War: A Reassessment* (University of Tennessee Press, 2021); Lebergott, "Why the South Lost," table 64; Sexton, *Debtor Diplomacy*, 157–74; Schwab, *The Confederate States of America*, 26–27; Sven Beckert, *Empire of Cotton: A Global History* (Vintage Books, 2015), 242–73; Robin Einhorn, *American Taxation, American Slavery* (University of Chicago Press, 2006), 220–21, 223–25, 250; Ron and Valeonti, "The Money War," 263–88.

46. William L. Shea and Earl J. Hess, *Pea Ridge: Civil War Campaign in the West* (University of North Carolina Press, 1992), 308–9; Alvin M. Josephy, *The Civil War in the American West* (Alfred A. Knopf, 1991), 336–49; Warde, *When the Wolf Came*, 100–102; Confederate States of America, Department of War, *Report of the Commissioner of Indian Affairs, January 12, 1863* (n.p., 1863), 1–3.

47. McCurry, *Confederate Reckoning*, 178–79; Hugh Rockoff, "Banking and Finance, 1789–1914," in *The Cambridge Economic History of the United States*, vol. 2, *The Long Nineteenth Century*, ed. Stanley L. Engerman and Robert E. Gallman (Cambridge University Press, 2000), 660; Schwab, *The Confederate States of America*, 75; Brig. Col. Gallopher to D. H. Cooper, May 4, 1865, Box 1, Folder 1A, District of Indian Territory Headquarters and Inspector General's Office, Letters Received and Other Papers, War Department Collection of Confederate Records, RG 109, NARA; Speech Given by Peter Pitchlynn Before Choctaw Council in 1865, Folder 2030, PPPH.

48. Circular to the Chief of the Choctaw Nation, April 10, 1865, Folder 2043, PPPH.

49. Bruce Levine, *The Fall of the House of Dixie: The Civil War and the Social Revolution That Transformed the South* (Random House, 2013), 193–217; McCurry, *Confederate Reckoning*, 258–61; Steven Hahn, *Political Worlds of Slavery and Freedom* (Harvard University Press, 2009), 55–114; W. E. B. Du Bois, *Black Reconstruction in America, 1860–1880* (Free Press, 1992), 55–83.

50. William Dole to William G. Coffin, February 10, 1862, LSOIA 67, 450–52; William G. Coffin to William Dole, October 15, 1862, in *ARCIA* 1862, 135–38; Henry Smith to William G. Coffin, July 16, 1863, LROIA 835 [277–80]; Justin Harlan to William G. Coffin, August 8, 1863, LROIA 835 [289–93]; William G. Coffin to Charles Mix, August 31, 1863, LROIA 835 [312–16]; Milo Gookins to William G. Coffin, October 17, 1863, LROIA 835 [369–70]; Pakoja, Tustamahemantha, Robert Smith, and Lewis to William Dole, September 14, 1863, LROIA 835 [508–9]; Billy Bowleg, Foshucheeehajo, Nokosolochee, Kochemeko to Oaktoha and Pascova, September 14, 1863, LROIA 835 [510–13]; William G. Coffin to William Dole, May 14, 1864, LROIA 835 [749–50]; William G. Coffin to William Dole, June 3, 1864, LROIA 835 [777–78]; William G. Coffin to William Dole, June 7, 1864, LROIA 835 [782–83]; William G. Coffin to William Dole, September 24, 1864, in *ARCIA* 1864, 447–51; Warde, *When the Wolf Came*, 68, 78–79, 86, 92, 105–10, 206–7; William G. Coffin Report, in *ARCIA*

1865, 253. Indian affairs officials estimated $4 million in losses suffered by the Cherokee; see James Harlan to W. G. Coffin, January 2, 1865, LROIA 836 [78–79]. See also Christine Schultz White and Benton R. White, *Now the Wolf Has Come: The Creek Nation in the Civil War* (Texas A&M University Press, 1996); and E. H. Carruth and H. W. Martin to William G. Coffin, July 25, 1862, in *ARCIA* 1862, 304–5.

51. Wilson, *The Business of Civil War*, 193, 202; Robert M. Utley, *The Indian Frontier, 1846–1890* (University of New Mexico Press, 2003), 71.

52. Winchester Colbert and Cha-ta-tomaha to Grand Council, June 12, 1865, Folder 2057, PPPH.

53. Clara Sue Kidwell, *The Choctaws in Oklahoma: From Tribe to Nation, 1855–1970* (University of Oklahoma Press, 2007), 79–80; Baird, *Peter Pitchlynn*, 146–47; 69–70; Choctaw Delegates to J. H. B. Latrobe, May 16, 1866, Folder 2120, PPPH; H.R. Rep. No. 42-98 (1873); "Treaty with the Seminole, 1866," in Kappler, *Indian Affairs*, 2:910–15; "Treaty with the Choctaw and Chickasaw, 1866," in Kappler, *Indian Affairs*, 2:918–31; "Treaty with the Creeks, 1866," in Kappler, *Indian Affairs*, 2:931–37; "Treaty with the Cherokee, 1866," in Kappler, *Indian Affairs*, 2:942–50.

54. Yarbrough, *Choctaw Confederates*, 191–92; Daniel Littlefield Jr., *The Chickasaw Freedmen: A People Without a Country* (Greenwood, 1980), 51; Christopher B. Bean, "Who Defines a Nation? Reconstruction in Indian Territory," in Clampitt, *The Civil War and Reconstruction*, 110–31; Steven Hahn, "Slave Emancipation, Indian Peoples, and the Projects of a New American Nation-State," *Journal of the Civil War Era* 3, no. 3 (2013): 307–30; Claudio Saunt, "The Paradox of Freedom: Tribal Sovereignty and Emancipation During the Reconstruction of Indian Territory," *Journal of Southern History* 70, no. 1 (2004): 63–94; Krauthamer, *Black Slaves, Indian Masters*, 101–18; Alaina Roberts, *I've Been Here All the While: Black Freedom on Native Land* (University of Pennsylvania Press, 2021), 41–71.

55. Chickasaw Delegation to D. N. Cooley, September 11, 1866, LROIA 857 [130–32]; H.R. Ex. Doc. No. 32-57 (1853).

56. James Riley, Allen Wright, Alfred Wade, John Page to D. N. Cooley, July 14, 1866, Folder 2133, PPPH; Peter Pitchlynn to D. N. Cooley, August 1866, Folder 2142, PPPH.

57. Secession explained most, but not all of the defaults. One state—Arkansas— had not paid interest on $162,000 in state bonds held by the Office of Indian Affairs since 1842. Indiana, still crushed by its canal debt, and Missouri, wracked by internal conflicts over secession, had both defaulted after the war, owing $210,000 and $158,000, respectively, plus overdue interest. See H.R. Ex. Doc. No. 40-59 (1867).

58. Ratchford, *American State Debts*, 159–60; H.R. Ex. Doc. No. 40-59 (1867).

59. Peter Pitchlynn, Holmes Colbert, Lewis Downing et al. to Columbus Delano, March 1, 1870, LROIA 857 [624–25].

60. Since most antebellum commercial debts had expired, the decision primarily applied to long-term debt obligations like state, municipal, and railroad bonds, which were now compelled to deliver interest payments in gold or silver. See Hepburn v. Griswold, 75 U.S. 8 Wall. 603 (1870); Unger, *The Greenback Era*, 176–78; and Richard H. Timberlake, *Constitutional Money: A Review of the Supreme Court's Monetary Decisions* (Cambridge University Press, 2013), 86–96. In cases where federal officials still collected interest in specie from securities, they sold it on the gold market and either reinvested the difference or distributed it to nations as part of their annuities. *ARCIA* 1871, 1074–76.

61. Wilson, *The Business of Civil War*, 8–11; Kyle S. Sinisi, *Sacred Debts: State Civil War Claims and American Federalism* (Fordham University Press, 2003), 9–10; O. H. Browning to Hugh McCulloch, October 9, 1867, LROIA 857 [335–36]; Conrad Baker to Hugh M. Culloch, November 5, 1868, LROIA 857 [455–57]; *ARCIA* 1868, 779–80; *ARCIA* 1869, 930; S. Rep. No. 45-476 (1878); H.R. Rep. No. 45-354 (1878); H. Mis. Doc. No. 45-66, at 42 (1878); *ARCIA* 1895, 2.

62. Elliott West, *The Contested Plains: Indians, Goldseekers, and the Rush to Colorado* (University Press of Kansas, 1998), 115–16, 157–58, 161–62; Unruh, *The Plains Across*, 156–200; Rodman Wilson Paul, *Mining Frontiers of the Far West, 1848–1880*, rev. ed., ed. Elliott West (University of New Mexico Press, 2001), 10–11, 37–55.

63. Stan Hoig, *The Sand Creek Massacre* (University of Oklahoma Press, 1961), 145–62; Ostler, *The Plains Sioux and U.S. Colonialism*, 45; Ned Blackhawk, *Violence over the Land: Indians and Empires in the Early American West* (Harvard University Press, 2006), 215–19; Utley, *The Indian Frontier*, 94. On raids as both economic and retaliatory, see Brian DeLay, *War of a Thousand Deserts: Indian Raids and the U.S.-Mexican War* (Yale University Press, 2008), 117–38. For a twentieth-century battle over commemorations of the massacre, see Ari Kelman, *A Misplaced Massacre: Struggling over the Memory of Sand Creek* (Harvard University Press, 2015).

64. West, *Continental Reckoning*, 167. On the legality of raiding, truce-breaking, and war, see Lauren Benton, *They Called It Peace: Worlds of Imperial Violence* (Princeton University Press, 2024). See also US Department of the Interior, *Report on Indians Taxed and Indians Not Taxed*, 641; and H.R. Ex. Doc. No. 5 (1866).

65. Hoig, *White Man's Paper Trail*, 140–41; "Articles of a Treaty Made and Concluded at Fort Laramie [. . .]," in *Papers Relating to Talks and Councils Held with the Indians in Dakota and Montana Territories* [. . .] (GPO, 1910), 19–20; William Tecumseh Sherman, quoted in Robert G. Athearn, *William Tecumseh Sherman and the Settlement of the West* (University of Oklahoma Press, 1956), 101.

66. James C. Olson, *Red Cloud and the Sioux Problem* (University of Nebraska Press, 1965), 60–67; Hämäläinen, *Lakota America*, 280–82; Weigley, *History of the United States Army*, 267.

67. John Lauritz Larson, *Internal Improvement: National Public Works and the Promise of Popular Government in the Early United States* (University of North Carolina Press, 2001), 192–93; Richard White, *Railroaded: The Transcontinentals and the Making of Modern America* (W. W. Norton, 2011), 16–17; Athearn, *William Tecumseh Sherman*, 223; Andrew C. Isenberg, *The Destruction of the Bison: An Environmental History, 1750–1920* (Cambridge University Press, 2000), 125–28. For the United States' "railroad colonialism" in a global frame, see Manu Karuka, *Empire's Tracks: Indigenous Nations, Chinese Workers, and the Transcontinental Railroad* (University of California Press, 2019), 40–59. For an account of the diverse responses Native people had to railroads, see Alessandra Nicole Link, "The Iron Horse in Indian Country: Native Americans and Railroads in the U.S. West, 1853–1924" (PhD diss., University of Colorado–Boulder, 2018), S. Rep. No. 40-219, at 15 (1869); William Steward, quoted in Link, "Iron Horse in Indian Country," 11.

68. Sean Patrick Adams, "Soulless Monsters and Iron Horses: The Civil War, Institutional Change, and American Capitalism," in *Capitalism Takes Command: The Social Transformation of Nineteenth-Century America*, ed. Michael Zakim and Gary John Kornblith (University of Chicago Press, 2012), 254–59; Richard Sylla, "Federal

Policy, Banking Market Structure, and Capital Mobilization in the United States, 1863–1913," *Journal of Economic History* 29, no. 4 (1969): 657–86; Michael Caires, "Building a Union of Banks: Salmon P. Chase and the Creation of a National Banking System," in *New Perspectives on the Union War*, ed. Gary W. Gallagher and Elizabeth R. Varon (Fordham University Press, 2019), 160–85; Matthew Jaremski, "National Banking's Role in U.S. Industrialization, 1850–1900," *Journal of Economic History* 74, no. 1 (2014): 109–40; William G. Roy, *Socializing Capital: The Rise of the Large Industrial Corporation in America* (Princeton University Press, 1997), 83–108; Sven Beckert, *Monied Metropolis: New York City and the Consolidation of the American Bourgeoisie, 1850–1896* (Cambridge University Press, 2001), 122–23; White, *Railroaded*, 21–24;

69. White, *Railroaded*, xxv, 16–17, 21–26; Carter Goodrich, *Government Promotion of American Canals and Railroads, 1800–1890* (Columbia University Press, 1960), 184–85, 202–3; West, *Continental Reckoning*, 180–81; Robert William Fogel, *The Union Pacific Railroad: A Case in Premature Enterprise* (Johns Hopkins Press, 1960).

70. Noam Maggor, "Escaping the Periphery: Railroad Regulation as American Industrial Policy," *Critical Historical Studies* 11, no. 1 (2024): 47–86; Richard Franklin Bensel, *The Political Economy of American Industrialization, 1877–1900* (Cambridge University Press, 2000), 289–354; Gerald Berk, *Alternative Tracks: The Constitution of American Industrial Order, 1865–1917* (Baltimore: Johns Hopkins University Press, 1994); Public Land Commission, Committee on Codification, *The Public Domain: Its History, with Statistics* [. . .] (GPO, 1881), 273; Paul W. Gates, *History of Public Land Law Development* (GPO, 1968), 377; U.S. Grant to W. T. Sherman, January 26, 1867, quoted in Olson, *Red Cloud and the Sioux Problem*, 62.

71. US Department of the Interior, *Report on Indians Taxed and Indians Not Taxed*, 641; H.R. Ex. Doc. No. 39-5 (1866); Francis Paul Prucha, *The Great Father: The United States Government and the American Indians* (University of Nebraska Press, 1984), 501–33; C. Joseph Genetin-Pilawa, *Crooked Paths to Allotment: The Fight over Federal Indian Policy After the Civil War* (University of North Carolina Press, 2012), 69; Emma Teitelman, *The Social Reconstruction of the South and West After the United States' Civil War* (Harvard University Press, forthcoming); US Department of the Interior, *Report of the Board of Indian Commissioners* [. . .] *for 1869* (GPO, 1870), 4–5; US Department of the Interior, *Report of the Board of Indian Commissioners* [. . .] *for 1871* (GPO, 1872), 11–13.

72. US Department of the Interior, *Report on Indians Taxed and Indians Not Taxed*, 641; Francis Paul Prucha, *The Great Father: The United States Government and the American Indians* (University of Nebraska Press, 1984, 473–78; C. Joseph Genetin-Pilawa, *Crooked Paths to Allotment: The Fight over Federal Indian Policy After the Civil War* (University of North Carolina Press, 2012), 78.

73. Cong. Globe, 41st Cong., 3rd Sess. 733–34 (1871).

74. Benjamin Madley, *An American Genocide: The United States and the California Indian Catastrophe, 1846–1873* (Yale University Press, 2016), 3; Cong. Globe, 41st Cong., 3rd Sess. 736 (1871).

75. Cong. Globe, 41st Cong., 3rd Sess. 764–65 (1871).

76. Cong. Globe, 41st Cong., 3rd Sess. 1502 (1871).

77. S. Rep. Com. No. 374-35 (1859); S. Ex. Doc. No. 87-42 (1872); S. Ex. Doc. No. 36-35, at 170 (1859); Brief Confidential History of Net Proceeds, Folder 3198, PPPH; Baird, *Peter Pitchlynn*, 132, 143; Kidwell, *The Choctaws in Oklahoma*, 121–36.

78. H. Rep. No. 40-63 (1868); Gates, *History of Public Land Law Development*, 369–71; White, *Railroaded*, 25–26, 60–61.

79. 16 Stat. 544, Pub. L. 41, Ch. 120 (1871).

80. Felix S. Cohen, *Handbook of Federal Indian Law* (GPO, 1942), 33; David E. Wilkins, *American Indian Sovereignty and the U.S. Supreme Court: The Masking of Justice* (University of Texas Press, 1997), 64–117; Nell Jessup Newton, "Federal Power over Indians: Its Sources, Scope, and Limitation," *University of Pennsylvania Law Review* 132, no. 2 (1984): 195–288; Maggie Blackhawk, "The Constitution of American Colonialism," *Harvard Law Review* 137, no. 1 (2023): 53–65; Sidney L. Harring, *Crow Dog's Case: American Indian Sovereignty, Tribal Law, and United States Law in the Nineteenth Century* (Cambridge University Press, 1994); Sarah H. Cleveland, "Powers Inherent in Sovereignty: Indians, Aliens, Territories and the Nineteenth Century Origins of Plenary Power over Foreign Affairs," *Texas Law Review* 81, no. 1 (2002): 1–284. For the plurality of Indigenous experiences after 1871, see Joel T. Helfrich, Michael Leroy Oberg, Alaina E. Roberts, Julie L. Reed, and Kevin Bruyneel, "No More Nations Within Nations: Indigenous Sovereignty after the End of Treaty-Making in 1871," *Journal of the Gilded Age and Progressive Era* 10, no. 1 (2021): 325–49; Jacoby, *Shadows at Dawn*, 127; *ARCIA* 1871, 418.

81. Vincent Coyler to Board of Indian Commissioners, September 5, 1871, in US Office of Indian Affairs, *Executive Orders Relating to Indian Reservations from May 14, 1855 to July 1, 1912* (GPO, 1912), 8. The Camp Verde Apache were granted permission to return to their homelands in 1898, and the government eventually granted them two small reservations, Camp Verde and Middle Verde. Ian Record, *Big Sycamore Stands Alone: The Western Apaches, Aravaipa, and the Struggle for Place* (University of Oklahoma Press, 2008), 27–30; Timothy Braatz, *Surviving Conquest: A History of the Yavapai Peoples* (University of Nebraska Press, 2003), 124–25, 172–77.

82. For an example of investment in federal bonds, see "An Act to Ratify an Agreement with Certain Ute Indians in Colorado, April 29, 1874," in *Indian Affairs: Laws and Treaties*, vol. 1, *Laws*, ed. Charles J. Kappler (GPO, 1902), 152. Some agreements stipulated that funds should not be invested in securities, but rather placed to the credit of the beneficiary nation in the Treasury, and bear a set rate of interest; see, for example, "An Act to Authorize the Sale of the Pawnee Reservation, April 10, 1876," in Kappler, *Indian Affairs*, 1:159–61.

83. 30 U.S. 5 Pet. 1 1 (1831).

84. David E. Wilkins and K. Tsianina Lomawaima, *Uneven Ground: American Indian Sovereignty and Federal Law* (University of Oklahoma Press, 2001), 65; J. G. Woerner, *A Treatise on the American Law of Guardianship of Minors and Persons of Unsound Mind* (Little, Brown, 1897).

85. Curtis M. Hinsley Jr., *Savages and Scientists: The Smithsonian Institution and the Development of American Anthropology, 1846–1910* (Smithsonian Institution Press, 1981), 81–292.

86. Frederick Hoxie, *A Final Promise: The Campaign to Assimilate the Indians, 1880–1920* (Bison Books, 1984), 16–17; Woerner, *A Treatise on the American Law of Guardianship*, 158–65, 180–82, 432–49, 484–98; Cohen, *Handbook of Federal Indian Law*, 169–73; David J. Wishart, *An Unspeakable Sadness: The Dispossession of the Nebraska Indians* (University of Nebraska Press, 1994), 191–295; W. T. Sherman to Gen. J. M. Schofield, November 9, 1871, in US Office of Indian Affairs, *Executive*

*Orders Relating to Indian Reservations*, 9–10, 33–34; *ARCIA* 1874, 314–15; Ostler, *The Plains Sioux and U.S. Colonialism*, 131.

87. *ARCIA* 1873, 372; *ARCIA* 1875, 527; 18 Stat. 420, 449, 25 U.S.C. 137; *ARCIA* 1877, 400; *ARCIA* 1880, 90; West, *The Last Indian War*, 104; *ARCIA* 1876, 388.

88. Beth H. Piatote, *Domestic Subjects: Gender, Citizenship, and Law in Native American Literature* (Yale University Press, 2013), 5–6; Amanda J. Cobb, *Listening to Our Grandmothers' Stories: The Bloomfield Academy for Chickasaw Females, 1852–1949* (University of Nebraska Press, 2000), 54–65; Julie Reed, *Serving the Nation: Cherokee Sovereignty and Social Welfare, 1800–1907* (University of Oklahoma Press, 2016) 115–95; Colin G. Calloway, *Pen and Ink Witchcraft: Treaties and Treaty Making in American Indian History* (Oxford University Press, 2013), 182–225; *ARCIA* 1884, 119.

89. Cathleen D. Cahill, *Federal Fathers and Mothers: A Social History of the United States Indian Service, 1869–1933* (Chapel Hill: University of North Carolina Press, 2011), 15–33, 79; Hoxie, *A Final Promise*, 54–57; David Wallace Adams, *Education for Extinction: American Indians and the Boarding School Experience, 1875–1928* (University Press of Kansas, 1995), 60–64; "Pawnee Indians," Indian-Pioneer Collection, Vol. 47, University of Oklahoma Libraries Digital Collections; Peter J. Powell, *People of the Sacred Mountain: A History of the Northern Cheyenne Chiefs and Warrior Societies, 1830–1879*, vol. 2 (Harper and Row, 1979), 807; Benjamin Madley, "Reexamining the American Genocide Debate: Meaning, Historiography, and New Methods," *American Historical Review* 120, no. 1 (2015): 119; Harring, *Crow Dog's Case*, 13, 204; Wishart, *Unspeakable Sadness*, 188, 196, 204, 219; Jacki Thompson Rand, *Kiowa Humanity and the Invasion of the State* (University of Nebraska Press, 2008), 85. A 2024 report from the Department of the Interior counted at least 973 deaths across the system between 1819 and 1969; see Bryan Newland, *Federal Indian Boarding School Initiative Investigative Report*, vol. 2 (US Department of the Interior, 2024), 15.

90. S. Mis. Doc. No. 83, 41st Cong., 2nd Sess., March 14, 1870; S. Mis. Doc. No. 76, 41st Cong., 2nd sess., February 26, 1870.

91. H.R. 1152, 40th Cong. (1867–69); 41 S. 679 (1870); H. R. 2635, 42nd Cong. (1872); *Protest of the Indian Delegates Against the Bill to Establish the Territory of Oklahoma* (Chronicle, 1872); The Omaha and Umatilla both lobbied Congress for allotments; see Emily Greenwald, *Reconfiguring the Reservation: The Nez Perces, Jicarilla Apaches, and the Dawes Act* (University of New Mexico Press, 2002), 27–28; and S. Mis. Doc. 45–52 (1878).

## Epilogue: The Past and Future of Trusteeship

1. *Indian Appropriation Bill: Hearings on H.R.1917, Before the Senate Committee on Indian Affairs*, 63rd Cong. 508, 511 (1913).

2. As K. Tsianina Lomawaima and others have argued, the Society of American Indians' views were not simplistically assimiliationist, and they did not believe the achievement of United States citizenship would nullify Native sovereignty; see K. Tsianina Lomawaima, "The Mutuality of *Citizenship* and *Sovereignty*: The Society of American Indians and the Battle to Inherit America," *Studies in American Indian Literatures* 25, no. 2 (2013): 333–51. See also Philip Deloria, "Four Thousand Invitations: Situating the Society of American Indians," *Studies in American Indian Literatures* 25,

no. 2 (2013): 25–43; Thomas Constantine Maroukis, *We Are Not a Vanishing People: The Society of American Indians, 1911–1923* (University of Arizona Press, 2021); Hazel Hertzberg, *The Search for an American Indian Identity: Modern Pan- Indian Movements* (Syracuse University Press, 1971); Laura Cornelius Kellogg, *Our Democracy and the American Indian and Other Works*, ed. Kristina Ackley and Cristina Stanciu (Syracuse University Press, 2015), 105; Cathleen D. Cahill, *Federal Fathers and Mothers: A Social History of the United States Indian Service*, 1869–1933 (University of North Carolina Press, 2011), 17, 30–31; Frederick E. Hoxie, *A Final Promise: The Campaign to Assimilate the Indians, 1880–1920* (University of Nebraska Press, 2001), 53–68, 189–210; K. Tsianina Lomawaima, *They Called It Prairie Light: The Story of Chilocco Indian School* (University of Nebraska Press, 1994), 1–7. On Kellogg, see Kristina Ackley and Christina Stanciu, "Introduction," in Kellogg, *Our Democracy and the American Indian*, 1–62; Laurence M. Hauptman, *Seven Generations of Iroquois Leadership: The Six Nations Since 1800* (Syracuse University Press, 2008), 143–63; and Cristina Stanciu, "An Indian Woman of Many Hats: Laura Cornelius Kellogg's Embattled Search for an Indigenous Voice," *Studies in American Indian Literatures* 25, no. 2 (2013): 87–115.

3. Kellogg, *Our Democracy and the American Indian*, 79–98, 151–52; Kristina Ackley, "Laura Cornelius Kellogg, Lolomi, and Modern Oneida Placemaking," *Studies in American Indian Literatures* 25, no. 2 (2013): 117–38; Doug Kiel, "Competing Visions of Empowerment: Oneida Progressive-Era Politics and Writing Tribal Histories," *Ethnohistory* 61, no. 3 (2014): 433–34.

4. Pub. L. 49-105, 24 Stat. 388 (1887); Pub. L. 59-149, 34 Stat. 182 (1906); D. S. Otis, *The Dawes Act and the Allotment of Indian Lands*, ed. Francis Paul Prucha (University of Oklahoma Press, 1973), 82–97; Leonard A. Carlson, *Indians, Bureaucrats, and Land: The Dawes Act and the Decline of Indian Farming* (Greenwood, 1981), 29–56; Hoxie, *A Final Promise*, 147–88; Hauptman, *Seven Generations of Iroquois Leadership*, 146. For early experiments in allotment, see Mary Young, *Redskins, Ruffleshirts, and Rednecks: Indian Allotments in Alabama and Mississippi 1830–1860* (University of Oklahoma Press, 1961). On the diverse experiences and unfinished legacies of allotment across nations, see Daniel Heath Justice and Jean M. O'Brien, eds., *Allotment Stories: Indigenous Land Relations Under Settler Siege* (University of Minnesota Press, 2022).

5. David A. Chang, *The Color of the Land: Race, Nation, and the Politics of Landownership in Oklahoma, 1832–1929* (University of North Carolina Press, 2010), 192–93; Felix S. Cohen, *Handbook of Federal Indian Law* (GPO, 1942), 216–17; Carlson, *Indians, Bureaucrats, and Land*, 157–59.

6. Laurence Schmeckebier, *The Office of Indian Affairs: Its History, Activities and Organization* (Johns Hopkins Press, 1927), 191. Present-day figures calculated as a share of gross domestic product per capita; "Purchasing Power of a US Dollar Transaction in the Past," MeasuringWorth, 2025, https://www.measuringworth.com/ppowerus/.

7. Cohen, *Handbook of Federal Indian Law*, 113, 196, 201–2; Schmeckebier, *The Office of Indian Affairs*, 192–96; Graham D. Taylor, *The New Deal and American Indian Tribalism: The Administration of the Indian Reorganization Act, 1934–45* (University of Nebraska Press, 1980), 1–7, 20–21.

8. Kellogg, *Our Democracy and the American Indian*, 92.

9. Ackley and Stanciu, "Introduction," 30; Laurence M. Hauptman, *Seven Generations of Iroquois Leadership: The Six Nations since 1800* (Syracuse University Press, 2008), 158–59.

10. Nancy Oestreich Lurie, "Ada Deer, Champion of Tribal Sovereignty," in *Sifters: Native American Women's Lives*, ed. Theda Purdue (Oxford University Press, 2001), 223–41; Ada Deer with Theda Perdue, *Making a Difference: My Fight for Native Rights and Social Justice* (University of Oklahoma Press, 2019, 3–43.

11. Charles F. Wilkinson and Eric R. Biggs, "The Evolution of the Termination Policy," *American Indian Law Review* 5, no. 1 (1977): 139–84; David Beck, *The Struggle for Self-Determination: History of the Menominee Indians Since 1854* (University of Nebraska Press, 2005), 129–49; Donald Fixico, *The Invasion of Indian Country in the Twentieth Century: American Capitalism and Tribal Natural Resources* (University Press of Colorado, 1998), 79–102.

12. Lurie, "Ada Deer," 225–27; Beck, *The Struggle for Self-Determination*, 147–48, 154–55.

13. Clara Sue Kidwell, *The Choctaws in Oklahoma: From Tribe to Nation, 1855–1970* (Norman: University of Oklahoma Press, 2007), 133–35; H. D. Rosenthal, *Their Day in Court: A History of the Indian Claims Commission* (New York: Garland, 1990), 15–32; Glen A. Wilkinson, "Indian Tribal Claims Before the Court of Claims," *Georgetown Law Journal* 55, no. 3 (1966): 511–28; David Wilkins, *Hollow Justice: A History of Indigenous Claims in the United States* (Yale University Press, 2013), 1–26. For an economic analysis of the issues plaguing the determination of judgments, see Leonard Carlson, *Ireedemable America: The Indians' Estate and Land Claims*, ed. Imre Sutton (University of New Mexico Press, 1985), 87–110. For the role of expert witnesses in claims cases and the impact of claims on the historical discipline, see Christian W. McMillen, *Making Indian Law: The Hualapai Land Case and the Birth of Ethnohistory* (Yale University Press, 2007).

14. Rosenthal, *Their Day in Court*, 30; Wilkinson, "Indian Tribal Claims Before the Court of Claims," 517–18; Sen. Rep. No. 92–97 (1971).

15. Rosenthal, *Their Day in Court*, 111–34, 165–74; Charles Wilkinson, *Blood Struggle: The Rise of Modern Indian Nations* (W. W. Norton, 2005), 57–86; David R. M. Beck, *Bribed with Our Own Money: Federal Abuse of American Indian Funds in the Termination Era* (University of Nebraska Press, 2024), 45, 75–77; Wilkins, *Hollow Justice*, 39–70.

16. *Menominee Restoration Act, Hearings Before the Subcommittee on Indian Affairs of the Committee on Interior and Insular Affairs*, 93rd Cong., 1st Sess. (1973), 32, 36.

17. Kellogg, *Our Democracy and the American Indian*, 203.

18. *Indian Trust Fund Management: Oversight Hearing on the Management of Indian Trust Funds by the U.S. Government, Before Senate Select Committee on Indian Affairs*, 102nd Cong. 36 (1992); Julia Whitty, "Elouise Cobell's Accounting Coup," *Mother Jones*, September–October 2005, https://www.motherjones.com /politics/2005/09/accounting-coup-0/; "Indians File Lawsuit, Charge BIA Mismanaging Trust Accounts," *Las Vegas Review*, November 10, 1996, 10A; *BIA Management of Indian Trust Funds: Oversight Hearing Before the Subcommittee on Native American Affairs of the House Committee on Natural Resources*, 103rd Cong. 98 (1993).

19. *Indian Trust Fund Management: Oversight Hearing on the Management Of Indian Trust Funds by the U.S. Government, Before Senate Select Committee on Indian Affairs*, 102nd Cong. 36–37 (1992).

20. *The Interior Department's Failure to Correct Serious Problems in the Management of the Indian Trust Funds: Hearing Before the Environment, Energy, and Natural Resources Subcommittee of the House Committee on Government Operations*, 103rd Cong. 87 (1994); General Accounting Office, "Responses to Questions Contained in October 29, 1996, Letter," memorandum, Document B-275522, December 10, 1996, 4–5, https://www.gao.gov/assets/aimd/ogc-97-23r.pdf; David E. Wilkins and Heidi Kiiwetinepinesiik Stark, *American Indian Politics and the American Political System*, 4th ed. (Rowman and Littlefield, 2017), 168.

21. *Review of the Bureau of Indian Affairs' Management of the $1.7 Billion Indian Trust Fund: Hearing Before the Natural Resources Subcommittee of the House Committee on Government Operations*, 101st Cong. 82–83 (1989); *Indian Trust Funds, 1995: Hearing Before the Senate Committee on Indian Affairs*, 104th Cong. 66–67 (1996).

22. *The Interior Department's Failure to Correct Serious Problems in the Management of the Indian Trust Funds: Hearing Before the Environment, Energy, and Natural Resources Subcommittee of the House Committee on Government Operations*, 103rd Cong. 39 (1994); Ada Deer, quoted in Michael Satchell and David Bowermaster, "The Worst Federal Agency: Critics Call the Bureau of Indian Affairs a National Disgrace," *U.S. News and World Report*, November 28, 1994.

23. Justin Guilder, "Focus on: *Cobell v. Salazar*," *Federal Lawyer*, March–April 2010, 31–33; Wilkins, *Hollow Justice*, 142–82.

24. Armen H. Merjian, "An Unbroken Chain of Injustice: The Dawes Act, Native American Trusts, and *Cobell v. Salazar*," *Gonzaga Law Review* 46, no. 3 (2010–11): 625; Todd Garvey, *The Indian Trust Fund Litigation: An Overview of "Cobell v. Salazar*," RL34628 (Congressional Research Service, January 3, 2011), 4.

25. Merjian, "An Unbroken Chain of Injustice," 653.

26. Guilder, "Focus on: *Cobell v. Salazar*," 33; Garvey, *The Indian Trust Fund Litigation*, 9.

27. Wilkins, *Hollow Justice*, 145; Edward Charles Valandra, "Objections to the Settlement, Cobell v. Salazar," *Lakota Country Times* (Martin, SD), March 30, 2011; Jerilyn Decoteau, "Why I Opted Out of the Cobell Settlement," *Indian Country Today*, June 5, 2011, updated September 12, 2018, https://ictnews.org/archive/why-i-opted-out-of-the-cobell-settlement. Alyosha Goldstein, "Finance and Foreclosure in the Colonial Present," *Radical History Review* 118 (2014): 42–63, situates the *Cobell* settlement's foreclosure of future litigation within a wider history of treaty abrogation and financial dispossession.

28. Elouise Cobell, quoted in "Elouise Cobell Dies At 65; Native American Activist," *Los Angeles Times*, October 17, 2011.

29. Rob Capriccioso, "Elouise Cobell, 65, Walks On," *Indian Country Today*, October 17, 2011, updated September 13, 2018, https://ictnews.org/archive/elouise-cobell-65-walks-on; Bethany R. Berger, "Elouise Cobell: Bringing the United States to Account," in *"Our Cause Will Ultimately Triumph": Profiles in American Indian Sovereignty*, ed. Tim Alan Garrison (Carolina Academic Press, 2014), 190.

Page numbers followed by an i indicate an illustration.

request, 170–71; Council Bluffs, Iowa, 114, 118, 119i, 120–21, 153; education funding and boarding school, 106, 120; Indiana canal funding, 108, 110; leadership of, 105–6; Maryland bonds and, 99, 122, 139; paper money or gold, 195; Relocation Treaty of 1846, 152, 168; removal campaign, 118; Sioux raids, 143; Treaty of 1821, 106; Treaty of Chicago (1833), 106–7, 118–20, 122, 139, 168, 269n17; Western resettlement and, 117–18, 124i
Upper Canada rebels, 141
U. S. Congress: annuity funding and, 58; Bureau of Indian Affairs mismanagement, 3–4; federal assumption of states' debts, 141; federally chartered corporations and, 15; Indian appropriation bill of 1917, 215; indigenous treaty-making and, 4–5, 182; Seneca treaty ratification, 34
US Constitution, 32, 69, 163, 200
US Mint, 37

Van Buren, Martin, 96, 113, 121
Vattel, Emerich de, 11–12
Virginia, 182–85, 197, 201–2

Wabanakis, 101
Wabaunsee (Potawatomi headman), 126
Wadsworth, Jeremiah, 29, 34–35
Wahpekute Dakotas, 194
Walker, Robert J., 150, 162
Wambditanka (Mdewakanton leader), 194
Ward, William, 62–63
War Department, 6, 15, 27–28, 38, 103, 130, 249n81
War of 1812, 38–39, 44
Washington, George, 19, 21, 24, 26, 28–29, 128
Wayne, Anthony, 25, 27
Weas, 180, 191
Weatherford, William B., 105
Webster, Daniel, 141
West Virginia, 201
Whitcomb, James, 150
Wolf, James, 80–81, 164
Woodbury, Levi, 82–84, 88, 90–92, 94, 264n57
Worcester, Samuel, 56
Wyandots, 19, 25, 48, 74, 101–2

Yankton Dakotas, 143